KOFI ANNAN

A SPOKESPERSON'S MEMOIR

FREDERIC ECKHARD

RUDER FINN PRESS

Copyright © 2012 Ruder Finn Press

Design: Brian Pearce | Red Jacket Press
Editorial Director: Susan Slack
Production Director: Valerie Thompson
Digital Imaging Specialist: Steve Moss

ISBN 10: 1-932646-56-6
ISBN 13: 978-1-932646-56-6

Printed in Korea

Published in French by Éditions du Tricorne, Geneva. [tricorne@tricorne.org] (May 2009)

Thank you for supporting CFC

[signature] Ed Elle

To my son, Jan — *Remember Vukovar!*

And to Kathryn, *in joy and pain.*

TABLE OF CONTENTS

FOREWORD 9

PREFACE 13
Sir Brian Urquhart

INTRODUCTION 15

GETTING TO THE TOP

INSIDE KOFI ANNAN 31
*Ghana; The Midwest; Titi; Addis Ababa; In and Out of Ghana;
Nane: The Essential Partner; Marriage and Roosevelt Island*

A NEW POLITICAL ACTOR 44
*The New World Order; Hostages in Baghdad; Taking Over Peacekeeping;
Black Hawk Down; Rwanda:A Genocide Foretold; The Shame of Srebrenica*

THE SEVENTH SECRETARY-GENERAL 56
*"No, He Won't"; Swept in on the Winds of the Sahara; Walks and Runs;
"He Was Strict with the Children"; The Social Secretary-General;
The Rock Star of Diplomacy; In the Air; A Job Like No Other*

CAMELOT

THE BILLION-DOLLAR DEAL 71

THE BAGHDAD GAMBLE 74

THE MIDDLE EAST 80
*The Israeli Withdrawal from Lebanon; Syria Leaves Lebanon; Lockerbie;
The Quartet; The Israel-Hezbollah War of 2006; Nuclear Iran; The UN and
Israel; Kofi and the Arabs*

SON OF AFRICA 93
Our Obama; The Harare Speech; A Visit to Rwanda; Angolan Dream; Nigeria;
Peacekeeping Turnaround in Africa; The African in Him; The Elephant

INTERVENTION — KOSOVO AND EAST TIMOR 105
The Annan Doctrine; Intervening in East Timor

DEMOCRATIZING THE UN 112
Civil Society; The Global Compact; Big Bad Pharma and HIV/AIDS

RELATIONS WITH THE PRESS 120

HARMONIZING THE SYSTEM 126
Barons and Baronesses; Getting Close to the IMF and World Bank; The Cabinet;
Coordinating Humanitarian Work; The Millennium Development Goals;
Peacebuilding

HUMAN RIGHTS AND THE RULE OF LAW 134
Making Human Rights Central; The Advancement of Women;
The Rule of Law

THE REFORM SECRETARY-GENERAL 142

STRENGTHS AND WEAKNESSES AS MANAGER 150

THE NOBEL CROWN 154

SECOND TERM BLUES

THE TURNING POINT: 9/11 159

"IT'S OBVIOUS; THEY'RE GOING TO WAR..." 161

THE DEATH OF SERGIO — AND OF NEO-CONSERVATISM 168

OIL-FOR-FOOD — HOW IT WORKED 178

ANNUS HORRIBILIS 182
Cotecna and the Conservative Media; The BBC and That Little Word "Illegal";
The Fallujah Letter; Depression?; More on Kojo

THE CASE AGAINST BENON 194

KOJO CLAIMS INNOCENCE 197

VOLCKER GETS TO THE MEAT 201

THE CARAVAN MOVES ON.. 208
Two Private Meetings; Firing the Faithful; The High-Level Panel Report;
The Tsunami and the Comeback

THE RESPONSIBILITY TO PROTECT 219
R2P; Darfur; Kenya

AFTERTHOUGHTS

HOW WILL HE BE REMEMBERED?.. 231

HAMMARSKJOLD AND ANNAN 241

SALUTES.. 245
Nelson Mandela, Colin Powell, Jacques Chirac, Tony Blair, Sergey Lavrov,
Li Zhaoxing, Javier Soldana

APPENDIX.. 250

BIOGRAPHIES.. 251

THANK YOU… 263

PHOTO CREDITS... 264

FOREWORD

BAILING OUT

In the spring of 2005, I had submitted a letter of resignation to Kofi Annan and hadn't yet heard back from him. After traveling with him throughout the Indian Ocean following the tsunami that hit the region at the end of 2004, I was struck at how physically tired I had become. The job of UN spokesperson is possibly one of the world's most interesting, if you're a news junkie, because all information flows through your office out to the public. It's also one of the most demanding, because you work in all time zones simultaneously and you give up a part of your personality to reflect the views of the person you speak for.

During Kofi's difficult second term, with the Oil-for-Food crisis hitting hard in 2004-2005, my job had become more and more stressful. I also had to ask myself whether I was part of the problem or part of the solution. Clearly, the UN and he were taking a beating over Iraq, especially from the right-wing press, and nothing any of us did or said seemed to make a difference.

So my offer to resign had two motives: first, to give Kofi the option of changing his spokesperson as part of a fight-back strategy; and second, to allow me to slip into retirement as I began to face my physical limits. After weeks of not responding to my letter, he finally called me into his office. He said, simply, "I would like you to stay on until the end of June. Would that suit you?"

The end of June I understood to be the time when he expected Paul Volcker's final report on the Oil-for-Food scandal to come out. That suggested to me that he saw me as part of the solution and not part of the problem, and I was reassured. But by asking me in a cool and almost accusatorial way, "Would that suit you?" he could almost have been saying, why are you bailing out now? During the Oil-for-Food crisis there were too many conversations that we didn't have and we seemed to have reached a point where we were having difficulty reading each other.

Once I left the office where I had spent most of the last 17 years, I began to look at Kofi in a new way. In 18 months, he would step down. How would he be remembered? How would I remember him? It was hard to judge because everything now was seen through the fog of Iraq. I had lunch with Kofi's chief speechwriter, Edward Mortimer, and asked him if anyone was making a list of Kofi's accomplishments as Secretary-General. Edward didn't know of anything specific, so I pulled a used envelope out of my pocket and said to Edward, well, let's make a list. And that list on the back of an envelope was the beginning of this book.

I had never intended to write a book. For that reason, I kept no notes. I wasn't sure it was appropriate for a spokesperson to write about what he had seen and heard in his privileged position. But a lot of anger welled up inside me at what I saw as unfair treatment that Kofi had received in the wake of the US invasion of Iraq. Then, out of the blue, a Geneva publisher called me and asked me if I would write a book on Kofi. I decided yes, here's my chance to speak up. That book was published in French in 2009. This book is an expansion and an elaboration of it.

WHO IS KOFI ANNAN?

Kofi Annan was not an easy person to get to know; and even after almost 10 years of working directly for him, I can't say that I feel I've touched the core. There is a refined formality about him that, coupled with his considerable charm, makes him easy to be with. But he does not intrude on your space and he expects you not to intrude on his.

In an insightful profile for *The New Yorker* magazine, Philip Gourevitch, now the editor of *The Paris Review*, wrote, "He is at once intensely present and personable and curiously detached." Yet in a different culture that detachment can be comforting, even admirable. Yves Oltramare, a Swiss banker and philanthropist who got to know Kofi from the time he became Secretary-General in 1997, told me, "I would say he's a reserved person, yes, but in the best sense of the term. And that's what I admire in him."

People often describe Kofi as centered — someone who knows himself and is comfortable in his skin. That is certainly so. The support of his extended family in Ghana could have been one reason for that. Another was most likely the position of privilege he enjoyed as the eldest son of a prominent Ghanaian. His father, Henry Reginald, was part of a royal bloodline that would have permitted him to claim the role of a tribal chief had he wished to. HR, as he was known, never showed an interest in exercising this right, nor did Kofi. But I think that Kofi sometimes thought of himself as a tribal royal.

For example, after the bombing in Baghdad that killed his close friend Sergio Vieira de Mello, along with 21 other UN staff members, Ahmad Fawzi, who had been Sergio's spokesperson, was in Kofi's office and broke down and sobbed. Kofi remained cool. When Ahmad asked him how he does it, Kofi told him that he had grown up in a tribal culture, and the chief of the tribe always maintained a posture of strength in order to inspire confidence in his people.

But the answer to who is Kofi Annan lies not just in Africa. From the age of 21, Kofi began an international formation that brought him to study in the US and Europe, and, except for a brief two-year stint in Ghana in the 1970s, he spent the rest of his professional life abroad. He said he felt profoundly African, but he absorbed so much from other cultures. And he was acutely aware of cultural differences and nuances when he interacted with people. He once told me that he doesn't speak to a Russian, say, the same way he speaks to a Chinese or a Brazilian.

Although there was always a reserve about him, he wasn't aloof. On the contrary, you always sensed he was aware of your presence. In a meeting with a dozen people around the table, if one of them frowned, even momentarily, Kofi would turn to that person and ask what was on his mind. And his memory was legendary; he would ask about your spouse by name, and how are the children? And never make a mistake.

Sir Kieran Prendergast, who was Kofi's Under-Secretary-General for Political Affairs, described this trait as "emotional intelligence". "He could read very well body language," Kieran said to me. "If you were in a meeting with him, you saw his eyes constantly scanning the other participants and, for example, if I had a headache or was feeling out of sorts, he would always notice it even though I would think I'd disguised it perfectly well, and he would ring me back afterwards and ask how I was."

"And part of his emotional intelligence," he continued, "was an exceptional degree of empathy. He got on very well with everybody. He got on with people of an extraordinarily wide range of backgrounds and an extraordinarily wide range of personalities, characters and policies. He was almost impossible to quarrel with.

"A third quality that he had in an exceptional degree was an ability to trust his colleagues and his subordinates. With most people, especially in the UN system, you have to earn trust and overcome distrust, and with Kofi I always felt that it was the other way around. He was inclined to trust you from the beginning. And for somebody who'd come up through the UN system, I think that was really quite exceptional."

"He didn't invent telephone diplomacy, but he turned it into a fine art."

Kofi was a master networker with a long Rolodex. His ability to connect with people shaped his life and his tenure as Secretary-General. Every fresh contact enriched him personally but was also an opportunity for him. He didn't invent telephone diplomacy, but he turned it into a fine art.

He was intellectually curious, had wide interests and picked up an enormous amount of finite detail that he stored away in his head. As his Spokesperson, I found it frustrating that it was so hard to tell him something he hadn't already heard somewhere else, whether it was a news item or a bit of gossip.

And he had a playful side. At boarding school in Ghana, he was known for teasing his fellow students by giving them nicknames. For example, J.S. Abbey, who as an adult became Ghana's High Commissioner to Canada and one of the nation's leading economists, was not a tall boy. So Kofi called him "Zacheus", after the biblical character that was so short he had to climb a tree to see Jesus. He called Mary Blay "Tadpole" because she was so thin and fragile. Today she is Mary Chinery-Hesse, a former principal adviser to the President of Ghana, and jokes about this nickname, given her now substantial girth. And Stanley Meisler, in his 2006 book on Kofi, recounts how on a trip to Africa in July 2002, Kofi invited the traveling journalists to his hotel suite for drinks, as he often did. I made myself useful by serving canapés to the guests. *CNN*'s Richard Roth asked whether I got an additional 15 percent for my services and Kofi quipped, "I'm training him for his next job."

Yet he always maintained an air of dignity. Dignity and serenity are the two words that emerged most often in the conversations I had with the more than 100 people I spoke to in writing this book.

John Ruggie, one of his closest advisers told me, "I don't know whether he would use the term, but he has a meditative capacity. He loves to socialize and to engage, but he also likes down time and quiet time; even if it's just by staring out the window at the East River or going for long walks, he was able to recharge." Kofi loved long walks in the mountains or woods, with his wife, Nane, or alone.

When he allowed me to retire a year and a half before the end of his mandate, I did a farewell interview for *CNN*. I was asked if I had any regrets, and I said yes, one. I told the story of being in his residence at five o'clock on the morning that the Nobel Peace Prize was to be announced. Kofi was there with Nane. An Oslo radio station reached me on my cell phone the moment the announcement was made that Kofi would share the prize with the UN. I turned to him to give him the news, and took one step towards him to give him a big hug. And then I stopped. What are you doing, I said to myself? He's the Secretary-General! My regret is I didn't hug him, I told *CNN*.

Kofi made no mention to me that he had seen that broadcast, but little escapes his attention. When the UN correspondents gave me a farewell party, and Kofi dropped in, he walked up to me in front of everybody, looked at me, then gave me a hug.

Kofi has such a rich and complex set of character traits it's not surprising that those of us who were closest to him still felt there was more to know. I hope through this book you'll get to know him better, as I think I did.

— *F.E.*

PREFACE

by Sir Brian Urquhart

It used to be said that no man was a hero to his valet. The same thought may well apply to the spokesperson of a public figure. In good times and in bad, and at all hours of the day or night, the spokesperson is in constant contact with the boss in order to represent him with the media and with public opinion. The spokesperson must find out daily what is on the boss's mind. In critical times the spokesperson must persuade him and his staff, who are often under severe stress, to agree to a public statement which is as informative as possible and which will avoid future misunderstandings while correcting past ones. With representatives of the media, the spokesperson must be prepared to maintain his equilibrium and temper in the face of a barrage of intemperate questions. All in all this is no easy job.

The office of Secretary-General of the United Nations attracts much public interest and at the same time must exercise the greatest discretion and confidentiality. The Secretary-General is involved in international matters of the highest importance, but his ability to get positive results depends to a large degree on the confidence and trust of over 190 member governments. If he is to maintain that confidence and to engage in significant dealings with those governments, he cannot indulge, as governments often do, in outspoken and critical public statements. Nor can his spokesperson. The spokesperson therefore requires a very special type of skill. Good relations with the media must be maintained; their legitimate right to information must be met as far as possible so that they can discharge *their* obligation to keep the world public informed; but none of this can be at the expense of the sensibilities or *amour-propre* of the member states of the UN.

The memoirs of a UN Secretary-General's spokesperson are of particular interest both as a first-hand account of the public life of the world's most senior international official and as a handbook on how to square the circle of contradictions and conflicting interests within which the UN Secretary-General has to function. Fred Eckhard worked for eight and a half years, during a historical period of great interest and considerable conflict, with a particularly congenial and successful Secretary-General. Kofi Annan was lucky to have Eckhard, and *vice versa.* Their time was haunted in particular by the situation in Iraq, the last years of Saddam Hussein and the ill-fated American invasion of that country, an operation intended to take a few months at most and only now, nine years later, is beginning to come to an end. The fact that a very large majority in the Security Council was opposed to the invasion put the Secretary-General in an unusually difficult relationship with the George W. Bush administration. Eckhard gives a lively account of this problem and of the incident that brought this relationship to its nadir, when a *BBC* correspondent managed to get Annan to say that the US invasion of Iraq was "illegal."

From the start Annan was an active and highly responsible Secretary-General, maintaining his independence of action on important matters even when the permanent members of the Security Council — supposedly the UN's most influential members — were not in agreement with him. In 1998 a major crisis was looming over Saddam Hussein's refusal to give the UN's weapons inspectors access to his numerous palaces, an issue that might well become the pretext for military action. Annan, in full knowledge that he would be blamed no matter what happened, insisted on going to Baghdad in a last effort to change the dictator's mind. For a short period he succeeded, until Saddam Hussein was again overcome by an apparent death wish, this time with disastrous results.

Annan was involved in critical situations in many parts of the world, negotiating a border dispute between Nigeria and Cameroon, saving East Timor from the rage of the Indonesian army, facilitating the withdrawal of Israeli troops from southern Lebanon, and negotiating solutions to scores of violent or potentially violent situations.

Kofi Annan was gregarious and outgoing. He was particularly successful in getting NGOs and the private sector more interested in and supportive of the United Nations. He was also more responsive to the media than most of his predecessors, so that the world came to expect thoughtful and constructive statements from him on important issues or events as they occurred. Drawing on his experience of earlier tragedies — Bosnia, Rwanda, Somalia — Annan also sought to bring new principles and standards into international affairs. Of these the most significant was the "Responsibility to Protect", an increased mandate for international action on massive abuses of groups within sovereign states. Governments accepted his proposal in principle at a summit meeting of the General Assembly, but have had difficulty so far in applying it in practice.

Fred Eckhard was an essential member of the team that assisted Annan in his ambitious and wide-ranging 10 years as Secretary-General. Nowhere was he more intimately involved with the Secretary-General than during two tragedies that marked Annan's tour of office — the assassination by terrorists of Annan's personal friend and representative in Baghdad, Sergio Vieira de Mello along with 21 of his colleagues; and the vicious and slanderous campaign against the Secretary-General and the United Nations that came to be known as the "Oil-for-Food Scandal." These events and their profound effect on Annan, described for the first time by Eckhard, were the downside of a very productive term of office. This book, among its many other strengths, will remind its readers that the Secretary-General, however eminent his service, is also a human being.

INTRODUCTION

THE GLASS HOUSE

One of the last things I did as Spokesperson for Kofi Annan was to get Kofi to agree to allow a photographer, Ben Murphy, to roam through the United Nations building, shooting at will. It was for a photo book called *The U.N. Building* that came out in 2006. Kofi had finally convinced the General Assembly to pay for an overhaul of the aging UN complex, removing asbestos, bringing it into conformity with the New York City fire code and so on. The building would have to be vacated for three years while this work went on and Ben wanted to make a photographic record before anything was changed.

Aaron Betsky wrote a marvelous essay for that book, describing how these extraordinary UN buildings came to be designed and built. He called it "a poem of bureaucracy in glass and stone." I spent 20 years working inside this complex and it's a world apart.

Going through the main entrance to the Secretariat, you enter a cool, high-ceilinged, marble lobby that is remarkable for what's not there. The architects did not include a UN logo, or the words United Nations, anywhere. The building itself is the logo.

My favorite spots

I had my favorite spots — the old press section at the back of the General Assembly hall with the two huge murals by Fernand Leger that looked like specimens under a microscope. In the adjacent Dag Hammarskjold Library building, the Reading Room has an undulating white pine ceiling that made me dizzy when I looked up at it. I liked to take walks in the garden to clear my head, especially in the spring, when I could stroll down a path lined with cherry trees, kicking up fallen petals. Tucked away behind the Secretary-General's conference room is a little kitchen, frozen in the 1950s, where Victor Arevalo, the butler, prepared lunch for Kofi Annan, as he did for the three previous Secretaries-General. And just next to that is the tiny bedroom, which, despite my best efforts, I could not get permission for Ben Murphy to photograph. I guess Secretaries-General are not supposed to nap.

A space very special to me is in a remote corner of the public lobby. Look for the glorious stained glass window created by Marc Chagall in honor of Dag Hammarskjold just after his death in a plane crash in Zambia on his way to negotiate an end to the Katanga secession during the Congo crisis in 1961. Stand in front of it and marvel. Then look to your left and you will see a double glass door that seems to lead to nowhere — there's a wall facing you just inside. Go in; the doors are not locked. Walk to your left around the wall and you will be in a surreal space called the Meditation Room. It was Hammarskjold's idea, bless him; he wanted just one room in the entire UN complex dedicated to silence. He designed every detail of the room himself, and personally commissioned every artist and artisan who worked on it.

It is small, about 15 feet wide at the near end, and tapering to about 10 feet wide at the back wall where there is a mural by a friend of Hammarskjold, the painter Bo Beskow — an abstract on a religious theme in hues of UN blue. In the middle of this space is a six-and-a-half ton rectangular block of iron ore, polished on the top, lit by a dim spot overhead. The mural is also lit; otherwise the room is dark.

The Meditation Room had been closed by UN security for more than ten years following a period of misuse and vandalism; security just didn't have the manpower to station someone there full time to guard it. Then Annika Savill, one of Kofi's speechwriters, led a one-woman crusade to get it reopened. Annika is a proud Swede, and she had also been diplomatic editor of the London *Independent* newspaper. You don't want to get in her way when she decides to do something. The Meditation Room was reopened, and Annika had a plaque mounted on the wall outside it with Hammarskjold's essay explaining his intent. That essay concludes, "There is an ancient saying that the sense of a vessel is not in its shell but in the void. So it is with this room. It is for those who come here to fill the void with what they find in their center of stillness".

I am grateful to Annika, because during the Oil-for-Food crisis I often retreated to that room. Kofi was taking such a terrible beating from the press, unfairly I thought, and I felt I was of no use to him. I was getting beaten up every day at my noon press briefing and the emotional pressure was mounting. So often on an afternoon I would go down to the public lobby, past Chagall and into that quiet space. It was almost always empty. I would sit on one of the few rattan-topped stools that creaked as I settled into it, and then listen to the silence. I thought of Dag and worried about the fate of the Organization that he had worked so hard to define.

The 38th Floor

The 38th floor is our West Wing, our Elysée. It is the top. The Secretary-General's office is at the northeast corner of the floor, with sweeping vistas of the East River and Queens, and the Deputy Secretary-General's is at the southwest corner with a breathtaking view of midtown Manhattan. In between are the mostly modest-sized offices of those who are privileged to work directly for the boss. It is very quiet. One never raises one's voice. You might say there's a 38th floor culture — a way of acting, of talking, of dressing. Secretary-General Kurt Waldheim carried this to an extreme — he would allow no woman to wear trousers and let it be known that he didn't approve of the color red.

But in fact the 38th floor is not the highest floor of the Secretariat building. There are three more, one with a large space with mirrored walls used by the ballroom dance club and the aerobic exercise club, another with ping-pong tables, especially popular with our Chinese staff members, and a third with miscellaneous offices.

I once asked Mark Hoffman, the chief of the Secretary-General's security detail for a time, if I could go up on the roof. He arranged it. A security officer took me up a flight of stairs from the 41st floor, inserted a key in a door and walked me out into the open air. It was a clear day, but windy. The building's aluminum grid rises another 20 feet or so above roof level to hide the water tank and other functional things that sit atop Manhattan skyscrapers. Peering out through one frame, I could see forever. Looking west, there was First Avenue below, then Second and Third. At Lexington, there was the exquisite Chrysler building, with its stainless steel crown glistening in the sunlight, then the Empire State a bit further south on Fifth and the cluster of tall new buildings rising in Times Square. And well to the south, the twin towers of the World Trade Center dominated the skyline.

I imagined the famous Saul Steinberg cover illustration for *The New Yorker*, and saw beyond Times Square to the Hudson River, New Jersey, Pennsylvania, California, then the Pacific with a small rock in it labeled Japan and a great expanse behind it that was China and Russia.

It was spring 2001. I had been Kofi Annan's Spokesperson for more than four years, during his first term when he could do no wrong, and the world looked pretty good.

YOUR VOICE IS NOT YOUR OWN

As a spokesperson, you have a curious job. When you open your mouth, it isn't your words that you're speaking. You're always expressing the views of somebody else. It's as if your tongue is not your own; your mind is not your own. You're the embodiment of another person, an office, an institution. Even in private conversation with a journalist, should you express a personal view, you would distort your message because the next time you speak in your official capacity your words will be filtered through the bias that you might have revealed in a weak moment. You always have to be guarded.

As Spokesperson for the United Nations, your time is not your own. You deal with journalists in every time zone. They get your cell phone number and punch it into their own cell phones so they can call you by pressing a single button. They do so easily, sometimes to ask the simplest question, without thinking that while it's daytime where they are, it could be nighttime for you. How many times did my cell phone go off at 3 o'clock in the morning? "Oh, sorry, did I wake you? I just wanted to ask you…"

As Spokesperson for Kofi Annan, I developed an instinctive sense of his presence. In a crowded room I tried never to lose sight of the top of his graying head for fear he would leave without me. I was the first person to see him at work in the morning, waiting for him at the loading dock in the third basement, handing him his morning news feed. When my cell phone rang, days, nights or weekends, I jumped for it, thinking it could be him. I judged his mood by the spring in his step and worried for his health if he sounded hoarse.

I came to think that the relationship between the boss and his spokesperson is like a good marriage. You get to know each other's thinking, you can complete each other's sentences, your lives become entwined inextricably. Your voice becomes his voice.

MEETING KOFI

I first met Kofi Annan when he was UN budget director, after I was hired in 1985 by Secretary-General Javier Perez de Cuellar to trouble shoot for the UN with the United States Congress. These were the Reagan years. It was morning in America and the sun seemed to be setting on the UN. Congress never saw a piece of legislation to withhold US funding for the UN that it didn't like. US arrears to the UN were mounting fast.

The Heritage Foundation in Washington was one of the new conservative think tanks that were springing up all over the country, inspired by conservative writer and publisher William Buckley and riding Ronald Reagan's coattails. One of Heritage's biggest moneymakers was its UN studies program. A day hardly passed by that Heritage didn't put out yet another press release revealing some UN shortcoming, outrage or scandal, and contributions from conservative supporters poured in to Heritage appreciatively. My job was to draft a rebuttal to each charge, get it cleared in New York, run off 150 copies and walk from one end of the Hill to the other, buttonholing Congressional staffers, and saying, "Did you see the Heritage press release this morning? Want to know the UN view?"

Three years later, around Christmas during President Reagan's last year in office, the White House issued a statement, that nobody read, saying that the President felt that the UN had sufficiently reformed and that he would be instructing the State Department to draw up a timetable for the repayment of US arrears. However, the Administration doesn't control the purse strings; Congress does. And repayment of arrears wouldn't start until more than 10 years later when Kofi Annan struck a deal with Congressional leaders.

As I usually spent three days a week in Washington and two in New York, I was seen as the guy just arrived in town with fresh news of the other place. In New York, it wasn't uncommon for a senior UN official to call me to ask about the latest prognosis for US funding of the UN. One of those who called was Kofi Annan.

Kofi made an impression on me in waves. First, there's his African-ness, including his Lumumba beard. Georges Abi Saab, an Egyptian who studied with Kofi in Geneva in 1961-62, said that the Lumumba beard, in the style of the assassinated Congolese leader Patrice Lumumba, was for many Africans in those days a badge of progressive African nationalism. Georges added that over the years his other African friends shaved their beards, while Kofi kept his and made it a sign of distinction. "For me," he said, "that symbolized his fidelity to his convictions."

His eyes are soft brown and expressive. He is slightly wall-eyed; his left eye can drift a bit, especially when he's tired. Kofi is so controlled that unless you're reading his eyes you're not getting the whole message.

When he starts to speak, you have to listen carefully. He talks just above a whisper. His voice is deep and soothing. It calms you. And he has something of a Caribbean lilt, to my ear, dropping the "g" on most words ending in "ing", so he says "talkin" and "listenin".

And he is very aware of *you*. He's reading your body language, listening to what you say between the lines. But you don't sense that this is aggressive attention, as if he's trying to gain strategic advantage over you, but rather sympathetic attention, as if he wants to get to know you better, to connect with you. You come to feel that he likes people; indeed, that he likes and is at home with himself.

And it seems he has always been this way. Abi Saab said of his former classmate, "Kofi had vivid alertness. He was intelligent and clever and very, very personable. Oh, that smoothness of his! He was friends with almost everybody. He knew how to get along with people. I appreciated this in him."

OFF ON MISSION

In the fall of 1988, I joined the Spokesperson's Office of Secretary-General Javier Perez de Cuellar. I was number three or four under François Giuliani, the Corsican Frenchman who was perhaps the most powerful UN Spokesperson ever. You can't go to school to learn to be a spokesperson, so I studied François. I admired his confidence and was impressed with how he intimidated the journalists. But his style was not mine.

One day I was listening to him brief the press at noon, a daily tradition that started in 1962 under U Thant, and I heard him say something inaccurate. With the righteous indignation of a freshman spokesperson, I ran down to the briefing room on the second floor and caught him coming out. "François," I said breathlessly, "what you said wasn't right. We'll have to issue a correction." François looked at me, amused, and said dismissively, "Once I said it, it became right." He didn't issue a correction.

Although I think François liked me — he used to invite me to his office after work, when he would open a bottle of wine or two for up to a dozen of his closest associates who would gather around to chat — he seemed more comfortable with me out of the office. In the spring of 1989, he recommended me as spokesperson for the UN peacekeeping mission in Namibia headed by Martti Ahtisaari of Finland.

The Namibia mission helped redefine peacekeeping. It wasn't just soldiers, it was civilian police, political officers, humanitarian workers, election supervisors, constitutional experts. In short, it was the beginning of complex peacekeeping. Martti and his top people were thinking on their feet, adapting to reality as we went along. And although the mission was touch and go at the start, it finished on time a year later with Namibia achieving its long-sought independence from South Africa. Those of us who participated in it returned triumphant and energized.

François, the consummate political operator, realized he needed to channel my energies in another direction. The UN Secretariat recommends a spokesperson to each incoming President of the General Assembly. In 1990, François pushed me to become spokesperson for Guido de Marco of Malta who, like Martti, later became President of his country. Guido didn't just want to preside over the Assembly, he wanted to lead it, and got extra-budgetary funds to travel to the Middle East just as the US was about to lead a multinational force to

Eckhard in Sarajevo 1992 in the basement of the Rainbow Hotel, temporary UN Headquarters, after it had been hit by Serb tank fire. "I found that being a UN spokesperson who couldn't say the Serbs were wrong, who couldn't comment on the rape of Foča, who couldn't express the moral outrage of the world at naked aggression, was to have no voice at all."

liberate Kuwait. I remember privately telling reporters, "Shhh! Listen, it's the Security Council, not the General Assembly, that's involved in this; we're just here on a friendly visit." It was fascinating to watch the Maltese team at work, though; they're hyper-political and know the Middle East like the back of their hand. They also adopted me as a member of their clan and took me to Malta with them, brought me into their homes, introduced me to their families, shared their wine.

When that was over in 1991, François recommended me for the UN peacekeeping mission in Bosnia. Did he not want me around? The mission had a military head, the refined General Satish Nambiar of India, who established mission headquarters in the Bosnian capital of Sarajevo in March 1992. So I packed my bags, hoping for another Namibia.

Before we left, we were given an orientation lesson, which included an impressive presentation on the age-old rivalry in Yugoslavia between Serbs, Croats and Muslims. The lecturer was Shashi

Tharoor, the special assistant to Marrack Goulding, then head of the peacekeeping department. Shashi had breezed through a Ph.D. at Tufts University in record time and was something of a boy wonder. When he finished his presentation, he asked if there were any questions. I couldn't help asking, "And what if war breaks out in Bosnia?" Shashi commented, François style, something like, "A typical journalist's question." He didn't answer it.

The Bosnian war erupted suddenly a month after our arrival, with the Serbs shelling Sarajevo wantonly from the surrounding mountains, forcing us to temporarily pull out in disgrace. The UN soon returned to Sarajevo with a new mandate — to accompany aid deliveries as the fighting continued, and I was rotated in and out of the city, first from Belgrade, then from Zagreb. I alternated with two other UN spokesmen, an Icelander and a Palestinian. I got a taste of war.

My time as spokesperson in Sarajevo was full of naked frustration. I set up the press office near the front door of our headquarters building for the convenience of the journalists, but that also meant that the security officers called on me each time someone knocked on the door asking to speak to someone from the UN. On one occasion a group of about a dozen people stood outside, anguished and agitated. They had had telephone contact with family or friends in the eastern village of Foča. The Serbs were attacking, they said, and terrible things were happening. Please do something. I told them there was nothing peacekeepers could do in time of war. I tried to guide them to the International Red Cross, but it was little solace. Eventually they left, more in disappointment than anger.

On another occasion, a lone woman came to the door. "I am a Serb," she said. "My neighbor, who is a Muslim, asked me to take her two children because with me they would have a better chance

Fred Eckhard and the BBC's Martin Bell chatting on the staircase of a bombed out building in Bosnia.

of survival." She then looked me in the eye and said in a low voice, "Don't let us do this to ourselves." Again, I explained why we were helpless, but she seemed to know what my response would be. She thanked me and walked toward the pole in front of the building where the UN flag was flying. She took a candle out of her pocket, placed it at the base of the flagpole, lit it and walked off, across the street and up the hill opposite from where I could hear tank fire.

Peacekeepers don't have enemies. But I found that being a UN spokesperson who couldn't say the Serbs were wrong, who couldn't comment on the rape of Foča, who couldn't express the moral outrage of the world at naked aggression, was to have no voice at all.

In Sarajevo, I built up a profound admiration for the war correspondents, like the *BBC*'s Martin Bell or *CNN*'s Christiane Amanpour, who covered that conflict and who, too, took their casualties. A reporter for the Catalan newspaper *Avui*, Eric Hauck, lost his photographer, Jordi

Pujol Puente, who at age 25 became the first foreign journalist killed in the Bosnian war. Margaret Moth, Christiane's camerawoman, lost a part of her face in Sniper Alley when a bullet passed through her cheek. Martin was felled with shrapnel in the groin.

WITH VANCE AND OWEN

As I was working in Sarajevo, sleeping in my office on a cot wearing a helmet and a flak jacket, briefing journalists when the shelling died down enough for them to make it to our headquarters, I was noticed by Ambassador Herbert S. Okun, the right hand to former US Secretary of State Cyrus R. Vance.

Vance, working as Secretary-General Perez de Cuellar's envoy, had successfully negotiated the first Yugoslav peace agreement between Serbs and Croats, before the Bosnian war broke out. Now, with war spreading like wildfire through the former Yugoslavia, the UN and the European Community had decided to launch joint Yugoslav peace talks in Geneva. These would be co-chaired by Vance, representing the UN, and Lord (David) Owen, former Foreign Secretary of the UK, representing the EC. They needed a spokesperson, and Okun threw in my name. Vance agreed and I said yes.

Marrack "Mig" Goulding, the head of UN peacekeeping at the time, was making a visit to Sarajevo. I accompanied his delegation on a tour of downtown. All of a sudden, shots rang out. UN security officers surrounded Goulding, who crouched behind a UN vehicle. "Bloody Serbs," I said to myself, walking to the front of the vehicle and staring off in the direction of the gunshots. I thought they were just trying to intimidate us by firing over our heads. I believe this is called being "shell-shocked"; it was time for me to leave Sarajevo.

"Working for Vance and Owen was like being in Spokesperson's Heaven." Eckhard here conferring with former US Secretary of State Cyrus R. Vance and former UK Foreign Secretary Lord (David) Owen, Co-Chaimen of the International Conference on the Former Yugoslavia, 1992.

Goulding was flying out the next morning to Geneva, where he was to meet Vance and Owen. I hitched a ride on his UN plane. I had never been to Geneva, and marveled at how clean and orderly it was. Unlike Sarajevo, there were no burnt out trams on the street, or bullet holes in the walls of buildings, or broken glass in window frames.

As Goulding entered the meeting room in the Palais des Nations to join Vance, Owen, Sadako Ogata, the UN High Commissioner for Refugees, and others, I paused at the door. Did I dare go in? But Okun grabbed my arm and ushered me into the room. "You will be in every meeting," he said. And I was.

Working for Vance and Owen was like being in Spokesperson's Heaven. The US State Department had always had a very progressive press policy — spokesperson Richard Boucher once told me that he saw every piece of paper that crossed Colin Powell's desk. Vance and Owen didn't go that far, but got close. Owen, who seemed unsure of me at first, maybe because of my nationality (I'm American), quickly warmed to me and kept me briefed on the European view of things. It was at these Geneva talks that I refined my sense of my job and my profession.

Vance and Owen did a masterful job, aided by Martti Ahtisaari, who crafted a new Bosnian map with a three-way split of the land in non-contiguous pieces that would have kept Bosnia whole. Within six months, in the spring of 1993, they had the Serb, Croat and Muslim leadership gathered in Athens for a reluctant signing of a peace agreement. But the Vance Owen Peace Plan had garnered enemies in Washington, who thought it was too pro-Serb and who, frankly, hadn't mastered the complex technicalities of it. (As a reflection of military reality, the Ahtisaari map gave the Serbs 51 percent of the land; militarily, they controlled more like 70 percent.) President Clinton got cold feet, Secretary of State Warren Christopher indicated only mild support, and without strong US backing, the plan, duly signed by all parties, collapsed. The war dragged on for two and a half more years before the US got serious and sent in Ambassador Richard Holbrooke to negotiate the Dayton Peace Agreement, which was even more pro-Serb because, of course, the world had continued to turn.

After the Athens signing, Vance left the peace talks, which then staggered on under Owen and Vance's replacement, Thorvald Stoltenberg, the former Foreign Minister of Norway. I left a few months later to return to New York. I had separated from my wife three years before and my son had just turned 17 and needed nudging to get into college. I had a lot of unfinished business on the home front.

The UN had changed while I was away. Boutros Boutros-Ghali had taken over from Perez de Cuellar, and from what I had heard of him he scared me. He joked about governing the UN "through stealth and sudden violence", and there seemed some truth to that. François Giuliani and his deputy Nadia Younes had both been pushed aside by him, and the new spokesperson was Joe Sills of the US, someone I knew well.

Peacekeeping was undergoing explosive growth, but not every mission was a success. Bosnia was going badly and Somalia was on the rocks. The peacekeeping department, now headed by Kofi Annan, was stretched to the limit with a record number of missions and personnel abroad. It was, in fact, a new UN. It was no longer just a talk shop. It had become an operational entity, regularly rotating tens of thousands of soldiers, experimenting with peace enforcement in Somalia, running a government in Cambodia. These were heady days at the UN, brought on by the end of the Cold War and the perception, wrong it turned out, that what was emerging was a New World Order with the United Nations at the center of it.

SPOKESPERSON ON PEACEKEEPING

I had now been at the UN for eight years and I had never received a promotion. At the UN you don't necessarily get a promotion for doing good work. You get a promotion when you change jobs, moving to a post with a higher grade and therefore a higher salary. There wasn't a more senior post available in the Spokesperson's Office; but frankly, I hadn't noticed. I was having too good a time.

But with my son thinking of going to college now, I had to get serious. The Spokesperson's Office was for me the most exciting place to be. You work with journalists, and that means working harder and faster, always following the news and being ready to jump when they ask you a question. Journalists are a good reality check. Most people in the Secretariat talk to each other all day and, maybe if they're lucky, to a diplomat. Nothing could be more different than talking to journalists, and I did so all day long. They keep you on your toes. They keep you honest.

How to get a promotion while staying in the Spokesperson's Office, I asked myself?

A morning staff meeting with Spokesperson Joe Sills. "He was probably the most laid back guy in the United Nations." (Left to right: Lili Schindler, Juan Carlos Brandt, Fred Eckhard, Joe Sills, Ahmad Fawzi, Hiro Ueki and Fabienne Seguin-Horton).

I was at a reception, one of those little wine and cheese things that happen at the UN all the time when someone is going away or has just come back or has a birthday or gets a promotion. Kofi Annan was there. I walked up to him and said, "Kofi, I need a promotion but I love my job. Why don't you top off my salary? I will work for both you and the Secretary-General and I will speak on peacekeeping out of the Spokesperson's Office?" He looked at me and smiled. "All right," is all he said. And the very next day his office began the paperwork to make it happen. I liked the way he operated — quick decisions, immediate follow-up.

Meanwhile, the journalists had recognized that I was back at Headquarters after three years' experience in the field. I knew peacekeeping; I had been there. I had been shelled in Sarajevo and had spoken for the Geneva peace talks. And peacekeeping, especially the Bosnia mission, was where the UN was making front-page news.

Evelyn Leopold of Reuters, the doyenne of the press corps, began rattling cages on the 38th floor, saying let Eckhard brief on peacekeeping; he's the only one in the Spokesperson's Office who knows anything about it. Boutros-Ghali hesitated; he first asked Alvaro de Soto, the patrician Peruvian, to do a feasibility study. After talking with journalists, Alvaro concluded that I should speak on peacekeeping, alongside Joe Sills, Spokesperson for the Secretary-General.

Surprisingly, Joe didn't mind. In fact, he welcomed the help. He and I had worked together in the 1970s at the United Nations Association. On a UNA visit to Nashville, Tennessee, his hometown, he had introduced me to mint juleps. He had helped me get my first job in the Spokesperson's Office. And he was probably the most laid-back guy in the United Nations. The new arrangement was going to work out fine.

So for the next two years Joe and I went down to the briefing room together every day at noon. Joe would brief on Boutros-Ghali's activities, and I would brief on the Bosnian war, the collapse of the Somalia mission, touch and go in Cambodia, the genocide in Rwanda and the near-impossible mission in the Democratic Republic of the Congo.

And for me to do that job, I needed access to the peacekeeping department. When I asked Kofi if I could sit in on his morning meeting, he said yes. When I asked him if I could talk freely to his staff, he said yes. When I asked if I could read the confidential cables that came in from peacekeeping missions around the world, he said yes again. Another Spokesperson's Heaven. So from 1993 to 1995, I became embedded in Kofi Annan's peacekeeping department and got to watch him up close for the first time.

Kofi once headed the UN personnel department, one of the world's most arcane institutions, and he knew how to use the rules to his advantage. When he was appointed head of peacekeeping, he took as his deputy Iqbal Riza, a former Pakistani diplomat who had distinguished himself in UN missions in Central America. He pried loose from Cambodia Hedi Annabi, the gifted Tunisian, who was helping to set up the UN peacekeeping mission there. And he brought along the Sorbonne-educated Elisabeth Lindenmayer, daughter of a French army officer, who had been a close aide from his days in personnel in 1987. He inherited a strong core of staff put together by Marrack Goulding, including the smooth and wily Russian, Dmitri Titov, who became Annabi's deputy, and Shashi Tharoor, the brilliant Indian who wrote novels on the side, and who followed Yugoslavia.

Iqbal said of Kofi, "He was handling up to seventeen peacekeeping operations with deployments around the world — an explosion in operational capacity with very thin staff. And everything used to run well."

At his morning meeting, Kofi rode herd over these strong, ambitious directors with understated mastery. I may have underestimated him because he made it look so easy. I thought he just sat there and listened while these overachievers jumped through hoops for him. But in 1995, Boutros-Ghali sent Kofi to Bosnia to hand over the UN peacekeeping mission to NATO. Kofi was away for months. As a temporary replacement for him, Boutros appointed the wise Iraqi Kurd, Ismat Kitani. Ismat had *gravitas*, but couldn't keep the directors from sniping at each other. The teamwork was not as strong. Finally Kofi came back, took his place at the head of the table, and everyone snapped back to attention.

Hedi Annabi told me later, "He had one exceptional quality that no other person I've worked with has had to the same degree: he had a knack for team building. He knows how to talk to people to motivate them. And those morning meetings with him were all about building a team, about encouraging people to engage, empowering them, giving them positive feedback — he wouldn't give negative feedback in front of everyone else. He had that quality of diffusing possible tension in the morning meeting, and there was tension, of course."

GETTING TO KNOW BOUTROS

The more I hung out in Kofi Annan's peacekeeping department, the better I liked it. In September 1994, I began sniffing around for a job there, but there were no suitable openings. Boutros-Ghali's Chief of Staff was Jean-Claude Aimé of Haiti. Jean-Claude had been an occasional guest at François's after-hours office gatherings, and although he struck me as somewhat dour, I found him likeable. But as Chief of Staff, he had become feared, and people said that he and Boutros brought out the worst in each other.

When word reached Jean-Claude that I was looking to join Kofi's department, he summoned me to his 38th floor office. I was nervous. Jean-Claude can be tough, but he has a nice smile, and he tried to put me at ease. "The Secretary-General is going on an extended trip to Egypt, South Asia and the Far East," he began. "He would like you to accompany him as Spokesperson."

Traveling in the Far East with Secretary-General Boutros Boutros-Ghali in September 1994. "I was beginning to warm to this man."

"Whoa," I thought. I was too junior to go on a major trip with the Secretary-General. The furthest I got with Perez de Cuellar was Montreal, and I had never traveled with Boutros. "Why me?" I blurted out — which is not how you're supposed to talk on the 38th floor. Jean-Claude smiled and said simply, "He likes to rotate his Spokesperson when he travels," which I knew was not true. There was a hidden agenda here, and I suspected it had to do with my desire to work for Kofi.

I prepared for the trip as best I could, asking Joe Sills for detailed advice. Then we were off. From Europe we went to Egypt, Boutros's home country. I knocked on the door of his suite to deliver him a news feed. I heard him say, "Come in!" He welcomed me, thanked me for the news update, and wandered over to a balcony. It was warm and pleasant and the balcony doors were open and he invited me to follow him out. We were on a high floor with a commanding view of the city. "My Parliamentary district was over there," Boutros said, pointing off into the distance. "I know every street." He talked about his constituents and their issues. "My God," I thought, "he's human after all."

The trip continued without a hitch as we went on to Japan and then China, where Boutros was to address the UN Women's Conference. In Japan, I again knocked on the door of his suite one evening to deliver a news feed, and a woman's voice commanded me to enter. Oh, no. It was his wife, Leah, a multi-headed monster, from what I had heard, who ate little boys for lunch. I went in cautiously; Leah had her feet up on the couch, her shoes off and a glass of whisky in her hand. Sitting opposite her was Lisa Buttenheim, a first rate political officer from the US who later became Jean-Claude's wife, with one of her colleagues. They were both sitting bolt upright, also with glasses in their hands. "The bottle is over there," Leah said, gesturing to a side table. "Help yourself; I'm not going to serve you." I poured a neat scotch, which I never drink, and sat rigidly next to Lisa. The conversation, led animatedly by Leah, was on politics and life. What a personality!

Leah came from the renowned Jewish Egyptian family of candy makers, Nadler. Boutros-Ghali was a Coptic Christian, who accompanied President Anwar Sadat on his historic visit to Jerusalem in 1977, for which Sadat was assassinated in 1981. Boutros-Ghali himself must have been on a dozen hit lists. He had the highest threat rating of any Secretary-General. I began to understand why he sometimes resorted to stealth and sudden violence.

Leah was habitually late. In Beijing, we were staying in a state guesthouse and were all gathered in the lobby. The motorcade was waiting to take us to our first official meeting of the day. Leah was missing, but Boutros seemed to be used to it. To help pass the time, I went up to him to hand him the morning news feed. "Ah!" he said, looking at the first page. He then took me by the arm, and walked away from the group. "What's going on here is…", he said, commenting on the first news item. From there he went on to the second and the third, lecturing me on the history of the events and providing political analysis. I was beginning to warm to this man.

When we returned to New York, I was again summoned to Jean-Claude's office. "I understand you've been looking for a job in the peacekeeping department," he began. "We would like you to stay in the Spokesperson's Office, and if you do I will see to it that we find a post somewhere to give you a promotion." Promises, promises. I said I would think about it overnight, but I had already made a decision. I called Jean-Claude the next day and told him I still wanted to work for Kofi Annan. In my gut, I trusted Kofi more.

MOVING TO THE 37TH FLOOR

In October 1995, Boutros struck me with stealth and sudden violence, declaring that I should not brief on peacekeeping anymore. No explanation given. This probably had more to do with Kofi than with me, because Boutros was approaching the fifth and final year of his first term. Although he had originally said he didn't want a second term, he was beginning to change his mind, even though he was already 72. ("Only a stupid person doesn't change his mind," he said.) Yet his relations with the US were strained, and his personal relationship with Ambassador Madeleine Albright was getting downright hostile. Kofi might have looked like a competitor if Albright was looking around for an alternative to Boutros. And she was.

Kofi wrote a letter about my suspension of duties to Boutros's communications director, John Hughes. "While I do not understand the basis for this sudden and rather surprising decision — nor do I need to know it," he wrote, "I wish to place on record my appreciation of the outstanding contribution he has made in that capacity [i.e. as Associate Spokesperson specializing in peacekeeping]."

He praised my record in the UN, concluding, "He is undoubtedly one of the best spokespersons I have come across in 33 years at the United Nations." He then asked that his letter be placed in my personnel file. He called me into his office and handed me a copy of the letter. Then he shook my hand, and with a sly smile, he said, "Don't let the turkeys get you down."

I stayed in the Spokesperson's Office, but I was running in low gear. I couldn't stand not having a noon briefing to deliver. Shortly afterwards, I heard of an opening for an information officer in Kofi's department at the next grade up, and I decided to take the plunge. I applied for it and got it. That was my first official UN promotion.

Being in the peacekeeping department had a certain buzz. News was coming in, but I had nothing to do with it once I had it in my hands. My job was to answer the calls of delegations and take their questions. But they never called. Governments had complained that the press was getting all the information first. (What else is new; that's their job, isn't it?) They wanted their own information channel within the peacekeeping department and they funded it, but then never used it.

So I sat in an office where the phone never rang. I decided to take up special projects. One was to draft media guidelines for the department. I made them very liberal, saying, in effect, that everyone in the peacekeeping department could talk to the press within their area of competence. Kofi liked the draft, and sent it up to Boutros's office for approval. The 38th floor promptly sent the text back down, refusing to adopt it because they said a single department shouldn't have media guidelines. So I went back to my computer, changed the word "department" to "secretariat" every time it appeared and gave it back to Kofi as a set of guidelines for the whole Secretariat. He again sent it up to the 38th floor, and this time we never heard back from them. So much for media guidelines.

This was 1996, and now the rumors about the US wanting to replace Boutros-Ghali were rife. Tension rose between the 38th floor and Kofi's office directly below it on the 37th, as Kofi's name was circulating throughout the building as a possible candidate. Things got so bad that Kofi went to see Boutros to assure him that he wasn't running for the office, but Boutros wasn't consoled.

THREE STRIKES

For Madeleine Albright, Boutros-Ghali had three strikes against him. First, he had been reluctant to authorize NATO air strikes against the Bosnian Serbs. This was an unfair criticism, in my view, because the Security Council was divided on the question of air strikes. The British and the French, each with veto power, had troops in the UN peacekeeping mission in Bosnia. There's an old adage in the UN that you can't make peace and war at the same time. If NATO were to bomb the Serbs with the blessing of the Security Council, the Serbs would declare war on the peacekeepers. Britain and France were not in favor of air strikes. The US, on the other hand, had no troops in Bosnia and was under domestic political pressure to get tough with the Serbs. Washington favored air strikes. Reflecting this underlying disagreement was the Security Council resolution that said that for air strikes to take place, two keys had to be turned — one by NATO and one by the UN Secretary-General. Pity poor Boutros.

The Serbs then outraged world opinion, first with the Srebrenica massacre of some 7,000 Muslim men and boys, and then when they fired mortars on Sarajevo's Markale marketplace, killing 37 people. Now the British and the French felt there had to be a NATO air strike and were willing to go along with the Americans. They regrouped their peacekeepers, circling the wagons in anticipation of the Serb response. The NATO hand was ready to turn the key. Madeleine Albright tried to get Boutros on the telephone to get him to turn it too. But he was in a commercial airliner en route to an official visit to the Caribbean. He was unreachable. Boutros had "passed the key" to Kofi during the brief time that he was unavailable. When Albright asked Kofi, he didn't hesitate. He said yes. Richard Holbrooke told Phillip Gourevitch of *The New Yorker*, "When Kofi turned that key, he became Secretary-General-in-waiting."

Strike two against Boutros came after the UN handover to NATO in Bosnia. The US realized it had bitten off more than it could chew and wanted the UN to maintain its presence in Eastern Slavonia, a Serb enclave in Croatia. Boutros said he wasn't for that; take all or nothing. Albright criticized him publicly for his stand. In closed Security Council consultations, Boutros referred to her criticism as "*vulgaire*" in French, meaning crude or common. Now in diplomacy, that's a pit fight.

Strike three involved Israel. Israeli soldiers had fired on a UN observation post in Qana, southern Lebanon, in April 1996, killing 106 civilians who had taken refuge there. Boutros asked his military adviser, Dutch General Frank van Kappen, for a report. Van Kappen wrote that the evidence pointed either to intentional targeting of the UN outpost or to gross incompetence. Madeleine Albright and the Israelis asked Boutros to not issue the report or at least to water

"There emerged a 'Transition Team' of about a dozen people. I was one." (Left to right: Fred Eckhard, Patricio Civili, Larry Johnson, Lamin Sise, Rolf Knutsson, Iqbal Riza, Elisabeth Lindenmayer, Kofi Annan, Gillian Sorensen, Shashi Tharoor, J.P. Halbwachs and Frederico Riesco).

it down. Boutros refused and issued the report as written — a brave and principled stance that amounted to political suicide.

Robert Orr handled the UN portfolio at the National Security Council then. He said, "We needed a partner. And in Secretary-General Boutros-Ghali, we had someone who did not seem to have a deep understanding of why he was in trouble with the US. We therefore needed to find an individual who could represent the best at the UN but also understand the US."

Kofi could no longer ignore the serious interest being shown in him by the United States. A friend, Ted Sorensen, the former speechwriter for and close adviser to President John Kennedy, volunteered to coach him in election politics. Kofi and Ted held several meetings with about a dozen people, and I was invited to the last one. At that meeting, Sorensen looked at Kofi and said, "If you have any skeletons in your closet, now is the time to tell us." Kofi looked down at his hands, as if he were embarrassed to be asked. "There's nothing, no," he said in almost a whisper. From these meetings there emerged a "Transition Team" of about a dozen people. I was one.

Madeleine Albright now had two uphill battles, one within the Clinton Administration and another in the Security Council. She won both. On 17 December 1996, the General Assembly voted Kofi Annan by acclamation as the seventh Secretary-General of the United Nations.

It's hard to imagine how unexpected this must have been for Kofi. No one from within the Secretariat had ever made it to the top post. (Perez de Cuellar had done a short stint in the Secretariat but before that had been a lifetime Ambassador for Peru.) In the past, Governments had looked to Foreign Ministers (Trygve Lie, Kurt Waldheim or Boutros Boutros-Ghali, who at the last minute was elevated to Deputy Prime Minister to increase his chances), or at least to Ambassadors or foreign ministry officials (Dag Hammarskjold, U Thant, Javier Perez de Cuellar). But Kofi was just a member of the UN Secretariat. He had no reason to think this would ever happen to him.

I went to see him on him on 2 January 1997, his first day on the job. He was standing in the middle of the Secretary-General's office, with only the essential furniture in place. The walls were almost bare. There were only one or two books on the otherwise empty bookshelves. His desk was clean. I sensed he was afraid. When I asked him about this 12 years later, he laughed and said, "No; if I had been afraid, I would not have gotten that far. I was more reflective, in anticipation of what was to come — where do we begin?" But a plan of attack would emerge quickly. More than any of his predecessors, he knew in detail what the job entailed before he took it on.

Kofi asked Iqbal Riza to be his Chief of Staff. Iqbal told me: "This was a very unexpected turn in his life. I remember, after the Security Council nominated him, he turned to me and said, 'You know, Iqbal, there's a hand somewhere that has brought me here. I don't know where it is or how it has got me here, but I haven't gotten here by myself.' So I said, yes, that's a good way to think about it."

I

GETTING TO THE TOP

CHAPTER 1

INSIDE KOFI ANNAN

GHANA

Kofi Annan doesn't speak about himself and seems uncomfortable when an interviewer asks a personal question. Julia Preiswerk, who has known Kofi for more than 45 years, told me, "Kofi has an extremely clear sense of limits and space. Getting past the point where you start invading his space is very hard to do. He has a way of maintaining distance in all circumstances."

Several good biographies of Kofi Annan have gone into the details of his life. We cooperated fully with the authors, and Kofi spent hours with each of them. There was the profile in *The New Yorker* by Philip Gourevitch in 2003; a book, in German in 2005, by Friederike Bauer, the foreign editor of the *Frankfurter Allgemeine Zeitung*; and then the books in 2006 by James Traub of *The New York Times* magazine and by Stanley Meisler former UN correspondent for the *Los Angeles Times*. Collectively, they present a pretty detailed picture of Kofi Annan the person, but let me try to fill in some gaps.

The Asante in him

Kofi's family was a mixture of Fante and Asante — his father, Henry Reginald Annan, was a fifty-fifty mix. Kofi's paternal grandfather was Fante, and his paternal grandmother was Asante. His mother, Rose, was pure Fante. The Fante were a group from the Ghanaian coast that gradually settled inland in Kumasi, the capital of the ancient Asante Kingdom. As coastal people, they had extensive contact over the centuries with Europeans and learned to get along with them. The Asante did not.

Patrick Hayford, a former Ghanaian ambassador who worked for Kofi at the UN, told me that the Asante are warlike; the Fante are laid back. Kofi has Fante qualities on the surface, he said — gentle, soft-spoken, relaxed — but Asante qualities underneath — strong, stubborn, fights for what he believes in. "When I was ambassador to South Africa," he told me, "Kofi went on this famous mission to Baghdad. And the *BBC* called me and asked, why is this man going on this very risky mission at this time? And my answer was, 'Kofi looks very gentle, very quiet, very soft, but there is an inner strength, and in times of testing that inner strength comes out." And then he laughed. "That, perhaps, is part of the Asante in him."

I realize now that the mild-mannered, easy-going man whom we all found it so easy to like would never have made a great Secretary-General without the Asante in him.

A Proper British Household

Henry Reginald, or HR, was a prominent Ghanaian of his generation who left a profound impact on all of his children. Kofi's younger brother, Kobina, told me that their father might have sought election as a tribal leader, had he wished. He was highly placed on both the Fante and Asante sides and became very close to the paramount leader of the Asante, the Asantehene. But instead he became an executive in a Unilever subsidiary, the United Africa Company, and went to work every day in a dark suit, purchasing cocoa for export.

He headed a proper British household with his wife, Victoria, and regularly attended services at the Anglican Church. But he gave all his children Ghanaian names, which at that time, for a person in his position, Kobina said, was almost revolutionary. HR's eldest daughter was named Nana Essie (Essie means born on Sunday) to distinguish her from his second daughter, Essie, who was also born on Sunday. He named the twins Kofi Atta (Kofi means born on Friday, Atta means "twin") and Efua Atta. And his youngest son he named Kobina.

In his book, Stanley Meisler says that Kofi's mother is Victoria, while James Traub gives her name as Rose. In a sense, they were both right. But the clue to the mystery was given to me by Kofi's daughter, Ama. "They all had different mothers," she said of her father's family, rolling her eyes upward in what I interpreted as a mild disapproval. In conversations with other family members the facts emerged. Indeed, it was not very British but certainly not uncommon for Ghanaians of HR's generation to father children by different women. And he did. Nana Essie was not born to Victoria, but Essie was. Kofi and Efua were the twins of Rose, a Fante woman from the coast. And Kobina's mother was Ama.

Yet, in the British tradition, HR raised all his children under his and Victoria's roof. Kobina was Ghana's Ambassador to Morocco until his retirement in 2009. I reached him by phone and asked him about his family. Victoria, he said, was HR's "English wedded wife", in other words his wife in the Western tradition. "She was the backbone of the family," he said, "being in the house but also getting very involved in church activities. She did some trading through Unilever as well. She was issued a passbook by the company, through which she advanced them money and then was given merchandise to sell. So she had a passbook and was doing trading in cloth and other things. You find that a lot in the upper class Ghanaian homes maybe about thirty years ago, a matriarch being a businesswoman in addition to being a housekeeper."

When I asked Nana Essie if the children's other mothers ever came into the house, she said, "Oh no; no."

Kobina then spoke about Kofi's twin sister Efua. "Efua finished school with Kofi," he said "and she was among the first Ghanaians selected by the Government to train as a bilingual secretary. So she studied in France and when she returned she was absorbed into the Foreign Service. She worked in Abidjan and Paris; and her last diplomatic position was in Washington, where she was the Ambassador's first secretary. She died in 1990. It was so unfortunate. They diagnosed it as crippling paralysis. She had quit the Foreign Service and was on her own, doing business. She used to come to New York to see us, and she died all of a sudden."

Those very close to Kofi sensed that he was deeply grieved by the early and unexpected death of Efua. I never heard him speak about it. Susan Linnee, who knew Kofi from the time he was at Macalester College in Minnesota, said to me, "He's a very private person, in that he doesn't talk a lot about personal things. For example, he never told me he had a twin sister, and yet that is so significant in West Africa, particularly in Ghana. But I found that out almost by accident."

Yet when Kofi learned that his twin sister was gravely ill, he closeted himself in his office and desperately phoned doctors and hospitals to try to get her the care that he felt she needed. "And when she died," Elisabeth Lindenmayer said, "it was like half of him died with her."

The Annan household included extended family members as well, in the Ghanaian tradition. One of these was Paul Keteku, who sent me this story from Kofi's childhood:

"Kofi's grandmother, Florence Wood, had the habit of sending us children to the farm on weekends," he wrote in an email. "To get to the farm, we had to cross the Aboabo River, which today is dried up. One weekend, after an especially heavy downpour, we were crossing a simple bridge over the Aboabo, when Kofi fell in. People in rural areas believe that a person will rise to the top three times before drowning. Kofi came up once, and then a second time, and it was only on his third rise to the surface that my sister Mary managed to pull him out of the river and revive him. She saved Ghana, and the world, from a terrible loss." This may have been a myth in the making — Kofi told me he has no recollection of such a thing happening.

Kofi felt very comfortable in his Ghanaian context. He told Philip Gourevitch of *The New Yorker:* "I feel profoundly African, my roots are deeply African and the things I was taught as a child are very important to me. Growing up in Africa, you had lots of people around you — cousins, aunts, grandparents, and friends of the family — so there always were people to talk to, people to seek advice from, people to play with, and a sense of friendship and love."

HR's work took him to different parts of Ghana, giving his children a larger view of their national roots. Kofi picked up other Ghanaian dialects growing up. HR and Victoria drew on Ghanaian and British traditions in raising their children and they all successfully straddled two worlds. Kofi told Gourevitch, "I grew up non-tribal in a tribal world."

HR and Home Rule for Ghana

HR was a player in Ghanaian politics; he actively campaigned for home rule for Ghana, which was then called Gold Coast and was under British rule. He helped found a party that picked a US-educated firebrand as their secretary-general; his name was Kwame Nkrumah. But Nkrumah's style didn't suit HR and his colleagues. Nkrumah wanted not a gradual transition to home rule, as they did, but independence and he wanted it now. He broke away from HR's group and formed his own party. His radical platform landed him in prison, but he eventually led Ghana to independence and became its first Prime Minister. He was a hero to his people, but HR never approved of his tactics.

Kobina remembers a house full of political figures and noted the risk. "Mind you," he said, "our father couldn't be out doing politics in the open, really. You know, he was the first African manager of the United Africa Company. And the white masters who were the owners of the company gave him a fair amount of free reign, but when you start kicking against colonialism, they naturally saw it as a threat. So he was sort of discreet."

After independence and retiring from Unilever, HR became chairman of the Ghana Commercial Bank and was later elected governor of the wealthy Ashante Province, the breadbasket of Ghana. His eldest daughter Nana Essie said to me, "Our father was always telling us that we have to be firm and stand on our feet. We shouldn't rely on anybody. So from infancy, we always tried to be hard, and as we went through life, whatever came our way, we tried to expect it, to prepare for it and to plan ahead."

Mfantsipim

Stanley Meisler, being the good journalist that he is, found the headmaster of Kofi's boarding school in Ghana, Francis Bartels, living in Paris, healthy and alert at 96. He interviewed him, and I chuckled when Stan quoted him as saying of Kofi, "He made so much of so little." I had to talk to Bartels myself, and I asked Stan for his number.

I had been living in northwest France with my wife, Kathryn, since we both retired from the UN in late 2005. Most people retire in the south, but Kathryn, a Scot, hates prolonged sunshine. She prefers wind and rain and changeable weather. So there we were in Brittany.

I reached Bartels by phone. His voice was steady; he had a soft British accent and spoke with the precision of a schoolmaster. He sounded 30 years younger than he was. When he heard we were living in Brittany, he said that he had an apartment in Trouville, in Normandy, just over a hundred miles to the east from us, where he went from time to time, and proposed having lunch at a restaurant there. We set a date.

Kathryn and I found the restaurant easily — it was on the harbor. The waitress knew Bartels, he must be a regular, and she showed us to his table. He was seated, and rose without difficulty to greet us. He apologized that his wife hadn't yet arrived; she was parking the car. He was casually, yet smartly dressed. He stood straight, with the posture of a young man. His face had symmetrical features; he was dark-skinned and handsome. His wife Monika then arrived, a tall, big-boned German woman thirty years his junior. She had worked at the Ghanaian embassy in Germany when he was Ambassador there. She had a big smile and a marked German accent, in both English and French. We liked them both.

Bartels did most of the talking. He said he had written a memoir, called *The Persistence of Paradox*, for which Kofi had done an introduction. In it, Bartels says he is descended from, and takes his family name from, a German slave trader.

Bartels was a close friend of Kofi's father. I asked him what he thought Kofi inherited from HR Annan. "He inherited HR Annan's calm," he said. "His father was a very collected person who could not easily be ruffled. I see that in his son." He thought a bit, and then added. "The job HR did as a United Africa Company agent in Kumasi would also make him somebody who would be careful in whatever he did or said. The job itself was a very tricky one; you had the British managers on the one hand; you had the Ghanaians on the other — all this at a time when the struggle for independence was on. Your choices are not many, and you have to be careful. And I think I notice that care and attention to what he says in his son."

Kofi was HR's eldest son. HR had sent his first two children, Nana Essie and Essie, to Adisadel College, but for Kofi he chose what was emerging as the leading secondary school in the country, Mfantsipim. His friend Bartels was Headmaster. Bartels insists there was no favoritism. "Kofi qualified on his own; this was not a favor," he emphasized. "We accepted 90 of about 3,000 applicants and Kofi finished among the top 90 in an entrance examination."

As lunch was ending, I had to ask him about his comment to Stan Meisler that Kofi had "made so much of so little", and he laughed. "I've had so many surprises with young people," he began, "including my own son. If you'd have asked me while he was in school whether he would get a degree, I would have said 'maybe'. Today I am able to say that he satisfactorily completed his post-doctoral studies in Paris and has several publications to his name. I think we make a big mistake if we read more than necessary into young people's performance in school."

He then looked at me with a grin and a sparkle in his eye. "So yes, I did say that. If you'd have asked me at Mfantsipim whether Kofi Annan was going to be…" — he stopped to laugh — "the person he's become, I would have said, 'No way'."

He then went on, "And he himself, I think, would probably agree, although he may not like the idea."

In the British system adopted at Mfantsipim, students again take an exam to pass from the Fifth to the Sixth Form, from which most would go on to the prestigious University College of the Gold Coast. But for the 90 or so students in Kofi's class, there were only sixty places in the Sixth Form, and Kofi didn't make the final cut. I asked Bartels weather it was because he wasn't bright enough. "No," he said emphatically. "It was a question of chairs and desks." The school just didn't have the capacity. "And remember," he said, "we were choosing from among the cream of the country in any case. So the potentiality was there. And he's proved it."

"Domo"

After our lunch, Bartels seemed bothered that he couldn't remember enough about Kofi as a student, and so when he got back to Paris, he e-mailed Andrew Arkutu, who had been a prefect at Mfantsipim when Kofi was a student there, to ask for more details. Yes, I said e-mailed. I came to exchange e-mails with Bartels often, and he always replied quickly. He was at home in the

21st century. In fact, over lunch, his wife Monika had expressed doubt about how to get some kind of information, and Francis admonished her, "Oh Monika," he said, "that's easily found on the internet." (Kofi has a deep respect for Bartels. When the former headmaster celebrated his 100th birthday in Paris in March 2010, Kofi set up a foundation in his name in Ghana to honor him.)

Arkutu found a couple of Kofi's classmates, interviewed them, and sent me a report. These classmates of Kofi's, he said, remembered him as independent-minded, with a strong interest in the politics and social issues of Ghana in the turbulent late 1950s. In fact, his nickname, which endures to this day, was "Domo", because of his right-of-center political views. In those days, "Domo" applied to any individual or party that was opposed to Kwame Nkrumah. "It's a corruption of "Demo", for democratic," Arkutu explained, "which is what the opposition considered itself, and Kofi's father was a leading opposition figure." The students at Mfantsipim used to organize mock parliamentary elections, and Kofi became deputy leader of the opposition. "So, like his father," Arkutu wrote, "he was a "Domo", which also became his nickname."

THE MIDWEST

When Kofi failed to get into the Sixth Form at Mfantsipim, he went to a new technical college in the town of his birth, the Kumasi College of Science and Technology. In his second year there, he was elected Vice President of the Ghana national students union, which got him invited to a student leaders' conference in nearby Sierra Leone, where a Ford Foundation talent scout spotted him. Ford was giving study grants to young Africans with leadership potential, and offered Kofi one to study at Macalester College in St. Paul, Minnesota. He accepted, and entered Macalester as a third year student in 1959 at the age of 21.

Kofi's time at Macalester is pretty well documented. But I loved this description by Susan Linnee of Kofi on the first night she met him. "It was in November of 1960 in a parking lot of an apartment building in Minneapolis. And there was this guy standing there in a trench coat with the collar pulled up and a hat pulled down over his eyes — it was raining — and he was standing next to a salmon-colored Studebaker. It was Kofi." Kofi shared the Studebaker with his roommate Roy Preiswerk and a friend, Charles Akin, whom Susan later married.

"He was the person who taught me how to dance the High Life," Susan went on. "You don't move your shoulders; you don't move the bottom. Very smooth. We also did the limbo. And all the time he was at these parties, he was very affable, very sociable, but certainly not a wild party person. And I don't ever recall seeing him drink." To this day, he's a moderate drinker.

1960s America was awakening to racial injustice, but was still a racially divided society. Kofi, from a privileged Ghanaian background, didn't understand racial injustice and was easily forgiving when he encountered it. Jim Traub in his book tells the story of Kofi taking a walk along Minnehaha Creek with a German girl, when some toughs shouted racial insults at him. Kofi was more impressed with the reaction of his friends, who were furious about it, than the threat itself. Traub concluded, "in his own mind he was not 'black'; he was African."

Susan Linnee says that on one occasion, a barber told him, "We don't cut niggers' hair." Kofi didn't understand. "I'm not a nigger," he said. "I'm a Ghanaian." He got the haircut.

"He was very easy in his own skin," Kieran Prendergast said to me. "I never saw the slightest sign of racial awareness or racial tension or racial prejudice or sensitivity on his part, though he was very observant about the way that other people regarded him."

In his first year as Secretary-General, I brought to Kofi's attention an editorial that I considered racist. His eyes betrayed a flash of anger. Then he said of the author, "That's his problem, not mine."

GENEVA

After two years at Macalester, Kofi got his bachelor's degree in 1961. One of his closest friends in Minnesota, his roommate Roy Preiswerk, was going to Geneva to do a doctorate at the Graduate Institute of International Studies. Roy suggested that Kofi apply for a Carnegie fellowship so that he could study at the Institute too. Kofi did, and got it.

He and Roy settled into a small apartment not far from the school, which is located in a villa right on the edge of Lake Geneva. Roy had been from a wealthy Swiss family; his father was in the import-export business between Africa and Europe. But his father divorced his mother when Roy and his elder brother were very young and then gave his former wife minimal financial support. She was forced to move from a mansion to a working class neighborhood overnight and to take two jobs to raise her boys. Roy developed a keen interest in the Third World and development. He got very close to Kofi.

Georges Abi Saab frequently used to spend evenings with Kofi and Roy in their apartment, where they talked politics with other international students, mostly from the Third World, many from Africa. Today Georges is a Professor Emeritus at that same Institute; I met him at the lakeside villa in 2006 to ask him to tell me more.

"There was a group of us who used to get together at that apartment to drink beer — that's all we could afford — and talk of what we could do to make the world better," he told me. "Kofi is not an abstract person; he finds fulfillment in action, in practical things." They all wanted to do something for Africa, for the Third World, he said, but they didn't know what.

Georges was anticipating that Kofi would not have the patience to pursue a doctorate and an academic career, and he was right. But if not, then what? One attractive option was international organizations, "because the countries we came from didn't have clout," Georges said. The United Nations had special appeal. "Hammarskjold was at his height," he said, raising his eyebrows. "He had such glamour and purpose! And people believed you could change the world through the UN."

While he was in Geneva, Kofi met a couple of "Smithies" — girls from Smith College in Northampton, Massachusetts — who would lend him support throughout his life. The first was Julia Falvy. He first encountered her at the UN library at the Palais des Nations, where she was doing research during a Junior Year Abroad. He invited her for coffee. "I thought he was handsome," she said to me, "and I accepted." After talking with her for a while, Kofi decided his friend Roy might like to meet her. He introduced them the next day and Julia and Roy eventually married. Kofi became godfather to their first child, a son, Frank.

A second was Toni Krissel, who later married Jim Goodale, a first amendment lawyer who became Vice Chairman of *The New York Times*. Jim and Toni became trusted lifelong friends, with Jim providing media advice to Kofi from time to time, notably during the Oil-for-Food crisis.

When Kofi became Secretary-General, Toni introduced him to her best friend, Sally Quinn, also from Smith, the *Washington Post* reporter who married the *Post*'s editor Ben Bradlee. Quinn and Bradlee helped Kofi break into the Washington social and media scene.

With his Ghanaian charm, his American style, and his European manners Kofi was becoming a master networker.

TITI

While in Geneva, Kofi met a Nigerian woman his age from a prominent Lagos family who was there studying French. Julia Preiswerk said that she loved to laugh as much as he did. Her name was Titilola Alakija — Titi to her friends. She was the daughter of Sir Adeyemo Alakija, a lawyer and businessman and the founder of a Lagos newspaper, *The Daily Times*.

Titi and Kofi were married in May 1965 in Geneva's Holy Trinity Anglican Church. Roy Preiswerk was his best man. In 2006, I visited Julia in her home in Geneva. (Roy died of a brain tumor in 1982.) She took out a black and white wedding photo. Titi is wearing a traditional white, Western-style wedding gown; she is petite, pretty and has a look of quiet determination on her face. Kofi is in tails, smiling, confident, stunningly handsome and looking as though he's about to conquer the world.

Titilola Alakija (Titi to her friends) and Kofi were married in May 1965 in Geneva's Holy Trinity Anglican Church. Roy Preiswerk (second from the right) was his best man.

Over the next eight years, Kofi and Titi had two children, a daughter Ama in 1969 and a son Kojo four years later. As adults, the two children often came to see Kofi when his official travel as Secretary-General took him somewhere near to where they were, either in Europe or West Africa. In his last year in office, I asked him if I could interview them for this book. He quickly arranged it. They were both at the official residence as he was packing up to leave the UN at the end of 2006.

I waited in the second floor library, which is mahogany paneled — a serene, dark space punctuated by two portals of light — windows overlooking the garden. After 10 years of the Annans' living here, this house had become a showcase for fine works of art, predominantly African. Ama was right on time. (Kojo is always late, I had the impression). She was then a young adult, 37 years of age, in business for herself in Lagos. She is slim, vibrant yet controlled, and has a stunning smile. I asked her about her family. She said that her mother's father was a returned slave from Brazil, from the state of Bahia, where they still have relatives. He was rich, apparently, because she said he rode around Lagos in a horse and carriage, "like his colonial masters".

I had never met Titi, but from what I'd heard, Ama was very much like her. I asked her if she wasn't more like her mother than her Dad. She speaks rapid-fire with complete self-assurance. "Probably," she said, "I think I'm a bit more like her than like Daddy. I'm not as…patient." Then she laughed. "She's a very direct person and, one could argue, like me — stubborn. I'll do everything in my power to convince you to think the way I think, otherwise agree to disagree, but not change my mind."

Kojo then joined us. He is ramrod straight, nicely built, with his head almost clean-shaven. He sat down next to me on the couch. I asked him about his relationship with his Dad. He thought for a minute, then said, "To be fair, my Dad never gets angry. The way he is as Secretary-General is the way he is." He uses more American slang than Ama does. "Even if he tells me off about something," he went on, "he tells me off very calmly. He doesn't scream or shout." He now seemed to be taking delight in imitating his father. "He would just say, 'Listen,'" Kojo said, pointing a long index finger, long like his father's, in the air. "He would put his finger up and say, 'Listen'. It's the same thing as my Mom breaking plates and smashing the whole place down. My Dad says, 'Listen', and that means it's all going to happen now."

"I Did What I Wanted to Do"

As Georges Abi Saab said, Kofi finds fulfillment in action. Staying around the Institute for the several years it would take him to get his doctorate was not his style. "He was intelligent," Julia observed, "but not an intellectual." That's true; but I would put it another way: he wasn't so much book smart as he was people smart. And this would serve him extremely well throughout his career.

Kieran Prendergast said to me, "he was very much an instinctive and intuitive person. I'm not implying that in any way that he wasn't rational or analytical, but I think his basic approach was one of intuition rather than looking for arguments to support the intuition."

At the end of 1962, after only a year of graduate study, Kofi left the Institute to take his first job, at the United Nations World Health Organization in Geneva. He started at the very bottom of the totem pole for professionals. He was what is known in the UN system as a P-1.

For Kofi, life in Geneva was comfortable, but after a couple of years at WHO, he was itching to return to Africa, he told me in a conversation I had with him in his 38th floor office in 2006. He looked into overseas vacancies in WHO, and found two — one in Congo Brazzaville and the other in Egypt. He applied for both and was ready to accept either. But the WHO personnel chief had other ideas. "You're going to Copenhagen," he said. "What's the difference between Copenhagen and Geneva," Kofi asked him? "Geneva is Headquarters and Copenhagen is the field," the personnel chief said. "I'm not going," Kofi replied. So he quit.

He took three months off ("the arrogance of youth," he commented) and drove through Europe while he sent out resumés. "I was sure something would come up," he said. "I drove up to Copenhagen to see what it looked like," he laughed, "and it definitely wasn't a Third World scene."

In the end he followed a distinguished Ghanaian diplomat and economist, Robert Gardiner, to the UN's Economic Commission for Africa (ECA) in Addis Ababa, Ethiopia, in September 1965, a few months after his marriage to Titi. He said with conviction, "I did what I wanted to do."

ADDIS ABABA

Kofi was in Addis Ababa in the early days of the Organization of African Unity, which was founded in Addis in 1963. He told The New Yorker's Gourevitch, "There was lots of political energy — electricity in the air. All these leaders came to Addis to talk about Africa and its development, and we were on the economic side, and you could see that if we all did what we were supposed to do and pooled our efforts and worked well, we could make a difference." Gourevitch called his article on Kofi, perhaps sardonically, "The Optimist."

MIT: A Walk along the Charles

Titi left Addis in 1969 when she was pregnant with Ama to give birth in Nigeria, then returned to join Kofi after the child was born. In 1970, Kofi was made head of personnel at ECA. His career picked up momentum in 1971 when he was offered an Alfred P. Sloan fellowship at the Massachusetts Institute of Technology. MIT is one of America's finest universities; Kofi didn't make the second cut against Ghana's best and brightest at Mfantsipim, so, frankly, he was unsure of himself at MIT. "How could I survive, let alone thrive, in this group of over-achievers," he said in a 1997 speech at MIT, remembering those days.

Kofi is deliberate. When he has a problem, he thinks it through, usually with the help of a long walk. He took such a walk along the Charles River, he said, and then the answer to that question came to him. He would *not* play by their rules. "Follow your inner compass," he told himself; "listen to your own drummer. To live is to choose. But to choose well, you must know who you are, what you stand for, where you want to go and why you want to get there."

I can see Kofi once again falling back on his self-confidence and in a clear-headed way marching forward. He got the Master's degree in management. This was a big experience for him. He told the MIT students in 1997 that what he took away from MIT was "not only the analytical tools but also the intellectual confidence to help me locate my bearings in new situations, to view any challenge as a potential opportunity for renewal and growth, and to be comfortable is seeking the help of colleagues, but not fearing, in the end, to do things my way."

This speech, drafted with American aide John Ruggie, perfectly sums up Kofi's philosophy. He is an optimist, for sure, but he is smart, firmly grounded, introspective and values the views of others, while realizing that, as a decision-maker, he stands alone.

Stan Meisler concluded from this speech that "at first meeting, it is possible to underestimate this good-natured, affable, non-scholarly man. But he knows himself, knows where he wants to go and knows how to go about getting there. He has surprised onlookers often by exceeding their expectations."

IN AND OUT OF GHANA

After MIT, Kofi returned to Addis in June 1972, but quickly began to bounce around the UN system once more. In August he was transferred to Geneva, where he was appointed Administrative Management Officer. Kojo was born in Geneva in July 1973. Then in 1974, Kofi got his first peacekeeping experience when he was assigned to Egypt for six months as chief personnel officer for the UN Emergency Force. He dragged Titi and the kids off to Cairo from where they went on to mission headquarters in Ismailia.

Unexpectedly, opportunity knocked in Ghana. Kwame Nkrumah, of whom Kofi's father had never approved, had run the Ghanaian economy into the ground, becoming an authoritarian and ineffectual ruler. He was overthrown in a military coup in 1966 and died in exile in 1972. Kofi seemed to identify with his failure. He told *The New Yorker*, "We could have given our people a much better life, and we failed them."

When Kofi's mentor in Addis, Robert Gardiner, returned to Ghana, Kofi followed him there in November 1974, accepting the post of managing director of Ghana's Office of Tourism. But the military were still in power and Kofi had a more refined sense of governance. Even with support from the leadership, his job would not have been easy. But the military wouldn't stay out of his hair. "There was constant interference," he told me. "The Minister of Trade and Tourism just couldn't stay out of things, you know? And so I decided this was not for me." He left Ghana two years after he had returned. "I left frustrated and disillusioned," he told me. He would never take another government post there.

Mr. Mom: Break-up of a Marriage

Julia Preiswerk told me that she and Roy had moved to Trinidad in 1969, where Roy had been appointed director of a new graduate institute. Kofi and Titi came to visit. But while Kofi stayed with the Preiswerks, Titi stayed with other friends there. Julia said that she felt there might already have been a problem in the marriage.

Kofi came back into the UN system as a personnel officer in New York in September 1976. Then he was seconded in August 1980 to the Office of the UN High Commissioner for Refugees in Geneva as head of personnel, a nice advancement. But these changes were wearing on Titi. In fifteen years, Kofi had changed locations twelve times, Meisler counted. That's a lot of moving.

Friederike Bauer, for her biography of Kofi, *Kofi Annan, Ein Leben*, interviewed Titi, and gave me this account translated from her book. She said that for Titi it was not easy after the two children were born, always packing up and starting over again, making new friends. Titi described waiting with Ama and Kojo for her husband to come home from work. At the same time, she didn't say that the marriage was unhappy. She spoke of "the wonderful time" they had together, and to this day respects her former husband as a great father for their two kids. She described him as balanced, sociable, even "a gift of God". But it was clear, Freiderike said, that the constant changing of jobs and continents was not good for family harmony. Titi told her of moments of loneliness, sitting on packed suitcases in hotel rooms after Kofi had already rushed to the next post. "The biggest problem for me were the moves," Titi told her. "I had had enough of them." The marriage fell apart. Julia Preiswerk put it tactfully: "They kind of grew out of each other."

Titi moved to London, taking Ama with her. Ama, then 11, was sent to a boarding school. Kojo, who was 7 and a bit too young for boarding school, stayed with Kofi in Geneva.

When I spoke to Ama at the residence in 2006, I asked her how it was in boarding school. She laughed. "Initially it was hard," she said. "I remember I had to have elocution lessons, because they couldn't understand my American twang." She showed no signs of unhappiness with the experience. And did she see her Mom often? "I just remember that during half terms and holidays," she replied, "she was always around."

When I visited Julia Preiswerk at her home in Geneva that same year, where today she is a practicing psychoanalyst, I asked her what she thought the impact of Kofi and Titi's separation had on the children. "I like Ama a lot, but she can be pretty aggressive, a bit like her mother," she answered. "The divorce probably made her tougher." And Kojo? "Kojo was an absolutely delightful child," she said, "although I'm not sure what was going on inside him. He may have been more sensitive than Ama; he might have suffered more."

Ama went to the Penrhos School in Wales. In 1981, Kojo was sent to nearby Rydal. I asked him in a 2008 e-mail how he liked it. "Boarding school separated me from both my parents, but I was with either of them every holiday," he wrote. "Many of my friends went to boarding school at an early age, so I never found it strange and have fond memories of my school days. Naturally, the first few weeks were spent missing the folks, but I think boarding school develops character, maturity and an early sense of independence." He then added, "I will definitely send my kids to boarding school too."

Julia Preiswerk told me that after their parents split up, Ama and Kojo would travel back and forth between them for visits. Mom would send them first class and Dad would send them back economy. When I interviewed them at the residence in 2006, I asked if it was true. They both laughed. " I think he just wanted to teach us the value of money and to appreciate what you have that others don't," Kojo said. "Yeah," Ama agreed.

Before Kojo went to boarding school, he lived with his father for about a year. For Kofi, who had spent years as a personnel officer in the UN system, single parenting was a revelation. "This was one of those times when you get to understand the difficult role of mothers, who often have to juggle jobs and children," he told me. But he knew that while his experience was similar, it still wasn't the same as for a woman. "And I thought maybe as a man working with other men," he added, "I had a bit of an advantage."

Those working with Kofi knew that, come hell or high water, he had to leave work at 4:00 to pick up Kojo at school. Shashi Tharoor says, "I've heard stories of his having to interrupt a meeting to say, 'sorry, now I'm going off to the school'. He never kept his kid waiting." Shashi remembers a story Kofi told him that once Kojo wanted him to come to an event for the parents at his school, and Kofi said that he just couldn't; he had something important at the office. And Kojo replied, "But Dad, all the other mothers will be there." Shashi observed, "Which in some ways is a lovely insight into the maternal touch of his parenting."

Kofi ended up going to that meeting. He told me, "I was the only father there."

NANE: THE ESSENTIAL PARTNER

Yves Oltramare, the Geneva-based banker and philanthropist, got to know Kofi in 1997. Yves had served for thirty years as a member of the Investment Committee of the UN Pension Fund. He told me that Kofi was the first Secretary-General ever to attend one of their meetings and then surprised him with an invitation for him and his wife to join him for lunch.

I went to see Yves in his Geneva office, and we got to talking about Kofi's relationship with Nane. "When you think of Kofi Annan, you think of him not only as a man but also as a couple," he said. "Kofi and Nane presented themselves in public in such a harmonious way." He asked me if I knew of a book called *Les Femmes Inspiratrices* (*Inspirational Women*). I said I didn't. "Nane, to me," he said, "has been a discreet but important *inspiratrice*."

Kofi met Nane Lagergren in 1981. She was a Swedish lawyer working for the UN High Commissioner for Refugees, a single parent herself, divorced, with a daughter, Nina. I interviewed Nane at the official residence, as she was packing to leave. She told me about her first significant encounter with Kofi.

"It happened on a very specific occasion, at a very specific moment," she said. "At a social event, I was on my way out. I turned around and our eyes met." She laughed. "Now that sounds corny, but it did happen that way without a word being uttered. It's not strange, because Kofi has a kind of aura about him. He projects a fascinating combination of the joy of life together with this very strong inner core, which are both very magnetic qualities."

Nane too has magnetic qualities. The first time I saw her was outside Kofi's office in the peacekeeping department. She had come to meet him. It was raining outside, and she was dressed very casually — maybe in a parka. Her hair was tousled and damp. What a stunningly attractive woman, I thought, not knowing who she was; obviously not a diplomat's wife. She seemed out of place, yet perfectly at home.

I can imagine Kofi being taken with her when their eyes met. Her blue eyes are large, moist and always talking, even when she's not. Kofi pursued her and courted her. He took her to meet Julia Preiswerk, a sign, Julia said, that he was very serious about Nane.

Then came another move. Kofi was promoted again, this time in April 1998 as a director in the management department in New York. Nane had a choice to make. She took a deep breath, abandoned her legal career and followed Kofi across the Atlantic. "It was the first time I had set out on uncharted waters with him," she said, "not knowing exactly what it would lead to or what would happen."

She started painting immediately, going downtown to the Art Students League. "But it wasn't easy giving up my economic independence, which had been so much a part of my life," she said. "It took long agonizing walks before I made that choice. In the end, it seems like a gift that it happened."

MARRIAGE AND ROOSEVELT ISLAND

Kofi and Nane lived in an apartment Kofi rented on Roosevelt Island, in the East River, connected to Manhattan by a Swiss-built cable car. It's a peaceful setting, just a stone's throw away from the busy Upper East Side shopping area and a mile north of the UN. In a children's book that Nane published in 2000, there is a photo of her and Kofi on the Roosevelt Island tram on their way to get married. Nane's blonde hair is long; she's wearing a simple white tunic over white slacks. Kofi, now 46, has flecks of gray in his hair and is wearing a powder blue Ghanaian robe to below his knees, with matching trousers. He looks happy and serene. The ceremony took place at the Church Center for the United Nations, across from the UN, on 10 September 1984.

Nane admits she's shy, "but I have a tenacious streak," she insists. She is the daughter of an esteemed international jurist, Gunnar Lagergren, who arbitrated the Taba boundary between Israel and Egypt. Gunnar Lagergren worked abroad for many years of his life, which meant that Nane had extended stays overseas until the age of 10, when she started Middle School in Stockholm. Her mother was the half sister of Raoul Wallenberg, the Swedish diplomat who, while assigned to Hungary, saved tens of thousands of Jews from the Nazis.

When Nane was in law school, she took art classes on the side at the art academy. As a young lawyer, she said, "I painted on vacation or stayed up until midnight working on self portraits." Of the painting, she said, "It was always there." She then touched on her family history. "The grandfather of my grandfather had wanted to be a painter too," she said, "but his father insisted he become an officer." But the father relented enough to allow his son one year in Paris to study art, "and so he pursued his dream." That became her dream too.

World's best-known unknown painter

From the Art Students League, where she started painting on her arrival in Manhattan, Nane moved to the Studio School set up on 8th Street in Greenwich Village by the second generation of abstract expressionists who emphasized drawing. Here she could paint from 9:00 in the morning until 10:00 at night, with artists coming in from the outside to criticize her work. Kofi was moving up the ladder at the UN, and was working later and later hours. After he became Secretary-General, Nane used to say she that had become the world's best-known unknown painter.

"So what I would do is go to that wonderful food store, Balducci's, on Sixth Avenue, and buy very nice take-out," she told me. "Then I would take the new subway line from West 4th Street right to Roosevelt Island, where we lived, and we would meet at 9:00 or 10:00 in the evening and eat together. He was very tolerant. I remember him one evening arriving especially late. I had picked up Chinese take-out and in reheating it I managed to burn the rice — he accepted this without complaint."

Nane now felt it was time to get her own workspace. Struggling artists had long since moved out of Soho, in Manhattan, which had become too expensive, to Williamsburg, Brooklyn. And from Williamsburg they were beginning to colonize the Polish neighborhood of Greenpoint, Queens, where Nane found a studio. She described it for me. "It was in the wonderful old factory right on the river — it was like entering a film about artists in New York. It was full of artists and artisans, and the building itself was like an amazing sculpture, with its big vents and pipes and old elevator. And there was a bread factory next door, so the smell of newly-baked bread that would come wafting through would make you hungry and you would have to climb down and go out and try to find something to eat. But finding take-out wasn't as easy here as on West 8th Street, where I could just cross the street to get a slice of pizza and a coffee."

From her window, she had a splendid view of the UN across the East River. "I knew Kofi's office was there someplace — sometimes I would try to count the windows to know where he might be sitting."

A big transition

Shashi Tharoor said of Nane and Kofi, "I think theirs is an enviable marriage. He first of all made her his priority, and she made him hers. There seems to be a lot of mutual understanding and respect. She accepts a vision of her place in his life that is loyal, supportive. There was never the slightest hint of any competition between them, of any discordance, of any different objectives." Then speaking as one whose first marriage also failed, he observed, "Often marriages don't work because people want different things out of life, out of their relationship. I never saw that with them. I really saw them as an absolutely perfect couple, with give on both sides."

Shashi Tharoor said of Kofi and Nane, "There was never the slightest hint of any competition between them, of any discordance, of any different objectives."

Kofi's Chief of Staff Iqbal Riza said of Nane, "In her own very quiet, self-effacing way she gave him an anchor. There's no question that his self-confidence rested on Nane." He then added, "She emerged from her shell with great grace."

Through his marriage to Nane, Kofi also became wedded to Europe. His African roots were undeniable, but he was now a man formed on three continents. His personal traits remained constant — calm, centered, confident — but his sensibilities were being shaped by indelible experiences in America and on the continent. It was this very unusual life formula that prepared him for the UN's top job.

CHAPTER 2

A NEW POLITICAL ACTOR

THE NEW WORLD ORDER

The late 1980s changed everything in international affairs — the fall of the Berlin Wall, the collapse of the Soviet Union, the rebirth of the United Nations.

In 1989, I was on my first UN peacekeeping mission in Namibia, in southwest Africa. Namibia was a trust territory taken over by South Africa from the Germans after the First World War; Pretoria held on to it for too long. When the South Africans finally decided to give in to international pressure and set Namibia on the road to independence, the UN was there as midwife. But the very first day our work officially began, 1 April, the Namibian rebel group SWAPO, heavily armed, poured over the border from their bases in Angola in violation of the peace agreement. It looked like more than a decade of preparations for a peaceful transition to independence was about to go down the tubes.

But then something remarkable happened. Senior representatives of the governments most involved in the Namibian peace process rushed in. They came from Russia, from the US, from Cuba, from South Africa and from Angola. What a cocktail. They gathered at a rural resort used by honeymooners; it was called Mount Etjo. They sat around a table, agreed that SWAPO had done something stupid and drew up a plan to send the SWAPO fighters back to Angola and get the peace process going again. And it was done.

What a pleasure to see what reasonable things can be achieved when Russians and Americans, Cubans, Angolans and South Africans, work together toward a common goal. This was my first concrete experience of the possibilities opened up by the end of the Cold War.

Presidents Bush and Gorbachev had declared that the emerging entente between their nations marked the beginning of a New World Order. The United Nations, stymied by US-Soviet rivalry for some 45 years, could now work as it was intended to. For us inside the glass house, it seemed too good to be true.

Russia and America voted together in the Security Council with the aim of cleaning up all the trouble spots created by the Cold War. China, France and the UK, the other veto-wielding members of the Council, went along, except for the occasional Chinese muttering about national sovereignty when things got a bit too intrusive for them.

HOSTAGES IN BAGHDAD

As the Berlin Wall came down, Kofi Annan was moving up. In 1987, Secretary-General Javier Perez de Cuellar made him Assistant Secretary-General for personnel.

After Iraq invaded Kuwait in 1990, and the Security Council was threatening retaliation, Saddam Hussein reminded the world that he was hosting thousands of foreign workers in Iraq and Kuwait, including 900 UN system staff and family members. He used many of them as human shields, placing them at strategic sites. Perez de Cuellar sent Virendra "Viru" Dayal, his Chief of Staff, to negotiate the release of these hostages, and asked Kofi to go along with him. It was Kofi's first political assignment.

Some people couldn't understand why Perez de Cuellar picked him. Iqbal Riza, who became Kofi's first Chief of Staff, remembers: "I had seen Kofi easily grow into ever more important management positions, but none of us who knew him ever thought of him as having a political mind — until he went to Iraq in 1991. I remember a very senior colleague said to me at the time, "What on earth have they sent Kofi for, he doesn't know the first thing about this. He's good at administration, but..."

I called Viru Dayal, who's retired and living in India, and asked him why Perez de Cuellar sent Kofi to Iraq. "It was because Kofi was in charge of administration and there were large numbers of UN staff members there, and also because Javier knew and recognized that Kofi wished also to be involved in political work. So both things were at play."

Viru and Kofi succeeded in getting all the human shields released and all the UN staff freed. But then Kofi surprised Viru by raising another issue that Viru hadn't thought of, and perhaps should have, that, he said, "reflected very profoundly on his character as a human being." While the media attention was focused on hostages from developed countries, there were thousands of workers, mostly from South Asia, and nobody was doing anything about them.

"And when we met the diplomatic corps in Baghdad," Viru said, "Kofi reminded the diplomats of the need to also act for the sake of the other stranded nationalities, who were facing a kind of a *cul de sac,* with the war advancing on them like an avalanche and having really nowhere to go and no one to care for them. They were in such numbers".

The guest workers too were allowed to leave, and Kofi helped arrange the airlift. He had made his debut on the political stage, going far beyond what he was asked to do, handling the assignment with sensitivity, and succeeding conclusively. Kofi told Stan Meisler, "It was exciting. It was interesting. You were doing something to help people directly. It was rewarding." He had found something he could sink his teeth into.

TAKING OVER PEACEKEEPING

Kofi was hankering for another political assignment, and an opportunity opened in peacekeeping.

When Boutros Boutros-Ghali became Secretary-General in 1992, he was immediately given a mandate by the Security Council to reshape the Organization in the peace and security area to adjust to the post-Cold War world. He started with peacekeeping; he moved the unit out of his office and set it up as a freestanding department with "Mig" Goulding at the head of it. He gave Mig a post for a deputy that he wanted, in addition to other staff and, in February of that year, named Kofi Annan to that post.

I thought that move made sense because the expansion in peacekeeping operations meant that you needed someone with Kofi's management skills to help administer the new department. But luckily for Kofi, Mig felt there were too many peacekeeping missions for him to handle alone; he decided to share the substantive workload. He gave Kofi responsibility for the missions in the Middle East and Africa. Kofi now had some of the world's leading hot spots on his plate, but that was just the beginning.

Boutros-Ghali then did more restructuring. Parallel to the new peacekeeping department, he created a political affairs department. In a sense the two were analogous to a defense ministry and a foreign ministry, respectively. Now that the Cold War was over, during which, for example, the Security Council could not deal with Vietnam because of US opposition, nor with Afghanistan because of Soviet involvement, the UN was now free to have desk officers for any threat to international peace and security, and the new Secretariat structure was beginning to reflect that.

Boutros-Ghali moved Mig laterally in February 1993 to head the new political affairs department, and he promoted Kofi to head of the peacekeeping department. Kofi was now an Under-Secretary-General in charge of a department that would be at the heart of the UN's security agenda at one of the most intense and exciting periods of UN history. In July of that year the number of peacekeepers would peak at 78,444. The UN had more troops abroad than any of its Member States except the United States.

Kofi's small staff was overworked, and Kofi himself was keeping longer hours. It was a challenge for his management abilities and for his political instincts as well.

Kofi pressed Shashi Tharoor, who was Mig Goulding's special assistant, to stay on the peacekeeping staff. Shashi began to become familiar with Kofi's approach to management. "One of the hallmarks of Kofi Annan's management style, which became even more apparent in the peacekeeping department," Shashi said, "was that he picked people he could trust to have around him and then he gave them the freedom to do their jobs. I mean, I signed so many cables on extremely important issues, and I did so feeling that he would back my judgment because he trusted it. And that's an incredibly empowering thing for a staff member. I grew professionally enormously by not having the sense that everything I did was going to be second-guessed."

Everyone who worked under him breathed deeply the freedom that he gave him or her to do their best as they saw fit.

Kofi also believed in what Shashi called "a healthy work-life balance." In Geneva, he thought nothing of leaving work at 4:00 o'clock to pick up his son at school, although he often went back to work afterwards. Family came first. In New York, where he was UN Controller from 1990-1992, some colleagues jokingly referred to him as the Remote Controller. Shashi said of his attitude towards work: "His logic was actually a sustainable logic, which is a) you've got to have a life outside the office and b) the reason you're keeping ridiculous hours is you're trying to do too much. You need to be able to delegate."

As the head of a UN department dealing with strategically important issues, Kofi also had to earn the respect of the most powerful Member States, some of whose envoys at the outset seemed to have reservations about him. Iqbal Riza, whom Kofi recruited as his number two, recalled: "When he started working for peacekeeping, there was an incident that was very revealing. In my first week as Kofi's deputy, I sat in on a meeting he had with the ambassadors from the Five Permanent Members of the Security Council. He had just taken over a few weeks before — this must have been his first meeting with them. And I remember so clearly, there was such an air of skepticism from many of them, and some were openly patronizing. This didn't faze him at all; he just answered their questions in a business-like way. In the second meeting, a week or two later, I noticed some thawing. By the third meeting, he had them totally with him. It was a grudging respect that came, and it came very early."

BLACK HAWK DOWN

At one point, a Pentagon team came to visit Kofi's peacekeeping department and they laughed at how understaffed it was. Kofi's people were, frankly, flying by the seat of their pants, while steadily increasing altitude.

As head of the peacekeeping department, Kofi had an almost undoable job. Paul Kennedy, in his 2006 book *The Parliament of Man*, identifies three reasons why this was so. First, the problems of collapsed states like Somalia or Haiti, where there was no government at all, were simply not foreseen in the Charter. Second, there were simply too many calls for UN help in too short a time. "For the Security Council to have understood and handled well one quarter of these cases would have been an outstanding feat of organization," he wrote; "to handle them all, even moderately well, was inconceivable." And third, there simply weren't the resources.

For the Secretariat, which had to do the Security Council's bidding, this was a recipe for disaster. And the disasters came one, two, three.

One was Somalia. Somalia had flip-flopped between the Soviets and the Americans during the Cold War, but with the collapse of the Soviet Union it lost its strategic importance. It imploded in 1991-92, triggering massive starvation. The media highlighted the humanitarian disaster and governments felt compelled to act. A UN peacekeeping mission already in the country could not prevent the warlords from interfering with the distribution of the relief aid.

In his final months in office, President George H.W. Bush offered to send in a large US military force, under the enforcement provisions of the UN Charter, to see that the aid got delivered. Boutros-Ghali, while saying it wasn't his first choice to have a UN force not under his command, went along and offered that option to the Council, which accepted it. You now had two UN missions in Somalia, a lightly armed peacekeeping mission under Boutros-Ghali's command and a heavily armed peace enforcement mission reporting to US Central Command in Tampa, Florida. The aid was getting through, but the lines of command were confused.

In October 1993, a US Special Forces unit attempted a raid to capture Somali warlord General Mohammad Farrah Aidid. UN mission headquarters wasn't informed; only Florida knew. The raid went wrong. In a fierce battle in downtown Mogadishu, two US helicopters were downed, 18 US marines were killed and the body of one was shown on television being dragged half naked through the streets. A popular movie, "Black Hawk Down", retold the tale.

President Clinton, who nine months earlier had taken over from President Bush, accurately read the mood of a horrified US public and pulled the plug on the Somalia UN mission. It shut down in March 1995. History will blame the Security Council for the failure of Somalia, and perhaps even President Clinton for his sudden about face. But the US blamed Boutros-Ghali, who felt it was his place to take the blame rather than to point a finger at a powerful Member State.

In 2005, before I retired, I invited all the living former UN spokespeople to come to the UN to discuss how the Organization's press relations had changed over 60 years. Ahmad Fawzi, the Egyptian who had been Deputy Spokesperson under Boutros-Ghali, remembered his frustration at trying to get Boutros to go public about the Black Hawk Down incident. "I begged him to let us tell the truth about what happened," he said. The Secretary-General refused, saying, "You cannot go out and blame a member state for an operation that goes wrong." It's often said around the UN that SG stands not just for Secretary-General but also for Scape Goat.

At the time, Kofi was hardly mentioned in the Somalia affair. Those who worked for him felt confident in his leadership in the face of so much that he was nominally responsible for. His department was humming along, well run but stretched. It was only later that his critics added Somalia to a long list of UN failures that they blamed on him.

RWANDA: A GENOCIDE FORETOLD

From Somalia, you can draw a straight line to the Rwanda genocide of 1994, which happened six months later. This was disaster number two, and this one eventually stuck to Kofi like Velcro. Some 800,000 Rwandans were killed in 100 days, and Kofi Annan's peacekeeping department had received a cable three months before it happened predicting exactly what would take place.

On 11 January 1994, Canadian General Romeo Dallaire, who commanded a weak and under-armed UN military force in Rwanda, sent a cable to UN Headquarters saying that an informant from inside the extremist Hutu militia known as the *interhamwe* had told him that all the Tutsis in Kigali had been registered for execution and that the *interhamwe* could kill up to a thousand Tutsi in twenty minutes. Weapons were secretly stored for this purpose. The informant also said that there was a plan to execute Belgian peacekeepers so that Belgium, which had the best-trained troops in the UN force, would pull out from Rwanda. This was a back-channel communication, a cable from Dallaire to his friend and fellow French-Canadian General Maurice Baril, the UN Military Adviser. The official channel was from the civilian head of the UN mission, Jacques Roger Booh Booh of Cameroon, but he was a weak and less than effective boss and was thought to be sympathetic to the Hutu. Dallaire broke the rules and sent a private cable to Baril.

So there it was. A clear and accurate prediction of what would happen in just three months. So why didn't Kofi Annan blow the whistle?

Isel: A sense of outrage

The desk officer for Rwanda at the time was Isel Rivero, a Cuban woman with a strong sense of outrage. I contacted her by e-mail in 2009; she's retired now and living in Europe. She told me that she had accompanied Dallaire on a preparatory mission to the country in the summer of 1993. She said that the capital, Kigali, was surrounded by French troops, with many displaced people in camps outside the French cordon. She worried for Rwanda when in October of that year the first democratically elected President of Burundi, Melchior Ndadaye, a moderate Hutu, was murdered by the Tutsi-dominated Army after only three months in power. 100,000 people, mostly Tutsi, were killed in the rage that followed. Burundi is the ethnic mirror of Rwanda and Isel saw in the assassination a loud warning call.

Isel reported up the chain to Hedi Annabi, the Africa director. Hedi had briefed Dallaire on Rwanda, and remembers clearly laying out for him the level of risk. Dallaire later wrote that Hedi was the only one who expressed concern that the peace agreement between the Government and the Tutsi rebels was shaky.

Hedi reported to Iqbal Riza, who oversaw this portfolio in a division of labor with Kofi, who was concentrating on Bosnia. Isel commented to me, "Kofi didn't have a role in any of this; he was busy with Yugoslavia and you know very well that he never micro-managed; he delegated." Iqbal and Hedi were both acutely aware of the Council's sensitivity to risk in peacekeeping since the Mogadishu massacre.

Isel says that she remembers screaming at Hedi about the risk, although neither Hedi, nor Iqbal, nor Maurice, nor Dmitry Titov, a desk officer with an office just two doors away from Hedi's, recalls this happening. Maybe it was a Munchian primal scream inside her head. But Dmitry, who knows Isel well, allowed that it could well have happened.

A trap?

Under Kofi's system of delegation of authority — and you could argue that this is a downside of it — Riza could sign cables in Kofi's name, a system that also exists in the US State Department. Riza studied the Dallaire cable. Dallaire allowed for the possibility of a trap, but urged action none-the-less. He wanted permission to seize the hidden weapons. Riza consulted colleagues, including Hedi and Maurice. First, they were alarmed by Dallaire's warning of a trap. Second, on the proposal to seize the weapons they agreed that, however well intentioned, this was out of the question. When governments lend their troops to the UN, they give them very specific guidelines, spelled out in a Memorandum of Understanding or MOU. There is no flexibility to start seizing weapons if it's not explicitly approved in the MOU. And in this case it wasn't. And third, after Somalia, the Security Council was in no mood to take more risks in Africa. Hedi told me, "While we were very concerned, Iqbal, Maurice and I all agreed that the proposed action by Dallaire was not consistent with the deliberately minimalist mandate given by the Security Council to the UN Mission in Rwanda."

At that time I was a member of Boutros-Ghali's spokesperson's office specializing in peacekeeping. Kofi had given me full access to his people. One day I was sitting with General Baril while he was on the phone to his friend, Romeo Dallaire, who was making his case for a raid on the weapons caches. They were speaking in French. Baril looked at me with clear blue eyes and a slight smile on his face as he told Dallaire, "But Romeo, you know you can't do that; it's not in your mandate." To me, that made perfect sense. It not only wasn't in the mandate, it was politically unfeasible. The mood in the Security Council was so foul that I was worried about the future of peacekeeping. I sensed we had no options.

Riza sent a reply to Booh Booh, following the proper communication channel, instructing him to show Dallaire's cable to the Belgian, French and American ambassadors in Kigali, as those three governments had the most influence in Rwanda. He also told Booh Booh to see President Habyarimana, a Hutu, and warn him that we had information that something awful was being planned and to say that the UN expected him to get his people under control. Riza, following the course of action agreed upon with his colleagues, did not approve the seizure of weapons. When he asked Booh Booh if he had any problems with these instructions, Booh Booh said no. And he did as he was instructed.

Kofi didn't see the cable until the next morning, Riza told me. And all cables were routinely sent to Secretary-General Boutros Boutros-Ghali's office. No one dissented. Everyone seemed to agree that Riza's formula was the most responsible way to handle the threat.

Why didn't Boutros-Ghali go to the Security Council and report on the cable? Well, first, Boutros didn't personally report to the Council, he sent a deputy to do that for him. And Boutros didn't want anyone else, least of all Kofi, reporting directly to the Council. Second, it appears that the deputy, Chinmaya Gharekhan, never specifically mentioned the cable to the Council, although he did report on the deteriorating political situation in Rwanda. And third, the Council didn't want to hear about it. It was just a few months after the Black Hawk Down incident and the Clinton Administration, which had come to power supporting active multilateralism, now, under strong Congressional pressure, was rethinking US policy on peacekeeping. There was no question of getting any more troops out of the Council at this time. No question. And no major power had a strategic interest in Rwanda.

The fact is, many members of the Council had better intelligence on Rwanda than the UN did. If they didn't pick up on the arms caches on their own, which seems unlikely, Booh Booh had briefed three ambassadors who most certainly relayed that information to their capitals.

The Ndiaye report

The UN had a chilling analysis of the situation in Rwanda from a Senegalese lawyer, Bacre Waly Ndiaye, who was then the UN Special Rapporteur on Extrajudicial, Summary or Arbitrary Executions. He visited Rwanda a year before the massacres began, in April 1993, and filed a report with the UN Human Rights Commission in Geneva.

In that 14-page report, Ndiaye laid out the historical background. The Tutsi minority had dominated Rwanda for centuries until the 1959 revolution that brought the Hutu majority to power. Many Tutsi were killed and many more fled to neighboring states. In the next eight years, the exiled Tutsi attempted at least 10 armed comebacks, each triggering renewed ethnic violence and retaliation. In 1973, Major General Juvenal Habyarimana, a Hutu, seized power in a military coup. He established a system of government based on ethnic democracy. Ethnic quotas determined access to schools, jobs and government posts; the Tutsi quota was 10 percent.

In October 1990, a Tutsi exile army that was formed in Uganda and included many former members of the Ugandan Army, invaded Rwanda from the north and marched to the outskirts of Kigali. Habyarimana, with the help of French troops, pushed them back and the fighting stalemated. A ceasefire was concluded in July 1992.

Ndiaye wrote that the Hutu of Rwanda feared the repatriation of the Tutsi for three reasons. First, a massive return of exiles would result in land disputes in a country that, after Bangladesh, was the most densely populated in the world. Second, they feared that the Tutsi, many of whom had prospered in exile, would dominate the Rwandan economy. And third, some feared the Tutsi would reestablish the feudal monarchy by which they had dominated the Hutu for centuries before 1959. Politicians, in order to cling to power, he wrote, often resorted to fueling ethnic hatred, usually in the form of spreading rumors about the Tutsi.

Violence in Rwanda was a feature of everyday life, according to Ndiaye. There was a high crime rate, a profusion of weapons (one could buy a hand grenade for $2) and it was common for opposition figures, journalists or troublesome witnesses to be murdered, with those political murders being passed off as violent crimes. Also, due to the fighting as well as the intercommunal violence, nearly a million people were displaced — one Rwandan in seven.

Later in 1993, in Arusha, Tanzania, a power-sharing agreement was reached between Habyarimana and the Tutsi from Uganda and the Security Council authorized a UN peacekeeping mission to help the two sides implement the accord.

It seems that the Ndiaye report never reached the peacekeeping department in New York. Isel said she hadn't heard of it. That's typical of the sprawling UN system; the left hand doesn't know what the right is doing. Iqbal told me, "Had we been made aware of this report, it might have given us a different perspective on Dallaire's message."

From January to April 1994, there were no more cables mentioning a genocide threat. The peacekeeping department was still trying to get additional staff to deal with an overwhelming workload. There was Bosnia. There was Cambodia. The situation in Rwanda was bad, but no one but Dallaire was predicting the worst.

Tom Franklin of the UK, who was the UNICEF country team director in Rwanda for three years and was evacuated at the beginning of the killings, is a friend of mine. "We were all engaged in the peace process," he told me. "I mean, it seemed totally logical to me that we should have been all trying to get that peace agreement to work. You can't go into a peace process and say, well I'm actually expecting a genocide. So it's so easy to look back when it seems all so obvious. It certainly wasn't at the time."

Dallaire continued to press for permission to seize weapons. As a concession, he was told he could cordon off the area where the weapons were located while the Government seized the weapons. But the Government had no interest in this idea.

And then it happened. On 6 April, a plane carrying the Presidents of Rwanda and Burundi, who were returning from a regional meeting, was shot down on its approach to the Rwandan capital. No survivors. The slaughter began immediately, including the killing of 10 Belgian peacekeepers, just as the cable had predicted. The Belgians were the best-trained soldiers in the UN peacekeeping force. One of their jobs was to protect the Prime Minister, Agathe Uwilingiyimana, a moderate Hutu. She too was killed.

The genocide begins

Radio Mille Collines was broadcasting incitement. Alison des Forges, the highly respected Human Rights Watch activist who was killed in a plane crash in New York in 2009, told Isel that she had asked the Pentagon to jam these incendiary broadcasts. Their reply: it would be too costly.

I was in the closed Council consultations when Ibrahim Gambari, the Ambassador of Nigeria, who was then Council President, put forward a motion by the Non-Aligned Movement to intervene with force, if necessary, to stop the killing. I watched, embarrassed, as US Ambassador Madeleine Albright raised her hand and said that that would be unacceptable to her government. The Council, which ironically had Rwanda on it as a two-year elected member, eventually voted to reduce the UN mission to a few hundred soldiers. The Rwandan ambassador was a known Hutu hardliner, Hedi remembers, and could have garnered support from some other Council members to block any action to intervene to stop the killing, had there been any support for that idea, but there wasn't.

On 17 May, while the genocidal killings were still going on, the Security Council reversed itself, calling for an arms embargo on Rwanda and expanding the mandate of the UN peacekeeping force to include the humanitarian task of protecting civilians at risk. Given the violent environment, they increased the troop level to 5,500. Isel said she was up all night sending faxes to 150 governments; there were a few offers of troops without equipment, which was the same as no offers at all.

Boutros-Ghali sent Iqbal and Maurice to Rwanda to report back to him on the feasibility of carrying out this new mandate. Their report, transmitted by Boutros-Ghali to the Council, has one paragraph that is graphically critical of the international community's "extreme inadequacy to respond urgently with prompt and decisive action to humanitarian crises entwined with armed conflict." The Security Council quickly reduced the size of the peacekeeping mission when the killings started, the report said, and now, two months later, appears "paralyzed" to act. "We have failed in our response to the agony of Rwanda," Iqbal and Maurice wrote, "and thus have acquiesced in the continued loss of human lives. Our readiness and capacity for action has been demonstrated to be inadequate at best, and deplorable at worst, owing to the absence of the collective political will."

"We were responsible"

Isel said that Iqbal talked to her on the phone from Kigali and asked her whether she thought the killing could have been averted in light of Dallaire's warning. She said yes; she volunteered to write up a chronology of Dallaire's situation reports to prove it. On his return she gave him the chronology, telling him "We were responsible". Isel told me that she considered leaking the Dallaire cable to a *New York Times* reporter she had been in touch with, but thought better of it. "This I regret immensely," she said.

When the Tutsi army finally got the upper hand and had cornered the *génocidaires*, the Council approved a French-led intervention force that interposed itself between the two armies, allowing the Hutu to slip into the Congo from where they were a destabilizing element for years to come.

Dallaire was left with a handful of soldiers to witness an atrocity. He was a sensitive soul inside the body of a professional soldier. Maurice said of him, "He is a brave man." I didn't realize until I had served in the UN peacekeeping mission in Bosnia that you could be a General without having experienced combat, especially if you were from a pacifist country like Canada. The UN military commander in Sarajevo was General Lew Mackenzie, another Canadian. He told me that before Sarajevo, he had never seen battle. I'm sure the same was true for Dallaire.

At the end of his mandate, Dallaire returned to Canada. In 2000, he was found under a park bench in Ottawa, nearly comatose. He had a bottle of booze in his hand, which, given the anti-depressants he was taking, could have been fatal. It almost was. With counseling, he pulled himself together and in 2003 published a remarkable memoir of Rwanda, *Shake Hands with the Devil*. In it, he contends that had the world given him the few more troops he needed, he could have stopped the killing. We all wonder, if, if, if…

Dallaire was appointed a member of the Canadian Senate in 2005. When I asked to interview him for this book, his office responded, in effect, "he doesn't want to talk about this anymore." I don't blame him.

A pre-emptive strike

In the mid-1960s, I was a student of African anthropology and linguistics at the University of the Congo. I did linguistic analysis of *kinyarwanda,* the common language of the Tutsi and Hutu of Rwanda. My professors had gathered and published thousands of lines of Tutsi oral poetry, some of which I also studied. I wanted to talk to these professors, whom I hadn't seen in 40 years, about what happened in Rwanda in 1994. One, the linguist Andre Coupez, had died a few years before. But I found the other, the cultural anthropologist Marcel d'Hertefelt, living in retirement in Tervuren, Belgium. I visited him at his apartment.

He spoke to me in a heavily Flemish-accented French, which I will translate roughly. "From what we know," he said, "the Hutu and the Tutsi have lived together for a very long time and they share the same culture. There is not a Hutu culture and a Tutsi culture. There is a Rwandan culture, and that's important."

So why is there such hate between them, I asked? "Hate?" he said. "One can't say that it is hate. What was very provocative, obviously, was the way the Tutsi, who emigrated to Uganda after the Rwandan revolution of 1959, formed an army and returned to invade Rwanda in 1993. The Hutu feared that all their gains in the revolution would be overturned by the Tutsi. And that triggered the very violent reaction, which was a genocide."

In that 1959 revolution, the Hutu majority took power for the first time. D'Hertefelt was a political supporter of majority rule. "If you like," he went on, "this genocide was a kind of — how do you say it in English — a pre-emptive strike. A pre-emptive strike against the Tutsi, which obviously was horrible. And why? The reason was military. It was a pre-emptive strike out of fear of losing everything they had gained in the 1959 revolution. And they lost a lot! So for me, it's an historic fact like many others."

But, I said, 800,000 deaths in 100 days!

"Yes, it's a lot. A lot," he admitted. "It's because they were blood-crazed, and they couldn't stop killing. They couldn't stop. It's a lot, of course. I'm not trying to excuse it. Let's say it started as a pre-emptive strike and then it became an orgy of blood. Yes, it was truly horrible."

THE SHAME OF SREBRENICA

Lose, lose

The third disaster to hit the peacekeeping department in the early 1990s was the Srebrenica massacre in Bosnia. It happened in 1995, as the war in Bosnia was getting worse and the UN mission there was in a hopeless bind. There was no peace to keep. Peacekeepers were escorting aid deliveries under an international effort led by the UN High Commissioner for Refugees, and trying to be friends with everybody — or at least enemies of no one. It wasn't working.

A fundamental tenet of peacekeeping is that you can't make peace and war at the same time. It's not a difficult notion to grasp. Peacekeepers are soldiers trained to be something else, because soldiers are trained to kill the enemy. Peacekeepers, on the other hand, have no enemies. They enter a sovereign territory at the invitation of the government. They work in an even-handed way with two sides to a conflict to help those two sides honor a peace agreement. They fire only in self-defense.

Hammarskjold, who invented modern peacekeeping, said it's not a job for soldiers but only soldiers can do it. Peacekeeping is so different from war-making that some modern armies, when their soldiers return from a peacekeeping mission, retrain them to kill, because while on a peacekeeping assignment they would have played by another set of rules entirely. They would have lost their killer instinct.

The Security Council couldn't agree on what to do in Bosnia. Bosnian Serb General Ratko Mladic pounded away at Sarajevo with artillery, and pushed tens of thousands of Muslims out of Serb-majority areas in what was called quaintly "ethnic cleansing". World opinion was appalled. Bill Clinton, who was elected US President on a platform that included a "get-tough-with-the-Serbs" plank, would not commit US troops but wanted to use NATO air power instead. The British and the French both had substantial troop contributions to the UN mission in Bosnia. If NATO bombed, their soldiers would, in effect, be entering the war. They wouldn't be peacekeepers anymore, and they would be put in even greater danger.

The media was on the side of the angels, of course, and the UN was the bad guy. I was the first UN spokesperson in Sarajevo in 1992, and went in and out of Bosnia on UN assignments until 1995. The press thought that the peacekeepers were neutral in the face of evil and only deserved contempt. Yet the Security Council preferred that compromising position to entering the war with both feet. It was lose-lose for the UN.

"Safe" Areas

There were a half dozen major towns where Muslims took refuge as the Serb assault continued unchecked. Sarajevo was one; Srebrenica, in the east of the country, was another. As the noose tightened around the Muslims in these enclaves, the Security Council decided to declare them "safe areas". Boutros-Ghali asked Kofi to estimate the number of troops he would need to make these six towns safe.

Maurice Baril, the Military Adviser, was with Kofi when he privately briefed the five permanent member of the Council on the need for 34,000 troops to protect the Safe Areas. "I vividly recall Ambassadors David Hannay of the UK and Madeleine Albright of the US telling us how incompetent and ignorant we were to think that we could not do the job with the number of troops we had," he said. "We now know what happened."

When Boutros-Ghali gave the number of 34,000 to the Security Council, they rebuffed him, saying 7,600 would be enough. Then when Kofi tried to recruit even these 7,600, he came up against stiff resistance. All he got on the ground was another 2,000, and that took him six months.

The Council, in approving a non-viable safe area plan, may have thought it was taking a stop-gap measure in the vain hope that the Geneva peace talks co-sponsored by the UN and the European Community under the joint chairmanship of Cyrus Vance and Lord Owen would succeed. I was spokesperson for Vance and Owen, who got about the best agreement possible from the Yugoslav parties in the spring of 1993, but who needed some tough backing from the US if the agreement was to be implemented.

US Secretary of State Warren Christopher said that the US would not back the Vance Owen Peace Plan with force. Owen was furious with him for saying this. "He was crass," he told me in a 2006 interview in his London townhouse, barely controlling his bitterness. "I think that diplomacy without the threat of force is so much for the birds. I mean, the Bosnian Serb leadership in Pale weren't stupid. They read this — the West were not going to enforce the peace plan. Why the hell should they agree to any peace plan? It was an absolutely crazy statement. And that statement of Warren Christopher, which was in the middle of February 1993, haunted Bosnia and Herzegovina for the next two and a half years."

Without determined US support, the plan died and the war continued.

General Philippe Morillon of France was the first deputy Force Commander of the UN peacekeeping mission. I remember when we first arrived in Sarajevo in 1992, before the war, we were looking for a site for our mission Headquarters. We were being given a tour of the penthouse floor of one of the twin towers that were the tallest buildings in the city. There were planters recessed about a foot and a half in the floor next to the windows that provided a thrilling view of Sarajevo and the surrounding mountains. On arriving at the floor, a group of us followed the agent, turning left. Morillon turned right. Suddenly, we heard a crash; Morillon had inadvertently stepped into one of the planters. We all turned toward him. With great panache, he leapt out of the hole in the floor, saying with a heavy accent and a smile, "Do not worry; I am a paratroop*aire!*"

In 1993, Morillon went into Srebrenica as the internally displaced from a nearby town overrun by the Serbs were flocking in, many of them wounded, all of them cold and hungry. He found himself effectively kept hostage by the desperate population. Still, he negotiated a deal to demilitarize the zone and evacuate the needy. I spoke to him by phone from Strasbourg, where he was serving as a member of the European Parliament. "In effect, I left only after an agreement was reached — with the approval of Kofi Annan — that a peacekeeping contingent would be deployed," he said, "and the wounded would be evacuated along with families, women and children who wished to go."

Part of that deal was that the Muslim defenders of the town, led by Naser Oric, would disarm or leave. Oric had been conducting raids on nearby Serb villages, which only added to the tensions. But this part of the plan was never realized, according to Morillon. "At that time, the agreement was that Naser Oric and his fighters should leave the safe area or turn in their arms, the zone would be demilitarized and peacekeepers put in place," he said. "None of that happened, because in the end the Serbs refused to cooperate, under the influence of Mladic, once the Vance-Owen plan failed."

With the failure of Vance-Owen, the safe areas concept was naked. Despite the agreement to demilitarize Srebrenica, the Muslim fighters inside the town remained armed and Srebrenica remained unsafe. Then, in July 1995, General Mladic, with about 2,000 troops, easily overran the city. An estimated 12,000 Muslim fighting-age men escaped into the hills and sought to trek overland 60 miles to the Muslim stronghold of Tuzla. 7,000 of them never made it; they were hunted down and killed by Mladic's soldiers, their bodies dumped in mass graves. The 600 UN peacekeepers in Srebrenica — 300 of them support staff — were worse than useless. The Srebrenica massacre has been called one of the worst atrocities committed in Europe since the Second World War, and the UN was to blame.

The Srebrenica Report

In 1999, Kofi Annan, now Secretary-General, called for an internal inquiry into the Srebrenica massacre. He wanted a clear analysis of where things went wrong, but he also wanted to fix what he could so this would not happen again. He chose two of the best and the brightest from among the younger generation in the peacekeeping department — David Harland, a New Zealander who describes himself as a dissident during his UN service in Bosnia, assisted by Salman Ahmed, a US national.

I spoke with David in New York in November of 2006. "The UN is enormously tolerant of internal dissent," he began. "I've never known whether it was a native disposition or it's just not a very tight bureaucracy." He said that he thought he was a surprising choice to conduct an inquiry on Srebrenica, because he was "almost bound to be critical of Kofi." He said that he and others were strongly dissenting from what they felt was a line of appeasement of the Serbs that, he said, "would end in tears." He added, "He must have known that mine would be a critical voice."

He speaks with firm conviction. "The Srebrenica report was a first effort to lay out the narrative of how the world got to that moment on the afternoon of Tuesday, 11 July 1995 when the Serbs stood in the center of the Safe Area. It's a coherent narrative that is used in all the court cases on Srebrenica."

"Any great disaster requires layers of things to go wrong," he went on, "and in Bosnia the one that I was most aware of was the UN Secretariat's own complicity." He said that the reports of Secretary-General Boutros Boutros-Ghali to the Security Council, for example, tended to equalize the sides "when there was no equality to be had."

He then thought for a few seconds. "But where my report might have done some harm is that it a little too easily let the countries off the hook. The view in the Secretariat at the time was, 'We told them they shouldn't go into Bosnia in the first place; then we told them that the Safe Area concept wouldn't work; then they didn't provide the necessary troops and finally when it failed they said, Ooh, that didn't work very well, that damned Secretariat.'"

He looked me straight in the eye. "With the benefit of a decade's hindsight, that's true. And I played down that line in the report. What I focused on in the report from the UN Secretariat angle was: Okay, UNPROFOR, you have been dealt, by the nature of the political machine, a bad set of cards. That's no reason to fold your hand and it's no reason to play those cards badly. Sometimes you have to work with what you've got. In a very constrained world, you still have to do what's morally right, what's politically right. And sometimes for soldiers, you have to do that even if it's dangerous, even if you're 300 Dutch peacekeepers and 2,000 Serbs are coming in.

"So I had focused on real failings, genuine failings, failings that had outraged me when I was in Bosnia. But in the scheme of things, and with a decade's hindsight, they were the least of the failings that caused that disaster."

In the end, he said, "We, in dissent, were right, but we were right on a smaller plane."

There were those very close to Kofi, such as his special assistant Shashi Tharoor, who felt that David's report was much too critical and should not be made public. Iqbal Riza, the Chief of Staff, told David he would argue with Kofi that although the report didn't reflect well on anyone in the UN, he should do the right thing and release it. David said, "So if Riza's story is correct, then he had that meeting with the Secretary-General, he prevailed and Kofi decided he would take the hit and that we should all learn from it."

The shock of Srebrenica shamed governments into taking a stronger position against the Serbs. The UK and France sent soldiers in — as soldiers this time not as peacekeepers — and they brought with them a radar tracking anti-artillery capability that could knock out Serb guns in the hills around Sarajevo. That was the beginning of the end for the Serbs.

Kofi is often personally blamed for Srebrenica, particularly by his enemies, and indeed as the head of peacekeeping at the time he has to take some share of the blame. He did, by accepting the Srebrenica Report as David Harland wrote it.

We the Secretariat have lots to answer for. Why didn't we stand up to the Security Council? Why didn't we point a long, sharp finger at the Serbs? Because we were in a compromising position, as peacekeepers, that's why. But maybe that's not an excuse.

For us, the only redeeming element was Kofi's release of the Srebrenica Report, in an effort to see that the same mistake not be made again. Chris Coleman, an American that Kofi brought into the peacekeeping department, said to me, "Of all the leaders who had any involvement in Rwanda and Bosnia, who's been the most forthcoming about what went right and what went wrong? Who's been the quickest to accept responsibility and to try to provoke an international debate just to strengthen things so it doesn't happen again? And I'd say, Kofi's the person who's done that."

CHAPTER 3

THE SEVENTH
SECRETARY-GENERAL

"NO, HE WON'T"

Kofi often used to spend holidays with his friends Toni and Jim Goodale in New York. On one occasion, Toni said to him over dinner, "Kofi, you are such a star, you are going to be Secretary-General some day." And Kofi replied, "Yes, and you're going to be President of the United States." He honestly didn't think it was a possibility. No one from the Secretariat had ever been named Secretary-General.

But Boutros Boutros-Ghali was in deep trouble with the United States, and Madeleine Albright was trying to nudge him to step aside. Richard Holbrooke, later the US Ambassador to the UN, then acting as a private citizen, decided to urge him to go. Holbrooke had been in Sarajevo the day that Boutros-Ghali commented in the Bosnian capital that there were 10 places in the world that were worse off. In fact, he was right. But those places weren't in Europe, which was his point. Still, he got zero for sensitivity that day and Holbrooke joined the ranks of those who thought he should not have a second term.

I met with Richard Holbrooke in his midtown Manhattan office. He described a dinner that had been arranged by Barbara Walters between him and Boutros and Leah Boutros-Ghali. "We went to the Four Seasons restaurant with his wife and had a very emotional dinner," he began. "I said to him, after consulting Secretary of State Warren Christopher, you know, we will support you for any other international position, World Envoy for Peace, whatever, but you have to leave this job if you truly care about the UN." Boutros wouldn't budge. He said he had been told by people like Congressman Lee Hamilton and Speaker of the House Tom Foley that this is just politics and after the Presidential election Clinton will relent. Holbrooke told him, "No, he won't."

Bob Orr had worked for Holbrooke and later became a strategic adviser to Kofi; he had been in a key position in the US National Security Council when Madeleine Albright was waging war against Boutros-Ghali. He handled the UN portfolio as the Clinton Administration was looking for an acceptable alternative. He described the problem as the Administration saw it. "The key issue then was the huge amount of US arrears to the UN that had been building for years, and a very difficult relationship with Secretary-General Boutros-Ghali," he said. "The question for anyone in the US Government who cared about the UN was how to get the relationship back on track."

So there were policy issues and personality issues, and to deal with the first they felt they had to address the second. And the US felt that Boutros just didn't get it. On the substantive side, Bob Orr said of Kofi, "We had all seen him in action in very difficult circumstances in his various jobs at the UN. I think he impressed most people with his handling of the most difficult issues in his peacekeeping days; clearly, Bosnia and his much more sophisticated understanding of the problems of the dual key approach was a prime example. He knew that the UN couldn't try to be NATO or NATO-Lite; it had a different role. He understood what the UN could do and what it could not. He was someone who made the most sense."

So Bob wrote the decision memo to President Clinton. "I knew exactly where all the main players in the US stood on this question," he said, "and Kofi Annan was the one unanimous choice."

SWEPT IN ON THE WINDS OF THE SAHARA

The Security Council nominates, but the General Assembly elects. On 17 December 1996, the Assembly officially made Kofi the seventh Secretary-General of the United Nations.

Nane watched him enter the General Assembly Hall. "He had such grace and dignity when he walked down the aisle," she told me. "There is such determination in those shoulders, in his gait and in the arch of his back. And an African representative called him a son of Africa, swept in on the winds of the Sahara. It was very moving and I knew he would handle his new tasks beautifully, but I found myself wondering, What about me, how will I handle it?"

Nane had received the news of the Security Council nomination while she was having lunch with a friend on the West Side of Manhattan. In a now famous interview with Reuters' UN correspondent Evelyn Leopold, she told the story of how she took ten minutes to collect herself. She then took leave of her friend and set out on the street. She repeated the story to me. "Instead of taking a cab, which I easily could have done to cross the city, I walked," she said. "And on the way I had three encounters."

"The first was in Times Square, where a woman walked up to me and said, 'Oh, were you in Beijing at the women's conference?' And I said, 'No, I wasn't. Why do you ask?' It turns out I was carrying a UNIFEM bag. And she looked so disappointed, so I was about to say, 'Yes, but my husband was just elected Secretary-General!' But she had already disappeared." Nane laughed at herself.

"The second happened a bit further across town," she continued. "As I was getting closer to the UN, I thought, Gosh! I should put on more presentable shoes. So I leaned against a mailbox and started changing out of my sneakers. Just then the wife of an ambassador came up to me and just hugged me. I immediately felt the support of the spousal community, which came to play such an important part in my life.

"And then the third meeting, just across from the UN — somebody said to me, 'Oh, are you walking around here without your security?'" That comment would presage a fundamental change in their lifestyles that was about to take place.

The Assembly paid tribute to the outgoing Secretary-General, Boutros Boutros-Ghali. Then Kofi walked to the lectern to deliver his acceptance speech. He began with the ritual honorifics, "Mr. President, respected Secretary-General…" and then he stopped. He spotted Javier Perez de Cuellar in the audience, the Secretary-General who had given him his first political assignment in Iraq. He looked down at him and smiled, then departed from his text: "or rather, respected Secretaries-General, as I see my old boss, Secretary-General Perez de Cuellar is here today — welcome home, Sir…

Welcome home, Sir. The greeting was warm and genuine. Of course, Boutros-Ghali was his old boss too, but the warmth, had there ever been any, had been squeezed out of that relationship in the last bruising year.

In his remarks, Kofi called attention to the fundamental political reality of the day. With the Cold War at an end, the UN, he said, was at a crossroads. Member States, while redefining relations among themselves, must now agree on what the United Nations should become. "The time to choose is now, for this Organization, along with the rest of the world, must change."

The speech, initially drafted by Kennedy speechwriter Ted Sorensen, had the Sorensen signature of clusters of three elements: "The United Nations is your instrument for peace and justice. Use it; respect it; defend it. It can be no wiser, no more competent and no more efficient than those Member States that now comprise and guide it.... Applaud us when we prevail; correct us when we fail; but, above all, do not let this indispensable, irreplaceable institution languish or perish as a result of Member States' indifference, inattention or financial starvation."

Of course, the financial starvation referred to the United States, which was withholding portions of its dues for political reasons. The largest contributor had accumulated massive arrears that had brought it to the point of losing its vote in the General Assembly, and the UN to the brink of bankruptcy. Relations with Washington would be high on Kofi's agenda.

Kofi asked Iqbal Riza to be his Chief of Staff. He called him "Iqie" (pronounced "ickey"), which for me somehow didn't go with Iqbal's refined, formal air. He was slim and dressed so nicely in an understated way. His voice was soft and slightly hoarse, except when he cleared his throat with an ear-splitting hack. He was a widower, tinged with sadness, I thought. He was from Pakistan and often lamented the deteriorating political situation in his home country.

It was Iqbal who first lectured Kofi on how his life would change. "I said to him, 'You know, Kofi, this is going to be a new relationship. On the 1st of January, I'm going to tell everybody in the office they cannot call you Kofi anymore. You're no longer a colleague and a friend and a boss, you're an institution, and everyone will address you as Secretary-General, including myself.'" And so it was.

WALKS AND RUNS

Kofi had taken a walk along the Charles to deal with his feeling of uncertainty at MIT. Nane had gone for long walks before deciding to give up law, follow Kofi to New York and start painting again. Walking is integral to their lives.

I asked Nane if it was more than just exercise, maybe a way to clear their heads and think things through. "Oh, I think for Kofi, definitely," she replied. "We often went out to Long Island for walks in the woods. Kofi particularly liked going out to Shelter Island, where there are huge nature preserves where you can walk and walk for hours, and he would do that." She then explained why. "He has this need, very often, to go into himself. As you know, he has such easy contact with everybody, but it's ultimately within himself he goes to find answers. And I think the walks, and reading and listening to music, are very much part of that."

For Nane, it seemed much more physical. "I walk because I love to move. I do it as a way of keeping healthy in a very determined way, and now I am talking more about the mind than anything else. I go bicycling in Central Park — I rent a bicycle at the Boat House. And I've been going up into the Swedish mountains to hike. I like that kind of thing, being out in nature; Swedes have been described as loving our stones."

As Secretary-General and First Lady, walking just wasn't the same. On an early trip to Germany, I heard Kofi tell the Foreign Ministry people that he and Nane would like to take a walk in the mountains. Right, no problem; the Ministry kicked into gear and arranged it. Kofi described to me the result: "Nane and I were walking through these deep woods, and suddenly there was a clearing with a dramatic view. We stopped to admire it. Our security also stopped, along with the German secret service, the German Foreign Service officer accompanying us, the secretaries, the interpreters and others in our party. We walked further and came across breathtaking mountain scenery. Again, we stopped, and stopping behind us to admire it were the security, the secret service, the interpreters and so on." He laughed. He must have thought they would never be alone again.

Even their bedroom wasn't sacred anymore. On a visit to Sweden, following receipt of the 2001 Nobel Prize in Oslo, Kofi and Nane were given the traditional wake up call for Nobel laureates on the feast of Santa Lucia. Young men and women in white robes, carrying lighted candles, come into your room singing sweetly. I wasn't aware of this and hadn't been warned. When I heard the voices in the hallway I came out to see what was going on. Nane and Kofi were in bed, their bedroom door open, and the carolers were filing into their room singing. A UN security guard, Paula Goncalves, was taking a photograph for herself. Without looking towards the bed, I passed her my camera and she took one for me. Later I felt ashamed that I had a picture in my camera of the Secretary-General and his wife in bed. I erased it.

Keeping up with the Secretary-General was no picnic for UN Security. Kofi is not tall, but he has powerful legs. He was a sprinter as a young man, after all, and he stays in shape. On trips, he would frequently opt for not getting into the official motorcade and instead hit the pavement to walk to the Parliament, or the Foreign Ministry, or wherever his next meeting was. Then he would kick into high gear, and his security guards, who were not uniformly thin, would end up gasping for breath, along with the rest of us, as we struggled to keep up with him. His security guys called it "the power walk".

Nick Panzarino, a security guard who did 38th floor security detail for 20 years, was one of the trim ones. He headed Kofi's security detail at the beginning and told me about an early visit by Kofi and Nane to Sweden. Nick usually got up at the crack of dawn to go out for a two or three mile run. With his former bosses, there was no risk of them rising early on him. But when he returned to the Palace (they were the house guests of the Queen), Kofi was standing at the front door in his jogging outfit. Nick apologized profusely, but Kofi reassured him there was no problem and asked him if he was up for another run. "By all means," Nick said.

So they took off together at a comfortable jog, when all of a sudden Kofi put on a burst of speed. "Jeez!", Nick said to me in his pronounced New York accent, "I thought we were going for a jog and this guy's sprinting. I can't handle this." But after about 30 seconds, Kofi went back to a jog and Nick caught up with him.

Nick says Nane was almost as bad. He remembers being assigned to her on their first trip to France. He had the distinct impression she was trying to lose him, as she walked through Paris. "She took off," Nick said. "I could just barely see her as she weaved through traffic and everything." But she didn't manage to shake him. "I'm pretty quick myself," Nick said proudly, "but she really tested me."

On a visit to Kosovo, Kofi was returning to the UN headquarters building in Pristina with the head of the UN mission there, Michael Steiner of Germany. Kofi and Michael were chatting about how they stay in shape. As they entered the five-story building, Kofi looked at the elevator, which was slow in coming, and then at the staircase. "Let's take the stairs," he said to Steiner. As he and Steiner began the ascent, Kofi said, "I'll race you." The two ran neck and neck up five flights, laughing like schoolboys. I took the elevator, and as I got out at the fifth floor, I saw that Steiner, who was trim, fit and younger, lose by a nose.

"HE WAS STRICT WITH THE CHILDREN"

Kofi, as a long-time UN administrator, knew the UN rules. As an ethical person, he respected them, even when it came to his kids. Ama and Kojo would come to New York to visit him at the Sutton Place residence with some regularity, but there was no question of sending a security detail out to the airport in the official limo to pick them up. Kofi insisted they take a taxi.

This was not exactly an established UN tradition. One of Kofi's predecessors, I was told, gave his wife an official car and driver to go shopping, had UN workmen restore antiques that she bought and then sent those antiques by official UN pouch back to their home country.

Nick Panzarino told me: "Kofi believed in obeying the rules and he didn't believe in exploiting the benefits of his position. He was very strict with the children. Whenever they traveled, he would not give them the official car. And sometimes they would be a little upset with him, you know, the fact that they couldn't get this or that, enjoy some of the little fringe benefits of his office."

Ama, in my 2006 interview with her at the residence, said that her father told them why: "His explanation to me about that was that he's trying to cut costs at the UN, so he can't on the one hand be cutting costs and on the other be keeping staff on overtime to pick up his kids. I mean, it's not a strange country to us; we lived here."

In the same interview, Kojo added: "He generally doesn't believe in excess. You'll see even in this house, he doesn't keep the cooks. The cooks go home at 4 o'clock every day, unless there's an official function. Most other Secretaries-General would have their cook serving them dinner at night. Not him. He doesn't believe in that."

THE SOCIAL SECRETARY-GENERAL

Kofi and Nane, more than any of their predecessors, went out on the New York social scene — with a vengeance. In the first term, a Sunday hardly went by when their photo didn't appear in *The New York Times* society section alongside Brooke Astor or some other prominent socialite.

Some UN staff cringed at what they saw as an indulgence, a pointless waste of time in an effort to be seen with the rich and the powerful. But *The New York Times* UN bureau chief at the time, Barbara Crossette, who wrote an article about it, saw it instead as shrewd and necessary

"She frankly was, you know, a regular person, and suddenly she had to adopt this very public persona," said Shashi Tharoor. "She changed her style of dress, her style of hair and everything else. And suddenly she became somebody she hadn't been."

politicking. Over lunch in midtown Manhattan, she said, "Kofi and his wife Nane told me that they felt that New York was such a rich city in so many ways in terms of the variety of people that you could meet, people that you could influence to pay more attention to the UN or to be more supportive of the UN, and that starts at Wall Street and goes right up to Harlem."

"Boutros Boutros-Ghali socialized grudgingly" she went on, "and was known, at least once, to flee a theatrical performance after the first act, but Kofi Annan and Nane have a great deal of social grace and they mix very well. They're enormously friendly people. And when they entertained they would have a very interesting mix of people from city life, and so he became a very popular figure in New York."

She acknowledged that he was criticized by some UN staff, who thought that it wasn't his job to be socializing so much, but, she observed, "Unfortunately New York is a city where socializing does matter a lot and where people make a lot of contacts. Because life is so complicated and busy here the opportunity to sit down over dinner or lunch and talk to people is very important. And I think through his personal effort, he made the presence of the UN rise considerably in New York."

I invited Toni Goodale to lunch and she told me that she had strongly urged Kofi and Nane to get out on the town. "When Kofi became Secretary-General, I said to both of them, look, the UN is a very isolated institution and the diplomats hang out with each other. And there are all these other people in New York and a lot of the press whom we hang out with. And I believe, if you want to, you should get to know a lot more people." Kofi agreed. Toni and her husband Jim then threw a big party for them — 200 guests — at the Four Seasons restaurant. Nane, who immediately picked up on what Toni was trying to do, worked with her on the guest list.

That was followed by a sit down dinner for 34 at the Goodale's home. This time the guest list was a Who's Who of the news world — Tom Brokaw, Dan Rather, Mike Wallace, Tina Brown, Harry Evans, Charlie Rose, Peter Jennings. Kofi and Nane were launched. They began to entertain on their own at the residence and quickly became fixtures in New York society. They were taken up by Brooke Astor and became social stars, according to Toni. "It's not that they tried; it's just that they're an impressive couple," she said. "They're friendly and interesting and, you know, people like them."

Toni called on her close friend Sally Quinn, and Sally and her husband Ben Bradlee threw a party in Washington for Kofi and Nane and invited the glitterati of the media scene there. "I thought it was important for Kofi," Toni added; 'but I thought it was even more important for the United Nations, that it not remain an isolated institution. A lot of people resent it, actually. You know, there have been mayors who've tried to kick the United Nations out of here. And there will be again."

As Kofi and Nane moved around the New York social world, something about him became apparent. He had an element of spontaneity that was refreshing. He could do the unexpected. At Lincoln Center, he was on stage with Wynton Marsalis, who had just performed for some kind of commemorative event. Kofi asked to see his trumpet, and then blew into it, producing an awful squeal. Everyone laughed and applauded appreciatively.

He was better at the drums. There was a fund raising concert in the General Assembly Hall, and the Brazilian star Gilberto Gil was on stage with his band. Gil called Kofi up and seated him in front of a conga drum. As Gil sang and played his guitar, Kofi accompanied him, his long fingers rhythmically tapping the drum like a pro. At one point, Gil turned to Kofi for a solo, and he let loose. He was a star.

And then there was the time he was at the Guggenheim for a private tour with the widow of Arthur Ashe. Nane was there, as was Julia Preiswerk, who told me this story. The director of the museum, who was to conduct the tour, showed up a few minutes late on a big Harley Davidson. Kofi's eyes widened. The director noticed his interest and said, "Would you like to go for a ride?"

Kofi was going to hop on the bike in a New York minute, when his security surrounded him. Mark Hoffman, the head of the detail, said, "Don't even think about it, Mr. Secretary-General."

These heavy social responsibilities were unexpected for Nane, and those close to her marveled at how she had adapted to her role as UN First Lady. Julia Preiswerk told me, "When I met Nane for the first time, her hair was long and she was wearing blue jeans and plastic sandals. She was like a flower child; all she wanted to do was paint." Julia thought that Nane had a hard time settling in after following Kofi to New York. "She's a very shy person," Julia said. "She wasn't really all that interested in social life, or hanging out with VIPs. That wasn't her thing. What did she know about cooking, or organizing staff or throwing large parties? Not much."

Shashi Tharoor also thought Nane changed dramatically in her new role. "Right up to Kofi's days as head of peacekeeping, she was often very casually dressed, nothing very fancy," he told me during an interview in his UN office. "She frankly was, you know, a regular person, and suddenly she had to adopt this very public persona. She changed her style of dress, her style of hair and everything else. And suddenly she became somebody she hadn't been. But she took to it. I certainly felt within two or three years she was very comfortable in her own skin, whereas she wasn't initially."

THE ROCK STAR OF DIPLOMACY

Kofi was being called the rock star of diplomacy. *TIME* magazine did a flattering cover story on him. One photo had him poised on a circular bench in the back yard of the Sutton Place residence under his "Thinking Tree."

I remember that when he was being given a tour of a shopping mall in Tokyo, a group of school children spotted him and burst into applause. This kind of thing happened all the time. People wanted his autograph, wanted to have their photo taken with him, gave him a friendly wave on the street. Kofi was becoming the best-known UN Secretary-General since Hammarskjold. He received an invitation to do a guest stint on Sesame Street. The script was that the Muppets were having a dispute over who would sing the alphabet song. Kofi comes along, introduces himself and suggests they all sing together. They do, and afterwards all gather around him and gave him a group hug. I can't say he was 100 percent at ease in this setting, but the breadth of his smile told me that he enjoyed it.

He rubbed elbows with movie stars, sometimes without knowing it. Farhan Haq was on my spokesperson's team; he was the son of the distinguished Pakistani development economist Mahbub ul Haq. I once assigned him to accompany Kofi at some celebrity event, and he later told me that a good-looking young man came up to Kofi and said breathlessly, "If there's ever anything I can do for you, man, just let me know," and then left as quickly as he came. Later in the evening, the same young man again ran up to Kofi and said, "I really mean it, man; I'm there for you," and again he left abruptly. Kofi leaned toward one of his security guys and asked in a low voice, "Who was that?" The security guy leaned down to Kofi and whispered, "Brad Pitt, Sir."

Kofi's social status peaked when he was invited to throw out the first baseball at Yankee Stadium during the third game of the 1999 World Series, an honor bestowed only on worthy celebrities. Kofi was good with his feet — after all, he had played soccer and run track. But he was not as good with his hands. So his American security guards volunteered to train him. They practiced with him over and over — left leg up, right hand clutching the ball back behind the ear, then with one motion, left leg is brought down, right arm swings forward, then a flip of the wrist as you let go of the ball. Kofi thought he had the hang of it.

Nick Panzarino was on security detail that day and went with Kofi to Yankee Stadium. He brought along his personal camcorder to film the big event. Kofi was given a Yankees jacket to put on before walking to the pitcher's mound. The mound is 90 feet away from home plate. That's a long throw. The catcher was behind the plate waiting for Kofi to pitch the ball. Kofi wound up. His left leg went up, his right arm brought the ball behind his ear, then leg down, arm around and the throw — "Ohhhh,

"Ohhhh, Noooo," groaned Nick, as the ball dribbled on the grass. UN/DPI PHOTO BY EVAN SCHNEIDER.

Noooo," groaned Nick. The ball dribbled on the grass. The catcher, experienced with celebrities who couldn't throw a baseball, ran forward to scoop it up and said something like, "Good throw, Sir." The crowd roared, eager for the game to begin, and Kofi walked off the mound with dignity. Nick showed us his home video Monday morning, and we heard his voice saying, "Ohhhhh, Nooooo" and laughed. "I better erase that," he said.

By the end of his second term, celebrity had become almost a joke for Kofi. He told me that after they moved out of the residence, he and Nane went off to Italy to do nothing for three months. They were in a mountain chalet, and after a few weeks started to get cabin fever. So they walked to the nearest village to find a newspaper shop. As they were gathering an armload of papers and magazines, Kofi noticed a couple of tourists looking at him and whispering. Finally, one of the tourists approached him and said, "I know who you are — Morgan Freeman! Can I have your autograph?" "Sure," Kofi said, and signed it K. Freeman.

Early in the first term, Iqbal Riza began to have reservations about this celebrity status. He said he would ask Kofi periodically, "SG, do you still have the same hat size?" And Kofi would reply, "Why? Do you think it's changed?" And Iqbal would then say, "No, I don't think it's changed. I can't see it. But only you can tell me." Then Kofi would reply, "No, I think it's the same." Iqbal once said to Nane, "Your husband's become a celebrity." And she said, "Please don't say that. He doesn't want to be a celebrity, I don't want him to be a celebrity." Whether she wanted it or not, that's what he had become. There had never been a UN Secretary-General like him.

Kofi receiving an AIDS pin in Beijing in 2004. "There had never been a UN Secretary-General like him."

But about this very public couple with very private instincts, *The New York Times'* Barbara Crossette said, "Nobody knows, who watched them from the outside, how much of a chore some of these social events might have been for Nane. She was always flawless and graceful, though, and I don't think she ever made anyone feel that she didn't want to be there. There was a lot about her that was perhaps hidden, and also about him. So to us outside, the reporters and others, they were both very private people, and together they were almost a unit — they exuded charm and grace but neither of them were people that gave away much about how they felt about these things that they had to do."

IN THE AIR

A Secretary-General is answerable to all the Member States of the UN, which during Kofi's tenure came to number 192, and he tries to visit as many of them as he can. Under the Charter, they are sovereign and equal, but obviously some are more equal than others. The five permanent members of the Security Council, for example, who wield a veto, have pride of place, and Kofi tried to visit each of them at least once a year. He went to Washington often, because it was close and easy — and important. And he often traveled through London and Paris en route to other destinations in addition to his official visits there. Ministry people would sometimes come out to Heathrow or Charles de Gaulle to confer with him while he waited for his next flight. He got to Moscow and Beijing less frequently.

Like his predecessor Boutros Boutros-Ghali, Kofi spent about a third of his time on the road. I traveled with him to some 100 countries in eight and a half years, and I can tell you it's a manic whirlwind. You might think this is a wonderful way to see the world, but frankly all we usually managed to see was an airport, a five-star hotel, the foreign ministry and the president's office and then we were gone. In 2002, we visited five countries that ended in "stan," and to this day, at any given time, I can only tick off four of them. At regional summits, Kofi met with up to a dozen heads of state a day. Traveling with him was the most exhausting part of my job.

His delegations were small and they moved quickly. The President of the United States travels with hundreds. Kofi had a dozen people with him on average — Nane, a trip coordinator, a senior political officer, a note-taker, a speechwriter as a back-up note-taker, a spokesperson, a secretary and three or four security guards.

When we were at an official reception, I never felt comfortable speaking to anyone or grabbing a bite to eat because I always needed to see the top of his graying head. Kofi had this habit of suddenly deciding it was time to go and making a beeline for the exit. And you were either with him or you were left behind.

In April 1997 (it was the 8th) he had just completed his first visit to India and was flying to Geneva, when we realized it was his birthday. One of us ordered champagne. The stewardess poured about 10 glasses and we stealthily followed her up to the first class cabin where he and Nane were sitting. "Happy Birthday," we whispered, trying not to disturb the other first class passengers, which was hard, given the number of us. Kofi smiled and said something like, "let's drink to that." He was sitting, and the stewardess was holding the tray of glasses in front of him. Nane took a glass, then he did, then one of us reached for a glass and tipped it over. And like bowling pins, one glass after another toppled and the champagne poured over the edge of the tray and right into Kofi's lap.

For me this was a moment of truth. If Kofi had a mean streak in him, this is when it would come out. We all held our breaths and, with mouths open, stared at him, horrified. "Oh, Gosh," he said, smiling, as the stewardess gave him a towel to mop up his trousers. "We'll have to order another round."

People are amazed that the UN doesn't have a private airplane, but it doesn't. Even the head of state of the world's poorest country must have a private plane or two, but the cost of buying it, servicing it, fueling it, paying to park it, salaries and benefits for a crew and a back-up crew is just more than the General Assembly would bear. We traveled commercial most of the time. Kofi usually had a first class seat, if the plane had a first class section. The rest of us flew under General Assembly rules — economy class if the flight was less than nine hours, otherwise business class. But we were such good customers the airlines would often bump us up to business class on shorter flights if seats were available.

Kofi was usually the star passenger, and willingly stood in the galley with stewards and stewardesses to have his picture taken with them so they could show it to their kids. But on one

British Airways flight the crew was all aflutter. Do you know who's on this flight, one of them asked me? "I know," I said; "Kofi Annan." "No, no," she corrected me. "Mr. Bean!" And indeed when the British comedian Rowen Atkinson walked off the plane with his son, who seemed about eight, all eyes were on him and nobody noticed Kofi. That was sobering.

Sometimes, when we traveled to more remote areas with less frequent air service, going commercial didn't make sense. In those instances we either chartered a plane, drawing on voluntary funds provided for that purpose by a few generous governments — Norway was one — or we borrowed a plane from a wealthy government, usually in the Middle East.

The most luxurious aircraft ever loaned to us belonged to Rafik Hariri, the billionaire businessman who helped rebuild Beirut after the Lebanese civil war, served as Prime Minister, and then was assassinated in 2005. Hariri's plane was a brand new Boeing 777, one of two he had recently bought. Mark Hoffman, Kofi's chief security officer on that trip, told me that at that time Hariri was the only one to own a 777 privately. It had a private bedroom for Kofi and Nane, a study for Kofi, a big, luxurious sitting room for them and anyone they wanted to invite in for a chat, and a lounge for us with Middle Eastern-style beds on the floor and lots of business class seats in the back. The menu included champagne and caviar and wondrous things to eat. We never had it so good.

On a visit to Nepal, we were offered a private tourist flight through the Himalayas. Lamin Sise was on board, crackling with excitement. He always — and I mean always — carried in his pocket three documents — the UN Charter, the US Constitution and the Universal Declaration of Human Rights. He was standing in the aisle, bending over to look out the window. And as we passed Mount Everest, his joy overflowed; he reached into his pocket, pulled out the three documents and waived them triumphantly in the air. Much later I asked him why he waved those documents over Everest. He thought for a moment and then replied, "To show the whole world from this highest peak three of the title deeds of human freedom and liberty."

Traveling in peacekeeping areas, though, was a different matter. We sometimes flew around in Russian cargo planes or big transport helicopters with Ukrainian crews. Many of these choppers had huge fuel tanks in the cargo hold where we sat, which seemed to me like an accident waiting to happen. In fact, a woman who worked for me as a press officer in Bosnia, Leah Zelnick, along with 11 others, was burned to death when one of those choppers went down in central Bosnia, igniting the 100-gallon tank on impact.

Elisabeth Lindenmayer put most of these trips together; she was a meticulous planner, and every minute of Kofi's day was accounted for. But others also took their turn, like Lamin Sise and Shashi Tharoor. I must say, when Shashi was trip captain, the pace was much more comfortable, often with sightseeing built in, but in the end it was Elisabeth who did most of the trips. When Elisabeth sneezed, it was with a little squeak. She told me her father, a military man, didn't approve of loud sneezing. She was very disciplined.

In the first year, before we figured out how these things should work, we allowed the foreign ministries of the countries Kofi visited to dictate the program. Those guys squeezed everything out of him, scheduling breakfast, lunch and dinner programs from the moment he arrived on their soil. Of course, we were all very gung ho in the beginning and happily jumped through the hoops that Governments held up for us. But then I began to notice a regular pattern — after going through a few hours of the program for a given day, Kofi would be leading his delegation up the steps of the Parliament or the Foreign Ministry and he would signal to one of the security guards and whisper in his ear. We would all stop, and the security guard would lead Kofi away. A few minutes later, he would return smiling. We had not budgeted time for him to make a pit stop!

Elisabeth eventually fought back with the ministries and established a workable pattern. Nothing official the first day we arrive — get over the jet lag. No early morning program if we could help it — start at about 9:30. Return to the hotel room for a pit stop every few hours, when possible, and no more than one official meal event per day. If the trip lasted more than a week, plan a day of rest in the middle. And that's how Kofi survived 10 years of official travel.

A JOB LIKE NO OTHER

Kofi grew into the job of Secretary-General, and steadily increased his work capacity. I asked Shashi if he thought Kofi's work patterns changed. "Yes, he replied. "First of all, it was a full time job like no other, because every moment of his time, including his social time, was now part of his role as Secretary-General. And one thing with which I was very impressed, and that he did much more of than I saw him doing in peacekeeping, was taking his work home with him in the sense of both paper and phone calls."

I used to meet him on his arrival every morning. Mark Hoffman, head of the security detail, would open the door for him and take his briefcase. It was always full. I would follow him up to his office, and he always invited me in. He took the briefcase back from Mark. And as we discussed what happened on the news overnight, he unloaded it, putting folder after folder into the "out" tray.

Shashi recalled that during the crisis on East Timor in 1999, Kofi was making calls around the world, even if it meant staying up all night. "His phone logs on East Timor are really striking," he said. "If those who called him the Remote Controller had seen him in action as Secretary-General, they'd change their tune. Already in peacekeeping it was a good step up in terms of how much he demanded of himself. And as Secretary-General, he demanded total performance, and I think he fulfilled that goal."

Iqbal saw Kofi's political instincts get more refined in his new role as Secretary-General: "What struck me was not just his political ability, which he had first demonstrated in Iraq in 1991; it was far more than that. He was politically astute. He showed a political instinct, and he would see under the surface and say, 'This is actually what's driving this situation.' And equally striking was how quickly he became familiar with the socio-economic field. And how aware he was of what was going on in the world outside the UN — in corporations, in development, in information technology. He had a very wide grasp of issues."

Kofi loved to talk to people and to learn from them. He was insatiable. And much of that was done on the phone — he came to excel at telephone diplomacy. But in the beginning, he just talked without taking notes. Andrew Gilmour, a deputy political director on Kofi's staff, described how that changed. "It was Kieran Prendergast," he said, "his top political adviser, who told him, on arriving at the UN from the British Foreign Office, 'Look, Secretary-General, a telephone call is effectively just like a face to face meeting where you would always have a note taker. You should know that when you're speaking to Foreign Secretary Robin Cook, don't imagine that it's just you two on the line. There will always be a Foreign Office note taker taking notes. And you should do the same thing, so that if there is any follow-up action to be taken by any of us, the relevant people can see from the note.' And so Annan initiated that procedure at the UN."

Kofi would then correct the note taker's account of the conversation, as needed, and send it to whomever he felt should see it. In fact, when Tony Blair's former international development minister, Clare Short, made an extravagant claim that her own government was bugging Kofi Annan's phone during the height of the Oil-for-Food scandal, I assumed that she had just seen the note of one of Kofi's phone conversations on someone's desk in London. It was most likely a leak, not a bug.

"He would ring up people indefatigably," Andrew said. "Sometimes when there was a major crisis, you would see on his telephone log in the morning that he'd called eight or ten Heads of State or Foreign Ministers over the weekend just to follow up on one issue."

Kofi also learned how to use the bully pulpit. John Ruggie once called him a "norm entrepreneur." In a telephone interview with him at Harvard, where he went after leaving the UN, I asked him to explain. "What I meant by that," he said, "was that he realized that the UN in and of itself doesn't have power and it doesn't have major resources, but what it does have is the ability to shape thinking and to give voice to aspirations and to legitimize certain norms or help delegitimize certain other norms or practices. And I think he understood the normative role of the UN much better than possibly any other Secretary-General except for Hammarskjold, who I think also understood it very well."

"But most of the other Secretaries-General have been much more focused on mediation efforts and bureaucratic things," he went on, "without understanding that the power of ideas and normative statements and programs is really what makes the UN unique."

Most people don't understand how little real power there is in the office of the Secretary-General. Mandela once jokingly referred to Kofi as "the boss of the world." Nothing could be farther from the truth. What Kofi seized and built on was the power to influence, which he exercised to great effect during his first term.

II

CAMELOT

CHAPTER 4

THE BILLION-DOLLAR DEAL

At the beginning of 1997, Kofi's first year as Secretary-General, Iqbal Riza advised him not to go to Washington too soon because in many parts of the world he was seen as Washington's man. But the US had been withholding parts of its UN contribution for decades, which was crippling the world organization financially. Kofi's reply: "I'll visit any capital that owes me a billion dollars." Indeed, that was the size of the US debt to the UN at that time.

The League of Nations had had a terrible time collecting its dues, and so when delegates wrote the UN Charter in San Francisco in 1945, they put some teeth in it on the question of payment. A Member State that falls behind by two year's worth of dues, the Charter says, will lose its vote in the General Assembly. For many members of the US Congress, losing the US vote at the UN was going too far, and by 1997, the US was on the verge of doing just that. The Congressional leadership was looking for a compromise. Bill Clinton was in the White House and UN Ambassador Madeleine Albright was making overtures to conservative Senator Jesse Helms, the Chairman of the powerful Senate Foreign Relations Committee. The stage was set for a change of policy.

Kofi went to Washington from 22-24 January, a little over three weeks into his first term. Clinton and Albright had done everything to make the visit a success. Kofi was greeted like a long lost friend. I thought he probably felt that he had to pinch himself. He was the toast of the town.

After meeting with Clinton, Kofi attended a reception hosted by Vice President Al Gore. He told Gore that Clinton had spoken of a new spirit of commitment to the UN, then commented, "We're in this together. It is a time of renewal for the US and the UN, a time of new promise." Kofi was confident and his impish humor surfaced. He said to the Vice President, "Please tell your people we have no black helicopters; in fact, we have no designs on the US at all. We're no threat; we couldn't even tame Somalia."

Black Helicopters

That was a funny comment, but not everyone in Washington would laugh. Right wing propaganda in the US had it that the UN had a secret army with black helicopters ready to take over the United States. As Spokesperson, I once received a panicked call from a staff member of a Congressman from Arkansas. White UN armored vehicles were seen in the state — was the UN invading? I looked into it and found that, in fact, the US had loaned the vehicles to the UN mission in Haiti for which they were painted white with UN markings; they were being returned to a supply base in Texas to be repainted US Army green and put back in service. But to some in Arkansas, that looked like a UN invasion.

Turning around popular opinion on the UN was going to be a tall order. The least Kofi could do was to assure them he wasn't going to invade.

At President Clinton's urging, Kofi made the rounds on Capitol Hill. It was rough going. Ted Stevens of Alaska, the Senate Appropriations Committee Chairman, told Kofi that repairing the US-UN relationship "was going to be difficult." Boutros Boutros-Ghali had left a bad taste here, he said. The 25-year-veteran of the Appropriations Committee then told Kofi that the Senate didn't think it was in arrears to the UN. Kofi made the understatement of the year when he told Stevens there was some misunderstanding.

The influential Representative from New York, Ben Gilman, was civil but accused Kofi of supporting a global tax. Kofi politely let him finish, and then said casually, "There's no support for a global tax." When the meeting was over, Kofi said to him, "You're from New York, come on by. It's your home." He meant, of course, that not only was New York the Congressman's home, but so was the UN.

Trent Lott, the powerful Senate Majority Leader from Mississippi, was courteous, if a bit condescending. In talking of UN finances, he made reference to his daughter abusing her credit card. Kofi had Joe Connor with him, his top manager and a former head of the giant accounting firm of what was then Price Waterhouse. Lott looked at Connor and asked him how he got his UN job. Connor always speaks with candor. "The Clinton Administration wanted an accountant who was a Democrat," he said. Lott seemed like he might give Kofi a chance. "I'm ready to work with you," he said.

Newt Gingrich, the Speaker of the House, prides himself on his knowledge of world affairs and his in-depth knowledge of Africa. He told Kofi that the US had to reshape its policy on sub-Saharan Africa. He said that Boutros Boutros-Ghali thought the UN was a substitute for world government. "You have a unique ability to change the UN bureaucracy," he said. Kofi and Gingrich spoke to the press afterwards. Gingrich was flattering. "The Secretary-General brings a remarkable depth of experience to the UN and a new attitude toward working with the US," he said. "We are deeply committed to a strong, effective, reformed United Nations. It's in the interest of the US; it's in the interest of freedom. We have a new partner."

Bob Orr was at the National Security Council at the time. Orr, a Californian with Midwestern roots, sees Kofi's success with Washington as linked to his Midwestern education at Macalester College. Orr told me, "My take on why Kofi has been a very effective steward of the US-UN relationship, some difficulties notwithstanding, is because he is essentially a wise African chief imbued with the common sense that comes from his education in the Midwest. He listens well and he's always taken a pragmatic approach to things. No one on the US side ever doubted that he always had the UN's interests in mind. But he understood the US and knew how to deal with it, and that enabled him to manage the relationship."

"Ah like you"

Kofi was off to a good start on this Washington trip, but still had to face arch UN critic Senator Jesse Helms of North Carolina. He walked into the Lion's Den and put out his hand. The aging Helms was gracious, oozing southern charm. He said to Kofi, in a deep drawl, "Ah asked my staff to find somebody who doesn't like you, and they couldn't. Everybody likes you." And then staring at him with a big smile, Helms said, "Ah like you." After the meeting, Helms guided Kofi out to a battery of TV cameras and jostling reporters, his hand reassuringly on Kofi's back.

Despite the encouraging start, Helms was not an easy person to negotiate with. He co-sponsored funding legislation with Democrat Joe Biden of Delaware, now Barack Obama's Vice President, placing tough "benchmarks" that had to be met if US dues were to be paid. He also said that some $500 million in US peacekeeping arrears was "contested" and therefore wouldn't be paid back. Those were arrears that built up after Congress unilaterally reduced the US share of peacekeeping without letting the Administration first negotiate the change at the UN with other Member States. But in the end, the benchmarks were met, much of the arrears were paid, and, most importantly, after a few years' work, all the withholding legislation of the past was wiped off the books. The US and the UN were off to a clean start.

But Kofi, with the help of his friend US Ambassador Richard Holbrooke, had to woo Helms over a period of years to achieve that final result. A high point came in 2000, when Holbrooke, as President of the Security Council for the month of January, invited Helms to visit the UN and address the Security Council. Most Council members were stunned by the prospect. To the surprise of many, Helms accepted.

As Holbrooke recounted the story for me during an interview in April 2007 at his office in a Manhattan investment firm, he frequently pointed to photographs mounted on the wall behind his desk. "There was a non-Security Council meeting, which the world remembers as a Security Council meeting because the only difference between it and an official meeting was that the country nameplates weren't there," he recalled. The Council's meeting with Helms had to be unofficial, yet almost all the trappings of an official meeting were there. "The Ambassadors sat in their normal places; he talked; they talked. It was an amazing show," he laughed. Helms delivered a blistering critique of the United Nations, and the ambassadors all listened politely, such is the discipline of their trade.

An invitation from Helms

Helms then returned the invitation to the Council Members to visit Washington, and they went. Richard pointed behind him. "The high point is this picture up here of Helms and all the members of the Security Council and about five key Senators when, two months later, Helms invited the entire Security Council to the Senate Foreign Relations Committee. That photograph is literally worth a billion dollars — the billion dollars of US arrears to the UN that were released by Helms the following year."

Richard then reflected on Helms's strategy. "Helms was a very shrewd man, much shrewder and more cunning than I originally realized," he said. "His ritualistic abuse of the UN in that speech at the Security Council that day was not, as reported by *The New York Times*, a warning to the UN. It was for his base. By being tough, he was creating an environment whereby he could compromise later on the legislation to restore US funding to the UN that he co-sponsored with Senator Joe Biden, known as the Helms-Biden bill, provided we produced real, tangible savings for the US taxpayer. And we ultimately did."

As the Washington drama played out, Bob Orr was working for Holbrooke, heading his Washington office. He said that he and Holbrooke carried out the most ambitious Congressional consultation on the UN in history. "But the key to our success," he said, "was, first, having senior American officials directly engaged, and second and equally important, having a likeable and a credible interlocutor on the UN side. Members of Congress felt a level of confidence in Kofi Annan; they felt that if a deal were done on reform for arrears, the UN would not simply pocket the money without taking action on reform. And I think it's not too strong to say that that deal in many ways saved the US-UN relationship."

CHAPTER 5

THE BAGHDAD GAMBLE

A UN Secretary-General has only one line in the UN Charter that justifies his involvement in political affairs, apart from just administering the bureaucracy. That's Article 99, which says that he can "bring to the attention of the Security Council any matter which in his opinion may threaten the maintenance of international peace and security."

In *The Parliament of Man*, Yale University's Paul Kennedy writes that this line in the Charter created an office, separate from the Security Council and the General Assembly, that could look at, and maybe even act on, threats to the peace. And it gave the Secretary-General's office "some claim to independent intelligence and assessment, even if it remained the servant to many masters."

Through that small crack, Secretaries-General have marched boldly from the very beginning. The first Secretary-General, Trygve Lie of Norway, sent the Security Council an unwelcome memo giving his view that Beijing and not Taiwan should sit in China's seat at the UN. His successor, Dag Hammarskjold, skillfully defused the Suez crisis of 1956, sending in UN troops, thereby creating a new UN institution — peacekeeping. Hammarskjold in fact intervened so often and so successfully, according to Brian Urquhart, that US tabloid newspapers starting running headlines like, "Leave it to Dag!" and "Let Dag Do It!" By the mid-1980s, when Javier Perez de Cuellar of Peru was Secretary-General, the beginnings of the collapse of the Soviet Union opened up new space for the Secretary-General to be an independent actor. Kofi Annan inherited this space and broadened it.

A Sacred Duty

Kofi's first big opportunity came early, when Saddam Hussein, in November 1997, declared his many palaces off-limits to UN weapons inspectors and also said he would no longer accept US nationals working as UN inspectors on Iraqi soil. The chief UN inspector Richard Butler pulled all his personnel out of Iraq in protest. The Security Council had called for Saddam to honor all Council resolutions and to give the inspectors unfettered access. President Clinton was threatening military action. Russia sought negotiation. Demonstrators came out into the streets demanding a peaceful solution. Kofi felt the pressure of public opinion, but also, he said, he had a "sacred duty" to act.

Afsane Bassir-Pour, who now works for the UN in Brussels, was *Le Monde* bureau chief at the UN at the time. I visited her in her home in Brussels in 2006. She described the mood in the US as extremely combative. "I remember day after day editorials in the press were creating a war-like atmosphere," she said, "and their argument was that Saddam Hussein is making the

UN Security Council look ridiculous by ignoring resolution after resolution." She then added, "although one Ambassador's answer to this was 'if the Security Council were to bomb a country every time its resolutions were ignored, it would be constantly at war'."

In France, she felt, the mood was different. On the one hand, everybody was getting sick and tired of Saddam Hussein creating crisis after crisis without any consequences. On the other, the French, as a nation, were so much against the economic sanctions on Iraq that the idea of adding bombs to sanctions was intolerable. "Very few people were in favor of a military solution," she said, "and in any case no one thought that bombings would bring about the end of the Saddam Hussein regime."

Kofi told me that he had conferred with the Deputy Prime Minister of Iraq, Tariq Aziz, who indicated that the Secretary-General would be welcome in Baghdad and hinted that Saddam would see him to find a solution. Kofi then called Security Council members to his private office to discuss a possible mission to Iraq. That had been done just once before, when Javier Perez de Cuellar called the Five Permanent Members into his office to challenge them to bring an end to the Iran-Iraq War. Kofi would do it many times during his two terms.

One private meeting took place between him and the Ambassadors of these privileged 15 Member States, and then another, and then another until he had a clear understanding of his negotiating parameters. A Secretary-General, if he values his job, will never get too far out in front of the Security Council. The US was nervous about this trip. Kofi told me that Madeleine Albright asked him whether he would still go to Baghdad if the US objected. He answered, "I would." Washington had "red lines" that they didn't want Kofi to cross if he negotiated with Saddam Hussein. Eventually, the "red lines" were spelled out; Kofi had limits, but he was more than just a messenger — he could negotiate.

For Kofi, the issue was clear. He told me in late 2005, when I interviewed him for a course I was going to give at Zhejiang University in China: "Honestly, I felt it would be unconscionable for Saddam Hussein to go to war because of refusal to open up the palaces."

We flew commercial to Paris, where President Chirac had a French Government jet waiting to take us to Baghdad. There was an advantage to France in this generous arrangement. Chirac got to talk to us before we left and, since we had to return his plane to Paris, he was one of the first to be debriefed on our way back.

Hans Corell's Sporran

One of the key players on this trip to Baghdad was Hans Corell, who was Kofi's Legal Counsel. Corell is a Swede whose brief stay in Scotland during his high school years changed his life. On special occasions, he dresses up in full Scottish regalia and plays the bagpipes. He takes the bagpipes very seriously, as he does everything else. He would practice for hours in New York's Central Park — it isn't the kind of instrument you can play in your apartment. Every 25th of January, my wife Kathryn, who was born in Scotland, used to help organize annual Burns Night celebrations at a Second Avenue bar on the occasion of the poet Robert Burns' birthday. She invited Hans, who showed up in kilt and sporran, played the pipes admirably and recited Burns's poetry with a convincing Scottish accent.

After Kofi had had a round of meetings with Tariq Aziz, it was Corell who followed up with his Iraqi counterpart, Riyad al-Qaysi, on the drafting of the agreement. Drafts went back and forth to Kofi and to Saddam Hussein, and then Saddam indicated through Tariq Aziz that he wanted to see Kofi personally.

Kofi went to the palace accompanied by political adviser Lakhdar Brahimi and Corell; his note taker was Rolf Knutsson. After a while, Saddam indicated he wanted to talk to Kofi privately, and the others left. Afsane Bassir-Pour, in her award-winning story called *"Les Havanes de Kofi*

Annan," describes what happened then. She told me that Kofi listened to a litany of complaints by Saddam that lasted nearly two hours. At one point, Saddam offered Kofi a cigar. (Afsane wrote that Kofi offered him a cigar, but Kofi denied this.) One of Kofi's secret vices is that he loves to smoke a cigar from time to time, preferably a Cuban Cohiba. He accepted the cigar that Saddam offered and they each lit up. Afsane reported that Saddam then said, "I only smoke with people I trust." It was then that the deal was cut.

The others were called back into the room. Corell had been confident that the text he had constructed with al-Qaysi would be politically acceptable to all members of the Security Council. But his stomach went to his mouth when Kofi told him that as a result of his discussion with Saddam there were to be a few changes to the text. Kofi saw the panic in Hans' eyes and reassured him that it was just a matter of tone, not substance, and he and al-Qaysi should rework the text slightly.

The two lawyers went to work on the text immediately and it was agreed that if final approval by Kofi and Saddam could be reached by 11:00 p.m. they would announce the agreement to the world then. If not, they would wait till morning. Kofi returned to his guest quarters. When the final draft was presented to him, he reviewed it and okayed it quickly. Saddam was not so quick; his final okay didn't come until 11:20.

Hans was the only member of our delegation still at the Palace when the decision was made to postpone the announcement till morning. He and al-Qaysi personally photocopied the final agreement so that each could have a copy. There were to be no leaks. Hans tucked his into his briefcase and walked out to his car to return to the hotel. It was almost midnight. But the car wasn't there; the driver must have misunderstood and returned with Kofi's motorcade.

"So al-Qaysi lent me his car and driver," Hans said. "But half way to the hotel, the car just stopped. It went stone dead. So the driver kindly walked me back to the hotel through the dark streets of Baghdad. And I was clutching my briefcase with white knuckles. I had the UN's only copy of this agreement. Suppose something happens to me, I thought? But we got back to the hotel safely and I fell asleep exhausted."

Afsane was impressed with how Kofi had organized his mission. "He had prepared his trip extremely well," she said. He had brought along a trouble-shooter, Staffan de Mistura, who was allowed by the Iraqis to visit all eight palaces in question. I organized a press conference for Staffan in Baghdad at which he explained the layout of each building. "He thereby demystified these places," Afsane said; "I thought that was a *coup de genie.*"

"Secondly, he understood what the Iraqis wanted and that was to be treated with respect," she went on, "that their palaces should be inspected with white gloves. And that is just what Kofi Annan gave them — respect. He treated them and their President with dignity and he got the results that he wanted in this way." She said that Lakhdar Brahimi later told her that Saddam Hussein said to Kofi, "I trust you," and that, she added, "was not an easy phrase for him to say to anybody."

"We've Got a Deal"

The guesthouse, a villa on the Euphrates River, was crawling with press. There were hundreds of them there from all over the world. In the time we had been there, I regularly walked out to the front gate to talk to them. Although I had nothing to say of substance and had been warned by Kofi not to say anything, I had learned from experience that it's best to feed the hungry beast.

On the day of the announcement, Kofi turned to me and said, "I think you should tell the press about the agreement." I was stunned. Here was a world-class news story and Kofi's first big political achievement. No politician in his right mind would pass up the chance to bask in the glory of it. But he was passing the job to me.

We set up a kind of podium on the grass in front of the villa. The journalists gathered around in their numbers. Shashi Tharoor, then Kofi's Communications Director, advised me not to take any questions, which I knew was a non-starter. I went before a sea of journalists and a battery of television cameras and said four words that went round the world. "We've got a deal." I took questions for 15 minutes or so, but those four words were the news. The next day they were the Quote of the Day in *The New York Times.*

"We've got a deal."

Kofi signed the agreement with Tariq Aziz, and we climbed back into our French jet and took off for Paris. En route, we stopped to refuel in Amman, Jordan. While waiting in the VIP lounge at the airport, the then-Crown Prince Hassan came out to congratulate Kofi. He walked with his entourage down the long corridor towards Kofi, a big smile on his face. And then he saw me. He veered away from Kofi and put his hands on my shoulders. "Ah!" he said. "This is the best-known face in the Middle East! Here's the man who said, 'We've got a deal'." Kofi was bemused, as if he hadn't thought about the media aspects of what he had just accomplished.

The US and the UK were tense over what Kofi had done. The stakes were high. Madeleine Albright had been on the phone constantly, and the night before the deal was announced she called Kofi at 4 o'clock in the morning, Baghdad time. Elisabeth Lindenmayer, who took the call, refused to put it through. She knew Kofi was exhausted. When Albright did get him the next morning, she was screaming, Elisabeth said. When I asked Kofi about this later, he said in a forgiving tone, "sometimes Madeleine can abuse friendship."

From Amman, we went to Paris, where we had dinner with President Chirac and spent the night. But Hans Corell had mail. "When I got back to my hotel, I found two faxes under my door, one from Washington and one from London," he told me. "And I think in all there were 40 questions. Why is it so? Why is this formulation? Why? Why? Why?" So he worked into the night drafting answers to those questions because he expected they would come up when Kofi briefed the Security Council on the agreement in New York the next day.

Kofi asked Iqbal, who was back at the office, if the General Assembly would approve of his taking the Concorde to get back to New York quickly to brief the Council. He proposed taking four members of his party with him — Hans, Elisabeth, a security guard and me. This would be expensive, but Iqbal got the clearance.

Those of us who had been traveling with Kofi regularly had taken to leaving our hotel room doors open during the day. That way you could hear when there was movement. The next morning we were up early. I heard the telltale noises in the corridor and rushed out to join the Secretary-General's small party to the Concorde. The elevator doors were open for us. The cars in front of the hotel were lined up and waiting, and whoosh, we were off to the airport. But then we realized we were missing somebody — Hans! He had had his door closed while he worked on the answers to those questions for the Brits and the Americans and he didn't hear us go.

From the car, Elisabeth called Hans at the hotel. He rushed downstairs, found a super French taxi driver, and said in perfect French, "Take me to the Concorde; I must join the Secretary-General!" And that driver ran lights and did what he had to do to get to the airport just behind Kofi's motorcade with police escort. As the doors to the Concorde were closing, in walked Hans, flushed and a bit embarrassed.

So Kofi, Hans, Elisabeth and I found ourselves in this oddly cramped, narrow-bodied luxury jet that whisked us off to JFK in under three and a half hours. During the flight, Kofi and Hans drafted his presentation to the Council.

Doing business with Saddam

We went directly from the plane to UN Headquarters, where the Security Council was waiting to be briefed. Hundreds and hundreds of UN staff filled the entry lobby to cheer their Secretary-General.

Kofi lingered in the lobby only a few minutes. He addressed the staff, thanked them for their support and advised them in a good-natured way to get back to work.

He took a few questions from the press. He was asked about his impressions of Saddam Hussein, and he said casually, "he's a man I can do business with." In his mind, I think he was looking to counter the demonizing of Saddam that was taking place in many Western countries, particularly the US. And for him, it was just a statement of fact. He had just negotiated an agreement with Saddam, therefore he had done business with him. But for the right wing, he had made a deal with the devil.

This so infuriated Congressman Gerald Solomon, a Republican from upstate New York, that he said on the floor of the House that Kofi should be "horse whipped," a blatantly racist remark.

Afsane observed, "With this trip, Kofi Annan took his place among *les hommes d'Etat* and became a hero in the eyes of his own staff. Unfortunately, the trip was also the beginning of his problems with the right wing in the US; he became their direct target."

"I think that the Security Council did not know what to do with Iraq," she went on. "Although bombing had been averted for a time, no one thought that that was the end of the cat and mouse game, as indeed it wasn't. This whole affair was also seen through the prism of the mood in the US at the time, which was the beginning of the rise of right wing, anti-UN press that we are still witnessing today. After that, the liberal press absented itself and the right wing press took over."

But while the right wing press was to be a longer-term problem for Kofi, he now had to face the Security Council. He took Hans with him into the chamber. Hans remarked how the tomb-like silence inside the Council contrasted with the cheering of the staff outside. The Ambassadors had only a few questions for him. No doubt the text of the agreement was being studied in capitals and the questions would come later.

When Hans returned to his office, two questioners were already waiting for him. "There were people both from Washington and the UK delegation waiting for me," he said, "and, I must say, they really grilled me on every detail in the agreement."

In the end, the Council blessed the agreement that Kofi had reached with Saddam. "This was a major achievement for Kofi Annan," said Hans, "an extraordinary achievement."

A Waste of Time?

Of course, the UN weapons inspectors went back to work in Iraq aggressively, and Saddam eventually balked on his deal with Kofi and the US went in and bombed in retaliation. I asked Afsane if she thought the Baghdad mission was a waste of time for Kofi. "No, it was not a waste of time," she said. "If he hadn't gone, he would have been blamed by everyone for not having given diplomacy a chance. And in any case, the trip will be remembered as one of Kofi Annan's triumphs."

Sir Jeremy Greenstock was UK Ambassador to the UN from 1998 to 2003. He had this to say about Kofi and Iraq: "Kofi pushed the edges out quite a bit on Iraq, and then drew back because 1998 was quite a searing experience for him. And I think that this, from his point of view, tested the limits of the degree to which the Secretary-General could be independent of the Security Council on a very difficult political issue."

CHAPTER 6

THE MIDDLE EAST

So many stars have to align just right for there to be any progress in the struggle for peace between Israel and its Arab neighbors. The US had been the trusted intermediary in the effort for the previous 30 years or so and had played that role alone. For Israel, Washington was the mediator of choice. But in Clinton's second term, Kofi would be invited to the table.

Kofi gazes out at the Old City of Jerusalem from his hotel room during the crisis of October 2000.

Kieran Prendergast, Kofi's head of Political Affairs, had served in Israel as a member of the British Foreign Service. He had come to know Martin Indyk, who had served two terms as US Ambassador to Israel. Indyk told Kieran in 1997 that in Washington there is a tendency to see people as either black knights or white knights, and that currently Kofi, former UN envoy Terje Roed Larsen of Norway and he, Kieran, were all seen as white knights. With the prospect of a return to power by the Israeli Labor Party, reawakening hope for a settlement of the Arab/Israeli dispute, he urged Kieran to have Kofi become engaged more in the Middle East peace process.

THE ISRAELI WITHDRAWAL FROM LEBANON

Another star came into alignment when the Labor Party won the May 1999 Israeli elections and Ehud Barak replaced Bibi Netanyahu of Likud as Prime Minister. Kofi saw an opportunity to take advantage of the opening offered by Washington, and he called Terje Roed Larsen back into UN service as a UN Middle East envoy. Terje was a veteran of the Oslo peace process on the Middle East and had served Boutros Boutros-Ghali as a Middle East envoy for two and a half years. The Israelis trusted him. Kieran said of him, "Terje gets on very well with both sides and he has ideas and he has enthusiasm and he has drive. All that was very important."

Kofi asked Terje to speak to Ehud Barak and to explore fresh openings in the peace process. I interviewed Terje in New York where he then headed the International Peace Academy. He speaks with animation, emotion running close to the surface. "I remember vividly," he said, "Barak invited me to come to his home. He had a bungalow just outside Tel Aviv and we spent an evening together. At one point I asked him, what do you want to do? And he said, I will tell you. The Middle East peace process is like an ugly dog. But when you look at this dog, it's actually a potentially beautiful dog. It's the tail that is ugly. So in order to beautify it, what do we have to do? We have to chop off the tail. But not the way you Oslo people did it — you sliced it like a salami. We have to chop it off in one go."

What Barak meant, he said, was that all the major issues had to be tackled at once — Syria, Lebanon and the Palestinian question, on a parallel basis, with a view to reaching a comprehensive agreement. When Terje reported this to Kofi, he immediately gave Terje a green light to pursue this goal vigorously.

Barak had made an election promise to pull out of Lebanon. More than 900 soldiers had died there since Israel's 1982 invasion. Even Netanyahu, before losing the election, was taking steps to prepare for withdrawal. "Kofi's political genius is that he sees opportunities," Terje said. "And what he saw was that the UN was the only one who could do this job, because only the UN could give the Israeli withdrawal from Lebanon legitimacy. Kofi convinced everybody, including the Americans, that he had to take the lead role. And the UN got the monopoly for negotiating with the Syrians, the Lebanese and the Israelis, provided we kept all the key players informed."

Terje had follow-up discussions with key Israelis on how it would be done. Initially, they wanted to continue to occupy a few "security areas" in Lebanon, but Terje argued that their withdrawal would not have legitimacy if they did this and would not get Security Council backing. It was all or nothing. He won the argument.

But if the Israelis were going to withdraw, the question arose, withdraw to where? The boundary between the two countries wasn't agreed. So the UN was asked to draw, not a boundary line, but what was called a "Blue Line". The UN's senior cartographer, Miklos Pinther, postponed his retirement to take on this assignment and diligently carried it out, using old colonial maps and modern GPS technology, and placed markers in the ground along the 49 miles of rugged border terrain.

This was an extremely delicate exercise, raising grave security questions for Israel. The Blue Line would pass very close to kibbutzim where there had been massacres of children by Palestinian terrorists 25 years earlier. And there was, as Kieran put it, hanky-panky on both sides, involving false maps, dubious territorial claims and a great deal of political pressure on both Terje and Kofi.

Kieran said, "Barak was being told by his military that the UN was cheating, whereas in fact it was they who were cheating. But in the end, facilitating Israel's withdrawal from Lebanon was,

I think, a major contribution to stability in the Middle East." The Security Council accepted the Blue Line, and they certified that Israel had withdrawn all its troops.

Dan Gillerman, Israel's Ambassador to the UN during the last four years of Kofi's second term, agreed. He told me, "One of Kofi's great achievements was facilitating the implementation of Resolution 425 and Israel's withdrawal from Lebanon in May 2000. There we worked very, very closely and I think he played a major role in giving Israel legitimacy after confirming that we did indeed leave every inch of Lebanon."

SYRIA LEAVES LEBANON

With Israel out of Lebanon, Kofi saw that it would just be a question of time before the issue of the Syrian presence in Lebanon would come up. Terje wanted to push on this issue, but Kofi told him to be patient. He asked Terje to visit Damascus and Beirut regularly, even if there was no particular reason for him to go there. So Terje traveled to the region every three months for several years, just to keep his foot in the water. Then in September 2004, the Security Council formally called for all foreign forces — meaning Syria — to leave Lebanon.

Terje, talking rapidly now, said to me, "There was a lot of skepticism inside the building. People said the Syrians would never leave; Kofi shouldn't get involved; this is suicidal; he will make a fool out of himself; this is self-defeating; it is dangerous. But Kofi very coolly said to me, pursue this carefully. And he was on the line absolutely every day when I was traveling. This was his working style, and he was always very encouraging, despite knowing that many of his political advisers were absolutely dead against everything that we did."

After the shocking assassination of Lebanese Prime Minister Rafik Hariri in May 2005, Kofi sensed the moment was right and sent Terje to Damascus, although Terje thought that nothing would move at that point. But, to Terje's surprise, the Syrians did a 180-degree turn, committing themselves on paper to a very precise timeline on their withdrawal from Lebanon. And they kept to that timeline.

LOCKERBIE

The Libyan leader, Muammar Qaddafi, took an ideological turn at the end of the Cold War and sought better relations with the West. Two Libyans, suspects in the bombing of Pan Am Flight 103, which went down in Lockerbie, Scotland, in December 1988 killing 270 people, were in prison in Libya. A deal was worked out whereby they would be tried in a special Scottish court set up in the Netherlands. Now all Qaddafi had to do was hand them over; he was nervous that the US and the UK might not be acting in good faith. Kofi went there to reassure him.

In early December 1998, we flew to Sirte, on the Libyan coast, and awaited word on what would happen next. I had a contingent of UN press with us, including *CNN's* Richard Roth. Kofi was expecting to see Qaddafi in the early part of the afternoon and the equivalent of the Minister of Foreign Affairs kept assuring us that he anticipated word from the Leader any minute. We sat and we sat until about 7 o'clock when it was confirmed that we would go to a place in the middle of the desert for the meeting.

Night was settling in as our official motorcade sped across the sands, security vehicles first, then Kofi's car, then one carrying Rolf Knutsson of Sweden, a senior political director in Kofi's office, and Awni Al Ani, the top UN Development Programme officer in the country; then Nadia Younes, who was Chief of Protocol; I was at the very back with the journalists, pens and cameras at the ready, excited at the prospect of seeing Qaddafi. But that was not to be. The journalists' cars were the first to pull away and return to the guesthouse. Then some of the other cars did the same.

Rolf described for me what happened next. "One by one your Libyan drivers peeled off, leaving just the Secretary-General, his security, myself and two others on the UN team, including Nadia Younes." The motorcade came to an abrupt stop in the middle of the desert. A second, smaller convoy of Land Rovers was waiting. The sky was clear and the air was cold. Kofi and his security were placed in the lead car and it sped off. Libyan security then had a debate about who else might be allowed to go. Rolf and Mr. Al Ani eventually were put in a second Land Rover, and it left with a screech. Nadia, who as an Egyptian had Arabic as her native tongue, followed the palaver of the security guards and aggressively argued that she had to go too. They weren't impressed. Her hoarse voice got louder and more threatening, spewing guttural sounds into the near-darkness but the Libyan security just instructed her to get into her car. And there she sat, cold and hungry, for the duration of Kofi's meeting with Qaddafi. "The least they could have done was get me a sandwich," she said later.

Rolf described what happened next. "We arrived at this weird site almost an hour's drive into the desert. There were huge, almost circus-sized tents, two of them, and some mobile homes and hundreds of camels making all kinds of funny noises. We were immediately led into one of the tents where Qaddafi was sitting with the Secretary-General. Each of us was introduced to Qaddafi, and then Qaddafi pointed at me and asked the Secretary-General very bluntly, 'Where is he from?' And the Secretary-General said, he's Swedish. Qaddafi responded, "Ah." He probably thought I was an American or a Brit or something. Mr. Al Ani was Iraqi and Qaddafi had met him before, apparently."

"After only a few minutes, Qaddafi said, I think I would like to be alone with the Secretary-General — this was in English. So then we went to the other tent, where we were sitting for at least an hour, or two hours — can't remember. We sat in the freezing cold, next to a fireplace, drinking tea. And then, when the meeting was over, we all left. No concrete agreement had been reached, but the Secretary-General was quite upbeat about the whole thing. He asked me to draft a letter to Qaddafi when we were on the plane on our way to the United Arab Emirates, which I did, thanking him for his hospitality and expressing optimism that a solution was near. And I remember adding something about how nice it had been to visit him in this fascinating, bucolic field environment."

The British had wanted the handover to happen for the tenth anniversary of the bombing, on 21 December 1998. But Qaddafi said he had to consult down to the grass-roots level on all important questions. It wasn't going to happen that quickly. Kofi had put his Legal Counsel, Hans Corell, in charge of the technical arrangements for the transfer of the two suspects to the Netherlands. Hans said it was probably the most dangerous operation he'd ever carried out. He began work on the transfer plan before Kofi's trip to Libya. It was to kick into gear on 24 hours' notice. He had made arrangements with the Italian authorities for an Italian plane, "and the whole thing was so secretive that not even the Secretary-General knew the details," he said.

He visited the Netherlands, where he rehearsed the transfer of the suspects with the Netherlands security and police. It was supposed to be at Rotterdam Airport and everything was in place by early November. He eagerly anticipated the call from Kofi while he was in Libya in December, but the call didn't come. And months passed. Finally, in April 1999, he got the signal to make the transfer.

"I and my security flew into Rome from three different locations, New York, Vienna and The Hague," he told me, "and we landed within 20 minutes of each other. We were whisked off to an Italian military airport, where we did one last rehearsal for the transfer." Hans had asked for an aircraft that had enough petrol to fly from Rome to Tripoli, then return to the Netherlands without refueling. It went off without a hitch.

"The atmosphere on board was dignified," he said. "The two suspects, who were passengers on board — not prisoners — were accompanied by one relative each. The seat assignment was carefully planned. My Chief of Security and I were at the back so we could observe everything. My Libyan counterpart, former Foreign Minister Kamal Hassan Maghur, was also on board." So far so good.

And then, 20 minutes before landing, the plane had to be redirected to another airport. A Netherlands newspaper had found out about the transfer to Rotterdam Airport and was staking it out. In the end, Hans safely delivered the two suspects to the Dutch authorities and called Kofi to report, "mission accomplished."

THE QUARTET

The stars in the Middle East fell out of alignment in September 2000, when the new head of Israel's Likud Party, Ariel Sharon, took a provocative and heavily guarded walk on the Temple Mount in Jerusalem. The Temple Mount is the holiest place in Judaism. But it is also the site of the third most sacred place for Muslims, the Haram e-Sharif (the Noble Sanctuary). Palestinians revolted, in what became known as the al-Quds intifada, or the Jerusalem intifada, and peace efforts were pushed back to square one.

President Clinton called for a summit in October 2000 at Sharm el-Sheikh, on the Red Sea in Egypt, to try to put peace talks back on track. Sharm is a place that has been the site of so many peace conferences it's been dubbed the City of Peace. Israel was eager for these talks, but the Palestinian leader, Yasser Arafat, was slow to say he would go. Kofi flew to Arafat's headquarters in Gaza one evening on an Israeli helicopter, without an appointment, and we waited two hours until Arafat could see him. After a long discussion, Arafat still didn't give a definitive "yes," but said he would call Kofi later that evening with his decision. Kofi went out to the hordes of press waiting outside and told them, "I firmly believe that that decision will be positive and that we will see him at the summit," giving Arafat a public push. Arafat in fact didn't call till 10 o'clock the next day, but he said he would go.

Sharm el-Sheikh laid the groundwork for the formation of the Quartet, a term that Kofi gave it, meaning that the US would work toward Middle East peace with three other partners — the United Nations, the European Union and Russia. Russia was Kofi's idea, and the Americans didn't like it at first. Moscow was not invited to Sharm el-Sheikh.

The Quartet began to take shape the following fall, after George W. Bush had succeeded Clinton as President and Bush's Secretary of State was Colin Powell. It was the beginning of the General Assembly in September 2001, when all the Foreign Ministers are at the UN. Kofi called Powell and European Union foreign secretary, Javier Solana, into his office. He proposed they work together towards peace in the Middle East. Thus the Quartet was born.

Kofi was now a player in an area of diplomacy where the UN had been excluded for decades. Kieran emphasized what a dramatic departure this was. "It established a new model, in which the US was obviously the most important element, the engine without which nothing would really drive, but with a balanced international representation. You had the power and the leverage of the US, which was now the sole superpower. The United Nations conveyed legitimacy, which is very important to the Arabs. The European Union provided the aid funds necessary to underpin a settlement. And the presence of the Russians was reassuring to both sides."

Powell embraced the idea of the Quartet and made it his own. In a telephone interview, I asked him why the US brought Kofi to the table.

"I wanted the UN in there, because it's UN resolutions that structure the outcome," he said, "and also because Kofi is such a gifted leader and conciliator and it would have been useless to try and move forward without having his active involvement, the active involvement of the United Nations."

Kofi, meanwhile, was of the view that the peace effort needed to be operationalized — in other words, that the international community needed to spell out clearly to the parties exactly what each had to do to move towards a final settlement. The broad outlines had been agreed in 1967, following the Six Day War. Israel would withdraw from territory it occupied in exchange for the recognition "of the right of all states in the region to exist within secure and recognized boundaries." It was called "land for peace" for short, but it wasn't as easy as it sounded.

Terje and Kofi discussed the need for a "Road Map" to peace. Eventually the specific elements of a comprehensive peace plan emerged and were embraced by the Quartet in October 2002.

"Kofi was on his top form in Sharm el-Sheikh," said Kieran Prendergast, here advising Kofi at the October 2000 peace conference organized by US President Bill Clinton. To Kofi's right is his Middle East Envoy, Terje Roed-Larsen.

But after years of effort by these four parties, Israel and the Palestinians are still miles apart. The Quartet itself gradually lost steam. There had always been those in Washington who didn't like the idea, and in Bush's second term, when Condoleeza Rice replaced Colin Powell as Secretary of State, those people eventually got the upper hand.

Kieran said to me, "You could see a sort of grinding down of the Quartet. Meetings became much more perfunctory. We managed to hold a couple of Quartet meetings that were followed by encounters with the key Arab moderates — Egypt, Jordan, Saudi Arabia. But Washington was not at all keen on these and they too withered away." Kieran argued with Kofi that the Quartet was in danger of becoming a fig leaf for a complete lack of any action. "In the end, I put it to the Secretary-General that the Quartet had to have some purpose, it had to have some substance," he said; "that it was not just a procedural thing to make us feel nice." After he left the UN in mid-2005, Kieran suggested that the UN should let the Quartet die a natural death. But it didn't.

In January 2006, Hamas, actively at war with Israel, unexpectedly trounced Fatah in the Palestinian Parliamentary elections. The US refused to deal with this legitimately elected party and Kofi, to preserve the Quartet, went along. His speechwriter, Edward Mortimer, in his notes for his 2008 Oxford lecture series, which he generously shared with me, said that he felt that while this was understandable and probably right, "it was surely a mistake for the UN to go along with it to the extent that it did." Edward endorsed the May 2007 end-of-mission report of Alvaro de Soto, the astute Peruvian who replaced Terje Roed Larsen as UN envoy in the Middle East. In that internal report, which was leaked to the *Guardian* newspaper in London, Alvaro argued that the US was wrong to boycott Hamas and that the UN did not need to go along with it.

Alvaro wrote, the US position "effectively transformed the Quartet from a negotiation-promoting foursome guided by a common document [the Road Map for peace] into a body that was all-but imposing sanctions on a freely elected government of a people under occupation as well as setting unattainable preconditions for dialogue." And Alvaro warned that the Secretary-General, by letting himself be used in this way, jeopardized the reputation and usefulness of the UN throughout the Middle East and indeed beyond.

Alvaro's report, Edward concluded, "is, in effect, an obituary of the Quartet and — a much more serious matter — it comes close to being one for the peacemaking role of the UN Secretary-General."

Kieran said to me, "The first key element of the Quartet was the fact that most right-thinking Israelis and the people in charge of Middle East policy in the second Clinton Administration liked Kofi and thought that he was somebody who had a real contribution to make and that the UN could make a serious political contribution to solving Arab-Israeli issues. And Kofi was on his top form in Sharm el-Sheikh; he was very engaged and looked up to and even relied upon by the Security Council on many important occasions. They tended to look to him to quite a remarkable degree for leadership. That's quite extraordinary. But nature has a tendency to revert to the mean, and with the Quartet I think nature has reverted to the mean."

THE ISRAEL-HEZBOLLAH WAR OF 2006

In July of 2006, the Middle East again erupted. Hezbollah fighters based in Lebanon fired Katyusha rockets and mortars at Israeli border positions and villages and kidnapped two Israeli soldiers. Israel retaliated massively with air strikes and artillery fire, including on the airport in Beirut, and imposed an air and naval blockade. The Israeli Defense Forces, which had recently pulled out of Lebanon with Kofi's assistance, now moved back in. The fighting was fierce but inconclusive, and in August Israel and Lebanon agreed to a Security Council formula for a cessation of hostilities, which included an expansion of the UN peacekeeping force in southern Lebanon.

As usual, Kofi was working the phones putting the deal together that the Security Council formalized in a resolution. First he reached agreement on a cessation of hostilities. Then he pressed Israel on a date for lifting the blockade. Israel wanted international monitoring of the sea routes. Kofi called the British, the French and others who had ships in the area. They agreed to patrol the coast. Israel then agreed to lift the blockade. And he received commitments from Western troop contributors for an expansion of the UN peacekeeping force in Lebanon.

Carlos Lopes, who was the senior political director in Kofi's office at the time, recalled how Kofi boldly intervened in the Security Council deliberations on a resolution on a cessation of hostilities. In the Council, France and the US led the negotiations, France representing Lebanon and the US representing Israel's interests. In private consultations, the members of the Council finalized the text of the resolution. The next day there was to be a formal meeting of the Council to adopt it, and it was to be a big show. Condoleezza Rice and the French Foreign Minister, Philippe Douste-Blazy, were to be there. In the private session, Kofi looked at the draft and said there was something missing. There was no specific time for the cessation of hostilities to go into effect and no modalities described for confirming its implementation. In his experience, he said, this was a recipe for disaster. The delegates looked coldly at Kofi, as if to say, why don't you mind your own business? But after their fury died down, they admitted that he was right.

Over the next 24 hours, Carlos said, Kofi worked with the Council and came up with wording that they could all accept. The Council members didn't dare reopen negotiations on the draft, and so they agreed that Kofi could include these additional details in his own statement. And so it was. At the formal session, speaking on behalf of the members of the Council, because he had no authority to do so himself, Kofi read out the time and the terms of the cessation of hostilities. And the fighting stopped and the cessation of hostilities held.

Terje Roed Larsen, still the UN envoy at that time, said to me, "Nobody around him thought it was possible to have a cessation of hostilities, but he just relentlessly pursued it. At one point, this was in August now, we were together and I used the phrase "if we succeed." He said, 'Terje, don't say "if", because if you say "if", you will fail. We will succeed; I don't want to hear any "ifs". You just put it into your mindset: we will succeed.' And, remarkably, he did."

Jean-Marie Guéhenno, the Frenchman who headed the peacekeeping department, analyzed Kofi's achievement on the blockade. "There was an element of gamble in the way he handled it," he said, "because he basically announced that the blockade would be lifted before he had a deal. Using his political nose, he sensed that by saying it was going to happen he could help make it happen. I mean, I was in his meeting with the Israelis and it was clear there was no deal there. So for him it was like carrying on pedaling so that you don't fall over."

"It was extremely difficult to pull off," he told me. "He went, I think, way beyond what his advisers thought he would be able to do. And that is an aspect of the Secretary-General that you shouldn't underestimate. One of his great strengths is his capacity to sense how a problem will unfold and also what the market will bear. He was braver than most of his advisers around the table, certainly myself, and it turned out he was right."

NUCLEAR IRAN

Kofi played a more dominant role in the Security Council than any of his predecessors. Carlos Lopes recalls the tension that existed as Iran went ahead with its nuclear program while the US and others feared that Teheran was fast moving toward the building of a nuclear weapon. Iran denied that, but there was talk in the Security Council of adopting strong sanctions against Iran.

Kofi felt that the atmosphere was overheated. He called the chief Iranian negotiator on the nuclear issue, Ali Larijani, and spoke to him for two hours about Iran's nuclear intentions. He then brought members of the Security Council into his office, in small groups, and briefed them on his conversation, hoping to moderate the climate of the discussions. US Ambassador John Bolton was furious. He and some other members of the Council felt that Kofi had stepped way over the line by entering into negotiations with Iran. Kofi replied, "I am not negotiating, but I think it is in everyone's interest that I use my good offices to try and influence the Council's discussions in a positive way."

The UN Charter, of course, only authorizes the Secretary-General to bring to the attention of the Security Council a matter that he feels is a threat to international peace and security.

And since the first Secretary-General, Trygve Lie, members of the Security Council have reminded the Secretary-General of the limits of his authority in the political area. "It's really very clear in the Charter," Carlos said. "These things are none of his business. But Kofi found new ways to influence the debate, and in the process significantly broadened the authority of the Secretary-General."

THE UN AND ISRAEL

In 1997, Kieran was being encouraged by Yossi Belin, a former Cabinet Secretary and future minister in the Israeli Government, to get Kofi to come to Israel and face head on the deep distrust of the UN that had taken root there. The result was the "Oom-schmoom" speech, which Kofi delivered on a visit to Israel in March 1998. Kofi worked on the speech with Richard Amdur, one of the three gifted speechwriters who later worked under Edward Mortimer.

The acronym for the UN in Hebrew is OOM, and David Ben Gurion once referred to the UN as "Oom-schmoom," giving vent to the feeling of Israelis that the UN was irrelevant and even hostile to them. At a luncheon in Jerusalem attended by a Who's Who of the foreign affairs establishment, including the entire Knesset, Kofi lifted his glass, and in his toast he reminded his audience of Ben Gurion's words. Well, those words had no sooner left his lips than the room erupted in good-natured laughter. But Kofi then added that without "OOM" (the United Nations), there would be "cloom" (nothing). He said it was an "anomaly" that Israel was excluded from regional groups at the UN and that this must be corrected. He invited his hosts to open their minds to a new era in relations between Israel and the United Nations, which he solemnly pledged to work towards. He left that room with a rather higher approval rating than when he entered it.

Kofi and Nane meeting with the families of Israeli soldiers missing in action (March 1998).

On that same visit, Kofi visited the Holocaust Memorial of Yad Vashem, as do all visiting dignitaries. The difference was that he had at his side his wife Nane, whose presence was symbolically important. She is the niece of Raoul Wallenberg, who has a special place in the hearts of Jews everywhere for his efforts to save Hungarian Jews from the Nazis. Wallenberg is thought to have been taken by Soviet troops who liberated Hungary and placed in a Soviet gulag. On exiting Yad Vashem, Kofi speculated about what might have happened during the Second World War if the Universal Declaration of Human Rights, which wasn't adopted until 1948, had already been in force. "Would there have been more Raoul Wallenbergs?" he asked.

We then went through the rain one evening to meet the families of Israeli soldiers missing in action, including that of Ron Arad, the airman who in 1986 parachuted from his plane, which had developed technical problems, over Lebanon and was then captured. We were in a small room; the families were tense, but composed. One member after another spoke, the anguish in their voices rising. Kofi and Nane could only listen in respectful silence. Kofi embraced them at the end, one after the other, and said he would do what he could, which they knew wasn't much. But they seemed comforted.

Kofi worked harder than any other Secretary-General to ensure that Israel enjoyed all the benefits of a Member State of the United Nations. Ambassador Gillerman told me in 2006, "During Kofi Annan's tenure, and especially over the last three or four years, Israel has become a more normal, a more accepted member of the United Nations. Israel feels that the United Nations is becoming more of a normal home, both for Israel and for the Jewish people."

That's a big statement. Gillerman mentioned several things that led to this improvement. First, Kofi fulfilled his pledge to work to get Israel into a regional group. Since most of the work of the UN is organized by five regional groups, including allocating committee chairmanships and other honorary posts, Israel had been left out of much of the action. In May 2000, Israel was accepted into the group known as "Western European and Other States," culminating in Ambassador Gillerman being elected in 2005 as one of the Vice Presidents of the General Assembly. The last time that happened was 54 years earlier when Abba Eban held that post.

Gillerman described as "very moving and emotional" two significant actions taken by the General Assembly in 2005. The first was the adoption on 1 November, for the first time ever, of an Israeli-initiated resolution marking the 27th of January as International Holocaust Remembrance Day. The second, on 24 January, was the first time in its history that the United Nations held a Special Commemorative Session of the Assembly marking the sixtieth anniversary of the liberation of the death camps in Europe. Kofi was supportive of each of these developments, often behind the scenes.

"In all, Kofi Annan has visited Jerusalem five times during his two terms, which is more than any other Secretary-General has," Gillerman added. "He has contributed to Israel's feeling more equal, more accepted. He has shown a very significant degree of sensitivity to the Jewish people. I'm sure that Nane may have had something to do with it, with her background as Raoul Wallenberg's niece."

Kofi and Nane were gracious with Gillerman and his wife, Janice. "We've had a very special relationship, which goes beyond, perhaps, what he had with most ambassadors. He's been a frequent visitor to our home; we've been to their home. We spoke on weekends; we shared our concerns about shoulder pain and other matters."

In my rather long conversation with Gillerman, he made it clear that he wasn't happy with Kofi all the time. Gillerman ticked off a number of gripes that Israel has against him. He said that Kofi's statements on the latest Lebanese war were "unfortunate," and his accusation that Israel had deliberately targeted four UN observers killed in southern Lebanon "irresponsible."

On Iranian President Ahmadinejad's statements denying that the holocaust took place, Gillerman said Kofi's moral voice was not loud enough or clear enough in condemnation. He felt Kofi was too soft on Iran and Syria, two countries that Gillerman described as "engines and generators of terror in our region and throughout the world." And Israel did not appreciate the way Kofi sometimes went beyond Quartet positions, staking out an independent line.

That said, Gillerman concluded with: "I've a lot of respect for Kofi. He's a very decent human being and an immaculate diplomat. And I think he's a very special person."

KOFI AND THE ARABS

His Royal Highness Prince Zeid of Jordan was a UN staff member — he worked in the UN peacekeeping mission in the former Yugoslavia — before he became his country's Ambassador to the UN. I asked him for an Arab assessment of Kofi's role in the region. He appeared cautious as he said, "In general, the Arabs will well appreciate how he was able to maintain the UN's role in the diverse peace efforts that were under way throughout the last ten years, but more specifically the Road Map and his role in the Quartet. It was clear for a long time that the Israelis would like to limit the UN's involvement in the affairs of Palestine/Israel and the Secretary-General was able to insert the UN in those negotiations in a meaningful way. After all, he's enjoyed excellent relations with all the leaders of the region and, generally speaking, he's shown courage and he has shown skill. And in very difficult circumstances was able to at least keep some focus on the Middle East, and I think he has to be commended for that."

"He's found to be quite affable by all the leaders from the Arab side," he went on. "I think they all like him as a man, and as a leader of the UN they respect him. His personality fits very

"His personality fits very much with the Arab style of speaking softly and showing humility, good humor and fortitude, and that he was calm in crises, or at least appeared to be, had a soothing effect."

much with the Arab style of speaking softly and showing humility, good humor and fortitude, and that he was calm in crises, or at least appeared to be, had a soothing effect."

Ahmad Fawzi of Egypt, a former Reuters television correspondent, often traveled with Kofi to the Middle East as a kind of facilitator; he also helped me with the Arab press. In his youth, he was one of Egypt's best-known disc jockeys, specializing in Western music, and to this day he tends to speak as if he's before a microphone, his deep, resonant voice articulating every syllable as if savoring a grape. When I asked him what he thought of Kofi's relations with the Arab world, he sighed. "I don't think he did enough to balance his efforts to improve relations with Israel. He tried, and he's very amiable as a person. He's on good terms with the leaders, on a one-on-one basis. But I don't think the publics really understand the complexities of being Secretary-General of the United Nations. And I don't think that we did enough as his advisers to try to promote a greater understanding of what we do in the Arab world."

"In the first place, if you're not a player, and you don't control events on the ground, you quickly lose the respect of the people," he said. "And there's an impression in the Arab world that the Israelis are walking over the United Nations and everything it represents. Every time we try to do something good, it is cancelled out by something bad that happens on the ground that is beyond our control — an Israeli attack on a Palestinian village, or Hezbollah kidnapping Israeli soldiers or a suicide bomb in a discotheque in Tel Aviv. It's a lose/lose game for the Secretary-General when he has to condemn one act of violence in strong terms, and then condemn the other act of violence in equally strong terms. If he chooses a word that seems to be weaker, immediately the other side will complain."

"So it's a very delicate balancing act and the perception is that he's come out in favor of the West and the Americans and the Israelis over the Palestinians and the Arab public."

Everyone who's anyone comes to Davos. Klaus Schwab, left, organizer of the World Economic Forum, with Yasser Arafat, Shimon Peres, Kofi and Amre Moussa.

Amre Moussa, the Secretary-General of the League of Arab States, considers Kofi a friend. I asked him how well Kofi explained to the Arab world why he felt it was necessary to repair the relationship between the UN and Israel. "It is only normal," he replied, "since the UN is expected to play an important role in addressing the Arab-Israeli conflict. The UN also has to ensure that international law is respected and upheld. It is only coincidental that you ask me this question while the UN is facing unjustified criticism by Israel for its report on the destruction of UN facilities in the Gaza Strip during a recent attack by Israel on Palestinians in Gaza. Yes, the Arab world had deep misgivings, but these were not directed towards Kofi Annan. They were rather directed towards the entire system that failed to respond to the legitimate rights and aspirations of the Palestinians."

And how did the Arabs view Kofi as a person? "Kofi and I know each other for a very long time," he said, "and I can be accused of being biased, but I know that he was highly regarded by the Arab public. He was respected and people felt that he was close to them. He and I worked together to avoid the war in Iraq, to advance a just peace in the Arab-Israeli conflict and to bring peace to the people of Sudan. Public opinion in the Arab world appreciated these efforts. I will always value the role he played as Secretary-General and I will always value our friendship."

CHAPTER 7

SON OF AFRICA

OUR OBAMA

Kofi was the first Black African to be elected Secretary-General. He was our Obama before most of the world heard of Obama. Still a young 58 when he took office, he was good looking, with a smart and artistic wife, Nane; he dressed impeccably, he was an insider who knew the UN to the core, yet an outsider in that he was no diplomat. He spoke candidly and he often thought outside the box. When I asked Catherine Bertini, who was Kofi's top manager in the second term, whether Kofi has Obama qualities, she responded, "I think maybe Obama has Kofi qualities."

And what did the Africans think of him? Carlos Lopes of Guinea-Bissau was a senior political director in Kofi's office during Kofi's last year in office. "There were two types of reaction about Kofi from Africans," he told me. "The people in the streets actually knew and were proud of him. And then there were the globalized Africans, including diplomats, who tended to be more mixed. They were more mixed, I would say, for reasons that derived from Kofi's impeccable modernity. Most of the African political elite argues African-ness on the basis of rural, or traditional, references. They ignore conveniently that Africans are mostly young and urban."

Carlos, as Kofi did before his election, lived on Roosevelt Island and often bumped into him on the tramway. "Kofi always preferred to appeal to the next generation and he projected the future into every speech about the continent," he went on. "He was not a man that dragged in the evidence of the past to excuse poor leadership. He was impatient with Africans that would not seize opportunities. I liked that from the beginning, when I first started meeting the Roosevelt Island older brother in the cable car. This was refreshing, someone who stands on his credibility. We have so much respect for him."

Carlos attended an internal UN meeting in Tarrytown, New York in 2003. "I remember a group of us, Africans, commenting how proud we were of this man being introduced to us as a moral authority," he said. "Many of us agreed that he was, together with Mandela, one of the bright stars compensating for so many unfortunate developments in the continent."

I also asked Ibrahim Gambari how Africans see Kofi. He is the former Nigerian ambassador to the UN, whom Kofi hired as political advisor and who eventually succeeded Kieran Prendergast as head of Political Affairs. Ibrahim is a clever diplomat and a shrewd negotiator with a ready laugh. Commenting on Kofi's giving him the coveted position of Under-Secretary-General for Political Affairs, a former preserve of the UK, he said, "People didn't think he could do it, but he did." Then he laughed. "Took the British out."

Was Kofi popular with Africans on the street, I asked? He surprised me when he responded, "I don't think so. But that's not the important thing," he explained. "I think he's respected; and they're proud of him. But to be popular in Africa is very difficult. First, you have to be there," he said with a laugh, "and even then there's no guarantee." Kofi had left Ghana at the age of 21. His college education was in the American Midwest followed by post-graduate study in Geneva and at MIT in Boston. He had divorced his Nigerian wife, Titi, and married Nane, a Swede. And his entire professional life, except for the two years with the Ghana Tourist Board in the mid-'70s, was spent in the UN. Apparently, that put a distance between him and his fellow Africans. He was a hybrid.

Initially, Kofi wasn't embraced by African leaders, according to Ibrahim. "A number of Africans who didn't know him before had reservations," he said. "They felt, here is somebody who is the first Secretary-General to be elected from within the ranks, who has never been ambassador of his country, who has never been a member of the government of his country."

"So the Africans did not see him as one of theirs, in that sense," he continued. "And at the beginning, he was probably handicapped, you know?"

I had picked up some disappointment among sub-Saharan Africans that Kofi didn't hand out more posts to them; he didn't play the patronage game. When I asked Ibrahim if there had been some grumbling about this, he said, "Yes, and I think it is unfair because, if you look at the record, you will see he appointed more mediators to African conflicts than any other Secretary-General; he pushed the Security Council to authorize more peacekeeping missions in Africa than any other Secretary-General. But more importantly, in my view, he has been courageous in speaking on behalf of the peoples of Africa, in fact over the heads of their governments on a number of issues."

"He never responded to the blandishments of the African Ambassadors that he must appoint this person, or that person out of African solidarity," agreed Kieran Prendergast. "On the contrary, I think he tended to be pretty hard on the African leadership. As a result, although they were proud of him, they really didn't feel that he was one of them, because he didn't play by those rules. He played by a completely nonracial, nondiscriminatory rule of merit."

THE HARARE SPEECH

When Kieran spoke of Kofi being hard on African leaders, he might have been thinking of Kofi's speech to an Organization of African Unity Heads of State gathering in Harare, Zimbabwe, in June 1997, barely six months into his first term. It was tough love. In that speech, Kofi described what he saw as three waves of history in independent Africa: the first was decolonization and the struggle against apartheid; the second was marked by civil wars and economic stagnation. He then saw the beginning of a third wave, which he said would be characterized by "lasting peace, based on democracy, human rights, and sustainable development."

He then said something only an African could get away with. "Africa can no longer tolerate, and accept as *faits accomplis*, coups against elected governments, and the illegal seizure of power by military cliques, who sometimes act for sectional interests, sometimes simply for their own. Armies exist to protect national sovereignty, not to train their guns on their own people." But he didn't stop there. "Where democracy has been usurped," he added, "let us do whatever is in our power to restore it to its rightful owners, the people. Verbal condemnation, though necessary and desirable, is not sufficient. We must also ostracize and isolate the putschists."

That Harare speech is a landmark in Kofi's 10-year tenure. It had gone through many drafts in New York, but Kofi wasn't happy with it. So at the last minute, he called John Ruggie and asked for help. I asked John to tell me the story. "Kofi really wanted to stress the idea that democracy and human rights were not exclusive to the West, and that the West was imposing on Africa," he said. "He understood cultural differences, obviously, but felt that leaders in many developing countries were using cultural relativism as a pretext for bad governance. He wanted to get that idea across. So that's what I picked up on."

"There were two main ideas," he went on. "One was that governments that come into office by military coups and the overthrow of democratically-elected governments should not be recognized by other governments. That idea had been kicking around, and I only dressed it up. The second dealt with human rights. And the inspiration for that came to me without my knowing it from the Shylock speech in *The Merchant of Venice*. I wrote, "Do not African mothers weep when their sons and daughters are killed and maimed by agents of repressive rule?" I didn't realize until a day or two later when I read the speech to my wife that I was paraphrasing Shakespeare."

The speech wasn't finished until Kofi was in Harare. When it was faxed there, the senior political officer on the trip, Ibrahima Fall of Senegal, immediately saw the political dangers in it and proposed rewriting it. But Kofi told him that he was happy with it as it was and would deliver it as drafted. When Kofi finished the speech, Lamin Sise told me there was a stunned silence in the room, and then some polite applause. OAU Secretary-General Salim A. Salim later told Kofi, "We would not have taken that speech from anyone else, but coming from you, we knew it came from the heart." President Mandela, in a meeting shortly after the speech, gave Kofi a vote of confidence, telling him it was "a brave speech, one that Africa needed to hear."

African leaders then followed up on Kofi's recommendation to isolate putschists. When the OAU was transformed into the African Union in 2002, the members adopted a protocol saying that any country that changes government by other than constitutional means will be ejected from the Union. "They kicked out Madagascar, when they had a military government," Ibrahim said, "then Côte d'Ivoire, Mauritania and the Comoros for the same reason. So as a result of this prodding and the wisdom of the African leaders, they have now gone ahead of the UN, because the United Nations does not have a rule that says if you change your government by unconstitutional means, you're out of here."

A VISIT TO RWANDA

Kofi was equally blunt with the post-genocide government in Rwanda. As part of an eight-nation tour to Africa in the spring of 1998, he stopped in Kigali for an official visit. He hadn't been in the country since before the 1994 genocide that ripped it apart. We had been delayed leaving Burundi, the previous stop, and arrived in Kigali after dark. Kofi had been scheduled to address the Rwanda Parliament, which was waiting for him, and he made the decision to go there directly from the plane.

His address to the parliament on the 7th of May contained a candid admission of the UN's colossal failure to stop the genocide: "We must and we do acknowledge that the world failed Rwanda at that time of evil. The international community and the United Nations could not muster the political will to confront it. The world must deeply repent this failure."

"Rwanda's tragedy was the world's tragedy," he said. "All of us who cared about Rwanda, all of us who witnessed its suffering, fervently wish that we could have prevented the genocide. Looking back now, we see the signs that then were not recognized. Now we know that what we did was not nearly enough — not enough to save Rwanda from itself, not enough to honor the ideals for which the United Nations exists. We will not deny that, in their greatest hour of need, the world failed the people of Rwanda."

But the speech had a heart-stopping line in it, one that Kofi himself had insisted on including. Referring to the genocide, he said, "The horror came from within." Unless Rwandans looked inside their souls to ask why the massacre of 800,000 persons had taken place, he reasoned, they could not deal with the question of how to prevent it from happening again.

Here is the full passage: "Four years ago, Rwanda was swept by a paroxysm of horror from which there is only the longest and the most difficult of escapes. It was a horror that came from within, that consumed and devastated entire communities and families. It was a horror that left you as survivors of a trauma, which to the world beyond your borders was unimaginable, even though we all now know how it happened. We will not pretend to know how you must overcome the unimaginable. We can only offer, in humility, the hope and the prayer that you will overcome — and the pledge that we stand prepared to help you recover."

Nader Mousavizadeh, a Dane who was a speechwriter for, but also a de facto political adviser to Kofi, drafted that speech. He told me, "Those words are mine. We struggled mightily to get the balance right in that speech — and arguably Kofi went further than Clinton or Albright in atoning for his sins. That said, [Chief of Staff Iqbal] Riza and I felt that we had to draw a line somewhere under the UN's responsibility — and I felt it was necessary for Rwanda's own process of reconciliation to acknowledge that this wasn't done to them by some alien force, or UN Blue Helmets for that matter, but by themselves."

"The horror came from within." Kofi laying a wreath on a table of skulls in Rwanda in 1998.

Elisabeth Lindenmayer was traveling with Kofi at the time, as was Lamin Sise. They were both uncomfortable with the draft text, as they were with the Harare speech, and agreed it wouldn't do. Elisabeth started rewriting, but Kofi again rejected the rewrite and delivered the speech as drafted by Nader. This was not what the Government wanted to hear. They wanted to point a finger outside — at the German and Belgian colonizers, at the UN itself.

After the speech, we went to an open-air reception hosted by President Bizimungu, except that the President and his Ministers didn't show up. When Kofi realized what was happening, he turned on his heels and left. Back in our hotel — the famous Mille Collines Hotel where in 1994 a scant contingent of UN peacekeepers had tried to protect moderate Hutu and Tutsi leaders targeted by the *génocidaires* we learned that Bizimungu's spokesperson was saying on the radio that the President had boycotted the reception because Kofi had made a speech "insulting to the Rwandan people."

Kofi's chief of Security, Michael McCann, wanted to turn around and leave. The government broadcasts amounted to incitement and he felt it wasn't safe to continue the program. Kofi, though, consulted a few of the local ambassadors on their assessment of the risk and then overruled his security. The next day he visited two massacre sites, one of which was 50 kilometers outside the capital. Witnesses described how they had called for UN help and it never came. Bones and skulls were stacked neatly on tables. Kofi asked to be left alone with Nane as they stood in silence before the gruesome evidence of the unspeakable.

The New Yorker Article

Just a few days before that visit to Rwanda, Philip Gourevitch highlighted the Dallaire cable in an article for *The New Yorker* magazine, building on a book he had just written on the Rwandan genocide, *'We wish to inform you that tomorrow we will be killed with our families.'* We issued a press statement that read, in part, "…the crucial issue today is not how to apportion blame with the benefit of hindsight. Rather, we should be asking how we can ensure that such a tragedy can never happen again…"

As Kofi's press spokesperson, I was worried. His popularity was high following his visit to Baghdad a few months before, and here was a respected journalist accusing him, in effect, of moral cowardice or at best moral blindness. The Gourevitch charge was, I felt, unfair. Did he not remember in 1994 the absolute opposition of key governments, notably the United States, to the idea of intervention in Africa? Had he not sensed then the Security Council's paralysis as the tragedy unfolded? Did he not appreciate Boutros-Ghali boldly calling what was happening in Rwanda genocide, when Boutros-Ghali knew that the Americans didn't want him to use that word for fear of highlighting an obligation to act under the UN's genocide convention, to which the US was a party? Did he not acknowledge, as General Dallaire would later in his book, Kofi's desperate efforts to recruit additional troops when no nation with capacity would offer any? Yet Gourevitch's core question hung in the air: Why did we not sound a loud warning call when we received Dallaire's cable?

When we returned to New York, I began to review the documentation that I knew the journalists would be looking at too. Boutros-Ghali had the information department publish a series of books on UN peacekeeping missions. The Blue Books, as they were called, were a kind of vanity press exercise. There was a Blue Book on Rwanda, and in it Boutros-Ghali, technically the author, writes that his representative, Chinmaya Gharekhan, had informed the Security Council of the Dallaire cable on 11 January 1994.

The texts for the Blue Books were drafted by the substantive departments, and the one for Rwanda had been handled by Kofi's peacekeeping department. I asked around the department if Chinmaya had briefed the Council. Those who had worked on the draft said that as far as they knew, he did not and that they had not written that; someone on the 38th floor must have added it.

In 2006, after he retired from the UN, Chinmaya published a book on his experiences in the Security Council, called *The Horseshoe Table*. He wrote that some Security Council ambassadors sought clarification of this line in the Blue Book, because the media in their countries had seized on it. "This infuriated some members of the Security Council," he said, "whose alibi for inaction on Rwanda was destroyed by a single sentence." He added that he had no personal recollection of briefing the Council on the cable, and had no notes from this period. In *The Horseshoe Table*, he writes: "This is where the practice of not keeping official records of informal consultations showed its worth. There was nothing to prevent the Secretary-General from claiming that the Council had been briefed, since it said so in the Blue Book."

That's true; there are no official records of the Council's closed consultations, which are confidential meetings. But there are and always have been unofficial records kept by us, the Secretariat. When Council members sit behind closed doors for a confidential discussion, a note taker from the Secretariat sits quietly in the corner, jotting down what each Ambassador says, and then does a summary note that gets pretty widely circulated in the Secretariat. We used to get them in the Spokesperson's Office, for example.

And they're kept on file.

So when I returned to New York, one of the first things I did was to see if I could find any record of Chinmaya having briefed the Security Council on the Dallaire cable. I looked at the unofficial records for the 11th of January, and then for two weeks after the 11th of January. I saw no mention of the Dallaire cable. The line in the Blue Book about briefing the Council on the cable seems to have been added somewhere in Boutros-Ghali's office.

Kofi's critics concede that to speak up might not have made a difference, but insist he was wrong to not even try. But there were two things at work here. First, Boutros-Ghali was Secretary-General; it was first and foremost his responsibility to speak up. His office was fully informed. And second, the peacekeeping department had briefed the key governments — Belgium, France and the US — on what we knew and we felt we had done what was necessary. They were the big boys; if anyone could make a difference it would be they.

The Carlsson Report

Kofi knew that, as Under-Secretary-General for peacekeeping when the genocide occurred, he had to accept some of the blame too, and even more important, as Secretary-General, to take steps to see that it didn't happen again. He commissioned the former Prime Minister of Sweden, Ingvar Carlsson, to analyze the UN's failures in Rwanda.

Carlsson was unsparing in his 1999 report. I talked to him about it by telephone. He said that the overriding failure was the lack of political will within the Security Council and a lack of resources given to the peacekeeping mission in Rwanda. "But we were also critical of the Secretariat for not following up strongly enough on the information provided by the informant," he said. "Boutros Boutros-Ghali could easily have taken more responsibility."

Regarding the information in the Dallaire cable, he said that if it were true, it was a clear signal that a genocide was being planned. "The cable mentioned that the names and addresses of all the Tutsi in Kigali had been gathered," he said. "That was a dangerous warning signal, even more important than the information about hidden weapons. Boutros-Ghali should have paid more attention to that. I still think that today."

In 2006, I interviewed Boutros Boutros-Ghali and asked him if he felt the Secretariat shared the blame for Rwanda, and he surprised me by his answer. "Certainly, we share responsibility," he said. "We did not put enough pressure on Member States. We didn't shout enough... Maybe if I had been more hysterical I could have gotten them to change their attitude, but I didn't push enough. I'm saying this with hindsight." Everything is clearer in hindsight.

The Carlsson Report hit the Secretariat pretty hard, a bit too hard in the eyes of some. I know I was one of those. But Kofi accepted its findings without exception and vowed to do better.

Chris Coleman was a young Texan whom Kofi spotted at the International Peace Academy and asked him to join the peacekeeping department. Chris, who wore the UN uniform, dark suit and tie, except with cowboy boots, served Kofi as a one-person think tank. He told me that he felt that for political reasons Kofi took more responsibility for Rwanda than he actually was answerable for, "because if you went back and reconstructed those events and you say, what could the Secretariat have done differently that would have made a difference? I don't see anything he could have done differently that would have made a difference. The realities were that the US had made very clear that it wasn't going to authorize a larger mission in Rwanda. It wasn't going to cross the so-called Mogadishu Line. The main troop contributors weren't about to get sucked into something like that."

To Chris, it was obvious that there wasn't going to be a Council mandate and there weren't going to be troops. "Somehow Kofi, in a very stand-up way, accepted his share of responsibility. But what the hell was his responsibility, really? Yes, this is a terrible thing to say, but if you look at it from that perspective, the main lesson for the Secretariat would have been, always cover your ass. Make sure you tell the Security Council things that you bloody well know they already know; they know better than you do; they know before you do, but tell them anyway. So, yes, Rwanda was awful; it was genocide; it was a tragedy; it was a major screw up of the United Nations, but of the Secretariat or the Secretary-General? I don't see it."

Despite what Chris said, the United Nations is a kind of church, and its head a kind of pope and everyone who works in it is supposed to be a kind of angel. At least that's how some people see it. The fact that we were overworked, that we told the Americans, French and Belgians who did nothing, that things were quiet for three months after the cable was received, that even after the killing started the Security Council failed to act, is no excuse why Boutros Boutros-Ghali didn't use his bully pulpit to speak up. So in the end, we are all guilty.

Dallaire concluded his book with a quote from his famous cable: *"Peux ce que veux. Allons-y."* ("Where there's a will, there's a way. Let's go.") For us in the Secretariat, our reading of the political reality around us was that there was no way the Security Council would intervene in Rwanda and therefore we had no will to act ourselves. That was, perhaps, a moral shortcoming.

Maurice Baril told me, "Of course, we were worried very much indeed that genocide could happen and that Dallaire was right. After all, it had happened in Burundi in 1993, at the same daily killing rate, and nobody did anything then either. As a matter of fact, no one was interested or worried, except for us in peacekeeping. Still, the lack of interest did not justify our not screaming out about Rwanda, even though we knew the Council would do nothing and would not give us the resources to do something ourselves."

When he testified before the Carlsson Commission, he was asked what he would do differently, if he had the chance. He told them, "I would nail a copy of Dallaire's cable to every lamp post within one kilometer of the United Nations."

ANGOLAN DREAM

Kofi's optimism came into play in March 1997, when he dove into the deep end with an early visit to Angola, an oil-rich country crippled by years of civil war. A tentative peace agreement had been reached between the Government and the rebels, and Kofi wanted to try and shore it up. After meeting with government officials in the capital, Luanda, we flew north to Huambo to see the rebel leader, Jonas Savimbi. The weather was awful, with rain pouring down; there was zero visibility. We circled over Huambo; there were no sophisticated landing facilities at the airport there; in fact, there wasn't even a paved runway. But the pilot wouldn't give up.

One of the veteran journalists with us looked nervously out the window and said, "The UN lost one Secretary-General in an air crash over Africa; let's not lose a second one." Eventually, we were forced to go back to Luanda. The next day the weather was clear and beautiful and we returned to Huambo, landing on a grass strip. Savimbi's enthusiastic supporters lined the route from the airport for kilometers, cheering and waving flags.

Kofi urged Savimbi to go to Luanda with him and join the unity government that had been agreed to in principle, but that Savimbi didn't have enough confidence in to leave his stronghold. He wouldn't go back, but he compromised. He said members of Parliament from his party, UNITA, could travel to the capital to listen to Kofi address that body the next day. So the rebel parliamentarians piled into our plane and the next day took their seats in the chamber. Kofi made an impassioned appeal to all of them to work together. He also argued from a practical point of view: with peace in South Africa, Namibia and Mozambique, should you pacify Angola, the whole region could benefit economically. Think of the tourist package you could put together, he said!

After Kofi left Angola, the rebel parliamentarians slipped off into the bush and back to the safety of Huambo. The war continued for five more years until Savimbi was killed in a firefight in 2002.

I asked Kofi if he had been too optimistic in 1997. "Probably. Probably," he said, in reflection. "It was a dream, a dream which can still be realized, from Congo to Angola. And I felt they had been fighting for so long, and the expectation was that the developments in South Africa that led to a peaceful transition should be an inspiration for them. They saw Namibia settled; they saw South Africa next. And with a bit of common sense, and the interests of their people and their country at heart, these were two wonderful examples for them to follow, and begin to develop a country that has so many resources and could be stable and prosperous. I was pushing them, because I really thought it was in the interests of their people and their country and that they should wake up to the possibilities around them."

Of course what he said was common sense. But there's no logic in war.

Nane was on that trip. It was a time when she was exploring what role she might play as wife of the Secretary-General. She listened to the pleas of Angolan war orphans being looked after by UN aid agencies and felt a tinge of despair at her helplessness. "In Angola, I went to a UN school for orphans of the war," she said, "and I first thought to myself, it's a good thing that they are in school. But then they sang this song to us. 'We are children who need a father to take care of us, what can you do about that?' What could I tell them? That their education is important? That they should take this opportunity and grow like trees from it? Yes. But their question hung in the air and I realized that I had to talk about them. I did not have any official role in the UN; I was not a UN person. But I could be an eyewitness to the work the UN is doing out in the field."

As part of that trip to Angola, Kofi and Nane also visited South Africa. Nane wrote two books for children and took up the cause of the advancement of women. "On my first visit to South Africa, I met with women's groups," she told me in 2006. "They had energy and enthusiasm and had come together to make a difference in their lives and the lives of their children. And I had the same experience over and over again in other parts of the world. We could sit down together and immediately relate to each other. And they gave me something; they gave me the energy I needed to speak to others about their work. The micro-finance groups, for example. They are so life affirming. And then there were the painful meetings where we met survivors of violence against women and girls. Whatever you do, you can't fix what is broken, but you can talk about it. And talking about it is the first step towards dealing with it."

Kieran Prendergast thought that Kofi had a keen sense of his historic role. "He had a strong feeling of the suffering caused by conflict," he told me in 2007. "He didn't like the argument that everything was too difficult. He liked to try to push the outer edges of the envelope and to encourage other people to show more initiative to resolve conflict, and where he thought there was a role for himself, to take a personal initiative to try and resolve things."

NIGERIA

Kofi gambled his personal prestige to help Nigeria manage a transition to civilian rule following the death of military strongman General Sani Abacha. You might well ask what a UN Secretary-General was doing meddling in the internal politics of a member state? I asked Ibrahim Gambari if he was surprised. "Well, I wasn't surprised because I was one of those who requested him to get involved. I was then the Ambassador of Nigeria to the United Nations. We just had a very traumatic experience of General Sani Abacha's rule and his sudden death. Meanwhile, of course, Chief Abiola, who presumably won the elections in 1993 but then ended up in jail, was still in detention and we felt Kofi Annan had a role to play as the Secretary-General of the United Nations but, more importantly, as a senior African leader, to try to help Nigerian leaders deal with this impasse."

So there we were in Abuja and the new Nigerian ruler, General Abubakar, was talking to Kofi about his plan to release Chief Abiola and other political prisoners and hold democratic elections. Kofi was to meet with Abiola and, he hoped, to escort him to freedom. Lamin Sise was with us on that trip, and after dinner he was visited by a member of the State Security, who informed him that there would be a meeting with Abiola that night. Lamin told Kofi, who decided to take no one else with him besides Lamin. The Security guys returned at 9:30 and whisked Kofi and Lamin through obscure corridors out to the back of the hotel, where they were driven away at high speed in a convoy of three black Peugeots to Aso Rock, the Presidential complex in Abuja. Abiola was in good spirits, Lamin told me. Kofi assured him that those in power wanted to return the country to civilian rule.

Kofi's friend, the journalist William Shawcross, was on the trip with us. He was working on his book *Deliver Us From Evil*, and Kofi briefed him fully. In it, William described a man totally cut off from the outside world. Abiola did not know who Kofi was. When Kofi told him, his reply was, "What happened to the Egyptian?", referring, of course, to Boutros Boutros-Ghali.

Shawcross wrote that Kofi asked Abiola what he would do if released. Would he claim the Presidency? Abiola replied no, he would not. Although he wouldn't put that in writing, he would give Abubakar that assurance on his word of honor. "I want to go the Mecca to give thanks for being alive," he said.

Abiola was not released to Kofi, however. Kofi and Lamin returned to the hotel. Ten days later, after we had left Nigeria, we were informed that Abiola had died in detention. But despite that, Nigeria managed a successful transition to civilian rule.

Ibrahim said, "I'm convinced that Kofi's intervention probably contributed to peace in Nigeria, because if it was not handled properly it could have been a disaster. And of course Nigeria, which is itself a peacemaker in the region — imagine if all mayhem had broken loose! So I think it was courageous on his part. I think some of the big powers didn't think it was wise for him to do this, but I'm glad he did, speaking even as a Nigerian."

The Bakassi Peninsula

Nigeria and Cameroon had a border dispute over the Bakassi Peninsula, which juts into the Gulf of Guinea and was thought to be potentially oil-rich. The two countries had had armed clashes over the territory before Cameroon submitted the dispute to the International Court of Justice (ICJ) in The Hague in 1994. The Court was about to issue its ruling and Kofi wasn't at all sure that the two countries could peacefully handle the verdict, whatever it would be. He decided to engage the parties in dialogue in 2002.

He called the two leaders together on several occasions, usually in Geneva. He met privately and separately, first with President Paul Biya of Cameroon and then President Olusegun Obasanjo of Nigeria. He then called together the full delegations, and all of this behind closed doors. But you could just as easily have left the doors open — there was almost no outside interest from the Western press.

And these two leaders, one Anglophone and one Francophone, initially highly distrustful of each other and having had hardly any personal contact until then, gradually warmed to each other. They agreed to accept the ICJ decision regarding their common border and, once it was issued, to then implement it responsibly under Kofi's guidance. I remember at one point, Obasanjo, smiling broadly, said to Biya something like, "And we must stay in touch. I will come see you; I will fly into Cameroon without even asking permission. And you do the same in Nigeria."

Ibrahim described to me what happened next. "And then after the judgment of the ICJ, he [Kofi] offered to assist them in implementing the decision," he said. "And he set up a Mixed Commission with his representative as the chair and they've been getting on with the process of delimiting not just the land border, but the maritime borders, including Bakassi, and supervising the withdrawal of Nigerian troops from Bakassi, which has now been completed."

I don't think it's an exaggeration to say that Kofi may well have averted a war. It was a model he used with less success in the maritime dispute between Gabon and Equatorial Guinea and the ongoing tensions between Ethiopia and Eritrea, mainly because his time ran out.

Andrew Gilmour, a deputy political director in Kofi's office, had spent three years working for the UN in West Africa. I talked to him in his UN office in New York. "Very few people will say to you, 'what a great Secretary-General, he solved this dispute between Cameroon and Nigeria'," he said. "And the history books won't focus on it, so he won't get a great deal of credit for what he did there. But he really ought to."

"One of the great things about him is that he concentrated on small disputes as well as the world's big ones," he continued, "and he expended an immense amount of effort trying to solve some of these issues that don't make it to the front pages, but which nevertheless create a lot of suffering and damage. Given how many issues were clamoring for his attention, it must have been tempting to focus on those where the media, or lobby groups, or the key Member States were most active and vocal. The fact that he often went beyond those issues and instead turned his attention to the world's 'forgotten problems' is not something that we should ignore."

PEACEKEEPING TURNAROUND IN AFRICA

Following the Mogadishu massacre of US troops in 1994, UN peacekeeping had almost ground to a halt. Things started to turn around in 2000, when Kofi persuaded the UK to seek Security Council backing for an intervention in their former colony, Sierra Leone. Revolutionary United Front (RUF) rebels controlled the eastern part of the country and were hacking off the limbs of men, women and children. The Council approved a large peacekeeping force, and then increased it in size until the rebellion was crushed and the RUF disarmed.

What's good for the Brits is good for the Americans, and when the former US colony of Liberia descended into a bloody civil war, Kofi again pressed the Security Council to intervene. They did. The President, Charles Taylor, who is accused of having supported the RUF in neighboring Sierra Leone in exchange for blood diamonds, eventually went into exile in Nigeria and is currently on trial for war crimes at the Special Court for Sierra Leone at the International Criminal Court headquarters in The Hague.

Peacekeeping in Africa was beginning to get a good name. In Côte d'Ivoire, which had been an economic engine in West Africa, an armed rebellion split the country in two in 2002, pitting a largely Christian south against a predominantly Muslim north. The President, Laurent Gbagbo, played not only the religion card but the ethnic one as well, and Kofi feared another Rwanda.

The US did not favor a UN peacekeeping role in the country, but Kofi pressed and won. The peacekeepers helped restore an uneasy peace that continues to this day.

African peacekeeping now looked like a train that couldn't be stopped. A civil war in the Democratic Republic of the Congo that started in 1998 came to be known as "Africa's World War" since it involved so many countries. Angola, Namibia and Zimbabwe backed the Government, and Rwanda and Uganda backed the rebels. The Congo is the size of the United States east of the Mississippi, Africa's second largest country after Sudan, and any peacekeeping mission had to be big and expensive. Kofi pressed for it and got it. It started with 90 military observers at the end of the "World War" in 1999. But the country was far from stable, and, under pressure from Kofi, the Security Council approved a major deployment in 2003 that continues today at a strength of some 20,000 troops and civilians.

THE AFRICAN IN HIM

I asked Ibrahim whether he thought Kofi took more of an African than a European/American approach to solving problems. He didn't hesitate. "Oh, absolutely," he said. "I can recognize us, as Africans, in him. He's brought the entirety of his experience and exposure to this job, but he never lost his African-ness. He doesn't wear it on his sleeve, but he doesn't need to."

And Africans recognize that, I asked? "I think he's proved that he is basically an African who likes consensus, who prefers talking to fighting over issues, has an inner strength that is not always visible," he replied, "and I think in the end they've accepted him proudly as one of theirs."

Ibrahim then went on to reflect on Kofi's personality. It was 2006. "He's easy to talk to," he said. "He's very humble, but it's a dignified humility. He's not someone you can walk over or disrespect. He never puts himself, or allows others to put him, in a position of disrespect. But he's not loud; he doesn't shout. And very few times have I seen him actually angry in a meeting. He manages to control himself, but at the same time, behind that, is a determination of steel, and also stubbornness, to defend what he believes in and to ensure that it actually happens — maybe not now, but he will come back to it."

There was no shortage of crises in Africa, and in his ten years Kofi saw what at times seemed like a continent imploding. But at his urging, the Security Council created one UN peacekeeping mission after the other, and these, over time, eventually put out the flames so that by the time he left office a fragile stability would prevail from Cairo to the Cape.

"He devoted a great deal of his time and energy to helping resolve conflicts in Africa," said fellow Ghanaian Patrick Hayford, "and helping to move the African agenda forward in the UN."

THE ELEPHANT

Even at the UN, a little fun creeps into your life from time to time. For Kofi, an early example was the gift of a 3,000 kilogram (6,600 pound) bronze elephant, which he unveiled in November 1998. This is a true story.

Alvaro de Soto is a distinguished Peruvian diplomat who has handled sensitive assignments for three Secretaries-General. For Kofi, he handled Myanmar, then Cyprus, then the Middle East. It was only fitting then that he take over from Brian Urquhart, the father of peacekeeping, as Chairman of the Arts Committee, when Sir Brian retired in 1986. Were it not for the Arts Committee, the UN would be awash with gifts of paintings, sculptures and other whatnot from Member Governments looking to place their name on a brass plaque on some wall within the UN grounds. But any government with such a wish must first apply to the Arts Committee, and it takes a skilled diplomat indeed to say no. Some think the Committee didn't say "no" enough.

The UN's North Lawn is a case in point. It is a vast and agreeably sunny space that is rare in Manhattan. If it didn't belong to the UN, a dozen apartment buildings would have been put up there. But every year, it seems, another hideous sculpture appears in that wondrous space, so that now it's beginning to look rather like a junkyard. There's the humungous St. George and the Dragon (gift of Russia) at the 47th Street Gate celebrating nuclear disarmament, and an oversized metal boat (gift of Ireland) commemorating Irish emigration. And then, in the northwest corner, amidst a cluster of trees and surrounded by a ring of waist-high bushes, is a life-sized bronze elephant (joint gift of Kenya, Nepal and Namibia) in salute of, I guess, elephants.

But this elephant has a rather prominent appendage. I asked de Soto to explain. "This sculptor had gone into the bush, in Kenya, and put an elephant to sleep with a dart. And while the elephant was asleep, a plaster cast had been made of it. And then the cast was removed and the elephant just sort of woke up and walked away. The cast was brought to New York and eventually the money was found to cast the elephant in bronze at a foundry somewhere in Brooklyn or Queens, I think. And it started to arrive in parts, to be assembled. Of course, when it arrived and we looked at one of the hind quarters, it became apparent and, uh, it became clear, uh, that it was anatomically true to life."

The elephant's penis, it seems, was semi-erect. So Alvaro did the obvious thing: he called the person responsible for mammals at the Bronx Zoo and asked for a consultation. The expert explained that the elephant's sex organ, when not erect, is fully retracted and not visible. He looked at the sculpture and said categorically that this elephant was not in full erection at the time of the taking of the cast, because the penis would be several feet long. He surmised that the dart that put the elephant to sleep may have contained some kind of muscle relaxant and as a result you had a partially erect penis.

Iqbal Riza, Kofi's Chief of Staff, was horrified at the thought of school children visiting the UN garden and seeing an elephant in such a state. He proposed a surgical operation to remove the offending penis. But this outraged the artist, who threatened to go public in denunciation. Iqbal backed off and quickly ordered the UN gardeners to plant shrubs a couple of feet high all around the elephant. It was done.

Kofi himself came to the unveiling, with remarks prepared by speechwriter Annika Savill. The press had picked up bits and pieces of the controversy and came along to the event. One journalist asked Kofi if it were true that he had given consideration to mutilating the elephant cast. Kofi, who was fully aware of all that had happened, with a little smirk, said, "I would not tamper with what God hath wrought."

Kofi then delivered his remarks. But it turns out that Annika had worked some *doubles entendres* into what she wrote, totally innocently, she insists. "But as we see this magnificent animal stand before us today, it was worth the wait," Kofi read. "The sheer size of this creature humbles us. And so it should. For it shows us that some things are bigger than we are."

Anne Penketh, an eventual successor to Annika as Diplomatic Editor at *The Independent*, London, was based at the UN at the time for *Agence France Presse*. She was a serious reporter, but few of her stories got recognized as much as the short three-paragraph item she filed for *AFP* under the draft headline, "UN Gets a New Member."

CHAPTER 8

INTERVENTION — KOSOVO AND EAST TIMOR

THE ANNAN DOCTRINE

When Kofi, as head of peacekeeping, was handing over Bosnia to NATO in 1995, he made a few modest remarks, which indicated to me that he was grappling with his own personal responsibility. "No modern man or woman can claim ignorance of what those who live here endured," he said then. "In looking back, we should recall how we responded to the escalating horrors of the last four years. We must each ask ourselves a series of questions: What did I do? Could I have done more? And could I have made a difference? Did I let my prejudice, my indifference, or my fear overwhelm my reasoning? And above all, how would I react next time?"

The Ditchley Speech

Those same questions were still turning over in his mind three and a half years later when as Secretary-General he was invited to give a speech to Britain's foreign policy elite at Ditchley Park, near Oxford, in June 1998. At this point, in the second year of his first term, he was at a high in his approval ratings following the stunning outcome of his trip to Baghdad a few months before. He accepted the invitation without at first knowing what he would talk about.

He had just hired Edward Mortimer of *The Financial Times* as his chief speechwriter, but Edward hadn't yet joined the staff. Kofi was on an official visit to the UK and gave Edward a call from London. "I got a message he wanted to speak about intervention," Edward told me. Edward had in fact written a paper for the International Peace Academy a couple of years before on "When should the United Nations intervene militarily in the affairs of one of its Member States?" He had no idea whether Kofi knew about the paper, but Kofi doesn't miss much. Edward met with him at the hotel to find out what he had in mind. Kofi said to him, "Well, I want to get across the idea that it's a matter of personal responsibility; it's not just great powers that can intervene; we can all intervene in some way or other."

Kofi advised Edward to look at his comments during the NATO handover in Sarajevo in 1995. Edward did so and saw the theme: instead of putting the blame on somebody else, each of us should ask ourselves, what could I have done that might have helped to avert this tragedy? "So that, I think, was very much a personal thing," Edward said. "Post-Bosnia, post-Rwanda, he felt that the UN was being judged on its inability to deal with genocide, ethnic cleansing, terrible violations of human rights, and he had to have something to say about that."

Edward graciously volunteered to work on the speech before he went on the payroll. The result was a landmark document that blew the doors open to the possibility, even the obligation, for States to help civilian populations threatened with genocide or ethnic cleansing. Governments must not hide behind the shield of sovereignty when the home government is unable or unwilling to help, he said. Not many people noticed at the time, but what later would be called "the Annan Doctrine" first emerged at Ditchley and stood on its own two wobbly legs.

In that speech, Kofi described a train that he could see barreling down the tracks towards the Security Council, and it had Kosovo written all over it. Here was a Yugoslav issue left unresolved at Dayton, which was percolating with the same violence that had rocked Bosnia, though on a smaller scale. Don't pretend you don't see it, Kofi warned, "This time, ladies and gentlemen, no one will be able to say that they were taken by surprise — neither by the means employed, nor by the ends pursued. This time, ethnically driven violence must be seen for what it is, and we all know too well what to expect if it is allowed to continue."

Kofi closed that speech by answering his own question of Sarajevo 1995, but which for him must have had echoes of Rwanda in it as well. "When people are in danger, everyone has a duty to speak out," he said. "No one has a right to pass by on the other side." And then he gave one of his favorite quotes, the unforgettable warning of Martin Niemoller, the German Protestant theologian who lived through the Nazi persecution. "In Germany, they came first for the Communists. And I did not speak up because I was not a Communist," Niemoller wrote. "Then they came for the Jews. And I did not speak up, because I was not a Jew. Then they came for the trade unionists. And I did not speak up, because I was not a trade unionist. Then they came for the Catholics. And I did not speak up, because I was Protestant. Then they came for me. And by that time there was no one left to speak up."

Kosovo: A Sacred Place to Serbs

Kosovo was one of those unlikely sacred places that people die over and kill for. It lies in a poor and dusty corner of southern Serbia, where it had enjoyed a significant degree of autonomy under Yugoslav President Tito's wiser brand of leadership. Following Tito's death, nationalist extremists like Slobodan Milosevic eventually took over and Milosevic imposed a chokehold over the province, triggering a low-scale war for liberation.

Ask any Serb anywhere the significance of 1389 and they'll tell you that in that year the Ottoman Turks defeated the Serbs at the battle of Kosovo Polie, leading to the Ottoman subjugation of the Serbs for nearly five hundred years. Like 1066 for the British, or 1492 for the Americans, or 1789 for the French, it's a date every Serb knows. Never mind that today the population of Kosovo is overwhelmingly Muslim Albanian; there was no shortage of Serbs ready to fight for the motherland when Milosevic, in a famous campaign speech in Kosovo in 1989, told the remaining Serb population there, "Nobody has the right to beat you." That sounds obvious enough, but Tito never spoke like that. Those words shattered the Tito myth of the "brotherhood and unity" of Yugoslavia and made Milosevic a Serb hero.

US Bombs Without Council Approval

In 1998, Milosevic began the ethnic cleansing of Kosovo, pushing large numbers of Albanian Kosovars over the borders and into Albania, Macedonia and Montenegro. For the European community, the situation got harder and harder to ignore. The UK began working on a Security Council resolution authorizing the use of force. But the US told the UK to back off. Stan Meisler, who knows Madeleine Albright well from covering her in New York and Washington, saw three reasons why as Secretary of State she wanted to keep Kosovo off the UN agenda.

First, the coherence of the Security Council that had appeared almost magically when President Bush got Council authorization to push Iraq out of Kuwait in 1991 had largely dissipated. The Russians, stout allies of the Serbs, would almost certainly veto this time. Second, although some of her closest allies felt that skillful diplomacy might bring Moscow around, Albright was not dealing from a position of strength; her President was under virulent attack over the Monica Lewinski scandal. And third, she would have to bring Congress along, and the mood toward the UN in Congress at that time was that the UN, in Meisler's words, "reeked of incompetence, inefficiency and defeat." She didn't have the strength to fight that battle too.

Albright sent US Ambassador Richard Holbrooke one more time to Belgrade to try his arm-twisting charm on the Serbian leader. It didn't work. What became known as "Madeleine's war" began on 24 March 1999, without Security Council endorsement but with the full blessing of NATO. Over 70 days of relentless NATO bombing had a devastating effect on Serbia.

Dissent Among the Advisers

The day the bombing began, Kofi issued a press statement that was widely interpreted as approving of the action. It read, in part, "It is indeed tragic that diplomacy has failed, but there are times when the use of force may be legitimate in the pursuit of peace."

Intervention on behalf of the Kosovars was exactly what Kofi had in mind at Ditchley, with one big exception. He assumed the Security Council would unite behind it. He now had to position himself as the guardian of the Charter in between an action he felt was morally justified — the defense of the Kosovars — and the military means resorted to by NATO, without Security Council approval. Russia helped ever so slightly after the fact by pushing to a vote a resolution condemning the NATO action, which was defeated 12 against, 3 for and 1 abstention. But this was not clean.

Edward Mortimer told me how Kofi's advisers differed on Kosovo. "There was a widespread feeling among international lawyers, and some UN officials, that the military action against Belgrade over Kosovo, without Security Council endorsement, was the end of international law as we know it" he said. "And that was the traditionalist view, that the Secretary-General should sort of rend his garments and say, you know, this is absolutely intolerable."

"And then there were a number of us who saw things differently who sort of said, well, hold on a minute," he continued. "You can't just say it shouldn't have happened because the Security Council didn't agree to it. Something had to be done. There is a need for international law to develop, and the Secretary-General has got to put himself on the side of history, as it were. And so that's how we eventually came to his speech before the General Assembly that fall, which put forward what Judy Miller of *The New York Times* had dubbed "the Annan Doctrine" — namely that sovereignty is not a shield behind which you can violate your citizens' human rights. That's not what it's for; that's not what it's about."

Kofi clearly was not happy that NATO had acted without Security Council authorization. But he was also unhappy that Milosevic didn't accept a compromise, that Moscow blindly supported the Serbs, thereby sacrificing a higher good, and that Madeleine Albright didn't fight harder against her internal adversaries to try and bring the Russians along. In a speech at The Hague in May 1999, Kofi issued a warning. "My regret then — and now — is that the Council was unable to unify these two equally compelling interests — and two equally compelling priorities — of the international community," he said. "For this much is clear: unless the Security Council is restored to its preeminent position as the sole source of legitimacy on the use of force, we are on a dangerous path to anarchy."

And then he added, "But equally importantly, unless the Security Council can unite around the aim of confronting massive human rights violations and crimes against humanity on the scale of Kosovo, then we will betray the very ideals that inspired the founding of the United Nations."

A 100-year-old Kosovar woman refugee asked Kofi and Nane, "Is this the way I'm going to end my life?"

A Visit to Kosovo

Towards the end of the NATO bombing campaign, Kofi made an official visit to Albania, and went up to the border with Kosovo, where thousands of Kosovar Albanian refugees were gathered. They were being looked after by the Office of the UN High Commissioner for Refugees, which was putting up tents as fast as the refugees arrived. Nane was close by him; they went into a tent and sat and spoke with a refugee family. A 10-year-old boy sat in the middle of them crying helplessly.

They visited refugees being treated in an infirmary, including a woman who gave birth as she was fleeing through the forest. She was shot in the leg, but she and the baby survived. Kofi signed her cast.

They then came across an old woman just sitting in the dirt in the middle of the unpaved road. Kofi and Nane crouched next to her, Nane helping to support her with one arm. The woman was disoriented, but through an interpreter she explained that she was 100 years old. She looked up at Kofi and asked if this were the way she would end her life.

Hard Questions for the Assembly

Kofi knew he had to put before the membership some hard questions on humanitarian intervention. He decided to do it in his annual speech to the General Assembly. I remember him telling me that the speech to the Assembly was not to articulate a doctrine but to put questions to the Member States so that an emerging policy could be rule-based and coherent. Without answers to those questions, our morality will be arbitrary and selective, he said to me.

In that speech on 20 September 1999, he told the Assembly, "While the genocide in Rwanda will define for our generation the consequences of inaction in the face of mass murder, the more recent conflict in Kosovo has prompted important questions about the consequences of action in the absence of complete unity on the part of the international community.

"It has cast in stark relief the dilemma of what has been called humanitarian intervention: on one side, the question of the legitimacy of an action taken by a regional organization without a United Nations mandate; on the other, the universally recognized imperative of effectively halting gross and systematic violations of human rights with grave humanitarian consequences.

"The inability of the international community in the case of Kosovo to reconcile these two equally compelling interests — universal legitimacy and effectiveness in defense of human rights — can only be viewed as a tragedy.

"It has revealed the core challenge to the Security Council and to the United Nations as a whole in the next century: to forge unity behind the principle that massive and systematic violations of human rights — wherever they may take place — should not be allowed to stand."

I spoke to Kofi after I retired at the end of 2005, as I was about to leave for China to teach. I asked him if he agreed that the NATO intervention was a second best solution after a political one. "It's an interesting question," he replied. "Obviously, a political solution would have been ideal. The drafters of the resolution [on intervention] felt that the Russian Federation may veto it, and so went without it. And given the situation on the ground, the reports that were coming out, I would say that that was the second best solution. And in the end, after the war, they came back to the UN and eventually even got the Russians to work with everyone as an international community to try and pacify the situation."

So the Council had done some patching up, but Kofi knew that what was needed were some hard answers to the questions he had posed. His staff debated whether he should push the Members further. Edward Mortimer remembers that "Kofi's initial instinct was to urge the Security Council to draw up criteria or guidelines. I and others urged him not to do this, since a) it would probably have been unable to agree on any, and b) any that it did agree on were likely to be very restrictive."

Edward argued that the function of a speech like the one he had just given to the General Assembly was longer term — to contribute to a shift in world public opinion and thus help to ensure that future decisions on intervention would be taken in a different atmosphere. Kofi accepted this. He started saying that he had handed the "talking stick" to Member States, following a practice used in Ghanaian village councils.

INTERVENING IN EAST TIMOR

Kieran Prendergast, Kofi's principal political adviser, says that when Kofi became Secretary-General he looked at a series of deadlocked conflicts to decide which ones he might like to try to invigorate. He chose four, one of which was East Timor. (The other three were Cyprus, Western Sahara and Georgia/Abkhazia.)

When the Indonesian military ran riot in East Timor in late 1999, Kofi pulled out all the plugs to get an international intervention by the book — that is, with Security Council approval. It was late in coming, but it eventually happened.

Indonesia, which was originally colonized by the Dutch, annexed East Timor, a former Portuguese colony, in 1976, after Portugal suddenly freed most of its colonies following the overthrow in 1974 of the Portuguese dictator, Antonio Salazar. The Indonesia takeover was something of a bloodbath; the UN estimated that one in seven of the East Timorese died. The UN never recognized Indonesian sovereignty over East Timor. And only Portugal, perhaps out of colonial guilt, and the UN, through the good offices of successive Secretaries-General, sustained any long-term interest in East Timor's right to self-determination.

In 1998, with the Cold War ending, the long-serving President of Indonesia, Suharto, stepped down and was replaced by B.J. Habibie. Habibie agreed in 1999 to let the East Timorese decide whether they wanted to remain part of Indonesia with special autonomy or become independent. The big powers didn't seem to care one way or another, leaving an unusual amount of space for Kofi to maneuver. He started by talking Habibie into letting the UN conduct the "popular consultation", as it was called, on independence. (The Indonesians wouldn't agree to a referendum, so Kofi proposed a referendum by another name.) Habibie agreed.

The UN was given just a few short months to organize it. Indonesia, in the meantime, refused to allow any additional international security for the referendum so as not to dilute the strong presence of its own forces in the territory. The Indonesian military, which didn't like the independence option, remained in control in East Timor and supported various militia, which were no more than marauding gangs that tried to intimidate the population into accepting autonomy. The UN had to postpone the referendum twice because of local violence.

For some reason, many in Indonesia felt the East Timorese would vote to stay part of Indonesia. How wrong they were. On 30 August 1999, virtually every eligible East Timorese voter went to the polls, and nearly 80 percent of them voted for independence. Stunned at their defeat, the Indonesian military sent their gangs on a violent rampage through the territory, killing and burning. Prendergast said, "It was sort of an orgy of destruction."

Kofi did what he does best — he worked the phones. Habibie may not have been getting an honest picture from his military of what was happening in East Timor. Kofi had to break the news to him. Kofi wanted to send in an international force to intervene, but China and Russia would veto anything that Indonesia didn't accept, and Habibie wasn't ready for a foreign intervention.

Then, on 5 September, the Australians informed Kofi that they would lead an intervention force. Australia had good relations with Indonesia and also a serious army. This was a breakthrough. Kofi pressured Habibie; he still resisted. On 8 September, gangs besieged the UN compound where over 1,000 refugees had taken shelter. Kofi agreed to evacuate the UN staff but was concerned about the East Timorese who had taken shelter with them. He asked his special representative there if any of his people would volunteer to stay. About 80 did. The militia in the end never entered the compound.

The US, concerned about the escalation, then stepped in and put financial pressure on Indonesia, threatening to block loans by the World Bank and the International Monetary Fund if the violence wasn't brought under control. On 10 September, Kofi used the bully pulpit to announce that the time had come for Indonesia to accept international help. And he raised the ante, saying those guilty could be charged with war crimes. His phone was hot. He was working it non-stop in what was probably his most impressive effort at telephone diplomacy. Prendergast commented, "This was a fantastic feat and I still don't know how he managed to do it."

On 12 September, Habibie gave in. He called Kofi and asked for a UN force to go to East Timor as soon as possible. By 20 September, the first Australian troops were landing, a record for timely deployment of peacekeepers not seen since the Congo over 40 years before. Order was restored and a UN mission, headed by the charismatic Brazilian Sergio Vieira de Mello, began working with the Timorese to prepare them for independence.

Tamrat Samuel, a UN political officer who handled the East Timor file, told me, "The successful holding of the popular consultation, despite the enormously difficult security situation, was in large part due to the vision and perseverance of the Secretary-General and his ability to rally international support. His integrity and others' trust in the soundness of his political judgment underpinned his success in persuading the international community to act in unison in the face of injustice and wide-spread atrocities."

In February 2000, Kofi visited East Timor. His friend Sergio met him at the airport. As we drove through the capital, Dili, Kofi saw half the buildings were burnt-out shells. But the clean up had begun and rebuilding was about to get under way. He then flew by helicopter to the town of Liquica, where the post-referendum killing had been so severe it was known as the "killing field" of East Timor. As he descended from the helicopter, I saw an old man come up to him, embrace him tightly and cry. Kofi and Nane walked to the village church, where hundreds had been massacred, and laid a memorial wreath. Survivors by the hundreds followed him there. A few began to cry, then dozens were crying, and Kofi and Nane stood there and embraced one after another who came forward to be comforted.

The crowd, which had now swelled to 5,000, gathered in the soccer stadium, where Kofi stood side by side with independence leader Xanana Gusmao. "Together, we can weather the current crisis and usher in a new era for East Timor," he told them; "an era in which East Timor takes its place in the family of nations, and in which its men, women and children can live lives of dignity and peace."

On 20 May 2002, East Timor became an independent nation and later that year became, as Timor Leste, the first new UN Member State of the millennium. Kofi was once again in Dili, this time for the celebration. At midnight on 19 May, the UN flag came down and the new Timor Leste flag went up. Kofi said, "I still recall the day, 45 years ago, when my own country Ghana attained its independence. Tonight, I am as excited as I was then."

NATO intervention to save the Kosovars, without Security Council approval, was swift, bloody and eventually led to an independent Kosovo. UN intervention on behalf of the East Timorese, which was authorized by the Council, was slow, was also bloody, and it too led to independence. I think Kofi must have wanted to find a way to have quick and clean intervention by the book.

CHAPTER 9

DEMOCRATIZING THE UN

CIVIL SOCIETY

Boutros Boutros-Ghali was a thinker; Kofi was a doer. Boutros-Ghali is remembered in universities around the world for his *Agenda for Peace*, which laid out the intellectual structure for a revised approach to UN peacekeeping. But he also wrote an *Agenda for Democratization*, in which he stressed the importance of the United Nations' engaging with what is now called civil society — public interest groups known as Non-Governmental Organizations, or NGOs. This Agenda was published at the end of his first and last term as Secretary-General, and got little notice. But if ever there was an agenda tailor-made for Kofi, it was this one. He was temperamentally suited to it.

Kofi put Gillian Sorensen in charge of external relations. She and her husband Ted were pillars of the New York foreign policy establishment. "Boutros Boutros-Ghali had spoken about the importance of civil society in thoughtful and eloquent ways," she told me, "but he was very preoccupied with other things, including his own political survival. It was Kofi Annan who really moved it forward."

Kofi asked Gillian to manage the UN's links with some 4,200 NGOs, such as Rotary, Chambers of Commerce, Doctors Without Borders and faith-based groups, especially in the United States where public support for the UN was in the doldrums. Gillian called them "a mighty, peaceful citizen's army that expands the work and potential of the United Nations in countless ways."

Kofi respected NGOs and what they were doing, she said. "He called NGOs 'our essential partners', and he meant it. He recognized that NGOs could dramatize and publicize and mobilize; that they could be politically savvy and media smart. They could raise awareness and raise funds. They could lobby. They could do things that the UN could not."

Kofi also asked Gillian to manage a program of Goodwill Ambassadors. Other UN entities, notably UNICEF, had successfully recruited actors, athletes, artists and writers as supporters. Kofi liked this idea and created his own Goodwill Ambassadors, whom he designated "Messengers of Peace." These included opera singer Luciano Pavaroti, former world boxing champion Muhammad Ali, conservationist Jane Goodall, actor Michael Douglas, and rock star Bono. I don't think Kofi expected the Messengers of Peace program to take off the way it did. And some Messengers sunk their teeth into it; Michael Douglas, for example, campaigned ardently for control of small arms and against nuclear proliferation. It quickly became too big to handle well.

During Kofi's tenure as Secretary-General, the number of NGOs grew like mushrooms. "They were coming into their own as a new and powerful political force that would not be denied," Gillian said, "and Kofi embraced them." Through Gillian and the UN information department, he addressed their demands for access, support, meeting space, guest speakers, information.

One of Kofi's more energetic Messengers of Peace was Bono of the band U2, here chatting with Kofi in Dublin during an official visit.

Every time he traveled, Kofi met with student groups, professional organizations, business people and editorial boards. He made himself accessible. His most controversial initiative, though, was to extend a hand to big business. Kofi befriended the founder of *CNN*, Ted Turner, who was embarrassed that his country, the United States, was behind in its UN dues by over a billion dollars. At the annual United Nations Association dinner in New York with Kofi in 1997, Ted took the microphone and stunned everybody, including his own lawyers, by saying he would give a billion dollars of his own money to United Nations causes. Ted made good on his word, spreading the gift over 15 years, and attracting an additional billion from others. Turner's generosity was infectious. Soon other billionaires were giving massive donations to health, environment and human rights causes, among them Microsoft's Bill Gates, investor Warren Buffett and Richard Branson of Virgin Atlantic and Virgin Records. This thing snowballed to a point where, in June 2010, Gates and Buffett called on their fellow billionaires to sign a "Giving Pledge" to donate most of their fortunes to the charity of their choice.

"There is a reserve about the Secretary-General," Gillian concluded, "but he reached out to people with grace and intelligence and warmth. That relationship will never go backwards, whatever the next Secretary-General does or says. The NGOs feel their power now. They've found their place and their footing. It's quite different from when we first came in 1997, when I heard a senior UN official refer to NGOs as 'a nuisance'. No official today would ever say such a thing, because it's just not true.

THE GLOBAL COMPACT

"It was with the private sector that Kofi made a pioneering effort," Gillian said. "Before Kofi Annan, there was a great distance between the UN and the private sector and rarely did the two meet. Kofi reached out to business executives, and they asked him how they could help. He took them at their word."

Indeed, in the 1970s, multinational corporations were a dirty word around the UN, and even today, in the eyes of those who work for a cleaner environment, human rights or affordable medication for those with AIDS, the corporations are often seen as the bad guys. Kofi thought differently. He saw they had money; they had talent; they knew how to organize to achieve a goal. In short, they had the kind of things he wished the UN had. He wanted a partnership with them to enhance the UN's capacity. He started courting big business at a ski resort in the Swiss Alps.

Davos, Switzerland, is a small skiing village that is taken over every January by Klaus Schwab, who invites everybody who's anybody to come join him to discuss the world's problems at what he called the World Economic Forum. And everyone who's anyone goes — the political elite, the business elite, the academic elite. Klaus had spotted Kofi as a rising star when he was Under-Secretary-General for peacekeeping and invited him to Davos. As Secretary-General, Kofi was keen to go again and his Communications Director, Shashi Tharoor, dealt with Schwab and made it happen. The first time Kofi addressed a plenary session in a cavernous room with a monster TV screen behind him projecting his live image, he hesitated, looking over his shoulder, and said, "I hope I never get used to this."

The first time Kofi addressed a Davos plenary session in a cavernous room with a monster TV screen above him projecting his live image, he hesitated, looking over his shoulder, and said, "I hope I never get used to this."

Kofi soon became a regular at Davos, and in 1999 he used the World Economic Forum to make a formal appeal to corporations to enter into a global compact with the United Nations. John Ruggie, then Kofi's director for strategic planning, was put in charge of drafting a speech.

Ruggie, a renowned political economist, discussed the intellectual content with Georg Kell and asked him to flesh it out. Georg is a happy German, with a great capacity for work and is absolutely single-minded in focus. Kofi hired him in 1997 to foster cooperation with the private sector.

"Well, it was in June 1998 that John Ruggie told me that Kofi Annan would be going to the World Economic Forum in Davos, Switzerland, in January and I'd better do something real good," said Georg with a laugh. "That's how it started; he said, 'something real good'."

Georg happened to have been focused for a long time on the UN-business relationship, and it always bothered him that the UN hadn't overcome the old ideologies; it was still caught up in the institutional framework of the Cold War, he thought. He wanted to find a pragmatic way to bring the UN's institutional advantage into play.

In June 1998, it was pretty clear to him that a backlash against globalization was about to take place. NGOs had posted strategies on their websites on how to derail the World Trade Organization, the World Bank and other international financial institutions. "And they very cleverly identified human rights, environmental and labor issues as the focus of their protest," Georg said. "It was clear to me that the UN's normative work in these three areas had a lot to offer: there was the Universal Declaration of Human Rights, the fundamental principles of rights at work defined by the International Labour Organization of the UN and the Rio Declaration on Environment and Development sponsored by the UN Environment Programme."

So the idea then occurred to Georg and John: why not challenge business to be part of the solution by agreeing to be guided by these norms that most governments had already in principle endorsed? "After all," said Georg, "they benefit a lot from liberalization, and for them to be part of the solution makes sense."

When Georg showed the draft of the speech to John, he loved it. He and Georg then gave it final shape. "Kofi read it," Georg said, "understood it, internalized it and embraced it."

The press gave good coverage to the speech. But then certain ambassadors, including the UK's Jeremy Greenstock and Switzerland's Jeno Staehelin, began urging Kofi to follow up with a program to put those words into action. For John and Georg, writing a speech was one thing; putting it into an operational framework was something else. "And we had no clue," Georg confessed.

Kofi had a trust fund, and he dug into it and gave Georg a pathetic $20,000 and told him to run with it, in consultation with John. Georg started by putting together a website and working with the three relevant UN agencies: the International Labour Organization, the UN Environment Programme and the Office of the High Commissioner for Human Rights.

Then he started to sound out business representatives. British Petroleum responded positively and hosted a meeting in London for about 15 companies. There was general interest in going forward. But business was nervous that there were no other stakeholders, and urged the UN to win over labor unions and NGOs as well.

Easier said than done. The Davos speech had some things in it that organized labor didn't like, so John and Georg had to massage the message to give it a more "positive articulation", in their words, with labor. NGOs were interested but skeptical, but gradually some "big brands" came on board: Amnesty International, Oxfam, the World Wildlife Fund.

Neither John nor Georg had yet grasped the size of their undertaking — or maybe they did and it scared them. "John and I were looking for an exit strategy at this point," Georg said, laughing. "Let's stage one event, we thought, bring them all together so everybody understands that it's important to internalize these universal principles that are endorsed by Member States already. We would affirm that business is now embracing these principles without waiting for every Government to come up with a perfect regulatory environment, and we would close shop."

So they planned a big event for July 2000 at UN Headquarters, thinking that would be the end. But the opposite happened. The participants agreed that there was a need for a long-term program in defense of the UN's principles in the areas of human rights, labor standards and the environment. So at that gathering, Georg said, "The Global Compact went operational."

Georg didn't understand how he could organize the Global Compact on a global level with no staff and no money, and more than once, he said, things looked "really bad". But then there was a grant from the Swiss Government, followed by contributions from nine other Governments that formed a group of "Friends of the Global Compact". Corporations started to kick in. By 2006, a private foundation was created for these funds and the annual budget of the Compact was $5 million, roughly half from governments and half from corporations.

The Global Compact launched a program called "Growing sustainable business in least developed countries". Participants worked together to overcome negative business environments and make sustainable investments in 10 sub-Saharan African countries. "That was a big hit," said Georg.

Then in April 2006, the Global Compact invaded Wall Street with a financial market initiative called "Principles for Responsible Investment," targeting pension funds and managers of assets of over two trillion dollars. This was now big time. "So now we have a market driver with real leverage," Georg said. He was optimistic that the UN would make the case that engaging in the Global Compact and internalizing the UN's principles in these three key areas makes good business sense.

"We also launched several new initiatives," Georg said. "Principles for Responsible Investment, now backed by more than 400 institutional investors driving environmental, social and governance issues into investment analysis; the Principles for Responsible Management Education, bringing the Global Compact into some 200 business schools; and individual networks which do a lot of work: Caring for Climate, the CEO Water Mandate and so on. And our network infrastructure has evolved — with over 80 country networks, the Global Compact now has ongoing activities in all parts of the world." Georg's face lit up with excitement. "You can't stop it anymore," he said.

"The journey of the Global Compact and its future is intimately linked with the UN's capacity to renew itself from within," he concluded. "Whether or not the Organization is learning to work with business and other private actors is arguably one of the most important questions that will define its relevance in the twenty-first century."

BIG BAD PHARMA AND HIV/AIDS

AIDS and Africa

Kofi carefully laid the groundwork for a global assault on HIV/AIDS, and he got a helping hand from his friend, Richard Holbrooke. As soon as Holbrooke was nominated as US Ambassador to the UN in 1999, Kofi urged him to make AIDS in Africa his priority. The pandemic was ravaging the continent; sub-Saharan Africa, with 10 percent of the world's population, is home to two-thirds of the world's HIV-infected people. The effects of the pandemic are mind numbing: it has created 11 million orphans, many left to survive on their own as heads of households.

Under the Security Council's rotating presidency system, Richard Holbrooke was scheduled to be President in January 2000. He called Kofi from Harare, Zimbabwe, and told him, "We're going to be President of the Security Council next month, which will be the first month of the new millennium. I want to hold a session on AIDS to start the millennium, and I want to devote the whole month to Africa, nothing but Africa."

Kofi was thrilled, but he anticipated trouble with the Security Council taking on a health issue, which is more properly the turf of the Economic and Social Council or perhaps the General

Assembly. Richard was blissfully unaware of this, and asked Kofi why should there be a problem. Kofi responded, "Because it's never been done before." Of course, that's all Holbrooke had to hear to want to do it.

Richard gathered political support for the meeting on AIDS and rammed it through. He successfully argued, with Kofi's concurrence, that AIDS is more than a health issue; it is a security issue. Governments have now come around to that view.

Kofi personally brought his AIDS message to Africa, where it was most needed. But the continent's leaders seemed to be in denial. They didn't speak about the disease. Kofi said when it comes to AIDS, "silence is death." Robert Orr, who was his strategic planner, said, "It was a visionary side of Kofi Annan to realize that very early on, despite the pain that would be caused to him personally by raising HIV/AIDS as a security issue, and as something that African leaders had to face up to. He saw it is a truly existential challenge to his continent and vulnerable people around the world, and he was willing to take on that pain that would be inflicted on him for breaking the code of silence in Africa."

On 26 April 2001, Kofi made a historic speech at the African Summit on AIDS in Abuja, Nigeria, laying out a five-point plan for addressing the disease. He demanded cheaper antiviral drugs. But he made a staggering proposal — that a "war chest" be created to permit "at a minimum, expenditure of an additional 7 to 10 billion dollars a year worldwide over an extended period of time."

Kofi's international profile was too high for this call to be ignored, and out of it grew The Global Fund. Stephen Lewis, the Canadian with the golden tongue whom Kofi named his Special Envoy for HIV/AIDS in Africa, said this about the Fund: "The Global Fund is something that he should be enormously proud of and is a major legacy of Kofi's because, in my mind, it has emerged as the most important new international financial facility that the world has created in the last several years. It has really been the anchor for the international response."

The UN's chief AIDS envoy worldwide was Peter Piot of Belgium, who had headed the UNAIDS program since 1995. Peter co-discovered the Ebola virus in Zaire in 1976 as a specialist in tropical diseases. He credits Kofi with much more than the creation of the Global Fund; it was the political groundwork he laid for it. "Through his total commitment, he put the AIDS issue on the top of the political agenda, making it, in a way, respectable," he said. "Thanks to him the Security Council took it up, the General Assembly held a special session on it."

Engaging the Drug Companies

Kofi used his new connections with big business to pressure the pharmaceutical industry to lower their prices for HIV/AIDS drugs for poor countries. This was not easy. The companies' lawyers were nervous about their CEOs talking to each other about drug prices because of laws against price-fixing. Some people around Kofi were nervous about him sitting down with these CEOs for fear of his being seen to be in bed with them. But Kofi took on "Big Pharma" with a surprising result.

A few weeks before he gave the Abuja speech, Kofi invited the CEOs of the world's chief pharmaceutical firms to sit down with him and talk about the problem of their pricing AIDS drugs out of the reach of the world's poor, the ones who needed them most. The CEOs initially hesitated, but eventually accepted Kofi's invitation. This was the first of several meetings that eventually led to the lowering of the prices of these medications for the poor.

Peter Piot organized the meetings for Kofi. "Getting the companies to lower their prices on AIDS medication was as important as raising money for the Global Fund," he said, "because when the price is reduced, more people can have access to life-saving medication."

Michel Lavollay is a French doctor who has worked for the UN not only in Iraq, but also in a variety of capacities, mainly on AIDS. "There were a number of us trying to put the access-to-drugs question on the table," he said. "In the mid- to late-1990s, the situation was that drugs were available in rich countries, where they were costing $15,000 per year per individual. And the assumption was that, well, that's the market. Africa? They'll never be able to afford that, so why even raise the question? Well, five years later, both the Security Council and the General Assembly held sessions dedicated to HIV/AIDS where the right to treatment was confirmed. And along the way, the prices of drugs went from $15,000 a year to $150 a year, or 50 cents a day."

Michel said he was deeply convinced that Kofi played a very important role by raising these issues. "He created political mobilization; he had a moral voice; he said it's unacceptable."

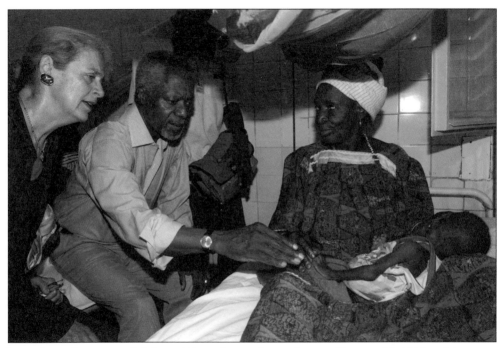

"Very often, when we traveled, he and Nane, frequently together, would meet with AIDS activists, or visit a clinic to talk with those with HIV. They met with sex workers and drug users. 'I mean, what Secretary-General has done that before,' Peter Piot asked?"

Kofi was active on AIDS early in his first term. "I think he started in 2000, when he gave the Princess Diana lecture on AIDS," Peter said. "And then he made a real breakthrough, in my view, when he convened a meeting of the so-called International Partnership on AIDS in Africa. It was there that, for the first time, African Governments, donor agencies, the UN system, business and civil society all came together in the same room and talked about AIDS. And it broke a taboo. And here we had Kofi, perhaps the most prominent African of his generation, saying, look, I'm concerned; this is a huge problem; we've got to get our act together; I'm personally committed. That was significant."

Peter thought that initially Kofi wasn't totally comfortable talking about condoms or about men having sex with men. "But he overcame that," he said. "And we mustn't forget Nane," he added; "she's been extremely important here. She was actually dealing with the AIDS issue before Kofi did. She was very pro-active on the AIDS issue."

Kofi and Nane both worked with civil society on HIV/ AIDS. Very often, when we traveled, he and Nane, frequently together, would meet with AIDS activists, or visit a clinic to talk with those with HIV. They met with sex workers and drug users. "I mean, what Secretary-General has done that before," Peter asked? "In many countries, it caused raised eyebrows, but he did it."

"Ah, he made an enormous difference," Peter concluded. "In terms of how the world looks at the AIDS epidemic, how the world is responding to it and how much money is being devoted to it."

CHAPTER 10

RELATIONS WITH THE PRESS

The best way to reach the public is through the press, and Kofi's reach was long. His predecessors were not always as good, I learned. In April 2005, just before I retired and with the help of Ted Turner's UN Foundation, I invited all of my living predecessors as spokesperson, and several journalists, to the UN for a full day of discussions on the UN's relations with the press over time. Some of the journalists, such as *The New York Times*'s Kitty Teltsch, had been around the UN since 1945.

For me, it was fascinating to hear these first hand accounts of how the different Secretaries-General dealt with the media:

Trygve Lie of Norway used to invite a select few correspondents up to his office at the end of the day, pour each of them and himself a neat scotch, and talk off the record about the events of the day. That's a pretty good start, at least for the select few.

Dag Hammarskjold of Sweden was sphinxlike and didn't talk to journalists one on one, for fear of appearing to play favorites. His press conferences, according to his biographer Sir Brian Urquhart, were a marvel of erudition, "in which few journalists knew what the hell he was talking about but they all seemed to enjoy it."

U Thant of Burma, the quiet Buddhist who is the forgotten Secretary-General, had been a spokesperson himself for his national government. He used to come into the office on Saturdays, and one enterprising reporter, the legendary Bill Oatis of *Associated Press*, would wait for him curbside. Without fail, Thant would stop and talk to Bill and give him a useable quote or two. Other journalists picked up on this and Thant ended up doing an informal press conference curbside every Saturday.

Kurt Waldheim of Austria seemed to think he could change the transcript of what he actually said in a press conference to what he had wanted to say, as if all the correspondents in the room didn't have tape recorders. Once, when he didn't like the verbatim transcript, he threw the papers at the head of the spokesperson, Bill Powell. He also lied about his Nazi past — not something that endears you to the media.

Javier Perez de Cuellar of Peru was more fluent in French than in English. When he spoke to the press in English, reporters would compare notes afterwards to see if anyone got something they could put in a news story. Often they couldn't. Vernon Walters, when he was US Ambassador to the UN, once repeated a quote by British columnist Rosemary Righter saying of de Cuellar, "He couldn't make waves if he fell out of a boat."

Boutros Boutros-Ghali of Egypt expected his spokesperson to handle the press for him and went for obscenely long periods of time without giving a press conference. He wasn't too careful about whom he gave interviews to, though. Once, after he left office, he ended up unknowingly in a one-on-one interview with the comedian Sacha Baron Cohen, who was in the guise of a hip-hop character he plays called Ali G. It was very funny — but not for Boutros.

Kofi was accessible. Josh Friedman, the Pulitzer Prize-winning journalist for *Newsday* who now teaches at Columbia University, says that he covered the UN during Boutros-Ghali's time and "in five years never even shook the guy's hand." Then, just after Kofi was elected Secretary-General, Josh was outside his office on the peacekeeping floor. Kofi signaled him in and they sat down and talked for a half hour. "From that time on, I was won over," he said.

James Traub, in an article for *The New York Times* magazine in 1998, wrote that Kofi had "gifts of character — attentiveness, self-possession, clarity, an utter lack of pretense and a kindness that seems to spring from an impulse of attentiveness."

"Soooo nice"

Evelyn Leopold of *Reuters* told me that when journalists traveled with Kofi and Nane to Washington in January 2007, one of her colleagues asked her, "How do we cover them? They are sooo nice, sooo attractive".

"That aura, his openness with the press, continued throughout most of his first term," Evelyn said. "In addition to giving press conferences, he would stop to chat in the corridors, or on his way into the building. He answered most questions as best as he could and, contrary to many a public figure, rarely dodged a query by giving a reply to something one never asked."

U Thant may have started the practice of the Secretary-General stopping curbside to talk to journalists on Saturday mornings, but Kofi never shied away from a question thrown at him in the corridor. He did this so often that I made a practice of always carrying a tape recorder with me, and my office would transcribe the recording of every informal exchange with the press. Jane Gaffney of my staff created a page on the UN website that she called "Off the Cuff", where she placed these transcripts of what Kofi had said informally to the press from 1999 onwards. We don't have records for his predecessors, but Kofi consistently did over 100 of what we came to call "press encounters" every year. In addition, he did an average of 7 press conferences a year at Headquarters and another 20 while traveling abroad, and most years gave more than 40 one-on-one interviews to the media. During his first year, 1997, he did an all-time-high of 168 interviews.

With the press, Kofi was the same as with everyone else. He remembered little details about you and asked after you. He once called Evelyn and said, "You looked tired today, Evelyn. Don't work so hard."

"On substantive policy issues," said Evelyn, "we were sometimes blinded by his charm, his genuineness and his use of the bully pulpit to put forth moral and sometimes politically controversial concepts. But he also was capable of looking back at UN disasters, such as in Somalia, and saying, 'We failed.' For the press this was startling, since the United Nations regularly took credit for successful ventures and blamed failures on the Member States."

With the Press on the Road

Whenever we made a trip in a private plane, and there were extra seats, Kofi let me invite journalists along. The *BBC*'s Rob Watson told me that on a trip to the Great Lakes region of Africa in 1998, Kofi made him smile a couple of times.

"The first night we were in Djibouti, I thought I was going to die, I felt so ill and dizzy," he said. "I remember asking Kofi if he traveled with a doctor as part of his team. (He didn't.) He looked at me in a very kindly way and asked me if it was my first trip to the continent, to which I said 'yes'. 'Ah', he said, 'then it's just Africa.'"

"Shortly after that," Rob continued, "when we were back on that funny propeller plane (we had borrowed a plane from a peacekeeping mission), he gave me his hot traveling tips for Africa. He said, 'Eat when you can, drink when you can, sleep when you can — and go to the can when you can.'"

Kofi casually briefing journalists on a private plane.

The New York Times's Warren Hoge traveled with Kofi to the Middle East in mid-2006 along with three other journalists, and was surprised when Kofi escorted them into the VIP lounge at the airport on arrival in country after country. And Kofi did the same thing everywhere. He would be seated next to the Prime Minister or the Foreign Minister and he would beckon the four journalists forward. He would then introduce each of them to the VIP next to him and ask him to give them an interview. And sure enough, the journalists got interviews with the Foreign Minister of Iran, the Foreign Minister of Qatar and the Prime Minister of Lebanon, to name just three. "No journalist has ever had a better agent," said Hoge.

Jim Goodale and his wife Toni introduced Kofi and Nane to a Who's Who of New York media. He told me, "Kofi was listened to because he had something to say. And it did not hurt him that he knew the media stars of America, centered as they were in New York City. Much of New York's social life pivots around these people. Kofi was able to use his relationship with this group to the U.N.'s great advantage."

Mistakes

When it came to media relations, Kofi and I had full compatibility. He expected me to help the press understand his objectives and for this they needed to be informed on everything. He invited me to sit in on delicate policy discussions, weekly cabinet meetings and his staff meetings. I was part of his team. He knew I would share with the press some of what I learned, on a background (quote me but don't identify me) or an off the record (no quotes) basis to help them understand our view of what was going on. And he trusted me to keep to myself what needed to be confidential in order to protect a diplomatic process.

He understood that governments tried to use the press for their own political purposes, that journalists spoke regularly to UN Ambassadors and others, and that to play that game you needed to be in it. He was ready to play, but only very selectively. He did not seek the media limelight for personal aggrandizement; that's not the kind of person he is. And he didn't need the media to help him get reelected. But he respected the role that the media play in the democratic process, and the way they could help him achieve his political objectives.

As with everyone else who worked closely with him, I felt I had his complete trust and confidence. He accepted my rules of the spokesperson's game, which included that I would not, and for professional reasons could not, lie or mislead. These were his rules too. He gave me close access to him. And he let me give my daily press briefing based on what I picked up from his meetings and from talking to his close advisers. He never asked me what I was going to say to the press at the daily noon briefing. He just assumed I would get it right.

He was also forgiving if you slipped up — just as long as you didn't make a habit of it. Once, on Good Friday 2002, Kofi was going to brief the Security Council on a trip he had just taken to Lebanon. With his approval, we routinely "leaked" to the press the text of his remarks to confidential Council meetings. The rationale for this was that Council members played the press like violins and would tell the media what Kofi had said, putting their own spin on it. I argued that the best way to combat this was to give the press the full text of what he actually said, and he agreed. I insisted that we not leak selectively so as to not play favorites among the media, so this was a very open process. We would squawk on the loudspeaker, "Now available in the Spokesperson's Office are copies of the text of the Secretary-General's remarks to the Security Council," and the entire press corps would sweep into my office to collect their copies. Each copy was carefully marked, "Check Against Delivery".

Good Friday is a UN holiday, and my staff rotated weekend and holiday duty. This particular day, Stéphane Dujarric was on duty and he asked political affairs officer Rick Hooper for an advance copy of Kofi's remarks for the press. Rick hesitated, because changes were still being made. But in the end, he gave Steph a copy. On that copy, Chief of Staff Iqbal Riza had added a sentence saying that Israel should stop using "disproportionate lethal force and other measures that violate international laws and standards in response to terrorist attacks." That line was a bit too hot for political adviser Kieran Prendergast and Kofi agreed to delete it.

The Spokesperson's Office staff runs with the news the way journalists do and the pace is fast. Olivia Ioannou of my office had already been at her desk for 12 hours and jumped the gun. She made the original version available to the press. Steph panicked and started running around to the journalists' offices to warn them about the change in the text. There are about 200 journalists who maintain office space at the UN and Steph decided not to talk to the major newspaper correspondents because he assumed they would be professional enough to check against delivery. But one, the *Los Angeles Times*, didn't check and led his story with the controversial quote that had been deleted.

Kofi is a news hound, and the *Los Angeles Times* is one of a half dozen papers he would read every morning before coming to work. All of us in the Spokesperson's Office had egg on our faces. I asked Steph to write a note explaining how the mistake happened and sent it up to Kofi with a cover note of my own saying, "I explained to my staff that we cannot function effectively without the total trust of the 38th floor and we must see that nothing like this happens again." I held my breath.

The same day, my note was returned to me with Kofi's handwriting on it. "Thanks," he wrote. "You and your team have provided excellent service. Mistakes might occur, and do occur, but that comes with responsibility. Let's put it behind us and carry on. Thank your staff for the long and dedicated service they have provided over the past five years." We all breathed a sigh of relief, and we never made that mistake again.

Spin

I remember attending a senior staff meeting on the 38th floor chaired by Kofi's Deputy, Louise Frechette, and Louise jokingly saying something like, "And Fred can put his spin on that." I stopped her cold. I said spin is deceit, and the Secretary-General does not expect me ever to deceive the press. To me that seemed self-evident, but judging from the surprised expressions on the faces of some people around the table, they seemed to be hearing something for the first time.

I realize that not every spokesperson believes this. In the high stakes political poker that democratic governments play every hour of every day, it must sound naïve to say never lie to the press. I was once invited for lunch at the home of the French Ambassador, Alain Dejammet, in honor of the new UN correspondent for Le Monde, Afsane Bassir-Pour. Dujammet is erudite and entertaining; he later wrote a very amusing little tongue-in-cheek book about the best places at the UN to take a snooze. He had also once been spokesperson for the French Foreign Ministry. "So Fred," he said, walking out to the kitchen to fetch something, "tell us your philosophy as spokesperson." I looked at Afsane and I said, simply, "Never tell a lie." Dejammet, in a high-pitched voice, said as he disappeared into the kitchen, "Hah!"

Several years later, when Tony Blair's spokesperson, Alastair Campbell, who spun at great heights, was eventually forced to resign in disgrace, I felt vindicated. All his little white lies about Iraq were exposed, and both his reputation and his boss's were seriously damaged.

You can tell a lie to buy a little time, but in the end the truth comes out. And when it does, your credibility with the media is shot. So the price for buying time is just not worth it. The press always, always finds out the truth. That's their job. Some of those around Kofi had a diplomat's instinct when it came to the media — the less said the better. One of those, for whom I have great respect, was Iqbal Riza, the Chief of Staff. I don't know how many times I picked up from a journalist news of an impending high-level appointment by the Secretary-General that had leaked out of the appointee's home country. My exchange with Iqbal would go something like this: "Iqbal, the press tell me that Kofi is about to name so-and-so as such-and-such." Iqbal would reply, "What! Are there no secrets in this house?" To which I would respond, "Thank you for the confirmation, Sir."

The Taiwanese Representative

In eight and a half years as Kofi's spokesperson, I had only one serious clash with him — at least I thought it was serious. The UN Correspondents' Association (UNCA) had invited the representative of Taiwan in New York, Andrew Hsia, to come into their clubroom at UN Headquarters and speak to them. They had guest speakers there regularly. Their president gave us a heads up, because he knew it would make the Chinese Government unhappy, as the UN didn't recognize Taiwan. I supported UNCA's right to invite whomever they wanted, which was a long-standing practice going back to the beginnings of the UN. But when I informed Kofi, he asked his Communications Director Shashi Tharoor to handle it, instructing him to sound out the Chinese.

"I tried to persuade the Chinese that their insistence on us banning the Taiwanese representative would be counter-productive and would guarantee the very negative publicity they wanted to avoid," Shashi told me. "If the individual was allowed into the building, I argued, no one would write about it; it wasn't news. But the Chinese obstinately dug in and our lawyers felt they had grounds to insist. Kofi's ban on the Taiwanese gave China and the UN unfavorable publicity, just as we had warned."

Boutros-Ghali once had blocked a UNCA invitation to a Chinese dissident, in what became an embarrassment for him. The dissident gave his talk outside the UN on First Avenue and got much more publicity than he would have had he been allowed inside. It also infuriated UNCA. I had been confident that Kofi wouldn't make the same mistake, but I was wrong.

Kofi asked us to inform UNCA that the Taiwanese representative would not be allowed on UN premises. I wrote Kofi an angst-ridden, two-page memo saying I had always been very proud of his good press relations but this decision of his regarding the Taiwanese "left me no proud ground to stand on." There was only silence at his end for what seemed like days. Finally, when I was in the elevator with him one morning, I said, "Did you get my memo?" "Yes," he said. (Pause). "Don't be a fundamentalist."

A fundamentalist! Years later, I tried to rationalize his position, without fully agreeing with it. As Bob Orr said, Kofi has a Midwesterner's pragmatism. China is a powerful country. He was working with Beijing on many important projects, and was pressuring them on key issues, such as their need to get more active in fighting AIDS domestically. He would expect UNCA to understand that and not make his job harder for him. He saw no compelling need for them to invite the Taiwanese into the building. I, as an American, was too purist on the press freedom issue, he thought. I wasn't being practical. I was a fundamentalist.

Free to speak

Whatever his ups and downs over 10 years in office, Kofi leaves behind one very concrete bureaucratic legacy for journalists — a directive saying that all members of the Secretariat have the right to speak to the press within their areas of competence. One of the first things I did as Spokesperson was to pull out from my computer the Media Guidelines that I had drafted for Kofi when we were in the peacekeeping department — the ones that Boutros-Ghali put in the deep freeze. I sent them back up to Kofi; they were massaged by Shashi Tharoor and then issued. This piece of paper opened doors for the press. If I were trying to arrange an interview for a journalist with someone in the Secretariat, very often the bureaucrat would say no, out of fear. I could then just point to Kofi's directive and say, here it is in black and white from the Secretary-General himself — you can talk.

Kofi's relations with the press would turn sour in the second term as the UN became engulfed in what is known as the Oil-for-Food scandal. But even during the peak "scandal" years of 2004 and 2005 he didn't duck, maintaining his average number of interviews, press conferences and over 100 press encounters a year. "There is no doubt that the press misses him," Evelyn said to me in 2007 after Kofi left office. "For better or for worse, he was rarely boring, whether he was the subject of denunciation or he came up with news angles. If the United Nations does not produce news, it disappears from the public mind — at least that's what journalists think."

CHAPTER 11

HARMONIZING THE SYSTEM

BARONS AND BARONESSES

We call the UN system a family, and perhaps it is, in the sense that it has many members, each doing its own thing and some not talking to others. Each UN agency, fund or program has its own board of directors, its own donors and its own mandate.

The agencies are actually autonomous. The funds and programs are less so because they report to the UN, and the UN Secretary-General even nominates their heads, but they too otherwise remain largely outside his sphere of influence.

The heads of these agencies, funds and programs are sometimes referred to as Barons and Baronesses because the Secretary-General does not control them. At best, he sits among them, sometimes uneasily, as the first among equals when they gather twice a year, once abroad and once in New York, to compare notes.

Secretaries-General have in the past tried to lead this competing band of UN entities, but without much success. Kofi had two things going for him. First, there's that charm of his that allowed him to bring so many different players under the tent. Second, he exercised the influence that derives from the superstardom that he would gradually achieve in the course of his first term.

GETTING CLOSE TO THE IMF AND WORLD BANK

In Washington, there are two members of the UN family that are so privileged that they seem a separate species. The International Monetary Fund and the World Bank are in theory part of the UN system, but with their enormous resources and their systems of weighted voting that allow the wealthy donors to wield power most confidently, they exist in a rarified world apart from the rest of their kin.

Kofi extended a hand to these two institutions in the very first month of his first term. He was in Washington in January 1997, where the Clinton Administration was treating him like royalty. He had already begun to acquire star power, and no one can sense this better than a politician. The politicians in Washington wanted to have their photos taken with him. He had a positive aura. And in a little-noticed corner of the agenda of that trip to Washington was a breakfast with two of the most influential men in the UN system — Jim Wolfensohn, President of the World Bank, and Michel Camdessus, Managing Director of the IMF. At that breakfast, Kofi laid the groundwork for an unprecedented degree of cooperation between the UN itself and these two powerful financial institutions.

Nitin Desai, the Indian economist who was Kofi's Under-Secretary-General for Economic and Social Affairs, said to me, "The World Bank always used to work at a certain distance from the UN. But Jim Wolfensohn wanted to be seen as part of the UN. He wanted to be seen with Kofi Annan. And I think Kofi's credibility with Washington institutions was probably higher than that of any Secretary-General's."

Jim Wolfensohn and his wife became close friends of Kofi and Nane's in the following years. He said that the relationship was both professionally and personally rewarding. "I have never found Kofi anything but accessible and open, even when there was a lot of pressure," Jim told me. "We would have private dinners together, and the thing was that there was a mutual dependence. We could help Kofi and Kofi could help us. And most importantly, we could exchange ideas about people and about policies in a way that it would have been very difficult for me to do with almost anybody else in the international system. And that brought a great harmony between us, and a great trust."

THE CABINET

Back home, Kofi instituted cabinet-style administration. Why had no Secretary-General done this before? Beats me. Its value seems obvious. But once a week, on Wednesday mornings, he sat down with his Under-Secretaries-General to discuss policy. And thanks to satellite technology that allowed him to hook up via videoconference with UN offices elsewhere in the world, he included the heads of funds and programs based in Geneva, Vienna, Rome and Nairobi. The Barons and the Baronesses were happy to spend an hour and a half with him every week. One Baroness commented to me that these weekly meetings also gave them "a chance to keep their eyes on each other." Catherine Bertini, who headed the World Food Programme during Kofi's first term, said "he brought the disparate parts of the UN system a lot closer together."

One time in the second term, Kofi was away and his deputy Louise Frechette was in the chair. She stayed in her normal seat, leaving Kofi's, at the head of the table, vacant. The room filled up quickly and the cabinet meeting began. Shashi Tharoor, who then was Under-Secretary-General for information and therefore a cabinet member, came bursting into the room late. In fact, he made such a habit of this that Louise called him "Kramer", after the Seinfeld character who made the crash entrance his signature.

Shashi scanned the room quickly for an empty chair and didn't see the one at the back of the room. So he confidently moved toward Kofi's chair and put his hand on the back of it. By this time, discussion had stopped as all present looked aghast at Shashi. Lamin Sise broke the stunned silence, saying with a twinkle in his eye, "He hasn't left yet, Shashi." A burst of nervous laughter eased the tension; Shashi then spotted the vacant seat at the back and took it. A few years later, in 2006, he would make a credible yet unsuccessful bid to succeed Kofi as Secretary-General.

Kofi got the agencies, funds and programs to accept that in the field the UN Development Programme representative would be the first among equals. He or she would be called the UN Resident Coordinator and would try to avoid overlap and duplication among the various UN entities. Kofi also picked up on an idea of Boutros-Ghali's, which had barely gotten off the ground, to put all UN agencies, funds and programs working in a country under a single roof, called UN House. With Kofi, the idea took off. Every time he traveled, it seemed he inaugurated another new UN House. He called those working from inside the UN House his Country Team.

COORDINATING HUMANITARIAN WORK

On the humanitarian side, Kofi energized the Office for the Coordination of Humanitarian Affairs for more effective response to complex emergencies and natural disasters. He named his trusted colleague Sergio Vieira de Mello of Brazil as the first head of this unit. Like Kofi, Sergio had charm and an iron will and he began to make a difference early on by getting all the Barons and Baronesses to pull in the same direction. Sergio's principal experience had been in the field; when he met resistance to change from among the staff that he inherited from Boutros Boutros-Ghali's days, he brought in people from the front line agencies to complement them. According to his biographers George-Gordon Lennox and Annick Stevenson, who wrote *Sergio Vieira de Mello: un homme exceptionnel*, "This immediately added to the credibility of the new office and allowed it to assume leadership in the humanitarian field in an unprecedented way."

Kofi then needed Sergio in Kosovo, after that in East Timor, then as High Commissioner for Human Rights and ultimately in Baghdad. He brought in Jan Egeland of Norway to head Humanitarian Affairs in 2003. Kofi's style of course is to pick good people, give them a challenging assignment, and let them run with it. Jan's deep experience in foreign policy, his keen moral sense, his habit of speaking out and his boyish good looks all made him a notable figure of the second term. He served till the end of Kofi's mandate.

I asked Jan how the cooperation of the Barons and Baronesses was going. "It's become increasingly good," he replied. "My predecessors met resistance even from the Secretary-General, but certainly from heads of agencies, in their efforts to make the Department of Humanitarian Affairs a robust coordinator, as called for by the General Assembly. It doesn't take a rocket scientist to see that you need to have a leader to coordinate humanitarian response when there are now virtually hundreds of actors, counting the NGOs. In the UN system alone, there are a dozen agencies that get involved."

So with Kofi's moral authority and Jan's upfront leadership, the UN agencies, funds and programs in Kofi's last years came to accept the UN's lead on humanitarian emergencies. "Kofi Annan said we have to work together," said Jan. "And at crucial moments, he would send out that message. But even more important, the people he chose to head these UN aid programs are really team players. So we have a more harmonious spirit among the UN people than ever before."

THE MILLENNIUM DEVELOPMENT GOALS

Economic and social issues are the bread and butter of the UN system and where the UN makes the biggest difference in the lives of ordinary people.

Kofi shook up the UN's economic and social areas in his first year as Secretary-General, when he merged three different departments of the Secretariat into one Department of Economic and Social Affairs. I asked Nitin Desai, who headed that department, what difference Kofi made in his area over 10 years. "When Kofi took over, we had had a string of major UN conferences," he replied, "such as the 1990 children's summit, the 1992 Rio conference on environment and development, the 1995 Beijing summit on the advancement of women, the 1995 Copenhagen world summit for social development. And a very ambitious program of developmental goals had emerged from them."

"These were great conferences because they mobilized a large number of people, they set goals and they formulated policy," he went on. "But when Kofi became Secretary-General, the challenge was to move from these sorts of things to actually getting results."

Nitin saw this as the leitmotif of Kofi's contribution over 10 years, moving from grand goals and policy statements to actually getting results on the ground. And the culmination of this effort was adoption of the Millennium Development Goals, which set precise objectives to be met within a specific timeframe.

Kofi spelled out the MDGs in a report to the General Assembly in the fall of 2000, which was a Head of State Millennial Assembly. John Ruggie led the effort, aided by Andy Mack of Australia, who spent months weaving together the various reform themes — the big-ticket items — to give a major push to the larger reform effort. Kofi invited the Heads of State "to step back from today's headlines and take a broader, longer view — of the state of the world and the challenges it poses for this Organization."

The report was called "We, the Peoples", taken from the opening words of the UN Charter, emphasizing Kofi's belief in a UN that works not for governments but for the people they serve. "We must put people at the center of everything we do," the report said.

"We, the Peoples" wove together a series of global agendas into a tapestry that was nothing less than a road map to a better future. It explored the globalization of the world economy and the need for better governance. In a section called "Freedom from Want" it laid out an attack plan against poverty. In one called "Freedom from Fear", it addressed people's security nightmares — conflict, weapons of mass destruction. In "Sustaining our Future", it took on global warming and other environmental concerns. In a section on "Renewing the United Nations", it called for a more people-oriented UN that is more results-based.

But the core of the report was the MDGs — a series of specific targets to be met by specific dates, such as cutting in half by the year 2015 the proportion of people living in extreme poverty.

I asked John to describe how the concept of the MDGs was born.

"Well, it was born out of very practical considerations," he said. "When I was down on the floor in the General Assembly selling the original reform program, and that included the idea of the Millennium Summit, I kept hearing over and over again that the 50th anniversary in 1995 was such a bust that we don't need another jamboree like it. And so we had to come up with a real practical program for the Summit, if it was going to happen. It couldn't just be another event celebrating yet another anniversary. And in fact we had substantive aims in mind to push in a variety of areas. And the resistance to celebration and our strategic objectives sort of combined to make it clear to us that we had to come up with very concrete things."

The dimension that lent itself most readily to concrete things, according to John, was the set of targets that became the Millennium Development Goals. "Now we could say that the Organization is dedicated to the eradication of poverty," he said, "but that wasn't enough; we needed something that was going to focus on results, not inputs."

John said that the MDGs were going to be a social mobilization tool. "They were a metric that civil society could use to judge governments," he explained, "that politicians could use to judge one another, and also that the business community could buy into. Business understands metrics, and so if we were going to get the business community engaged in poverty alleviation and other UN goals, this was a useful vehicle to get them involved."

Nitin said that we should not underestimate what John achieved with the MDGs, which was to connect the development agenda and the broader political agenda of the UN in that famous Millennium Report. "And one of the reasons I think the MDGs have acquired so much status," he said, "is because John very successfully connected the development agenda, the human rights agenda and the broader political agenda of the UN. So I would put the MDGs at the peak of Kofi's achievements during his tenure."

Even the World Bank found them useful. Jim Wolfensohn told me in 2006, "I think it's fair to say that by setting common goals, which everybody accepted, Kofi took a very constructive step. What was not clarified, of course, was how you work together to achieve those goals. But the fact that there were common goals meant people would be more ready to work together in fields like education or health, in which both the Bank and the UN have a heavy interest, and there was an acceptance of where we were trying to get to. And I think that was helpful. I'm sure it was helpful."

Follow up by Jeff Sachs

But Kofi wasn't going to just let the Millennium Report sit there and collect dust. He told the Heads of State he was going to issue them a scorecard periodically, telling them how they were doing at achieving the Goals. And he invited them all back to a World Summit in 2005 to take stock of how they'd done in the first five years.

He then hired an outspoken young professor from Columbia University, Jeffrey Sachs, to provide intellectual underpinnings for achieving the Goals and to keep the ball rolling. He named Jeff the head of the UN Millennium Project. That project involved a global mobilization of expertise among various expert groups, such as agronomists, AIDS experts, climatologists and so on, to make specific recommendations on how to achieve the Millennium Development Goals. "We presented a report to Kofi in January 2005," Jeff told me, "14 volumes on all aspects of the MDGs. And those recommendations in essence were then adopted at the UN World Summit in September 2005. That is a step forward, but it still is not the same as achieving the Goals. It just helped to get certain ideas and plans under way."

Actually achieving the Goals is the object, and so far the world is lagging behind. I asked Jeff why that is. "The problem is not that the Goals are unachievable," he said. "The problem is that we don't have the adequate level of global cooperation to achieve them right now. The world is terribly distracted by war and by short-sightedness, so that even what would seem to be very straightforward — fulfilling the longstanding commitment of rich countries to provide 0.7 percent of their gross national product as aid in order to achieve the Goals — is not fulfilled. And it's a tremendous struggle even to raise the aid levels by fractions of one percent of rich world GNP."

"And this, in my view, is the absolute essence of the problem," Jeff continued, "because the biggest problem is in the poorest countries, precisely those who can't look after themselves."

A Challenge by Bolton

Nitin saw Jeff's work get bogged down in the controversy over the Iraq War. "My suspicion is that Kofi's one regret is that this Oil-for-Food stuff distracted attention from what he would have liked to do, which is to use that last half of his second term to really put some 'oomph' in the MDG effort."

I asked Jeff about the impact of the Oil-for-Food issue on the Goals. "I think that the Oil-for-Food scandal was used basically to pillory the UN, in my opinion, by a lot of the American right, but more as an excuse than as a real analysis. It was part and parcel of the overall absence of US leadership on the MDGs. The Iraq war launched a controversy between the US and the UN, and the Oil-for-Food scandal and how it was used politically were all part of, in my view, a period in which the US simply did not play a constructive role to achieve the globally agreed goals adopted by the UN; the MDGs were among them."

"Indeed," he continued, "it reached a point where the US Ambassador at the time, John Bolton, actually proposed to take the MDGs right out of the final agreement of the 2005 Summit. This was a proposal that led to a worldwide furious reaction, and the proposal was withdrawn. It signified not only the lack of US commitment to the Goals, but actually working against them at a diplomatic level."

John Bolton was perhaps the only person Kofi genuinely didn't like. He never told me that, but I just feel it. Kofi got on with Saddam Hussein, Jesse Helms, Muammar Qaddafi. He even liked George W. Bush. "I didn't like his policies," he once commented to me, "but I always got on well with both him and his wife." But Bolton was a house-wrecker at the UN; he almost single-handedly undid the years of work that Kofi had put into the major reform proposals that he put before the 2005 Assembly.

At the end of 2006, President Bush hosted a private farewell dinner for Kofi. Protocol dictated that John Bolton be there. Bolton too was leaving because there was so much opposition in the US Senate to his appointment two years earlier that the President had to appoint him during a Senate recess, and recess appointments are limited to two years. After the dinner, a reporter asked Bolton if there wasn't "more of a healing process" between him and Kofi as each of them prepared to leave the UN. Tough to the end, Bolton replied, "Nope, nobody sang 'Kumbaya,'" referring to the song with the theme of "coming together". The next day, another reporter asked Kofi about Bolton's comment on "Kumbaya". Kofi laughed and replied, "Yes, but does he know how to sing it?"

The style of the man

Carlos Lopes of Guinea Bissau, the senior political director in Kofi's office in his last year as Secretary-General, sees in the subtle way the MDGs emerged a measure of what he called "the style of the man". He pointed out that the Millennium Declaration adopted by the Heads of State at the 2000 General Assembly nowhere mentions the Millennium Development Goals. It just approved the principles on which the goals are based. Once he had the principles approved, Kofi asked four organizations — the Organization for Economic Cooperation and Development, the IMF, UNDP and the World Bank — to work on the statistical side. In fact, Carlos said, UNDP had a team of 10 people working almost full time on the MDGs. And it wasn't until the summit in Johannesburg nearly two years later that the MDGs appeared officially in a UN document. "It was all basically internal advocacy based on the Millennium Declaration," Carlos declared in May 2009 at a press conference in Geneva to launch the French edition of this book. "It took a lot of persuasion; it took a lot of effort behind the scenes to get the final outcome, which is the shifting of the debate on economics from prescription to objectives."

"And that is a major contribution to the international debate on economics," Carlos said. The experts no longer just prescribe what needs to be done; since adoption of the MDGs they specify the objectives they want to reach by when. "Nobody really challenges it," he asserted. "When the G-20 met this year [2009] to discuss the world economic crisis, they described objectives, not prescriptions. So it has become the norm."

The MDGs survived US indifference and John Bolton's assault in 2005 and they remain in place. Through them, Kofi pulled the UN system together and pointed it in a concrete direction. Those working in the field see that as a permanent improvement.

PEACEBUILDING

The MDGs were not the only major harmonizing reform by Kofi that survived John Bolton's ax at the end of 2005. Another was peacebuilding.

Carolyn McAskie had 30 years' experience as a Canadian diplomat and aid expert when Kofi brought her into the UN to be the Deputy Emergency Relief Coordinator. He then appointed her head of the UN peacekeeping mission in Burundi. And when the General Assembly approved his idea of creating a new Peacebuilding Commission to help countries in conflict rebuild themselves economically and socially to solidify the peace, he asked Carolyn to head the Secretariat office that would service the new Commission.

"It was Boutros Boutros-Ghali, in his landmark report of 1992, who first talked about the need for peacebuilding to bridge the gap between peacekeeping and development," she told me. "And since then, we have been refining the concept. But it was during Kofi Annan's time that we were galvanized into actually doing something about it. And I think this is going to be one of his abiding legacies, the fact that he seized this idea and turned it into something that actually happened."

Carolyn said that Kofi's success in getting Member States to do something entirely new was the result of two things. First, more than ever before there was a shared agenda on development. There was no longer much controversy. "The policy coherence," she said, "has been growing over time and culminated with Kofi Annan defining the Millennium Development Goals."

Second, Carolyn cites the growing success of peacekeeping after the frightening events of the 1990s — Somalia, Rwanda, Bosnia. "The Brahimi Report — another important part of Kofi Annan's legacy," she went on, "galvanized both the Secretariat and the Security Council, in my view. The kinds of things we're doing in peacekeeping now would be unimaginable 10 years ago." When I asked for examples, she said, "I would say that Kosovo was a turning point. Kosovo and then Timor and then Afghanistan and Congo paved the way for a new found confidence in the Security Council to address these issues."

Human Security Report

To further put things in context, Carolyn cited the 2005 Human Security Report by Andrew Mack. Andy Mack was the Crocodile Dundee of Kofi's brain trust from 1998 to 2001, when he was Director of the Strategic Planning Unit that Kofi had created under John Ruggie. I say Crocodile Dundee because in addition to being head of the Human Security Centre at the University of British Columbia, where he wrote this report, and doing stints at a string of first-rate universities, this Aussie's resumé includes being a pilot in the UK Royal Air Force, a meteorologist in Antarctica, a diamond prospector in Sierra Leone and a journalist for the *BBC*. Andy's Human Security Report pointed out what many people overlooked, that since the end of the Cold War, international efforts at peacemaking and peacekeeping and peacebuilding, spearheaded by the UN, had produced the first downward trend in political violence — apart from international terrorism — after nearly five decades of steady growth. Wars today, he concluded, are fewer and less deadly.

Carolyn said that when we look at Lebanon or Afghanistan or Iraq today, we think the world's going to hell in a hand basket. But she invites us to look at the next level down, where real progress is being made in places like Haiti, Liberia, Sierra Leone, the Congo and where she headed a UN peacekeeping mission — Burundi. "So, if you accept my premise," she concludes, "that on development we're clearer now on what we have to do, and on peacekeeping, that we're making real progress, then, for me, that throws into relief the realization that you have to do something very specifically institutional about that gap between peacekeeping and development."

Protecting the Investment

Carolyn then mentioned another study, this one by Oxford University economist Paul Collier, which showed that half the countries that come out of political conflict fall back into crisis in the first decade. That study, she said, made her and others realize that we were not doing enough to protect the investment in peacekeeping. Her mission in Burundi cost $300 million a year. The UN mission in Liberia cost something like $750 million. "Where is our commitment to protect that investment?" she asked.

And the idea was born of creating a Peacebuilding Commission to take countries in conflict from the peace negotiations to peacekeeping to the development investment. However, this new effort was going to rely on an unprecedented degree of cooperation among the Barons and the Baronesses of the system. "Peacebuilding should not be something new that we do on the ground; it should be something different," Carolyn said.

"So in answer to my colleagues from the UN agencies who say, well, what does this mean for us, my answer is, it means that we will now work together on how you are doing what you are doing. It's no longer business as usual. Peacebuilding is not something in addition to the country program for UNICEF or WHO or UNDP. Peacebuilding is how they will implement their country program within their existing resources."

Tough words. But one of Kofi Annan's last significant acts as Secretary-General was to issue the report of his Panel on Coherence, aimed exactly at this issue of coordination among UN agencies, funds and programs that should help as well. That report said that the UN system, in its work in the field, should "deliver as one." "And the issue is that when you deliver as one in a post-conflict situation," Carolyn said, "you should be doing it with the objective of keeping country X on track and not increasing the risk that it will fall back into conflict."

CHAPTER 12

HUMAN RIGHTS
AND THE RULE OF LAW

MAKING HUMAN RIGHTS CENTRAL

Human Rights advocates tend to see Kofi as something of a patron saint. Joanna Weschler, who represented Human Rights Watch at the UN for more than a decade, said this to me: "No Secretary-General has openly said he was against human rights, although at least one, Annan's immediate predecessor Boutros Boutros-Ghali, in my view was hostile to the notion. And all of them, with the notable exception of Kofi Annan, essentially considered state sovereignty sacrosanct, as always trumping human rights".

Joanna commented that in 2006, when candidates to succeed Kofi were for the first time openly campaigning for the job of Secretary-General, not one was forthright regarding his position on human rights. "You don't win popularity contests at the UN by promoting human rights," she commented. "I actually think it is difficult, and sometimes politically costly, for a Secretary-General to be publicly and adamantly *for* human rights. Kofi Annan showed considerable courage by tackling the issue head on, when from his very first press conference he started talking about the centrality of human rights."

Mary Robinson

In 1997, Kofi made a bold choice in nominating Mary Robinson, the former President of Ireland, as UN High Commissioner for Human Rights. He told her not to be afraid to be an independent voice, and she wasn't. She spoke out against what she saw as the disproportionate use of force by NATO in Serbia in the spring of 1999 and about the infringement of civil rights in the US in the wake of the attacks of 9/11 in 2001.

She had initially told Kofi she would serve for only one four-year term, and the US and possibly others seemed happy when that term was nearing an end. They saw her as too outspoken. But then she changed her mind. Kofi had to really squeeze Washington to go along with an extension, and the most he could get their consent for was one year. At the end of that year, Mary again said she would stay on until the end of the second four-year term, but Kofi had no political capital left. He had to replace her. But in choosing Sergio Vieira de Mello to succeed her, he kept the bar high for her office.

I spoke to Mary in New York in 2006 where she heads a human rights NGO, Realizing Rights/The Ethical Globalization Initiative, and asked her how she evaluates Kofi's contribution to human rights. She regrets that he sometimes let political obstacles get in the way of his defense of human rights as she would have liked to have seen it, but otherwise gives him high marks. "Kofi Annan was the first Secretary-General to recognize that human rights were central," she said to me. "I think the political barriers he faced were very strong and at times I felt that the Secretary-General could have been stronger in practice on human rights issues while I served as High Commissioner. If I could have gotten to him personally, he might have been more supportive; sometimes the barriers were those surrounding him who felt that concern for human rights would only complicate political and peacekeeping challenges."

I asked her for an example. "I happened to be visiting Serbia in 1999 during the US-led attacks," she replied, "and I saw the results of a cluster-bombing of a poor housing complex in Niš minutes after it happened. I spoke out about it and got a bit of a rap. This isn't something that you interfere with, I was told. Similarly, during the bombing of Afghanistan, I supported the call of civil society groups for a humanitarian corridor for relief aid and was really criticized for that, and directly so by Kofi. I found that very hurtful. It was as though the political pressure was such that I was dispensable, that political considerations overrode the principled human rights approach." She paused a moment. "Maybe it has to."

"Having said that," she added, "I feel that Kofi acted on behalf of human rights with increasing strength, and that he's made huge progress for human rights at the UN. In his report, *In Larger Freedom*, he makes the link between security, development and human rights — that nexus is incredibly important — and I hope it will be carried forward by the new Secretary-General."

The canton of Geneva offered the United Nations the magnificently restored Palais Wilson on Lake Geneva and Kofi decided to make it the headquarters of the High Commissioner for Human Rights. Symbolically, Mary said, that was important. After she left the post, Kofi successfully lobbied the General Assembly to vote new resources for the office of the High Commissioner. She gave him points for that as well.

The Human Rights Council

In bureaucratic terms, Kofi's main contribution was getting Member States to shut down the Human Rights Commission in Geneva, which had become a total sham. Governments teamed up with each other to block serious human rights assessments of one another, and many human rights advocates had lost confidence in it as an institution.

Kofi's High-Level Panel made passing reference to the idea that sometime in the future a Human Rights Council might replace the Commission. But in fashioning his report, Kofi seized that idea and ran with it. He proposed giving the new Council limited membership and real teeth. But human rights in the United Nations is so politicized that Kofi's proposal became a political football. The General Assembly watered it down considerably and US Ambassador John Bolton entered the fray in a way that just made things worse. What emerged was not much better that what existed before, and some say it is worse, although optimists still hold that in the long run it will be an improvement.

"The new Human Rights Council, which Kofi worked so hard to get governments to accept, is not off to a promising start," said Mary, "although that is no fault of his. I lay the blame in part with the United States and Europe. They should have been more vigilant and worked harder; it's the baddies that get up earlier in the morning and work hard. That's heartbreaking."

Kofi's voice on human rights was buttressed by his chief speechwriter, Edward Mortimer, who not only found the right words, but also helped refine the concepts in a string of inspiring speeches that laid down the intellectual and moral framework for those on the front lines in the field. Mary said that part of Kofi's legacy stems from the importance of language. "In speech after speech," she said, "he highlighted the central role of human rights – whether in tackling HIV/AIDS, poverty or deeply entrenched conflicts. He rejected convincingly any suggestion that human rights are a 'Western' construct, and gifted human rights defenders worldwide with many quotations to inspire them and others to speak truth to power, and to strengthen the moral authority of human rights values everywhere."

Sergio de Mello's tour as High Commissioner was of course cut brutally short when Kofi, under pressure from Washington, sent Sergio to Baghdad for what was to be a short stint of a few months and where a suicide bomber killed him and 21 others.

Louise Arbour

Kofi's next nominee as High Commissioner was Louise Arbour, a feisty Canadian jurist who took on a high international profile in 1996 when she became the Chief Prosecutor for the International Tribunals for the Former Yugoslavia and Rwanda. Three years later, she left that job to become a justice of the Supreme Court of Canada.

Kofi had a run-in with Louise when she was at the Tribunals, she told me. The High Representative in Bosnia, Carl Bildt, had apparently complained to Kofi that Louise was not indicting enough Croats and Bosniaks and that the Tribunal was therefore looking very anti-Serb. Kofi conveyed Bildt's concerns to Louise in a letter, asking her to explain what her prosecutorial strategy was. Well, that was like a red flag to a bull.

"And I wrote back and I said, no, I can't account to you because this is within my discretion," she told me. "I run these investigations and the statute says that I shall not seek nor receive instructions from any government nor anybody else, and that includes you. Well, I didn't say it quite that way, but that was the gist of it." That said, she did him the courtesy of giving him an explanation of her strategy, but she said that she told him, "But I just want to put on the record that I don't account for how I proceed — except eventually to the Security Council, which appointed me and presumably could dismiss me — but I'll explain why we're moving this way, so that you can feel at ease." She said that he understood and that "he respected these kinds of clean lines in our work."

I spoke to Louise in her office at the Palais Wilson. She told me that Kofi almost gave her "a heart attack" in 2004 when he asked her to give up the Supreme Court — which no one in Canada ever does voluntarily — to become the new High Commissioner for Human Rights. "I think he quite didn't get it," she said to me laughing. "I said, now you don't understand, when you go to the Supreme Court of Canada, you come out in a casket, or on your seventy-fifth birthday they drag you out. Nobody leaves the Court. He really blew me away and caused me headaches for several months."

But Kofi is hard to resist. He negotiated with the Canadians and eventually convinced Louise to take the job of High Commissioner. She brought both integrity and dynamism to the office. I asked her how she assesses Kofi on human rights; she didn't hesitate. "I think he's the greatest human rights Secretary-General that the UN has had so far," she said. "Particularly in his reform agenda, where he articulated the centrality of human rights as the third pillar of the system, which is coming right back to the roots of the Charter."

Louise said that Kofi was supportive of her efforts in two important areas. First, he moved the system from "the dusty normative framework in which we were happily stuck, to the great delight of Member States" to the implementation of human rights. "He's always been supportive of making the Office of the High Commissioner for Human Rights stronger, more visible, more operational, more active," she said. And the second is the financial growth of her office, which Mary mentioned. "And I think he gets it," she added. "I think he's very intuitive about human rights, which is, again, not true for much of the system."

"He had the most intuitive sense of the importance of individual rights — that this was not just about states and governments," she concluded. "He has an almost personal relationship with the people we call rights-holders, people who have the right to assert what the Universal Declaration of Human Rights contains for them."

THE ADVANCEMENT OF WOMEN

You would think that the advancement of women would be an easy cause to advocate. After all, in theory, it should get you 51 percent of the vote. The problem is that the power is largely concentrated in the other 49 percent.

Kofi was a strong advocate of women's rights, up to a point. His symbolic actions were strong, starting with the creation of a post of Deputy Secretary-General, which he said in advance he

Nane maintained an active program, speaking out primarily on women's rights and AIDS awareness and prevention.

would give to a woman. And he did. Once the General Assembly approved of the new post, he gave the job to Louise Frechette, the Deputy Defense Minister of Canada. He named a number of impressive women to key posts, where he had the authority to do so, but these appointments were small in number compared to the overall total, and advocates of women's rights were frankly disappointed that he didn't do more. That said, they did see him as on their side.

Kofi appointed Rachel Mayanja of Uganda his Special Adviser on Gender Issues and the Advancement of Women. "It was during his time in personnel that we first had a serious policy on sexual harassment," she said, "so that even before his tenure as Secretary-General, we can credit him for progressive work on gender equality."

Rachel visited southern Sudan to meet with women who had been involved in the peace process there, and when she introduced herself as Kofi Annan's representative, she was surprised at how many knew his name. They told her that Kofi had been extremely helpful to them when he visited the region. "He took the women aside," said one woman, "and asked us to organize ourselves to negotiate and urged us to be firm." Rachel said, "We have seen his commitment to women in conflict situations, encouraging women to become players and putting them at the table for peace negotiations."

Under Kofi, the UN's personnel policies evolved to a point where the Organization began thinking like a good employer, Rachel said. And by becoming a good employer, it began paying attention to issues of interest to women in a way that would attract them to work for the UN and keep them there.

Noeleen Heyzer and UNIFEM

A real dynamo of the UN system in the struggle for women's rights was Noeleen Heyzer of Singapore, who headed the UN Development Fund for Women, better known as UNIFEM.

She told me that her first encounter with Kofi involved violence against women, an issue, she said, with which the UN had not been very comfortable. Her objective was to help governments review their laws on domestic violence and rape, and she organized a black-and-white photo exhibit called "Wall of Shame, Wall of Hope" that included graphic images of women of different cultures being subjected to abuse.

She had invited Nane Annan to open the exhibit, and some people around the Secretary-General started pushing the panic button arguing that Nane shouldn't go because the photos were too controversial. On the day of the opening, Noeleen said, Kofi went down to look at the photos himself. "If violence is a problem," he said, "we should admit it." Nane opened the exhibit, which was a big success; the exhibit then launched a campaign and that resulted in the General Assembly creating a system-wide Trust Fund to End Violence Against Women.

Using the Trust Fund

Noeleen then wanted to showcase some of the successful strategies supported by the Trust Fund money and so organized a UN inter-agency multi-media event using the latest technologies to link five sites around the world in order to urge an end to violence against women. She wanted Kofi to participate. Again, she said, those close to Kofi urged him to stay away from the event, which was being staged in the General Assembly Hall on International Women's Day in 1999. Those same aides told Noeleen that if he came at all, it would only be for two or three minutes. But Kofi surprised them by showing up and staying for more than an hour. And then in 2001 when he was awarded the Conrad N. Hilton Humanitarian Prize of $100,000, he donated that money to the Trust Fund. "I was impressed by the way he took personal risks," Noeleen told me. "He didn't just listen blindly to his advisers; he checked and then he decided for himself."

Women, Peace and Security

The women's movement was getting increasingly involved in women's role in peacekeeping and peacebuilding, and Noeleen saw the opportunity to try to get a Security Council resolution recognizing that role. Kofi could easily have stopped her from addressing the Council, but he didn't. She brought women from conflict zones to meet with Council members. As a result, the Council adopted in 2000 Resolution 1325 on women and security, which is described as a watershed in the evolution of international women's rights.

After 9/11, the fall of the Taliban in Afghanistan provided a test case for Resolution 1325, and Noeleen sought to engage Afghan women in the peace process and on demanding their rights as a new government was formed. Those on the political side of the UN weren't thrilled with her involvement, but Kofi didn't tell her to back off. Instead he included her on his team for the donors' conference on Afghanistan.

Noeleen was on a roll, and looked longingly at what Kofi had done for human rights. He made it a central pillar of the UN and he got substantially greater funding for the High Commissioner. She thought he could have done the same thing for women's rights, and that he missed a great opportunity to do so in 2005 when there was a major review conference on women's issues. But Kofi dropped the ball, she said. "At that time there were so many things on his mind; there was Iraq; the Oil-for-Food issue. There were so many things that disengaged him."

McAskie on Women in the UN

When I asked Carolyn McAskie of Canada what she thought of Kofi's record on women's issues, she told me, "I think he's done his best, but I'm not entirely convinced he's always had the best advice. And maybe we haven't done enough to ensure that there are good women candidates up there." Still, she said, "I think that the profile of women in the UN has improved during his tenure, but we still have a long way to go. There are a lot of women in my generation who have moved up the line and who are available for senior jobs. The pool is growing. And the UN has to know that."

THE RULE OF LAW

Just as economic and social issues are at the heart of the UN agenda, although totally obscured by the headline issues of war and peace, the rule of law is that agenda's soul. Member governments use the UN to build up, gradually and over time, international rules or norms to live by. It's called the UN's normative function, and it is essential.

Hans Corell, Kofi's Swedish Legal Counsel, loved to quote the Romans: *Ubi civitas, ibi jus* — where there's a society, there is also a legal order. He also relishes reminding us that the oldest known collection of laws dates from 2100 B.C. in Sumer — in other words, Iraq.

International Criminal Court

During Kofi's 10 years as Secretary-General, dramatic advances in international law took place. The most notable was the coming into being, on 1 July 2002, of the International Criminal Court (the ICC). The ICC was the missing link in the international justice system. It was created to prosecute those who commit genocide, crimes against humanity or war crimes, when their home government is either unable or unwilling to do so.

Kofi was a big supporter of the ICC concept. The US was not. When the treaty was almost finalized, Kofi convened a conference in Rome in June/July 1998 to try and wrap it up. It was to last for five weeks. There was a lot of horse-trading and weakening of the draft text to get more support.

Hans Corell was in Rome while Kofi was paying an official visit to Argentina as the end point was near. As convener of the conference, Kofi needed to be in Rome for the signing, if an agreement was reached, and he was on the phone regularly with Hans. It got to the point where Kofi was going to have to interrupt his official visit and fly out of Buenos Aires that night if there was a breakthrough in Rome. A Secretary-General *never* interrupts an official visit, but this was important.

In one phone call, Hans told him that they were still counting the votes, but advised Kofi to go to the airport. Kofi's security bought the tickets and Kofi called Hans again. "Is there an agreement," he asked? The results of the vote had just been announced — the treaty on the ICC had been adopted. "There was such joy in the room," Hans told me. "People were hugging each other, some laughing, some in tears. And I held my phone in the air so that Kofi could hear all the excitement, and he said to me, 'I guess there's a treaty', and he flew to Rome to address the signing ceremony the next day."

I was not with Kofi in Latin America; one of my Spanish-speaking deputies was. But I flew to Rome to join him for the signing. There was electricity in the room the morning after the vote — here were delegates, lawyers, NGOs celebrating a great breakthrough while the US delegation sat in their seats unsmiling. There were many speakers, but Kofi's words were the most quoted. "No doubt many of us would have liked a Court vested with even more far-reaching powers, but that should not lead us to minimize the breakthrough you have achieved," he said. "The establishment of the Court is still a gift of hope to future generations, and a giant step forward in the march towards universal human rights and the rule of law."

Washington threw obstacles in the way of the march toward the signing of the ICC statute, but it just kept rolling, with Kofi cheering from the sidelines. President Clinton had signed the statute as one of his last acts as President, but the Bush Administration, spurred on by John Bolton, who had been made a senior official in the State Department, "unsigned" the treaty in May 2002.

Three-and-a-half years after he left office, Kofi continued to press powerful governments that had not signed the treaty to do so. These included the US, China and Russia. In an Op-Ed in the *International Herald Tribune* on 31 May 2010, he wrote, "There must be no going back or lessening of momentum. Our challenge is to protect the innocent by building a court so strong, universal and effective that it will deter even the most determined of despots."

Special Courts and Extraordinary Chambers

In June 2000, the President of Sierra Leone wrote to Kofi to ask for a UN tribunal to try those who had carried out atrocities against his people, including lopping off the limbs of men, women and children. Kofi forwarded the letter to the Security Council, which in August asked him to negotiate an agreement with Sierra Leone to establish a Special Court. A deal was signed in January 2002, and the court is functioning nicely — witness the Charles Taylor trial.

Hans Corell, who led the talks on the Special Court for Sierra Leone, also negotiated long and hard with the Cambodian Government to set up something like a UN tribunal to try Khmer Rouge leaders, whose fanatical rule resulted in the deaths of more than an eighth of the population, or 1.7 million people. The talks were tough, and at one point Kofi lost confidence in the process and withdrew from the negotiations. However, the General Assembly pushed him back in and a less-than-perfect agreement was eventually signed in mid-2003 establishing the Extraordinary Chambers in the national court system to carry out trials of former Khmer Rouge leaders. After years of delay and doubt, in February 2009, the first trial got under way when a senior Khmer Rouge leader by the nickname of Duch was put on trial for the torture and murder of some 15,000 people at a prison in Phnom Penh.

These special courts come on top of the International Tribunals for the former Yugoslavia (1993) and for Rwanda (1994), created by the Security Council on Boutros-Ghali's watch, and together form impressive building blocks of the rule of international law.

Kofi and the Rule of Law

In early 1999, Kofi called his Under-Secretaries together for a retreat to discuss the priorities for the new millennium. He asked each of them to write a paper, which he circulated a few days in advance of the meeting. Hans, of course, wrote his on the rule of law. He said it was his determined opinion that the root of all the world's conflicts was a lack of democracy and no rule of law. As Hans read the papers of his peers, he felt that although they didn't use the term "rule of law", their ideas were similar to his. So he cut a few lines from this paper and a few lines from that and pasted them together. I'll let Hans tell the rest of the story.

"At the retreat, each of us presented our papers, and when it was my turn, of course, everybody smiled and said, you know, what can you expect from the Legal Counsel, and all that. But then I distributed my second paper, the one made up of snippets from 15 or 16 other submissions, and that hit the meeting like a bomb. They saw the common thread. In the ensuing discussion, we started listing the issues on the board. And at the end of the meeting, we concluded unanimously on two priority themes for the new millennium: number one, obviously, peace and security, and number two, the rule of law. And the Secretary-General was faithful to that ever since; he reverted to this topic time and again in his tenure."

The profile of the rule of law gradually rose within the UN. In September 2003, the United Kingdom put the subject on the agenda of the Security Council — the first time that that ever happened. Then in June 2006, the Council adopted a statement that starts off, "The Security Council reaffirms its commitment to the Charter of the United Nations and international law, which are indispensable foundations of a more peaceful, prosperous and just world." The increased attention to the rule of law also found its way into the General Assembly. In September 2005, heads of state adopted the so-called Summit Resolution committing them to actively protect and promote all human rights, the rule of law and democracy.

When Leona Forman of the Information Department came up with the idea of setting up a treaty-signing table at the 2000 Millennium Summit, Kofi seized on it. In April of that year, he sent out letters to all Heads of State inviting them to sign or ratify certain treaties when they came to New York in September. Hans created a media-friendly setting just inside the Delegates' Entrance to the UN, and the Heads of State or Government could be seen on television at home signing this or that international treaty. It was such a success that treaty-signing events became an annual fixture at the UN, with a different treaty area being emphasized each time.

On Kofi and the law, Hans concluded, "He is not a lawyer, but I must say I was impressed, as his legal counselor, at the sensitivity he showed to legal matters.

CHAPTER 13

THE REFORM
SECRETARY-GENERAL

UN reform is a perennial issue. Every Secretary-General has taken a crack at it. I was told that Boutros-Ghali once said to a journalist, "I've been here two years and I still haven't figured out how this place works." And Ban Ki-Moon, speaking to UN agency chiefs in September 2008, vented his frustration with trying to get the UN to work right. "We all know the UN is a huge bureaucracy," he said in Turin, Italy. "Coming here, 20 months ago, that prospect didn't bother me. After all, I was Korean foreign minister. I spent many years in large organizations. Trust me. I knew how to play the game. Then I arrived in New York. There is bureaucracy, I discovered...and then there is the UN."

Mike Berlin, who covered the UN for the *Washington Post* from 1973 to 1988, once did a freelance piece for my UNA publication *The Inter Dependent* based on an interview with Secretary-General Javier Perez de Cuellar. Perez de Cuellar lamented that half his meetings with Ambassadors had to do with appointments — in other words, the Ambassadors lobbied regularly to get their nationals jobs at the UN. The UN Charter emphasizes that in hiring one should take into account "the necessity of securing the highest standards of efficiency, competence, and integrity". But it adds that recruiting on as wide a geographical basis as possible is also important. Through that door march the lobbyists. It's a miracle that we got any good people at all. In that same interview, Perez de Cuellar muttered that only 1 in 10 staff members do useful work.

So Kofi faced the same mess as all other Secretaries-General. But three things made him special. First, he was a trained manager, not a diplomat. Second, he had the inside track; after more than 30 years in the UN, he knew the system inside and out. And third, he made UN reform a major priority during his 10 years in office. He also put his foot down on lobbying. Ambassadors came much less frequently to ask for jobs for their nationals. When a journalist asked him in his first few months whether he was disappointed in the outcome of his reform efforts, he gave one of his classic quotes, "Reform is a process, not an event." He had to say that over and over.

"Something doable"

Kofi initially placed Canadian millionaire Maurice Strong in charge of steering the reform effort. Strong had chaired the Stockholm environment conference in 1972, had headed the UN Environment Programme and knew the UN system well. To energize the process, Kofi then asked the much younger John Ruggie to join the effort; he had recruited Ruggie from Columbia University's School of International and Public Affairs, where he was dean. John first came to my attention when he was at Berkeley, writing innovative pieces on international political economy. I asked him to be an adviser and contributor to my publications at the UN Association, before I joined the UN. John once told me that university politics is one of the roughest games in the business. If that is so, he had good training to work at the UN. One of the first jobs Kofi gave him was to sell the reform agenda to the General Assembly.

"The game plan was to begin with something that was doable," he told me in a telephone interview. From there, the proposals would become increasingly ambitious. So at the outset, he and Kofi "resisted addressing questions related to the big political picture and what the UN's role in the new era will be in order to focus on some pretty clear and straightforward — administrative, budgetary and other issues that needed to be done no matter what." But they built into the process follow-up activity, including, most important, "a commitment by the General Assembly to convene the Millennium Summit, for which we had grander plans".

After Kofi put the July 1997 agenda on the table, Ruggie followed up. He did what's called in American politics, "working the floor". I don't think it was ever done at the UN before. "There had been a tradition of blindly sending recommendations down to the General Assembly," John said, "and as somebody who follows American politics, I was sensitive to the fact that anything could happen once you send this thing down there. You've got to work the floor; you've got to create the informal contacts. And so Kofi said, go ahead." So John circulated among delegations, chatting them up, answering their questions about the reform agenda, picking up intelligence. When he saw a problem only Kofi could fix, he arranged for him to talk to a group of Ambassadors in a private meeting to sort it out. And it worked. The General Assembly approved Kofi's reform proposals at their fall 1997 session.

Included in that package was the organizing of the Secretariat's work around five themes: peace and security; economic and social affairs; development cooperation; humanitarian affairs; and human rights. Kofi set up four sectoral committees to coordinate policy in the first four areas, insisting that human rights, the fifth, cut across all of them. His emphasis on human rights was unprecedented, and would eventually become an important part of his legacy.

Kofi kept slugging away at reform on two tracks — things he could do under his own authority, and things he needed Member States' approval to do. He didn't just cut staff and clean up management; he tried to get the Member States to overhaul the UN's institutions, including Security Council reform, then General Assembly reform, and Human Rights Commission reform.

In the category of things he could do under his own authority, he created cabinet-style administration, as I already mentioned, meeting weekly with his senior advisers and department heads, but also including the heads of funds and programs, such as UNICEF, or the UN Environment Programme. He brought the UN family closer together.

Catherine Bertini is an American who headed the UN's World Food Programme and later served as Kofi's senior manager. I spoke to her by phone in early 2009, and she said of the cabinet meetings, "We were all doing our own thing up until then and that really pulled us all together in a way that I think was very important for his ability to manage a very disparate group of organizations and people. So I found those very, very useful." Kofi insisted that the cabinet meet weekly, even when he was away. Catherine commented, laughing, "But parenthetically, Fred, they were always more useful when he was there than when somebody else was chairing the meeting. Because he always lent a perspective that we needed to hear and learn from."

The Security Council

Kofi eliminated Boutros-Ghali's management approach, which concentrated power in the hands of just a few people. Under Boutros-Ghali, Department heads did not report directly to him but to one of three deputies who worked with him on the 38th floor. As I said earlier, Boutros usually did not brief the Security Council himself; he had one of his deputies do it for him. Kofi eliminated the three deputy posts and had Department heads report directly to him; they also sat around the table with him once a week at the cabinet meeting.

As for the Security Council, Kofi sensed the strain that existed between the Council and Boutros and moved to change things. He attended all important Council meetings himself, and he allowed anyone, no matter how junior, to report to the Council if that person was the best qualified person to brief the members. This policy greatly improved the quality of the Secretariat's briefings to the Council because it was no longer concentrated in the hands of a single individual. As a result, relations with the Council improved.

David Malone, a Canadian diplomat who has written widely on the Council, told me, "Boutros-Ghali, in retrospect, made a significant tactical error in deciding that he would limit his personal engagement with the Security Council and communicate with the Council through an intermediary in the person of Chinmaya Gharekhan, a very accomplished Indian diplomat. This set the backs of the Permanent Five ambassadors very much up and because the Secretary-General didn't follow their debates as closely as he might have, even though I'm sure Gharekhan reported faithfully what was going on, he was often somewhat tone-deaf in his communications with Council members, particularly, of course, and famously, Madeleine Albright."

Kofi wasn't going to make this same mistake, nor was he temperamentally inclined to. "Kofi Annan," Malone went on, "having observed all of this unfold, and being inclined anyway towards a multiplicity of human contacts — Kofi is nothing if not open to people — decided to junk that approach, which had not served Boutros-Ghali well, and to engage personally and much more frequently with the Security Council."

The General Assembly

Kofi also streamlined his servicing of the General Assembly, putting page limits on reports and time limits on the servicing of meetings. He actually told Member States that if they were going to meet after 6:00 p.m., he wasn't going to provide interpreters and note-takers. It worked.

I spoke about General Assembly reform to Chen Jian of China. He was one of the lesser-known UN officials, but the UN could not function without his staff. They service meetings of the General Assembly and its committees, of the Security Council, of the Economic and Social Council and other bodies, including editing, translating, typing, printing and distributing all parliamentary documentation.

Jian is soft-spoken with a playful sense of irony. He remembered the first time he came to the UN as a member of the first Chinese delegation from Beijing in 1972, following the General Assembly's ouster of Taiwan. The head of that delegation, Qiao Guanhua, who later became Foreign Minister, said to Jian, "The United Nations is a place where we have mountains of documents and sea waves of meetings, one after another." Jian then said to me, "Now after more than 30 years, I've come back to head this department which helps to produce these mountains of documents and sea waves of meetings."

Jian ended his first year as head of a UN department, 2001, with a big budget deficit and he was profoundly embarrassed. He called in a consultant who told him he needed to change his approach. He had to stop saying yes every time delegates asked for a meeting or for something to be translated into six languages. He had to stop servicing and start managing.

So Jian drew up a plan and presented it to Kofi; Kofi liked it and told him to go for it. Jian began by declaring that there would be no more night meetings or weekend meetings, with the exception of the plenary of the General Assembly, the Security Council and high-level meetings of the Economic and Social Council. Then he announced that all intergovernmental bodies must each live within an entitlement of a limited number of meetings per year, otherwise he would not service them. "Through this procedure, we put discipline into this intergovernmental process," he said.

After some grumbling, everybody fully grasped the concept. And Jian was actually told by some diplomats that they appreciated it because their families could now know when they would be coming home to dinner. Another major plus was that he was living within his budget.

Jian then imposed order on the production of documents. He asked General Assembly committees, for example, to draw up a plan of work in advance, estimate when the committee report would be needed and he would then give that report a production "slot".

Kofi started something he called an Annual Compact with his department heads, by which they would commit to him what they would produce in the next 12 months. At Jian's suggestion, Kofi started putting in those Annual Compacts a commitment to meet their production slot deadlines. It took a couple of years, but eventually everyone was working in their slot.

The General Assembly has long sought to impose limits on documentation, and during Kofi's term they formally set two limits. The Secretariat should hold its reports to 16 pages each and delegations should try to hold theirs to 20 pages. Jian said, "By this means we were able to reduce the number pages of documents, and also make them more concise."

Jian also proposed, and the General Assembly agreed, that, where possible, different reports on similar issues should be combined. Jian was obviously pleased. "So by using these three methods, slotting, page limits and consolidation of reports," he said, "our department has turned from deficit to surplus over the past four years. And in all this, the support of Kofi Annan was indispensable." Kofi approved Jian's proposal to change the name of the department from "General Assembly Affairs and Conference Servicing" to "General Assembly Affairs and Conference Management".

The Deputy

Kofi created the post of Deputy Secretary-General, named Louise Frechette to the job, and gave her key portfolios to manage, including overseeing the reform agenda. He spread the workload.

I spoke to Louise by phone after she had left the UN and asked her if she thought her job made a difference to Kofi. "I think it relieved him and the rest of his staff from the need to tackle day in and day out all kinds of coordination and management problems," she said. "I saw myself, really, as a helpful fixer more than anything else." She too complained that people failed to see the nature of the UN as an intergovernmental institution rather than a corporation. "The only thing that I realized very late in the day is that while I knew what my role was — and I think most people in the Secretariat understood in what capacity I acted — the outside world assumed that I was the Chief Operating Officer of the Organization," she said, "that I had the authority to run the organization. I had no such authority, just the confidence of the Secretary General to resolve problems and make people work together."

Catherine Bertini thought that the appointment of Louise was useful, "because she took on a lot of issues that needed to be solved that were just too complicated to have gone to Kofi, or too time consuming, but for a smooth-running organization needed to be dealt with and she did that well."

The Brahimi Report on Peacekeeping

Kofi knew from his experience running the peacekeeping department that the mistakes made in Somalia, Rwanda and Bosnia needed to be digested and analyzed if future peacekeeping missions were to be based on sound practice. He called on Lakhdar Brahimi to head a panel to provide that analysis.

The Brahimi Report, as it became known, was released just before the Millennium Assembly in the fall of 2000. It became an instant classic. Lakhdar himself was surprised by how well it was received. "Current wisdom had it that it was one more well meaning exercise that would produce a nice report which would join countless others to gather dust on the shelves of our esteemed organization," he said to me dryly.

The Brahimi Report had three recommendations that caught everyone's eye. One was that the Security Council had to give peacekeepers mandates that were achievable and the resources to make that possible. A second was that the Secretary-General should stop telling Security Council members what they wanted to hear and instead tell them what they needed to know. And a third was what came to be known as the "light footprint", that the UN shouldn't send in more people than is necessary to do the job.

Kofi's strategic thinker in the peacekeeping department, Chris Coleman, said that one result of the Brahimi Report was that Member States gave the department badly needed additional funds. Before Brahimi, peacekeeping was so short staffed it was dysfunctional. Another was that the culture of the relationship between the Secretariat and the Security Council changed.

"Pre-Brahimi, the Secretariat, in dealing with the Security Council, was quite cautious — I would say bullied, probably, was a better term," he said. "If you take the fact that there was that overall attitude toward the Council, number one, coupled with the fact that we had very little internal capacity, it meant that in many cases — to use Brahimi's terms — we told the Council what they wanted to hear, maybe because we were afraid to tell them otherwise, or maybe because we really didn't know what else to say." With that culture change and that additional capacity, the peacekeeping department reached a situation where much more frequently they could tell the Council what it needed to know. And that made a huge difference. "We were quite blunt on a number of occasions, post-Brahimi," said Chris, "which I think made for a better debate in the Council and in many cases made for better policy decisions by the Council."

There was a third element, Chis said, "which was our ability and readiness to look at circumstances where impartial, even-handed peacekeeping wasn't the right answer and to say so. And also a much greater readiness to deploy the credible deterrent capacity, where impartial peacekeeping was needed but with enough 'oomph' to make clear to the parties that we were to be taken seriously and not to be pushed around."

Jean-Marie Guéhenno was a distinguished French diplomat who was hired by Kofi to head the peacekeeping department in October 2000. Under Guéhenno, the number of peacekeepers hit a new peak in October 2006 of over 100,000 soldiers, police and civilians. I asked him how peacekeeping changed after the Brahimi Report.

He paused and reflected. "Big question," he said. "I think that the Brahimi Report forced governments to recognize that peacekeeping is not some kind of exceptional activity, where you scramble to bring together a group of talented people to address a security threat that has suddenly emerged, but rather that it is a core activity of the UN that has to be professionalized. It has made all of us more aware of that need for discipline and rigor."

Without the additional resources triggered by the Brahimi Report, Jean-Marie said, "We would not have been able to cope with the surge that we've had, with now close to 100,000 people deployed in the field. We would have collapsed a while ago if the Brahimi architecture had not been put in place. So that's a real achievement." But there is a downside, he added. "As the confidence in peacekeeping has increased, so have the demands. And frankly, the demands are now outstripping our resources, meaning that our operational risk remains quite significant."

Jean-Marie thinks that the strength of the Brahimi Report "is this combination of a very solid political vision, one that certainly reflected the conclusions the Secretary-General had drawn from the period when he was running peacekeeping, and an operational experience of the realities of a peacekeeping mission."

One of those who worked closely with Brahimi on the report was Salman Ahmad, an American who was also a co-author of the Srebrenica Report. He is a quiet, soft-spoken young man with great gifts. He was working in Guéhenno's office when I asked him where Kofi's fingerprints are on the report. "First, his choice of Lakhdar Brahimi was brilliant," he said. "And on the panel, he said we needed people who had actually done this before, who knew the business and who actually had a field perspective."

The second reason Salman cited was that Kofi gave the panel a lot of latitude. "He told them, I'm not going to censor you; I'm not going to tell you that you can't be critical. But what I am telling you is that you've got to give me something that can actually work. And he told them to go as far as they could, be bold, be innovative, be frank but be realistic. For people like Brahimi, those are pretty good instructions and pretty generous parameters. And I think that accounted for why the report had legs."

Sexual Abuse and Peacekeepers

Deep into Kofi's second term, as the Oil-for-Food "scandal" percolated along, a serious reform issue emerged with the discovery of large-scale sexual abuse on the part of peacekeepers. Nothing could be worse for the reputation of the United Nations than for a peacekeeper to sexually abuse a young girl. And yet it happens. In the eastern Congo, the UN military were camped right next to a refugee settlement full of poor, hungry and desperate people. A banana could buy a peacekeeper sex.

Troop contributors often don't want to face this problem. "When reports of sexual abuse in the Congo were coming out in the media in 2004," Salman Ahmed told me in his office in the peacekeeping department, "we didn't have everyone on the same page, particularly the membership, as to whether or not there was a problem. So the first challenge for us was to say to troop contributors, look, we have a problem; it's real; it is happening; and maybe some of the reports you're getting up through your national chain are not telling you this information. But you couldn't possibly talk about structural reform or other initiatives without first getting everyone to agree and understand that there was a problem out there."

I was very nervous about how the press would play this issue, because for me it was worse than Oil-for-Food. The problem had been around for decades and had never been tackled seriously. So we were at fault. Yet the journalists covered the story in a direct and professional way. That may have been due to how Jean-Marie Guéhenno, as head of peacekeeping, handled it.

"We saw very quickly that this issue had the potential to do enormous damage to peacekeeping and beyond peacekeeping to the United Nations itself," he told me. "And because there are people who would want to destroy the United Nations, we faced a strategic choice. We could try to minimize the issue and sweep it under the carpet, we could point a finger at the troop contributors or we could recognize it as a major threat and deal with it substantively. And in fact, the problem went well beyond the Congo; it was structural, not just a case of a few bad apples. The Secretary-General immediately recognized that the right approach was to deal with it substantively."

Jean-Marie saw a second strategic choice. "If we were going to deal with it structurally," he said, "to address the issue in substance and not just spin, we were going to have to bring the troop contributors on board. And that was not going to be easy, because it was clear we would meet some resistance from them. But you cannot meaningfully deal with sexual exploitation and abuse without working with the countries that give us the troops."

Jean-Marie's deputy, Jane Holl Lute, a former US Army officer, briefed the press regularly and candidly on the nature of the problem and what we were doing to try to deal with it. "The press recognized that there was some serious work being done," Jean-Marie said.

Kofi was distracted by Iraq and Oil-for-Food when the sexual abuse issue emerged in 2004. His Royal Highness Zeid Ra'ad Zeid al-Hussein stepped into the breach. When the Prince worked for the UN in peacekeeping in Bosnia, we just called him Zeid. He was down to earth, friendly and accessible. He became Jordan's Ambassador to the UN; after a failed 2006 bid to succeed Kofi as Secretary-General, he was appointed by his Government as Ambassador to Washington.

In the summer of 2004, Kofi appointed Prince Zeid Advisor to the Secretary-General on Sexual Exploitation and Abuse. The Prince began by visiting troop-contributing countries and, as someone representing a major troop contributor, to talk about "our problem". Kofi was totally supportive, the Prince said, "but you sort of felt he was under a lot of pressure from Oil-for-Food at the time."

The troop contributors were defensive at the beginning, the Prince told me, "but I tried to encourage them all to be as honest and as open about this as possible. So when I spoke in the Security Council on two or three occasions, I would discuss the problems that we've had with Jordanian peacekeepers and speak openly about it. And then a couple of them, the Pakistanis and the Moroccans, started to speak openly about it as well."

In the spring of 2005, the Prince submitted his report to the General Assembly. It was widely praised by international NGOs for providing, for the first time, a comprehensive strategy for the elimination of Sexual Exploitation and Abuse in UN Peacekeeping Operations. 191 Heads of State and Government in September 2005 endorsed the report in its entirety.

The Prince was confident that the situation would gradually come under control. "I think once we get the fundamentals of this comprehensive structure to eliminate sexual exploitation and abuse in place," he said, "then over the next few years, we should see a reduction in the number of complaints and allegations as the culture also begins to change regarding peacekeepers' respect for women."

Problem solved? Not quite. "I wouldn't say that today it's been fully resolved," said Jean-Marie, "because it's like a river with clean water — it's never the same water from one day to the next. With our troop rotations and civilian turnover, we have maybe 200,000 people a year serving in peacekeeping. So every year you have like a mid-sized city that you want to see behaving; it's a never-ending job."

A 10-Year Effort

Kofi's reform efforts continued over 10 years. He changed the budget process so that it was based on results. He overhauled personnel policy, initiating web-based recruitment and flexible hours for better work/life balance. He made the appointment of senior officials fairer and more transparent. He created the post of Staff Ombudsman. He upgraded security, naming a senior Security Manager to oversee all aspects of security worldwide. He rewrote the rules on procurement. He created an Ethics Office, expanding the requirement for financial disclosure by senior officials and protecting whistle blowers. He launched the UN website and made UN documents available free of charge over the internet.

When I asked Louise Frechette whether these reform efforts made a difference, she said, "They made a big difference. Management reform is a never-ending process, and the reform cycles and patterns in the Secretariat were not that different from reform cycles I had gone through in the Canadian administration."

"Did it leave a perfect organization behind? Of course not," she said. "Did it leave a better organization? Absolutely, starting with the peacekeeping area, for instance, which was, you know, a "man and his dog" kind of operation at the beginning and quite a professional set-up at the end."

Ten years of effort by Kofi may have made a difference, but many opportunities for change were wasted by Governments that just could not agree among themselves on Kofi's sweeping proposals. He asked Governments to undertake major steps towards UN reform in areas where only they had the authority to act. He went beyond what was prudent in pushing Member States to update the composition of the Security Council, saying it reflected the geopolitical realities of 1945. They balked. He challenged the General Assembly to introduce sunset clauses to remove obsolete items from their agenda. He suggested that they not consider every item every year, to simplify the agenda. They refused on both counts. And, he made a bold proposal to replace the Human Rights Commission by a stronger Human Rights Council but Governments torpedoed that one too.

Jean-Marie Guéhenno concluded that "on the question of his major reform effort, you can say that while it was more needed than ever, the political conditions for it to succeed may not have been there. And so the focus on management was a fallback, because the broader political reform could not be pushed through. Is he completely satisfied with that? I think he has accepted it. Like a *compagnon de devoir* (or master craftsman), he has done the best he could do with the tools at his disposal."

In a 2006 interview with Edward Mortimer, I asked him if he thought Kofi had set the bar too high on UN reform. "Personally, I don't," he said, "because it's a case of who dares, wins, in the game of international politics. You will always get less than you ask for, and if you ask for little, you will get very little. "I think it would have been unrealistic to imagine that everything he said in his report would be implemented by Member States," he went on. "But on the whole, I'm favorably surprised. I think that more of it has been taken up and is being worked on now than I would have expected. I think it did pay off." Catherine Bertini agrees. "He came out of the box running really fast in 1997 with very serious, in-depth proposals," she said. "You're never going to get everything, and he got a lot."

Oddly, Kofi ended up being criticized by some as a bad manager. Ban Ki-moon, on taking office, indicated that he was going to clean up the mess that Kofi couldn't. In April 2008, Kofi traveled to New York to receive the first MacArthur Prize for his support of the International Criminal Court, the Responsibility to Protect and his out front position on human rights generally. He was introduced by Ban, who made a little joke in his introductory remarks. He said that Kofi's shoes were hard to fill — and his suits too; he's always so nicely dressed. There was polite laughter. He then gently complained that Kofi had left him the daunting task of renovating the UN building. Kofi took the podium to make his acceptance speech. But first he looked down at Ban, smiling with the wisdom of over 40 years' experience in the UN. "Let me know when you finish the renovation," he said, "and I'll give you the name of my tailor."

CHAPTER 14

STRENGTHS AND WEAKNESSES AS MANAGER

There's much confusion over just what a Secretary-General's role should be and what it can be. As recently as 2006, US Ambassador to the UN John Bolton argued that the Secretary-General should be an administrator, not a political actor. But that argument has pretty much been erased by history, and virtually all governments, even Ambassador Bolton's, accept that the Secretary-General's job, as it has evolved, includes an important responsibility for helping to maintain international peace, and not just being a paper pusher.

The Secretary-General is sometimes criticized for not administering the UN the way a Chief Executive Officer would administer a corporation. The problem with that is that the UN, for better or for worse, has little in common with a corporation. It is a political organization of 192 governments — 193 with the admission in July 2011 of South Sudan, and the Secretary-General serves them all. There is little executive authority.

John Ruggie, Kofi's strategic adviser for four years starting in 1997, said to me: "There are different styles of leadership in management. Some are very hierarchical, but Kofi was at the other end of the spectrum. He was an enabling, an empowering leader and manager. He let you know what he hoped to achieve and he tried to pick the right people to do what he wanted done. His style was to say, do it! And if you need any help from me, let me know. And he would expect that you would come back to him to brief him regularly and if you had a problem, to ask his help."

You might say that Kofi's management style was high-risk, too trusting of the people under him. He would be criticized later for not taking a hands-on approach to managing the Iraq Oil-for-Food Programme, for example. But the up side was that people loved to work for him and most worked their hearts out for him.

Doesn't Get Down in the Weeds

Kevin S. Kennedy worked for several years in Kofi's Executive Office. He had to use his middle initial "S" because there was another Kevin Kennedy in the Secretariat with the middle initial "M" who was a former military guy who handled a number of sensitive assignments for Kofi. They always used to get each other's phone calls. To distinguish them, Kevin S. used to say that the other Kevin's middle initial was M. for "Military" while his was S. for "Sivilian". He's American. I interviewed him in his 38th floor office and asked him about Kofi's management style.

"He certainly is a leader," he said, "somebody who identifies opportunities, who gets the best out of the people around him, but he is not a hands-on manager who is inclined to get down in the weeds and to look at the technical details of something as mundane as the management of an office. He is a manager who sets the big agenda, sets the objectives, lays out the priorities, identifies where the weaknesses are, looks at where the opportunities are, but not a manager who then says, well, to get from here to there, we have to go through all these intermediary steps. But I think he was very good at identifying people who could do such things.

"So in that sense, yes, a fabulous manager and perfectly suited to the kind of overall work that the UN has on its plate," he went on. "But he's not a shop floor manager; he's not a bureaucrat. For somebody who's often been called a bureaucrat, who's come out of the UN system, he's about as unbureaucratic a character as you could ever find in any governmental or quasi-governmental organization."

Kieran Prendergast remarked on how Kofi grew in his role. "If you look at his performance as Secretary-General," he told me, "in the early first couple of years, he had a reputation for being very cautious and very methodical. As he grew in office — and he did grow very much in office — increasingly he relied on his own judgment. And I noticed an increasing willingness and readiness by him to act on that instinct and on that judgment, even if everybody around him was telling him not to do it. And I would say in his first six, seven years, he was much, much more often right than wrong."

When I spoke to Nane at the residence I asked her view of her husband in the workplace. "You know," she began, "people say he was an insider, just sort of a UN person all along. But if I were describing him, I would say he is a man who went his own way. Although he comes from the ranks of the Organization, he does not think in bureaucratic terms. Someone said he is the most rebellious spirit on the 38th floor. So it's not just that he was promoted from one step to the next because he was sitting still. He was creating his own environment. He is never one to complain that he has nothing to do and has not been given direction. He creates his direction, what he wants to be and what he wants to do."

She then turned to the subject of Kofi and ego. "With Kofi," she said, "you never deal with his ego; you deal instead with someone trying to find solutions and you don't have to go past his ego to get there." A number of people said that about him. John Ruggie, for example, who was one of Kofi's closest advisers, said of him, "Of all the major leaders I have met, either in the private or public sector, he is among the least ego-driven."

Accountability

Jane Holl Lute, the ex-US Army officer and member of the US National Security Council whom Kofi brought on as number two in the peacekeeping department, once hissed at me, "There is no accountability in this place." I had never thought about that or been bothered by it, but it bothered me now. Is that true? When UN headquarters in Baghdad was bombed, killing 22 people, Kofi fired Tun Myat, his Security Coordinator, but refused the resignation offered by his Deputy, Louise Frechette, on the grounds that there was a collective failure. Some UN security officers in Baghdad were suspended, but successfully appealed. The journalists were unimpressed.

A few years later, I was talking by phone with Joachim Hutter, a retired senior director in the peacekeeping department, and asked him about Jane's comment. "Accountability," he said, "is a term that has come into its current usage only in the last 15 years or so. Its original meaning was that you could account for a sequence of steps that produced a given result. I prefer the word 'responsibility'. The UN has an institutionalized diffusion of responsibility."

And why is that, I asked? "All bureaucracies tend to avoid individual responsibility; it's their nature," he said, "but this is more pronounced in an international one like the UN. The Secretary-General has limited power; he reports to over 190 governments. The Security Council gives the Secretary-General a peacekeeping mandate, let's say, but then the Secretary-General has to get both resources and political support from the Council in order to carry it out. Hence the responsibility is collective and as a result roles are not clearly defined."

"It was almost routine, for example," he went on, "for the Secretariat to claim credit when a peacekeeping mission succeeded. But when there was a failure, the Secretariat would blame Member States. And of course the opposite was true. President Clinton blamed the 1993 failure in Somalia on the UN, when it was entirely the fault of the US. And so it goes."

The more I thought about it, the more it made sense.

Management Style

At the end of each day, Louise Frechette and Iqbal Riza would sit down with Kofi to review the events of that day and to look forward to the next. On his management style, Louise was critical. "I was surprised by how loose and informal his approach to decision-making was," she said. "Meetings that he chaired often lacked a clear agenda or ended without a clear conclusion being drawn, which in my opinion is a very important trait of a good manager at that level. He tended to rely on personal interaction with the chiefs of departments rather than on more transparent, explicit instructions. This left room for divergent interpretations among his managers leading to lingering disagreements between departments."

Shashi Tharoor takes issue with those who argue that Kofi was loath to take tough decisions. "I did not see that," he said. "But I think he had a philosophy of leadership that involved extensive consultation. This could in part come from this African style of trying to bring the village along with you but then ultimately it has to be the wise old man who has to finally call the shots. So those who criticize him may be coming at things from a different ethic and culture. I would argue that Kofi Annan's approach is very much more what fits and works in a multinational organization."

Louise echoed one of the most common criticisms of Kofi as a manager. "He also was very reluctant to replace poor performers," she said, "or call his senior managers to account." Kieran Prendergast agrees. "He was not ruthless enough," he told me. "You know, if you're going to be a great general, sometimes you have to sack people. I think he was too kind; I think he was too trusting. I think that when people didn't measure up, or when they became stale, he didn't do what a really good general or leader would have done, which is to get rid of them. I don't think he refreshed the team often enough."

This said, Louise went on, "one should not make too much of these weaknesses. People have funny notions about what it is to manage at the level of Secretary-General. He's a leader; he has to set strategic direction, be clear as to where he wants to go, but it's not his job to attend to the day-to-day management no more than it is the job of a President or a Prime Minister. His job was, however, to make sure that he had the right people at the head of his various departments and to hold them accountable if they were not producing the results that he expected. Kofi was great at setting the broad vision and inspiring people but he did not always do what was necessary to ensure that the Secretariat acted in accordance with the vision."

Catherine Bertini said that part of the problem with the senior managers is that too many of them reported directly to Kofi. She advised him to limit those with direct access to him to between 8 and 12, but Kofi likes people too much to close his door to anybody. I think he must also have felt he could keep his hand on the pulse of the Organization by talking with as many people as possible.

And Kofi knew just about everyone's portfolio. "He was a terrific boss," Catherine said. "He knew the issues we were dealing with. You didn't have to brief him. He would absolutely focus on my rather small issue, given everything else he had on his plate, because he knew it was important to me and he dealt with it."

Another thing he was known for was supporting his people. "I would give him advice," Catherine Bertini said; "he didn't necessarily take it but he would always back me up if I made a decision and someone else was critical of it." So many of his senior managers told me similar things.

As for replacing poor performers, in the United Nations every employee wears a flag on his or her back and you can't just fire people the way you can in the corporate world. And Kofi seemed to accept that everyone could make a mistake. He had the most subtle way of letting you know you had let him down — with his eyes, or his body language — that you really didn't want to mess up again.

John Ruggie sees a parallel between Kofi's management style and that of British Petroleum CEO Lord Browne, who also gave a lot of latitude to those under him. Eventually BP ran into trouble. One of its senior executives said about Browne, "He was great on strategic issues but didn't pay enough attention to the operational." One of Kofi's weaknesses, according to John, was: "He didn't put in place close monitoring systems, and things were pretty soft in that dimension. So it was great in the enabling and the empowering dimension; it was pretty weak in the accountability dimension unless you took it upon yourself to be held accountable. And if you didn't, then bad things could happen."

And they did.

CHAPTER 15

THE NOBEL CROWN

The remains of Manhattan's Twin Towers were still smoldering when the Norwegian Nobel Committee announced its selection for the 2001 Nobel Peace Prize.

At about 5:00 a.m., New York time, on 12 October, I went over to the Secretary-General's residence on Sutton Place. There had been so much speculation that Kofi was a candidate that I needed to be there, just in case. I was not alone; I found three or four television crews standing at the front door in the dark autumn morning chill for the same reason.

Familiar UN security guards let me in and told me that the Secretary-General was still sleeping. I was greeted by Lamin Sise, the scholarly Gambian lawyer who was one of Kofi's most trusted aides; he had been there since 4:00. Lamin crackled with energy; he showed no signs of fatigue despite the early hour.

I received a call on my cell phone from Norwegian Broadcasting saying that there was speculation that the Peace Prize would be awarded to the United Nations and to Kofi personally; did I have a comment? I said, sensibly, that we would have no comment before an official announcement was made. Lamin asked security to awaken Kofi and Nane. In 20 minutes or so, they came downstairs; they were dressed casually, Kofi in an open-neck shirt.

My cell phone rang. Again, it was Norwegian Broadcasting. "They're making the announcement now," the reporter said. "Listen." I could hear something being said in what I assumed was Norwegian, of which I understand not a word, and then I heard familiar phonemes — "Kofi Annan". The reporter said that the Secretary-General and the UN would share the prize. I covered my cell phone and gave Kofi the news. I was so proud, I moved toward him in a reflex reaction to give him a hug, and then awkwardly pulled back. But Nane did it for me; she was thrilled, Lamin was ecstatic. I left the room briefly to give a short interview to Norwegian Broadcasting, to which I felt very grateful. In citing Kofi for the prize, the committee said "He has made it clear that sovereignty cannot be a shield behind which Member States conceal their violations." The Annan Doctrine was getting traction.

The other Nobel Prizes are awarded in Sweden. Alfred Nobel was the Swedish inventor of dynamite. But in his will, he specified that the Peace Prize should be awarded by a Norwegian Nobel Committee appointed by the Norwegian Parliament and that the prize should be given in Oslo.

Kofi was scheduled to accept the Nobel Prize on 10 December, and the acceptance speech, we all knew, had to be a good one. Edward Mortimer took it on. But the prize was shared by the entire United Nations, and it seemed like the entire United Nations wanted to get in on the drafting of the speech. In fact, the writing of all of Kofi's speeches was a collective effort. Edward would discuss the central ideas with Kofi. He might ask a substantive department to give him a first draft, or else he would send his own draft to the substantive department for comment. Kofi's various advisers would weigh in, depending on the topic of the speech. The Nobel speech was all of that, squared, and you know the expression "too many cooks...."

Nader Mousavizadeh, one of Edward's speechwriters, had not even seen a draft of the speech when Chief of Staff Iqbal Riza called him into Kofi's office about two weeks before the award of the prize. Kofi and Iqbal had Edward's draft in front of them and Kofi, shaking his head, said, "It's just not right." Riza then said to Nader, "This is going to be awkward, but would you take a stab at a different draft?" Nader went home, and with no other cooks looking over his shoulder, he banged out a speech. When he showed it to Edward, Edward graciously admitted it was a better product. Kofi made a few minor changes and it was done.

I went to Oslo with Kofi and Nane. Ama and Kojo were there, along with Nane's parents and her daughter Nina. The Nobel Committee rigidly sets a ridiculously low number on the amount of guests the honoree can bring. Kofi's only non-family invitees were Richard Holbrooke and British journalist and writer William Shawcross and their wives. Oslo is a magical place in winter. The city center is organized around a long, rectangular park with a skating rink in the center. The Grand Hotel, where we stayed, overlooks the park. And Kofi and Nane stood on a balcony as hundreds of people carrying candles paraded in the night under his window, a Nobel tradition.

On the day of the award, we all filed into the grand hall and waited for several minutes. Then with the blaring of trumpets, the Norwegian King and Queen were ushered in and the ceremony started. The President of the General Assembly for that year was the Foreign Minister of the Republic of Korea, Han Seung-soo, who would accept the prize on behalf of the United Nations. It was agreed that Kofi would give the acceptance speech.

"Today, in Afghanistan, a girl will be born," Kofi began. "Her mother will hold her and feed her, comfort her and care for her — just as any mother anywhere in the world. In these most basic acts of human nature, humanity knows no division. But to be born a girl in today's Afghanistan is to begin life centuries away from the prosperity that one small part of humanity has achieved. It is to live under conditions that many of us in this hall would consider inhuman."

Let me give you the next few paragraphs to get a taste for the speech.

"I speak of a girl in Afghanistan, but I might equally well have mentioned a baby boy or girl in Sierra Leone" he went on. "No one today is unaware of this divide between the world's rich and poor. No one today can claim ignorance of the cost that this divide imposes on the poor and dispossessed who are no less deserving of human dignity, fundamental freedoms, security, food and education than any of us. The cost, however, is not borne by them alone. Ultimately, it is borne by all of us — North and South, rich and poor, men and women of all races and religions.

"Today's real borders are not between nations, but between powerful and powerless, free and fettered, privileged and humiliated. Today, no walls can separate humanitarian or human rights crises in one part of the world from national security crises in another.

"Scientists tell us that the world of nature is so small and interdependent that a butterfly flapping its wings in the Amazon rainforest can generate a violent storm on the other side of the earth. This principle is known as the "Butterfly Effect". Today, we realize, perhaps more than ever, that the world of human activity also has its own "Butterfly Effect" — for better or for worse.

"Ladies and Gentlemen, we have entered the third millennium through a gate of fire. If today, after the horror of 11 September, we see better, and we see farther — we will realize that humanity is indivisible. New threats make no distinction between races, nations or regions. A new insecurity has entered every mind, regardless of wealth or status. A deeper awareness of the bonds that bind us all — in pain as in prosperity — has gripped young and old.

"In the early beginnings of the 21st century — a century already violently disabused of any hopes that progress towards global peace and prosperity is inevitable — this new reality can no longer be ignored. It must be confronted."

The speech was very well received. Kofi's stardom peaked in Oslo. But the attack on the World Trade Center was in the process of fundamentally changing international politics in a way that would bring into question the basic concept of collective security embedded in the United Nations Charter. And Kofi's second term, which was about to begin, would prove the measure of the man.

Kofi joking with his daughter Ama, who holds the Nobel medal, while son Kojo and Kofi hold up the Nobel certificate just after receipt of the Nobel Peace Prize. Nane is at right.

SECOND TERM BLUES

CHAPTER 16

THE TURNING POINT: 9/11

On the 11th of September 2001, at about 9:00 a.m., I was putting the finishing touches on the Secretary-General's news summary from the night before. We "fed" him three times a day with news updates, the first by fax just before he left the residence to come to work, so he could read it in the car on the way in.

One of my deputies, Stéphane Dujarric, came into my office a bit breathless — I must say, he's always a bit breathless — saying his wife had just called and said a plane had hit the World Trade Center and we could see the building burning live on TV. We all have TVs on our desks, but none of us had the right channel. A quick channel surf picked up the local news station with the iconic image of one of the Twin Towers streaming smoke against a clear blue sky.

I went to the top of my news update and started drafting a new article for the Secretary-General's press review. As I was typing, I had one eye on the TV, and this time I saw a second plane banking toward the second tower and BAM! It crashed right into it. Although the news commentary still wasn't talking about a terrorist incident, I rewrote the short first item. Given the perfect visibility, there could be only one explanation for what was happening. The US was under attack.

Kofi's security detail had been notified, of course, and they had him locked down at the residence. From the upper levels of the UN building you could see the smoke from the towers filling the sky over lower Manhattan.

An invitation from Giuliani

Leaders are defined by crises, and out of 9/11 the Mayor of the City of New York, Rudolph Giuliani, emerged as the hero of his people. He was composed, ever-present, feeling, showing the way. Every politician wanted to visit the site of the bombing, and Giuliani hosted as many of these visits as he could. He was no admirer of the UN, but Kofi was one of the first non-Americans that Giuliani invited to tour the site. On 18 September, in a tightly controlled event, we went downtown by boat. Kofi stepped onto the dock, approached Giuliani and embraced him. It was a warm, emotional expression of solidarity shared between two men from opposite sides of the world, who could have made a speech but didn't.

The World Trade Center was just what its name implied. Among the nearly 3,000 victims were citizens of 90 nations, whose remains like all the others were incinerated as two of the world's tallest structures collapsed in flames. When one New York City fireman was asked about the victims' remains, he famously responded something like, "they're under my fingernails, they're on my clothing, they're in my lungs."

Kofi would come to see his ten years as Secretary-General as cleaved in two by 9/11. "What some have not realized is how the world changed during that second term," he said to me in 2006. "In fact, you can almost draw a line, pre-9/11 and post-9/11, where the bitterness and the acrimony were introduced into the Organization. That has not healed yet. And this was reflected in the wider world as well."

A Second Term

Earlier in 2001, Kofi faced the choice of whether or not to run for another five-year term. His friend Richard Holbrooke said that the decision was up to the Security Council and Nane. Everyone knew what a strain the role of First Lady was on Nane and some thought she would pressure Kofi to step down. I too thought there was a chance he would stop. He was at such a high, it was a perfect time to call it quits. Besides, frankly, I was tired too. But my friend Thorvald Stoltenberg, the former Foreign Minister of Norway who was one of my bosses in the Geneva peace talks on the former Yugoslavia, introduced a splash of cold-water reality. In his playful, Norwegian lilt, he told me, "I've never known a politician who didn't want a second term."

In the end, Nane and Kofi went for it. "Nane was hoping one term would be enough," Kofi said to me in that 2006 discussion. "In fact, I myself at the beginning felt that we would do one term, then we'd move on. But by the end of the first term, I was in the middle of so many things, and quite a lot of delegations encouraged me, saying there's need for continuity, there's a need to bring these things to their logical conclusion. And probably I also optimistically thought that there was a lot that could be done in a second term, so I went along with it. But, you're right, Nane wasn't keen on it."

I asked him if he had any regrets. "No," he replied. "I think it was a challenging assignment. It was a duty. There were frustrations and it was very difficult, but there were also exciting, fulfilling moments."

On the 30 of June 2001, the General Assembly unanimously elected Kofi to a second five-year term. In January of that year, George W. Bush had begun the first of two terms in the White House. Bush and 9/11, separately and together, would shape Kofi's second five years as head of the United Nations Secretariat.

CHAPTER 17

"IT'S OBVIOUS;
THEY'RE GOING TO WAR..."

President Bush's decision to invade Iraq was probably the most divisive foreign policy decision of his eight years in office. The 2001 attacks on the World Trade Center and the Pentagon had initially generated a worldwide wave of sympathy for the US, which many people say Bush squandered when he went into Iraq.

The UN Charter says that Member States don't have to wait for Security Council approval to hit back in self-defense. The US had traced the bombings of the World Trade Center to al-Qaeda, and its leader, Osama bin Laden, who had been running terrorist training camps in Afghanistan. As early as October 1999, the Security Council had called on the Taliban to stop supporting international terrorism and to turn over bin Laden. They refused. The US wanted to strike out at the Taliban and bin Laden, the Security Council and the UN Charter provided a comfortable legal underpinning for it, and Kofi Annan lent his moral authority to it.

The day after 9/11, the Council said that the attack on the US was a threat to international peace and security. Just over two weeks after that, they set out measures to fight international terrorism. A global cooperative effort was under way. On 15 September 2001, the US declared bin Laden the prime suspect in the 9/11 bombings and on 7 October launched air strikes against Taliban positions. There were no protests. In surprisingly quick order, the Taliban retreated in defeat, abandoning Kabul by mid-November.

That was the easy part, it turned out. Putting together a new government was going to be hard, and the Bush Administration decided to ask Kofi Annan for help. In July 1997, Kofi had named Lakhdar Brahimi his special envoy for Afghanistan, but after two years of failing to get the country's factions to cooperate, Brahimi had given up. He had wanted to quit. He was an experienced political operator — he had been Foreign Minister of his country, Algeria — and he was also a no-nonsense guy. But Kofi wouldn't give the job to someone else, so Brahimi suggested he be put "in deep freeze" because he could not see any purpose in carrying on.

The fall of the Taliban gave Kofi an excuse to take Lakhdar out of the "deep freeze". Brahimi toured the region and then proposed an Afghan-led process that would eventually result in the creation of a broad-based government. He first garnered the support of the Russians and the Americans, the Iranians and the Pakistanis; and then he brought together the Afghan factions in a castle outside of Bonn, Germany, where he banged heads together for nine days. It worked; the Bonn Agreement was signed on 5 December 2001, paving the way for the establishment of a government over a period of two to three years.

The Invasion of Iraq

The invasion of Afghanistan did not yield Osama bin Laden, and so talk in Washington began to focus on Iraq. Although there was no known link between Iraq and al-Qaeda, some people in Washington began to talk of one. And so US planning for the overthrow of Saddam Hussein got under way; the drumbeat for war against Iraq picked up steadily throughout 2002.

Political opinion in the United States, even on the right of the spectrum, was divided. Some advisors of President Bush the father, like former National Security Advisor Brent Scowcroft, started to speak out against going after Saddam Hussein. Scowcroft wrote in *The Wall Street Journal* that an invasion of Iraq "could turn the whole region into a cauldron, and thus destroy the war on terrorism".

Kofi talking with US Secretary of State Colin Powell. He got on well with most members of the Bush Administration, even while disagreeing with some of their policies.

Within President George W. Bush's cabinet, Secretary of State Colin Powell was a lonely voice urging the President to consider a peaceful option, using UN weapons inspectors to keep Saddam Hussein in his box. UK Prime Minister Tony Blair was asking Bush to do the same. Bush gave Powell the green light to pursue the UN option.

In the Security Council, opinion was deeply divided. The UK had long ago made a policy decision to stand behind the US, and continued to do so. Yet there was a strong anti-war constituency in the UK, and Prime Minister Tony Blair was trying to be an intermediary between anti-war Europe and pro-war US. France and Russia were fundamentally against military action. Kofi Annan threw his weight, such as it was, behind engaging the US in finding a peaceful solution through the Security Council. Annan's advisers, though, were pessimistic. I remember Chief of Staff Iqbal Riza shaking his head, despite all this talk of Security Council involvement, and saying with quiet resignation, "It's obvious; they're going to war."

The bellicose rumblings in Washington, led by a President who believed that the United States should use its unparalleled military and economic power to advance its own agenda, made a lot of people nervous. There was talk of a unipolar world following the collapse of the Soviet Union, but now that world was beginning to take concrete shape. America could do anything it wanted. Most other nations supported the attack on Afghanistan, but in many capitals, the targeting of Iraq was going too far. But could it be stopped?

The Emperor and the Pope

Kofi went before the General Assembly on the 23 September 2002 to give one of his finest speeches. Edward Mortimer, in his notes for a series of lectures at Oxford University in February and March 2008, wrote, "We decided well in advance that this must be a landmark speech, a ringing defense of the multilateral principle in world affairs." And indeed it was.

Traditionally, the host country speaks after the Secretary-General, and Edward was worried that coverage of President Bush's address would drown out that of Kofi's. So he suggested that we release the text of the speech the night before without embargo. This was a normal tactic in press relations, but not one that the UN had ever adopted before. Edward recalls that both the Deputy Secretary-General, Louise Frechette, and Kofi's information chief, Shashi Tharoor, were against the idea. But I supported Edward and Kofi went for it.

It worked brilliantly. *The New York Times* played the speech on page one on the day Kofi delivered it and ran most of the text inside. This was a bit of a coup in media relations terms, since it was Kofi who was drowning out Bush, and the Americans were not amused. I received an irate phone call of protest from the US mission's press office, and I'm sure others up the UN chain received similar calls.

In his speech, Kofi warned Iraq of the dangers of not complying with Security Council resolutions. The UN inspectors had been shut out of Iraq since August 1998. "If Iraq's defiance continues," he said, "the Security Council must face its responsibilities."

And he reaffirmed the right of self-defense, but with a caveat: "Any State, if attacked, retains the inherent right of self-defense under Article 51 of the Charter. But beyond that, when States decide to use force to deal with broader threats to international peace and security, there is no substitute for the unique legitimacy provided by the United Nations."

The terrorist attacks of 9/11 were not an isolated event, he said. "They were an extreme example of a global scourge, which requires a broad, sustained and global response. Broad, because terrorism can be defeated only if all nations unite against it. Sustained, because the battle against terrorism will not be won easily, or overnight. It requires patience and persistence. And global, because terrorism is a widespread and complex phenomenon, with many deep roots and exacerbating factors."

"I believe that such a response can only succeed if we make full use of multilateral institutions," he went on. "I stand before you today as a multilateralist — by precedent, by principle, by Charter and by duty."

On the fight against terrorism, his message was clear. "Individual States may defend themselves by striking back at terrorist groups and the countries that harbor or support them," he said. "But only concerted vigilance and cooperation among all States, with constant, systematic exchange of information, offers any real hope of denying terrorists their opportunities."

Kofi then concluded, "...for any one State — large or small — choosing to follow or reject the multilateral path must not be a simple matter of political convenience. It has consequences far beyond the immediate context.... The more a country makes use of multilateral institutions... the more others will trust and respect it.... And among multilateral institutions, this universal Organization has a special place."

Edward wrote that wonderful speech, and after it French Ambassador Jean-David Levitte commented to him, *"C'était le discours du Pape à l'Empereur."* It was a speech by the Pope to the Emperor.

But the Emperor wasn't listening carefully, or else he didn't want to hear. In his speech, President Bush portrayed Iraq as a nation bristling with weapons of mass destruction, a nation that had defied United Nations resolutions for a decade and that would be held to account. To the other members of the Security Council, Bush said, in effect, you can either join us in this fight or lose your relevance and disappear, like the League of Nations, into the dustbin of history.

Iraq Does an About-Face

President Bush's case against Iraq began with Baghdad's defiance of Security Council resolutions, notably its refusal for some four years to readmit UN weapons inspectors. The Iraqi Foreign Minister, Naji Sabri, was in the Assembly Hall and heard the speeches by both Bush and the Secretary-General. Kofi had tried unsuccessfully until then to get Iraq to change its mind and readmit the inspectors. He even gatecrashed a meeting at the UN of Arab ministers, including Sabri, and told them that Iraq had to comply with Security Council resolutions or face war.

Baghdad decided to compromise. Arab League Secretary-General Amre Moussa accompanied Sabri to a meeting with Kofi. Sabri had a draft letter in his hand saying Iraq would now accept the return of the UN inspectors. The draft, however, was full of "ifs, ands and buts". Kofi told him it wasn't good enough. It had to be clear and unconditional. He sent them back for a redrafting exercise.

They only went down the hall to Michael Moller's office. Michael was a senior political director in Kofi's office and at various points looked after the Iraq portfolio for him. He has a dry voice with a hard edge and speaks in staccato punches like Dragnet's Sergeant Joe Friday. I called him and asked him to describe what happened that afternoon.

"After a while, the Secretary-General left us to sit and come up with some sort of sensible draft," he said. "And that's what we did. We went down to my office for a couple of hours, effectively typing it straight into my computer. Sabri then called Baghdad from my phone to get clearance. It was very much a product of teamwork between Moussa, the Iraqis and myself. And that's how we got the letter, that same afternoon."

I asked him if he sensed Washington would be unhappy with Kofi for facilitating Saddam Hussein's compliance. "Well, that was pretty much out in the open at the time," he replied. "So it was sort of two opposing objectives that clashed here, but there was nothing much we could do about it."

And did the Secretary-General still have confidence that sending the inspectors back could work, I asked? "I don't know if the right word is 'confident'", he said. "I suppose 'hope' would be the better word. But he certainly felt that at the very least it would give us some time to try and find a more peaceful solution and give us some space, and more importantly to give the Security Council some space, a certain calm, to find a diplomatic solution."

Buying time

Kofi was trying to pull Washington into a Security Council consensus, although most people around him believed he was only buying time. On 8 November 2002, the Security Council finally agreed on a resolution authorizing the return of the inspectors to Iraq that provided for the Council to convene again to consider Iraqi non-compliance and called on Iraq to submit a complete declaration of its weapons of mass destruction program.

Hans Blix of Sweden, the chief UN weapons inspector, sent his inspectors into Iraq on 22 November, but even after a four-year absence, he found little new in the way of evidence of weapons of mass destruction. In December, the Iraqis submitted a 12,000-page report supposedly revealing all. It did nothing of the sort, Blix told me. "At the time, my gut feeling was, like everybody else, that they had been hiding something and lying to us," he said. "But Mohammad ElBaradei (the head of the International Atomic Energy Agency) and I were both disappointed and said so. I remember telling the Iraqis that it's five minutes till midnight and that time was pressing. Perhaps we should have done that even earlier."

Dramatic Council Debates

In a Ministerial-level meeting of the Security Council on the subject of combating terrorism on 20 January 2003, French Foreign Minister Dominique de Villepin surprised US Secretary of State Colin Powell by threatening to use a veto against military action in Iraq if UN weapons inspectors weren't given more time to finish their work. This embarrassed Powell and strengthened the hand of pro-war conservatives in Washington.

In Paris, French President Jacques Chirac and German Chancellor Gerhard Schroeder jointly pledged to oppose war with Iraq for the time being, prompting a comment by US Secretary of Defense Donald Rumsfeld that France and Germany were "problems". He then caused a furor when he referred to them as "old Europe".

President Bush decided to recreate an Adlai Stevenson moment at the UN by asking Powell to do a drop-dead power point presentation to convince the world that Saddam Hussein was a threat to international peace and security. Stevenson had Council Members riveted in October 1962 when he showed photographs proving that the Soviet Union had placed nuclear missiles in Cuba.

The Council met on 5 February 2004. It had drama — Powell made a sophisticated presentation laying out what he called the evidence that Saddam had weapons of mass destruction and implied a link to the al-Qaeda terrorist network. It had eloquence — Dominique de Villepin argued that UN inspections could still be useful to disarming Iraq and proposed tripling the number of inspectors. Regarding the war option, de Villepin asked:

"How do we make sure that the considerable risks of such intervention are actually kept under control? This obviously requires a collective demarche of responsibility on the part of the world community. In any case, it must be clear that in the context of such an option, the United Nations will have to be at the center of the action to guarantee Iraq's unity, ensure the region's stability, protect civilians and preserve the unity of the world community."

The Guernica

A custom has evolved that members of the Security Council, on coming out of a meeting, may talk to the press informally in the corridor outside the chamber. To facilitate this, the UN information department had set up a microphone in a "stake out position" just under the words "Security Council" mounted on the concave wall at one end of the corridor. This arrangement was fine for the size of the press corps that normally covered the UN.

The Powell presentation on Iraq though was going to draw a record number of journalists to the UN. The US Mission to the UN had called my office to say that Powell would want to talk to the press at the stakeout. I studied the space to see how to accommodate the maximum number of journalists and decided that we would have to move the stakeout position to the middle of the concave wall. But there was a small problem. At that point on the wall was a tapestry version of Picasso's *Guernica*. Was I going to put Colin Powell in front of an iconic anti-war work of art for him to defend his argument for going to war against Iraq?

The TV guys from the information department worked with me. I asked them, innocently, what they thought of the backdrop. "Too busy," said one of them. Exactly. I now had a technical reason to solve a political problem. My deputy Stéphane got Iqbal Riza's permission in writing, and we had the *Guernica* covered with a UN-blue cloth, then flanked it with the 15 flags of the Security Council members. It was colorful and it was clean.

The next day, Powell came out to the stakeout and spoke to the press. From a technical point of view, it was impeccable. Then there ensued a media firestorm. The fact that the UN could cover up the *Guernica* during a debate over a war that a majority of the world didn't want to happen was judged as craven. Both *The New Yorker* and *Harper's* ran cover art of the *Guernica* partially hidden by a curtain. The UN was discredited and I was mortified. Shashi berated me in an angry phone call. I deserved it. I tore off the covers of those two magazines, framed them and hung them in my office. "Next time, let's think twice," I told my staff.

Today the stakeout is just to the right of the *Guernica*. It accommodates fewer journalists, but it is as it should be.

Applause

A week later, the Council was to hear a report by Blix and Mohammed ElBaradei. The whole world was watching. There was still no smoking gun, and there was no verification of the evidence presented by Powell on the 5th. In that presentation, Powell did not use an allegation put forward by President Bush in his State of the Union address the week before that Saddam had tried to buy "yellow cake" uranium from Niger. Even Powell thought that one was unsubstantiated. I remember ElBaradei whispering about the Niger documentation, "But that was an obvious forgery." ElBaradei later told the Council that forcefully, but until then no one was willing to say it out loud. Gradually it became established that almost everything Powell had presented as fact was unverifiable. We all found out later, and too late, that there was no case.

De Villepin laid bare the depth of anti-war feeling with a rousing speech. While he did not argue against military action, he asked for a pause to allow the UN inspection regime be given more time to complete its work. "In this temple of the United Nations, we are the guardians of an ideal, the guardians of conscience," he said. "This onerous responsibility and immense honor we have must lead us to give priority to disarmament through peace." His words were greeted by a round of applause, which was stunning because protocol dictates that such should never happen in the Security Council. He then drew appreciative laughter, when he said, "This message comes to you today from an old country, France," an obvious reference to the Rumsfeld insult.

Kofi listened stone-faced to the debate. He did not clap when de Villepin spoke although his heart must have taken flight from those words. When I asked him afterwards if he was tempted to clap, he said impatiently, "That would be stupid." Edward's notes read, "As I suspected, journalists were watching Kofi much more carefully than we were. Felicity Berringer of *The New York Times* wrote, 'Kofi Annan pushed the points of his fingers against each other, bending and straightening them in a slow series of mini push-ups.'"

Just over a week later, Blix and ElBaradei gave a follow-up briefing to the Security Council on their latest inspection activity. Still no conclusive evidence of weapons. The US and the UK went for a resolution to go to war. France, Russia and Germany said they would not let such a resolution pass. That was the end of the debate. Washington and London withdrew the draft resolution, and we all knew that war was inevitable. Kofi told the press: "If this action is to take place without the support of the Council, its legitimacy will be questioned, and the support for it will be diminished." That was an understatement.

The Iraq Steering Group

Kofi set up an Iraq Steering Group to plan the UN's systemwide humanitarian response to war, should it come. He asked his deputy, Louise Frechette, to chair it. Kofi used her in a variety of support roles, and this was one of her most important.

The UN system, as usual, was having a family quarrel. Many UN agencies felt that by preparing for war we were accepting it as inevitable. "Humanitarians felt 'gagged'," Edward wrote, "and talked about the need for advocacy." Louise asked, "what were we advocating?" The implication — never quite stated in so many words — was that what the agencies were really trying to do was engage in political advocacy against the war. "It's an ironic situation," Edward said. "We are all against the war, yet we are afraid to say so publicly for fear of alienating the US."

Kofi finally seemed to accept that war was likely. He said as much at a press conference on 14 January when asked whether the UN was doing contingency planning. A politician would have ducked that question, but Kofi took it head on. "Obviously, we live in the real world," he said, "and we have had lots of experience handling post-conflict situations, or what some call nation-building: from Kosovo to Afghanistan to Bosnia...So, obviously, we are doing some thinking, without assuming anything. But it will be prudent for us to look ahead."

The Iraq Steering Group started meeting three times a week. Kofi named Rafeeuddin Ahmed of the UN Development Programme (UNDP) as his special adviser on Iraq. Rafee presented the initial thinking of a sub-group he headed that favored a UN Assistance Mission for Iraq on the Afghan model. Edward wrote in his diary: "It seems more and more clear that, in promising to bring democracy to Iraq, Bush, Wolfowitz and company have no real idea of what they are taking on." Indeed, there was a broad body of opinion both inside and out of the UN that was of the same conviction.

The US Goes to War

On 20 March 2003, the US began the invasion of Iraq.

Kofi issued a statement, saying, "Despite the best efforts of the international community and the United Nations, war has come to Iraq for the third time in a quarter of a century. Perhaps if we had persevered a little longer, Iraq could yet have been disarmed peacefully, or — if not — the world could have taken action to solve this problem by a collective decision, endowing it with greater legitimacy, and therefore commanding wider support, than is now the case."

Nader Mousavizadeh, who was often a note taker for Kofi's confidential phone conversations, said to me, "What was hard for him was that he fundamentally is someone who abhors war and would find it very difficult to accept the use of force, more so than he is now given credit for. But I also think he was genuinely surprised that he was so wrong. He really thought that this war was going to be avoided; he believed it when Rice and Powell were saying they really didn't want war. And then when it was obvious that war was coming, I think he felt that he'd been had a little bit."

Kofi remained anchored by his belief in the importance of the unity of the Security Council, Nader added. "I remember telling my pro-war friends, Kofi isn't against holding Saddam accountable — even through the use of force — but he's against doing so without Security Council support."

CHAPTER 18

THE DEATH OF SERGIO —
AND OF
NEO-CONSERVATISM

Neoconservatives are a relatively recent phenomenon in American politics. The movement grew up in the 1960s and '70s and its members strongly supported Ronald Reagan's election in 1980. They are primarily intellectuals, once moderates or liberals, who embraced certain conservative political positions, notably virulent anti-communism, and gave intellectual energy to the country's far right. The godfather of neoconservatives, Irving Kristol, is said to have described them as "liberals mugged by reality".

At the end of the Cold War, neocons felt that the US should use its now uncontested military and economic might to defend democratic states under threat, such as Israel, and to export democracy and human rights worldwide, starting in the Middle East. They believed less in the rule of law than in unilateral action to defend their principles. They were not fans of the UN.

Neocons had been on the periphery of mainstream US politics, but the mainstream was shifting right. With the election of George W. Bush, prominent neoconservatives, such as Paul Wolfowitz and Richard Perle, were given key positions in his Administration, although they were not yet dominant. It was only after the attacks of 9/11 that their philosophy of hitting out militarily and unilaterally at the enemies of America gained traction.

Paul Wolfowitz had long favored ousting Saddam Hussein by force. After 9/11, from his influential position as Deputy Secretary of Defense, he took the lead in convincing President Bush to take military action against Iraq, an action that before then would have seemed too extreme even for conservative policymakers. Bush's decision in the neocons' favor was their finest hour. When the US opted for war in a region as volatile as the Middle East, it split the Atlantic Alliance and divided the UN Security Council. And in the aftermath of the attacks on the World Trade Center and the Pentagon, a surprising number of US lawmakers went along with this new hard line policy. It was as though it would have been unpatriotic to question the President's strategy.

Freedom Fries

As the US prepared to go to war against Iraq in 2003, Richard Perle, a leading neo-conservative and Chairman of the Defense Policy Board at Donald Rumsfeld's Pentagon, told a British newspaper, "We're going to get a twofer in Iraq — Saddam Hussein and the United Nations."

Perle relished the thought of driving Saddam from power and diminishing the United Nations at the same time.

The fear that Perle's scenario could actually be realized was palpable around the UN. France, Russia, Germany and others, with Kofi's full support, sought to slow the US juggernaut in favor of a peaceful solution in Iraq. The reaction across the US was over the top. *The New York Post* ran on its front page a doctored photo of a Security Council meeting, with the heads of weasels on the bodies of the French and German delegates, accusing them of wanting to let Saddam Hussein "off the hook". The headline read, "Axis of Weasel", echoing President Bush's now famous phrase, "Axis of Evil", referring to Iraq, Iran and North Korea. In California, people were invited to a rally at which they poured French wine into the gutter. Consumption of French wine subsequently plummeted in the US. In Washington, a member of Congress, Bob Ney, a Republican from Ohio, used his position as Chairman of the House Administration Committee to rename French Fries "Freedom Fries" in the House cafeteria. (Years later, he was indicted on fraud and conspiracy charges and was forced to resign.)

If the neocons were right, the collective security agreement enshrined in the Charter of the United Nations would be shredded. The world would become unipolar, revolving around Washington.

The Roof Falls In

But the neocons turned out to be wrong. The US charged into Baghdad, and with amazing speed the regime of Saddam Hussein collapsed. There was the somewhat contrived scene of jubilant citizens tearing down Saddam's statue in Baghdad with the help of the US military. George Bush declared "mission accomplished" and then the roof fell in. In 2012, more than nine years later, Iraq was somewhat calmer but still chaotic and the US had lost more soldiers there than there were civilians killed in the World Trade Center bombing.

To many of us at the UN, the initial US success filled us with foreboding. As Edward Mortimer wrote in his notes, "People at the UN were afraid that Rumsfeld and company would now carry all before them, and seek to change other regimes by military force." In fact, the neocons also had Syria and Iran in their sites. But the US reversals in Iraq, unfortunate as they were for Iraqis, as well as for President Bush, had a comforting side. The military option was being discredited and the unipolar world was looking ever more multipolar.

Before it was clear just how bad it was going to get in Iraq, the US went back to the UN for formal recognition as an occupying power and for help with reconstruction — and maybe too with an eye to repairing the transatlantic relationship. President Bush and Prime Minister Tony Blair, at a press conference in Northern Ireland in April 2003, said that the UN would have a "vital role" in post-war Iraq. Kofi was caught in the middle, as Edward observed in his notes. "But our main concern right now," he wrote, "is to position the SG correctly between the US and the UK, who are trying to hijack him to win international legitimacy for what they have done and are doing in Iraq, and others — France, Germany, Russia — who are proclaiming that the UN must now be put in sole charge of the country."

The air was unsettled. There was a steady deterioration of the security situation in Iraq. For those who opposed the war, a majority in the Council, there must have been a gnawing urge, which had to be resisted, to say, "We told you so." But the Ambassadors' instructions from their capitals seemed to be, "cool it".

Kofi advised the Council members to reconcile and work together to rebuild Iraq, arguing that "a stable Iraq is in everybody's interest." And, needless to say, it was in the UN's interest to reunite the Security Council. Council members resumed dialogue with the US over Iraq, with no overt bitterness although with underlying resentment. A resolution was adopted unanimously in late May 2003 recognizing the US-led coalition as an occupying power and asking Kofi to name a Special Representative for Iraq.

As they drafted the resolution, though, diplomats bickered over language to describe the UN role in post-war Iraq. Would it be a central role, a vital role, an essential role, a leading role? But that was all nonsense. The US hadn't admitted defeat yet; it wasn't ready to hand over Iraq to the UN. It just wanted a little international help with a job that would be harder and take longer and be more expensive than they had anticipated. However, at home, Bush began to distance himself from the neoconservatives who got him into this mess.

Washington and London were pressuring Kofi to name a Special Representative for Iraq quickly. But at the same time, there were voices counseling Kofi not to crawl into bed with the victors. *London Times* columnist Simon Jenkins was one of those. In mid-April 2003, he wrote that Kofi should let the US and the UK clean up their own mess in Iraq until they begged him to take it off their hands. "Then, he can name his price," Jenkins wrote. Kieran Prendergast discussed the Jenkins column with Edward Mortimer. Edward highlighted it and Kieran sent it up to Kofi to read. But Edward wrote in his notes, "KP and I agree, however, that the SG will not take this advice. He is too eager for the UN to play 'an important role', and too soon."

Kofi, I believe, had come to the decision early on that he had to jump on this train. The US went into Iraq without Security Council approval. Had they succeeded, it could have spelled the end of the UN. With the US now knocking on the UN's door, Kofi wasn't going to risk letting George Bush stand out in the cold too long, no matter what his advisers said. There was too much at stake.

Defining the UN role in Iraq

Kofi's advisers debated what kind of role the UN should play in Iraq. According to Edward's notes, an alliance emerged between Rafee Ahmed and Mark Malloch Brown, who was then head of the UN Development Programme, in favor of a more forward-looking policy. "Instead of waiting for the Council to tell him what to do," Edward wrote, "or for the US to present everyone with a *fait accompli*, shouldn't the SG come forward with some suggestions of his own?"

In late April, Rafee sent Kofi a strictly confidential note advocating just such an approach, according to Edward, who was allowed to read it. In the note, Rafee argued that the US-led process in Iraq was too narrowly based and was not going to produce a credible, representative Iraqi government. The UN could help, but would the US accept that help? Rafee suggested that Kofi talk to Powell by phone.

But Edward feared that Powell was not strong enough in the Iraq debate in Washington. Rumsfeld seemed much more powerful. Mark Malloch Brown knew Paul Wolfowitz from his days in Washington as a political consultant and while handling public affairs for the World Bank. He said he could talk to Wolfowitz directly. "He's not hostile to the UN," Mark said, according to Edward's notes, "but knows little about it, and is too busy to bother finding out more."

Edward sent Kofi a note recommending that he make use of Mark's contact with Wolfowitz. Late in the evening of 1 May, Mark sent Edward an e-mail saying that Kofi had authorized him to see Wolfowitz and a date for a meeting in Washington had been set for Saturday, 3 May. The following Monday, Mark told Edward that the meeting had gone quite well and that Wolfowitz was quite keen to involve the UN in Iraq.

On Tuesday, 6 May, Kofi had a small meeting to discuss how far the UN could go in cooperating with, and therefore legitimizing, the occupiers of Iraq. Edward, who attended, noted that Kieran Prendergast and Jean-Marie Guéhenno urged caution, while Mark Malloch Brown and Shashi Tharoor favored getting involved. Kofi seemed to have already made up his mind. Edward wrote, "The SG is frustrated that we seem to be re-hashing arguments about the war instead of focusing on practical next steps."

Sergio's selection

Sergio Vieira de Mello had film star qualities and a towering reputation at the UN. Kofi once told me, "Sergio could go all the way," meaning that he could succeed him as Secretary-General, even though it was not Latin America's "turn", such were his strengths.

The Bush Administration zeroed in on Sergio as their first choice for UN representative in Iraq, but Kofi had just named him High Commissioner for Human Rights the previous year. Sergio was in the process of overhauling that office and neither Kofi nor human rights advocacy groups wanted to see the seat vacated.

Sergio had been drawn to danger his whole professional life. He served in Lebanon, Cambodia, Rwanda, former Yugoslavia and East Timor, where he had his greatest success. The High Commissioner for Human Rights job might have been a bit too bureaucratic for him, but he threw himself into it. When he was invited to Washington and wooed personally by Condoleezza Rice and George W. Bush to take an ill-defined job in a dangerous place, he couldn't resist. Kofi agreed to let him go to Iraq, but only for four months.

Sergio worked with Paul "Jerry" Bremer, head of the US-led Iraq Transitional Authority, to broaden the reach in the search for what Bremer wanted to call an advisory council. Sergio convinced him to call it a governing council. Sergio could talk to people that Bremer couldn't and helped get all seven leading Iraqi political parties onto the council. Reporting to New York by phone on 8 July, Sergio said that things were going well politically. His deputy, Jamal Ben-Omar, said that there was no hostility towards the UN but that he feared it was only a matter of time before UN staff were directly targeted.

Edward's note of that phone conversation then goes on, "I said maybe Sergio should do more to publicly differentiate himself from the Americans and the British and show that he's playing an independent role in the political process. But this apparently is the one thing Bremer does not want, though he seems very receptive to Sergio's advice in private. I guess one is the price of the other."

When the Security Council unanimously adopted Resolution 1483 on 22 May, recognizing the US/UK-led coalition as the legitimate governing authority in Iraq as the occupying power, it also recognized the Iraqi Governing Council, lifted sanctions against Iraq and dissolved the Oil-for-Food Programme. The Council had been pieced back together again. Kofi had lost his voice following the invasion of Iraq and some suspected it was the result of emotional stress. But now his voice was back and he was in the game. Edward wrote, "The SG seems to have recovered his health and bounce, and there's a feeling that the UN is back in business."

Kofi even gloated a bit at a press conference that he gave in New York on 30 July. Edward wrote: "The SG was in unusually bold form, and actually said he had warned the UN bashers months ago that they would need the UN. The general impression he gave was that he was definitely over the depression or exhaustion he suffered from in the immediate aftermath of the war, that he felt vindicated by the course of events and that he even hoped the shock might lead to a strengthening of the multilateral order."

After that press conference, Mark Turner, the UN correspondent for *The Financial Times* of London, told Edward he planned to write an article for the next day on the theme "Annan is back!"

The attack on the UN in Baghdad

The UN isn't used to being targeted as the enemy in places where it carries out humanitarian tasks. Sergio's team, housed in the old Canal Hotel on the outskirts of the Green Zone, had received warnings of security threats, but didn't want the UN compound surrounded by US troops and barbed wire. They actually asked the US military to dismantle what was already in place, including a barrier to a small road that ran right by Sergio's office. And they failed to request that any alternative measures be taken.

Nadia Younes was a senior member of Sergio's staff and a former colleague of mine in the press office under Secretary-General Javier Perez de Cuellar. Kofi liked her, and her career was advancing rapidly. As part of that advancement, Kofi named this chain-smoking, wisecracking woman head of protocol. Not exactly a good match. At one point, at a head of state summit of the Organization of African Unity, she was setting up meetings for Kofi with up to 15 leaders per day. She ushered in one Head of State, and in her gravelly voice announced, "Mr. Secretary-General, the President of Burundi." Actually, there had been a slight confusion in the line-up, and the person with her was the President of Burkina Faso. Kofi knew both Presidents well, and smoothed over the gaffe. Lamin Sise, the Gambian lawyer on Kofi's staff, had a friendly relationship with Nadia, and couldn't help teasing her about her mistake. But Nadia never got flustered. She just laughed heartily and, with a twinkle in her eye, said, "You guys all look alike."

Sergio recruited her for Baghdad, but the place gave her the creeps. She was on the phone to Lamin often, commenting on one occasion, "I know this region. The history of this country is written in blood." On another, she said, "Get me out of this hell-hole," and pleaded with Lamin to convince Chief of Staff Iqbal Riza to allow her to return to New York Headquarters immediately. Kofi had recently appointed her Assistant Secretary-General for General Assembly Affairs and she was eager to take up her new duties. Lamin scrambled to find someone to replace her, which he knew Iqbal would insist on. He finally came up with Chris Elfverson, who volunteered to relieve Nadia right away. But by then it was too late.

On 19 August 2003, a suicide bomber drove a truck laden with explosives down that road next to the Canal Hotel, stopped under Sergio's office, where Sergio was having a meeting with several people at the time, and detonated it. Sergio lay in the rubble, conscious, his legs crushed and pinned. UN security were trying to move the debris with their bare hands, but without heavy equipment it was impossible. Martin Griffiths, a friend of Kofi's as well as of Sergio's, told me that when a guard offered to pray with him, Sergio, who still had the rebellious spirit of the 1968 student riots in Paris, which he had participated in, shot back a profanity. A few hours later, he had bled to death. Twenty-one other UN staffers died with him.

At first, we had no news of Nadia. Jimmy Breslin, the legendary New York reporter, came into my office unannounced and sat down and started taking notes as I was on the phone trying to get news of her. It was the day after the bombing and we had received conflicting reports, one that she was in a hospital somewhere and another that there was no news. Nadia, a lifetime smoker, had a husky voice and a huskier laugh and you always knew when she was around. "It's not normal that we shouldn't know where she is," I said. Nadia was one of the 21.

Another was Rick Hooper, the American right hand to Kieran Prendergast who specialized in the Middle East, a devastating blow to Kieran personally and professionally.

Sergio attracted the best and the brightest, and some of the best died that day.

An investigation

Almost immediately questions arose about Kofi's judgment in leaving UN staff in such a dangerous place. Edward wrote, "Indeed much of the debate since then has been a tug-of-war between the SG's responsibility for the lives and safety of his staff and pressure on him from the US, the UK and Iraqis themselves not to desert Iraq in its hour of need."

In late 2006, in a private conversation with Kofi in his office, I asked him about this. "It was a difficult period," he said. "You knew my position on the war. I never supported the war, nor defended it. And I was not bashful about it; it was clear to everyone. And then at the end of the war, I felt that one could not leave an unstable Iraq in the middle of that region. That would be extremely dangerous. The international community had to come together to get Iraq right, regardless of the divisions and one's view of the military action. But of course that implied that the US and the coalition forces were prepared to play it that way. I mentioned that they did in Kosovo and in Afghanistan. But in Iraq, that was not to be.

"And then, I had to send my friends and colleagues to help Iraq. What made it so difficult was, for a long time I resisted sending Sergio. I kept telling the US and UK that he has a job, a very important job. He's the High Commissioner for Human Rights; he's not available. And then they got to him personally; he signaled his willingness to take on the assignment for a brief period; and finally we agreed he could go for four months."

After the attack in Baghdad, Kofi once again lost his voice. When I asked him what the events of 19 August meant to him personally, he responded, "Sergio and a group of wonderful colleagues and friends went to Iraq to serve, to help, and got blown up. You can imagine my pain, melancholy, agony and the questions and doubts. And I spoke to Sergio the day before he died. We were laughing and talking about his holiday plans in October. He was going to take one month off to be with his mother in Rio, and I said fine. The death of these friends affected me deeply. I had to step back and regroup — and then I came back."

Kofi hesitated before ordering the UN out of Iraq, but after a second attack on the Canal Hotel a few weeks later that killed an Iraqi security guard at the UN compound, he had no choice. He told Washington that the UN would still work with them, but from a distance. He then sent in Martti Ahtisaari to investigate the security situation at the UN headquarters in Baghdad prior to the attack.

Martti, who won a Nobel Peace Prize in 2008 for a long series of peace assignments in and out of the UN, found severe security lapses. I had been his spokesperson in 1989-90 in Namibia. He showed me a draft of his report before he submitted it to Kofi and it was devastating. In a conversation much later, he told me, "I was basically furious when I produced that report because I felt that the lives of our friends and colleagues could have been saved. And I had absolutely no sympathy whatsoever for those who failed to do their jobs properly. The security failures in Baghdad must have increased Kofi's agony like it increased mine over the loss of Sergio and the others. And it must also have made him angry that there was a, sort of, bureaucratic inertia that was a factor. Whatever people said, it could have been prevented."

Chris Elfverson was Benon Sevan's Swedish deputy who oversaw from New York, and at times also administered in Iraq, the Oil-for-Food program in the Kurdish north. He told me that he had put protective film on all the glass in all UN buildings in the north and had recommended to both Benon Sevan and Tun Myat of Myanmar in their successive roles as Security Coordinator that the same be done at the Canal Hotel in Baghdad. The Ahtisaari report said that had that been done, the lives of most of the victims would have been saved. "I fervently believe this should trouble their consciences," he said to me more recently in Geneva.

Kofi reeled under the weight of these losses. He asked Tun Myat to step down in the wake of the Ahtisaari report. His Deputy, Louise Frechette, had overseen the Iraq portfolio; she chaired the high-level Steering Group on Iraq that coordinated daily UN policy. She sent Kofi a letter of resignation, but he rejected it, saying that the failures were of the group as a whole, not hers alone. If he fired all of them, he would wipe out half his cabinet.

When I asked Louise if she thought Kofi made a political mistake in not accepting her resignation, she said, "Only he can say whether it was a political mistake. The inquiry had not fingered me personally. It pointed the finger at the whole of senior management, which included him, of course. It said that we should have known, we should have anticipated. In response, Kofi sent a letter to all members of the steering committee through me as chair, expressing regret and disappointment that we had not advised him better. I thought: you can't have all your senior management receive a letter like that and nothing happen. So I offered my resignation.

"I think, in his mind, he was clear that this was a collective responsibility, not a personal one, and I don't think he wanted to personalize it. Was it a mistake? I don't know. The anger really was at him in the Secretariat. If he had accepted my resignation, I'm not sure it would have eased the pressure. It might have had even the opposite effect."

Loss of Voice

Kofi was obviously carrying a great emotional strain. After the US invasion of Iraq in 2003, the first signs of it began to emerge. He started to withdraw; he lost his voice.

He went to Geneva to give a speech to the Commission to Human Rights. He could hardly speak. Did he have laryngitis? A cold? On his return to New York, he did not come into the office and instead went to see a doctor about his throat. On 30 April, the Quartet (US, Russia, the EU and the UN) unveiled its "Road Map" for peace in the Middle East and Kofi was so hoarse he could hardly get through his speech. On the 1st of May, in a meeting with the Security Council on Iraq, Louise Frechette had to read Kofi's talking points for him. His voice was gone. The following day, she had to stand in for him for World Press Freedom Day.

Kofi then decided to cancel all travel and most of his speaking engagements for the month of May. Sometimes when I looked him in the eye, I sensed he wasn't there. At meetings, he seemed vacant, as if his spirit had gone somewhere else to seek counsel on what to do with the shattered United Nations, whose Charter it was his job to defend.

Those of us closest to him talked about it to each other in hushed tones, but didn't dare mention it outside that little circle. The press was slow to pick up on it. They noticed his hoarse voice, of course, but thought it was due to a cold or overwork.

Iqbal scrambled to build recovery time into Kofi's busy schedule. There was a bit of vacation, several weeks, actually, on doctor's orders.

Gradually, we saw improvement. But it wasn't 100 percent. He was carrying a burden and it was pushing him down.

Then came the bombing in Baghdad in August. Mental anguish, I thought, was added to that burden. But, remarkably, he

"Kofi was obviously carrying a great emotional strain. After the US invasion of Iraq in 2003, the first signs of it began to emerge. He started to withdraw; he lost his voice."

didn't stumble; he slogged on. He went through the memorial service for the 22 victims without his voice cracking. He ordered an inquiry into the security of the UN compound in Baghdad. And although he eventually pulled all his staff out of Iraq, he maintained a toehold in the political arena there.

I asked Iqbal Riza if Kofi sought psychological help, and his answer was, "I don't think so". I then asked Louise Frechette. "Well, I assumed all along that he sought medical attention," she said, "which is the smart thing to do. He lost his voice a couple of times, so I think he needed medical attention. Elisabeth [Lindenmayer] hinted that he was getting some psychological attention as well, which also would have been the smart thing to do, frankly. After a while, the campaign abated so he started spending less time worrying about the bad publicity over Oil-for-Food and more time on all the issues of the day. In my recollection, the time when he showed clear signs of distress was fairly short and it never stopped him completely from dealing with those issues."

Fork in the Road

Despite the torment he must have felt over the seemingly avoidable loss of his friends' lives, Kofi kept functioning. He knew he had to deal with a constitutional issue that was staring member governments full in the face. Could one of them use force preemptively, as the US had done in Iraq, without prior agreement by the Security Council? Was there something about the threat of international terrorism that changed the ground rules of collective security laid down in the UN Charter in 1945? He decided to put these questions before the Members in his speech to the General Assembly in the fall of 2003. It is one of his finest, and came to be known as the "fork in the road" speech.

Kofi started that speech with an appeal to all Member States to pull in the same direction. "The last 12 months have been very painful for those of us who believe in collective answers to our common problems…," he began. "It is vital to all of us that the outcome is a stable and democratic Iraq — at peace with itself and its neighbors, and contributing to stability in the region."

He then laid out the constitutional dilemma that was before the United Nations. "Article 51 of the Charter prescribes that all States, if attacked, retain the inherent right of self defense. But until now it has been understood that when States go beyond that, and decide to use force to deal with broader threats to international peace and

"I can recall many occasions," said Kieren Prendergast, "where the Security Council…tended to look to him to try and come up with some formula that might restore their unity, which is not really the role of the Secretary-General."

security, they need the unique legitimacy provided by the United Nations." He acknowledged that some now say that this understanding is no longer tenable, since a clandestine group could launch an armed attack with weapons of mass destruction at any time, without warning. "Rather than wait for that to happen, they argue, States have the right and obligation to use force preemptively," he said, "even on the territory of other States, and even while weapons systems that might be used to attack them are still being developed."

According to this argument, States are not obliged to wait until there is agreement in the Security Council, he went on. "Instead, they reserve the right to act unilaterally, or in ad hoc coalitions. This logic represents a fundamental challenge to the principles on which, however imperfectly, world peace and stability have rested for the last 58 years."

The problem with this argument, he said, is that "it could set precedents that result in proliferation of the unilateral and lawless use of force."

He then posed an interesting question — why does a State feel so vulnerable that it takes action on its own outside the Charter? "But it is not enough to denounce unilateralism," he said, "unless we also face up squarely to the concerns that make some States feel uniquely vulnerable, since it is those concerns that drive them to take unilateral action. We must show that those concerns can, and will, be addressed effectively through collective action."

And then came the punch line, calling the Security Council to face the bottom line challenge. "Excellencies, we have come to a fork in the road. This may be a moment no less decisive than 1945 itself, when the United Nations was founded…. The Council needs to consider how it will deal with the possibility that individual States may use force 'preemptively' against perceived threats."

But he wasn't going to just leave the question in their laps because he knew full well they could sit on it for years and not take action or even reach agreement. He announced his intention to set up a High-Level Panel to look at these questions and report back to him. He would present his recommendations, based on their report, to the General Assembly Summit called for the fall of 2005.

Lakhdar Goes In

The occupying powers, the US and the UK, had pledged to hold elections in Iraq for the transfer of sovereignty by 30 June 2004. It turned out that that was too optimistic and Paul Bremer needed to buy time. The Grand Ayatollah Ali al-Sistani said he would not accept that elections could not be held by 30 June unless the UN told him so. Bremer needed help.

While Kofi did not feel he could send a team back into Iraq full time, he reached for his remaining ace in the hole — Lakhdar Brahimi. Lakhdar was not at all eager to accept the assignment, he told me.

"I have the impression that Kofi is painfully aware that the presence of Sergio and his colleagues in Iraq at that particular time was not even that indispensable. Frankly, the UN had no business being in Iraq at all in August 2003. That is why Kofi Annan and everyone in the UN feels so much regret, so much bitterness about this tragedy. Kofi knew this better than any of us. I had discussions with him before. As you know, he thought of me going there. But before they offered it, I told him that there was no job for us in Iraq at that particular time: the US-led coalition invaded the country. They went to the Security Council and got a resolution that gave them the status of occupiers. What is it that you want to do there?"

But of course Paul Bremer and members of the Iraq Governing Council had personally come to see Kofi to ask for the UN to return to Baghdad. "They said they wanted really to put an end to the occupation, to restore sovereignty to Iraq and that they needed UN help for that," Lakhdar went on. "They said clearly that they would not be able to do it alone. Again and again they said they needed the help of the UN. In these conditions, the Secretary-General found it simply impossible to say no."

Lakhdar would have had no difficulty saying no, he told me. "And my inclination was to say no. The UN had to go back to Iraq, but why should it be me? I had been against the war. But both the Secretary-General and I were put under unbelievable pressure. Not only the US, but also the United Kingdom and quite a few Iraqis, including not only some of the honorable members of the Governing Council, but also some who had been strongly opposed to the invasion, wanted the UN back and wanted me to be its point man in Baghdad."

But then the US pressure came from the top. Kofi called Lakhdar from London, while on an official trip. According to Lakhdar, Kofi said, "Look, the President of the United States has spoken to me several times; we really cannot say no. Please go. 'Just go for a few days', he said. I told him, you know very well that if I go, I am not the type of man who would just go for a few days. If I go, I will try and do the job. So, I went there very, very reluctantly, but I did go. And once there, of course, I did my best. But my best was not good enough."

Lakhdar went to Baghdad and consulted widely on who should be the members of the new Iraqi government. But it was not easy, he said. "It was an impossible job because the Americans had empowered a number of people who were not at all representative. We tried to push the walls out as much as we could, but there was a limit to what could be done. And you had to deal with what I called all the vetoes that were there. You couldn't have anything if the Kurds were not on board. You couldn't have anything if the Shi'ite leader Sistani wasn't on board. And you couldn't have anything if the Americans weren't on board. So, you know, navigating in these kinds of waters was not very easy."

Still, Lakhdar weeded out some people who were totally unacceptable. He said, "Yet I think we managed to get rid of quite a few very fundamentalist people, quite a few very corrupt people and form a government that on paper looked a little bit better; but ultimately, it did not prove that much better."

Lakhdar helped shape the Iraqi Interim Government, but in the end the Americans had their way. Thanks to him, it was better, but it was not as good as it could have been. Lakhdar convinced the Shi'ite leader Ali al-Sistani that the 30 June election date wasn't realistic, and that helped the Americans, and the process, a lot. The UN at this point, though, was playing a more important but still not a central role in post-war Iraq.

No Weapons of Mass Destruction

President Bush had sold the idea of invading Iraq to the American public on the grounds that Saddam Hussein had hidden caches of weapons of mass destruction. Members of his Administration had spoken derisively of the UN chief weapons inspector, Hans Blix of Sweden. With the US now the official occupier of Iraq, Washington asked David Kay, a former UN weapons inspector and an American, to go into Iraq and find the weapons that Hans Blix couldn't. He went and found nothing. On 29 January 2004, he reported to Congress, "We were all wrong on WMD". He resigned, saying that US intelligence had "goofed". Not content with that, the US sent in a second team under American Charles Duelfer, who had for years been the number two man on the UN weapons inspection team. In early October, after an exhaustive search, Duelfer reported that it appeared that Saddam Hussein had destroyed all such weapons.

This was profoundly embarrassing for the Bush Administration. In Washington, key neoconservatives began slipping from their positions of power. To his credit, Richard Perle admitted in an interview with *Vanity Fair* magazine in 2006 that things might have been done differently. "Could we have managed the threat by means other than a direct military intervention?" he told the magazine. "Well, maybe we could have." But it was now too late.

In April 2007, *The Economist* wrote: "The tragedy of neo-conservatism is that the movement began as a critique of the arrogance of power. Early neocons warned that government schemes to improve the world might well end up making it worse. They also argued that social engineers are always plagued by the law of unintended consequences. The neocons have not only messed up American foreign policy by forgetting their founders' insights. They may also have put a stake through the heart of their own movement."

CHAPTER 19

OIL-FOR-FOOD — HOW IT WORKED

When Saddam Hussein invaded Kuwait in August 1990, the Security Council, energized by the sense of unity that followed the end of the Cold War, adopted a dozen resolutions, steadily raising the cost to Iraq of remaining in Kuwait and culminating in the authorization of "all necessary means" (i.e. war) to drive Saddam out.

One of those resolutions, number 661, imposed economic sanctions on Iraq. Saddam shrugged at these threats and arrogantly predicted "The Mother of All Battles". That's what he got. On 24 of February 1991, the US led an impressive international military force, sanctioned by the Security Council, that routed the Iraqi military in short order.

Devastating Damage

Secretary-General Javier Perez de Cuellar sent Martti Ahtisaari to assess the damage after the fighting. The Americans weren't happy with his language. Martti described "near-apocalyptic results on the economic infrastructure" of Iraq. "Most means of modern life support have been destroyed or rendered tenuous," he said, adding, "Iraq has, for some time to come been relegated to a pre-industrial age." The tension over the Ahtisaari report reflected two different ways of looking at what had just happened. The militarists saw a brilliant victory, and some among them felt the job was left unfinished because Saddam was still in power. The humanitarians agreed that good had triumphed over evil, but were more upset about the consequences for the civilian population, which were severe.

The US led the drafting of the terms of surrender, which emerged as Security Council Resolution 687. It spelled out in great detail everything Saddam would have to do as a result of having lost the war. Diplomats jokingly called 687 "The Mother of All Resolutions". It said that Iraq had to destroy all its weapons of mass destruction and the means, that is, missiles, of delivering them; he had to pay reparation to Kuwait for war damages and restore all stolen Kuwaiti property; he had to repatriate Kuwaiti and third country nationals, and so on. Until these things were done, UN sanctions would stay in place. Iraq had no choice but to accept, and did so on 6 April 1991.

But then the US hinted that it was moving the goal posts. The very next month, officials of the first Bush Administration began to say that the sanctions would not be lifted against Iraq as long as Saddam Hussein remained in power. When President Bill Clinton came to power, senior members of his Administration said the same thing. So we now had two agendas for the lifting of sanctions — one from the US and one from the UN.

Under UN sanctions, the Iraqi economy began to shrivel. One of the world's leading exporters of oil was hardly exporting any, and was living off dwindling reserves. Real earnings dropped, imports declined, the exchange rate for the dinar plummeted. It was an economic and humanitarian disaster.

The Oil-for-Food Idea

The Security Council, under pressure from the Ahtisaari report and humanitarian groups, came up with the Oil-for-Food idea in August 1991. Iraq once again would be permitted to sell its oil, they proposed, although in amounts approved by the Council. The Council would also approve all contracts of sale. The money from the sales would not go to the Iraqi Treasury, but to a UN administered escrow account, eventually set up in a Paris bank.

Iraq could then buy badly needed humanitarian supplies — but not directly. If the Government wanted to buy potatoes, for example, it could sign a contract with a potato supplier, but that contract would have to be approved by the Council. Once approved, the potatoes could be shipped to Iraq only through certain points of entry, where UN inspectors would control that they were indeed what was ordered and in the proper amount. The Government could distribute the potatoes, except in the Kurdish north, where the UN did the distribution. (After the war, the Coalition continued to protect the Kurds, whom Saddam had persecuted brutally.) The UN certified that the potatoes had been delivered and authorized the Paris bank to pay the potato vender. And that was how Oil-for-Food was to work, in simplest terms.

These terms were so intrusive that Saddam Hussein at first refused to consider them. The national economy continued to grind down. Five years passed before he broke down and allowed Oil-for-Food to go forward in 1996. Gradually, Iraq's oil industry got up and running, oil was sold, the money went into the Paris bank, and Iraq began buying food and humanitarian supplies, working through the Security Council.

UN humanitarian workers went into Iraq to help set up the program. One of them was Michel Lavollay, who described the program to me. "Well, it started out as a fairly straightforward job, if you want; difficult, but straightforward, in the sense that we had to create from scratch a mechanism for monitoring the arrival and distribution of food and medicine. So we did that, and it worked pretty well.

"The Iraqis were complying. They seemed eager to demonstrate that they were efficient about this program but at the same time they were reflecting their intrinsic qualities as Iraqis, which was very striking. They were both very kind and open with us, the UN observers. They judged us to be fairly neutral in their issues with the outside world and with their internal situation. They have a high education level; they are a people who have a very solid past, and they are very good mathematicians and excellent engineers. Others have described them as the Prussians of the Middle East.

"So, that was one aspect. And the other aspect was that we did have access to every single little village in the country. So there was no obstacle to us visiting any part of Iraqi society, within the marshes in the south, or along the Iranian border in the refugee camps. And so we had a good sense of what was going on."

"Our experience in the first year of Oil-for-Food showed that the Iraqis were complying and were not meddling with the program," he went on. "What it also showed for us was that the population was indeed suffering. And as neutral UN staff, we felt an obligation to describe exactly the state of the population in Iraq at that time. We had access; we could develop questionnaires and get straightforward answers, sometimes angry answers, from mothers, from ordinary citizens, who described a country which had reached levels of development equivalent to the poorest countries in Africa when it had been one of the thriving countries of the Middle East just 10 years before."

Halliday and von Sponeck Step Down

The desperate condition of the Iraqi civilian population was becoming a growing political problem for the US and the UK and others whose strategic goal was to contain Saddam Hussein. The civilian cost of UN sanctions was great. UN humanitarian agencies sent more and more alarming reports to New York, as did the humanitarian workers for the Oil-for-Food Programme. A Humanitarian Coordinator oversaw the program in Iraq, and Kofi was embarrassed twice when his Humanitarian Coordinator resigned in protest against the inhuman effects of UN sanctions. The first to resign, in September 1998, was Denis Halliday of Ireland. I asked him why he quit.

"I volunteered to head the Oil-for-Food Programme in Iraq," he answered, "to work with the government in Baghdad and the Kurdish authorities in the north to put it in place. And it was a struggle but it was also a success. It was a success not thanks to the Security Council or the Member States, but thanks to the Iraqi government, which had technocrats of great skill who worked with us under great difficulties and eventually got the program to work."

Denis realized that this success was having the effect of allowing the Security Council, and Washington in particular, to claim that the humanitarian problem had been solved, relieving the pressure to lift sanctions. "The hidden agenda of the United States," he said, "was always the removal of Saddam Hussein." He did not want to be party to a program that took the pressure off the Security Council to, in his words, "take an honest look at sanctions, evaluate their impact on Iraqis, particularly the children, and not keep them in place forever without any sense of responsibility as to their genocidal consequences." Denis stepped down and then, in February 2000, his replacement, Hans von Sponeck of Germany, did the same thing for the same reason — UN sanctions were unfairly hurting the innocent people of Iraq. Tensions were running very high; political pressure to lift the sanctions was mounting.

Eventually the Security Council increased the size and scope of the Oil-for-Food Programme, although it was not as efficient as it might have been because the Council, mainly the US and the UK, were checking contracts for dual-use items. A dual-use item is something that could have a humanitarian use but also a military one. For example, chlorine can be used as a water purifier but also as an element in a chemical weapon. Or atropine, which is a widely used muscle relaxer in surgery, can also be used as an antidote for nerve gas poisoning. There was such sensitivity to dual use that by early 2001 some 2,000 contracts worth a total of over $5 billion were on hold.

Saddam milks the program

Some of those involved in the program saw two phases in terms of Saddam's attitude towards it. Darko Mocibob worked for Benon Sevan, who oversaw the program for the UN. "Saddam complied with the rules of the Oil-for-Food Programme in the first few phases," he told me, "believing that it would be short-lived and that sanctions would be lifted soon. Indeed, the Iraqis never agreed to extend the program for more than six months at the time. It's clear to us now that once it became obvious to Saddam that sanctions would not be lifted as long as he remained in power, he began looking for ways to use the program to stay in power. I concluded that much of the kickbacks and income from smuggled oil ended up financing a parallel state budget, paying for salaries of civil servants, the military and other loyalists as well as buying additional food to supplement the UN food basket."

Chris Elfverson, who was deputy to Benon Sevan, agrees. "Saddam's government was the recognized government of Iraq and was expected to run the country," he said. "But he was not allowed to use his oil revenue, the only legal source of income he had, to pay civil servants, hospitals, road maintenance and so on. I raised this several times in the Security Council's sanctions committee and the reply was, 'He can use his revenue from smuggling.'"

Even before the Oil-for-Food Programme began operating, Saddam Hussein was managing to sell some oil under the table, mainly to neighbors Jordan and Turkey. The US and the UK and others were aware of this, but since those oil imports benefited two allies of the West and helped offset for them the negative affects of sanctions on Iraq, it was decided to turn a blind eye to it. The Council eventually "took note" of these shipments, arguing that Article 50 of the Charter, by which third parties hurt by sanctions can appeal to the UN for financial relief, made these imports legitimate. In Washington, both the Bush and the Clinton Administrations officially exempted Jordan and Turkey from penalties for their illicit trade with Iraq.

In any case, the UN controlled only a small portion of Iraq's trade. "It's important to note that the UN sanctions against Iraq were in no way all-encompassing," Chris said. "We could control only merchandise coming across the border that was purchased through the Oil-for-Food Programme. Everything else, maybe 80 percent of the traffic across the Turkish-Iraqi and Jordanian-Iraqi borders, went unchecked. We had no authority to look at it."

Under Oil-for-Food, the Council, in token deference to Iraq's sovereignty, agreed to let Saddam choose the oil purchasers and the suppliers of imported humanitarian goods. He was like a kid in a candy store. He had leverage over companies, which allowed him to extract kickbacks from importers and surcharges from exporters. "And many British and American firms played this game," Chris commented, "acting through European, and in particular French, subsidiaries, meaning that a good portion of Iraqi imports came from US firms. In addition, much of the oil eventually ended up in the US."

With his illicit wealth, he also tried to win friends and influence people with the objective of getting sanctions lifted, selectively bribing this one and that. He seemed to think, well, if the US is not going to lift sanctions no matter what we do, unless I relinquish power, which I'm not going to do, then I can play this game too. Members of the Security Council, especially the US and the UK, were aware of this activity, but seemed to have made the calculation that tolerating it was an acceptable price to pay for keeping sanctions in place and maintaining the pressure on Saddam.

Clean Hands

In the end, despite Saddam's sticky fingers, and the tie-ups over dual use, the Oil-for-Food Programme oversaw the sale of $64.2 billion in oil sales and delivered some $39.7 billion worth of humanitarian supplies to Iraq. (The balance of the money funded the weapons inspectors, compensation to Kuwaitis and others, and so on.) It placed food on every Iraqi table, dramatically increasing caloric intake and reducing malnutrition among children. Health care improved significantly, water quality and sanitation was upgraded, agricultural output was boosted, school enrollment increased, power was restored and the quality of housing improved.

After the US invaded Iraq in 2003, the Oil-for-Food Programme was shut down, its books audited and the balance in the bank — initially some $8.1 billion — was turned over to the US-led Coalition Provisional Authority to be used for the reconstruction of Iraq. The auditors found that not a dollar was missing. With regard to the more than $10 billion of Iraqi oil money that was eventually handed over to the CPA by the UN, however, auditors later found that $8.8 billion of it was unaccounted for. No one seemed to care much about this.

The UN Secretariat had taken on the biggest assignment of its 55-year life, ran it reasonably well, with a few blips, and had a good degree of success in achieving what it was set up to do. Yet UN critics, in the US in particular, would growl about the Oil-for-Food scandal, which, in the end, was their scandal.

That was the Oil-for-Food Programme for Iraq.

CHAPTER 20

ANNUS HORRIBILIS

Kofi called 2004 his *annus horribilis*, a term he borrowed from Queen Elizabeth II, referring to the year 1992 when two marriages in the royal family broke up, the Queen's daughter-in-law was photographed by the tabloids topless with a new boyfriend, and a devastating fire swept through Windsor Castle.

COTECNA AND THE CONSERVATIVE MEDIA

By the beginning of 2004, the Bush Administration's dream of a stable Iraq was fading fast. The US presence in Iraq was generating precisely what the President said he went in to prevent — a haven for terrorists. Amidst the embarrassment of the deepening quagmire, President Bush met with Kofi in Washington in February, frankly, to ask for help. Kofi obliged, pledging to work with the US to stabilize Iraq. Even Jerry Bremer, head of the Coalition Provisional Authority, paid a call on Kofi in his office to ask for assistance.

Kofi's political enemies on the American right now turned their sights on him. The conservative media in the US spearheaded their attacks, and leading the charge were Rupert Murdoch's *Fox News* and *The Wall Street Journal*'s editorial page.

The first signal that the UN was vulnerable on Oil-for-Food came from the other side of the Atlantic, though, and much earlier. In January 1999, the *Sunday Telegraph* of London contacted my office regarding an article they were writing on corruption in the Benazir Bhutto regime in Pakistan. An official of a Swiss-based trade inspection company, Cotecna, had been linked to illegal kickbacks to Bhutto. And the *Telegraph* noticed two things — first, that Kofi's son Kojo worked for Cotecna, and second, that Cotecna had the UN Oil-for-Food contract to inspect humanitarian goods coming into Iraq. The *Telegraph* asked about conflict of interest.

Fair enough. My office relayed the inquiry up to Kofi's office, and Chief of Staff Iqbal Riza took charge. He asked the UN's senior manager, Joseph Connor, who oversaw procurement, to look into it. Connor had his people do a cursory check. I say cursory because he came back to Riza the very same day with a one-page note saying that Kojo had worked for Cotecna's West Africa operations, had severed his employment toward the end of 1998, about the time Cotecna got the UN contract, and that no one in the UN's procurement unit knew that Kojo worked for Cotecna. (Connor later commented to me that some of them didn't even know who Kojo was.) They had awarded the contract to Cotecna because it was the lowest bidder.

Kofi asked his Legal Counsel, Hans Corell, whether there was anything he should do about it. Based on information that Hans had received from Joseph Connor, Hans advised him no. Hans told me in 2009 that the important question was whether the Contracts Committee knew that Kojo worked for Cotecna. When Joseph Connor informed him that they did not, this for him was the determining element. "If they didn't know about his employment," he said, "there could be no doubt about Cotecna having won the contract on its own merits." He then added, "The overriding issue is whether the body reviewing the bids and offering the contract is acting in accordance with the law and that a relative of the boss has not attempted to exercise undue influence on the decision makers."

In the spokesperson's office, we were satisfied with the guidance we received and gave the information to the *Sunday Telegraph*. Edward Mortimer suspected that someone from Lloyd's Register in London put the *Telegraph* onto the story. Lloyd's had lost the contract to Cotecna. When no other media picked it up, though, we assumed there was nothing more to it and were relieved when the story seemed to die. "With hindsight," Edward wrote in his notes, "one wonders whether it would have been a good idea to somehow bring it to public attention at that point, rather than wait for others to do so." Indeed, it would have.

A Warning from Chalabi

On 3 June 2003, Edward had received a friendly warning from an unlikely source. He had coffee across the street from the UN at the Millennium Plaza Hotel with exiled Iraqi leader, Ahmad Chalabi, whom he had known for some 10 years during his days as a reporter. Chalabi was bitter that the UN had not supported the military overthrow of Saddam Hussein and that the Secretariat had not made greater efforts to highlight Saddam's skimming of the Oil-for-Food Programme. Edward argued back that there was nothing that Kofi could have done to stop it, since Saddam struck these deals privately with companies — the money never passed through UN hands. Chalabi wasn't satisfied and warned Mortimer that he was going to launch a public campaign against the UN. In December, an Iraqi newspaper close to Chalabi published a list of people and companies that had received oil vouchers from Saddam. One of those names, in Arabic, looked very much like Benon Sevan's, the man who ran the Oil-for-Food Programme for Kofi.

My heart sank. I considered Benon a friend and didn't think he would take illegal kickbacks. If it were true, however, it would smear the entire Secretariat — and the UN itself. Of course, Chalabi was a questionable source. He had been tried in absentia and convicted of 31 counts of embezzlement, theft, misuse of depositor funds and so on in connection with his role in the Petra Bank in Jordan and was sentenced by a Jordanian court to 22 years in prison. And he had sold much of Washington on the idea that Saddam had weapons of mass destruction, which turned out to be false. My hope against hope was that he was setting a political trap for Benon and had no hard evidence. Benon issued a categorical denial, which I read out at my noon press briefing.

Safire and Rosett

In early 2004, Claudia Rosett reopened the question of Kojo's employment with Cotecna. She was unknown to us until then, although she had worked for *The Wall Street Journal* since 1984 and been on its editorial board since 1997.

Rosett wrote that Cotecna had continued payments to Kojo beyond the end of 1998 when Joe Connor told us that Kojo's links to the company had been severed. We had to scramble. Lamin Sise was tasked by Chief of Staff Iqbal Riza to look into it. Lamin told me that he first called Kojo to clarify the precise dates of his employment with Cotecna. He reached him on his mobile phone in Nigeria, but Kojo said he was not at his office and could not consult his files. Lamin knew that I would need to say something at the noon briefing. Kojo suggested that he call André Prunieux, a Vice President of Cotecna in Geneva, to get the exact dates. Lamin spoke to Prunieux, who told him that while Kojo had stopped working for the company on a regular basis at the end of 1998, he was given what is commonly known as a Non-Compete Agreement.

I was not familiar with Non-Compete Agreements, but I dutifully explained to the press that indeed Kojo had continued to receive payments from Cotecna as part of such an agreement. Non-Compete Agreements, I was told, and I repeated to the press, were standard in the business world, and are given to certain departing employees so that they will not compete with their former employer. Prunieux told Lamin that these payments ended a year later at the end of 1999 and I, unwisely, relayed this information to the press. Other Cotecna executives, in later testimony before the US Congress, would contradict what Prunieux told Lamin, admitting that the payments had gone on longer.

In my heart, I was not confident in what I was putting out. I was already back-pedaling on what I had said previously. The mainstream media began to take an interest in the story. It was no longer just a battle between the UN and the ideological far right. We were in trouble now, and the far right was on a roll.

On 17 March 2004, the *annus horribilis*, William Safire wrote about "Kofigate", a reference to the Nixon Watergate scandal. On Monday the 21st of April, Safire had a provocative piece in which he urged the Bush Administration to "Follow the Money". In it, he wrote that Saddam Hussein "skimmed a huge bundle and socked it away in Swiss, French and Asian banks." Journalists began to uncover details about Saddam's "illegal smuggling" of oil to Turkey, Jordan and Syria, companies paying Saddam kickbacks for contracts and Saddam bribing influential people he felt could help get the sanctions against Iraq lifted.

Kofigate soon snowballed into what Safire later referred to as the "heftiest heist in history". The Oil-for-Food Programme had managed the sale of roughly $64 billion in oil, and with part of that money oversaw the purchase of $39 million in humanitarian goods. Some of the UN's critics illogically added these two figures together and talked about a $100 billion scam. Things were getting way out of control.

Rosett did an Op-Ed in *The New York Times* on Friday 18 April accusing the UN of secrecy on Oil-for-Food. "Putting a veil of secrecy over tens of billions of dollars in contracts is an invitation to kickbacks, political back-scratching and smuggling under cover of relief operations," she wrote. We came to know Rosett as the master of the half-truth. She did admit in her article that, "Mr. Annan's office does share more detailed records with the Security Council members, but none of those countries makes them public." So is she criticizing the UN, Kofi Annan or governments? Through innuendo, all three.

With these articles and others, conservatives fired the first shots across the bow of the UN as the US was turning back to the world organization for help in Iraq. For conservatives, this change of tack by the Bush Administration was a severe setback. Their political objective, I assumed, was to discredit the United Nations by any means, and Oil-for-Food gave them a lot of ammunition.

I felt I was being hit by a truck. After 16 years of working in the UN Spokesperson's Office, I had developed a fundamental respect for journalists and had become convinced that they are an essential ingredient in the balance of power; their greatest service is working to keep politicians honest — or more honest. But they do have a nasty herding instinct, and when they all start running in the same direction they can lose perspective. I felt that was happening on Oil-for-Food, over which we, the Secretariat, had minimal control; it was a show run by governments. But we failed to explain to the mainstream press how Oil-for-Food worked and how governments were in charge. That gave the conservative media a lot of running room.

Have a taste of the headlines during 2004:

8 March: Oil-for-Food is a global scandal, says *The Wall Street Journal.*

29 March: There was never such a rip-off as Oil-for-Food, wrote *The New York Times* columnist William Safire.

8 April: Conservative Republicans say Oil-for-Food casts doubt on UN's ability to help the US in Iraq — *Los Angeles Times.*

22 April: If the UN can't be trusted to run a humanitarian program, how can it be given a political role in Iraq? — *Times* of London.

28 April: The UN is a menace to security, writes Claudia Rosett in *The Wall Street Journal.*

19 July: Oil-for-Food money is fueling the insurgency in Iraq — *New York Post.*

22 September: Oil-for-Food stole food from the mouths of hungry children, says Claudia Rosett — *The Wall Street Journal Europe.*

14 October: Kojo Annan is up to his eyeballs in Oil-for-Food says *Fox News*'s Bill O'Reilly.

20 October: Oil-for-Food is the heftiest heist in history, writes William Safire.

2 November: The UN is rotten to the core, says columnist Kevin Myers — *Irish Times.*

17 November: Saddam used Oil-for-Food money to pay Palestinian bombers — *New York Post.*

19 November: What did Kofi Annan know and when did he know it? asked the *New York Post*, echoing a phrase from the Nixon Watergate scandal.

23 November: The White House is protecting the UN from the Oil-for-Food scandal because it wants the UN's support in Iraq — *The Wall Street Journal.*

29 November: Kofi Annan must resign, says William Safire.

Ouch! These guys play rough.

How to Fight Back?

One of those counseling Kofi on media matters was Jim Goodale, a former Vice Chairman of *The New York Times*. Jim's view was that the conventional wisdom as it applied to an American politician didn't apply to a UN Secretary-General.

"As we learned from the media-centric presidential campaigns of the 1990s," he told me, "the only way to deal with a political attack is to return it in kind immediately. This was genius of the Clinton presidential campaign and its manager, James Carville. Since Kofi was now, in a sense, in a domestic political campaign, the only way for him to protect himself was to do the same thing. But how could he? Was it appropriate for someone who had Pope-like status to fire off instant responses attacking those who attacked him? And was it appropriate for a Secretary-General to attack those who attacked his son? And should he?

"Further, if he hired a domestic public relations crisis firm, that act would appear to be defensive and, more to the point, quite undignified for the Secretary-General of the United Nations to do."

Kofi's "Pope-like status" was fading fast; he needed to do something dramatic.

The Volcker Panel

In March 2004, Kofi decided to ask an independent panel to investigate Oil-for-Food, and he was able to convince Paul Volcker to chair it. Volcker, an American and the former Chairman of the Federal Reserve Board, is a figure of towering integrity. It was miraculous that he accepted, I thought.

Lamin Sise told me that when Volcker first heard the scope of the project, he said to Kofi, "This is going to cost you." Volcker had chaired a panel looking into holocaust accounts; that inquiry had cost over $200 million. When Kofi heard that figure, he looked at Volcker and smiled and said, "We don't talk in those terms here." When Kofi discussed with his senior managers how to cover the estimated original cost of the inquiry, which was over $30 million, someone suggested using Oil-for-Food money. But deputy Louise Frechette disagreed. "That would look terrible," she said. "The Member States should be assessed for it." But when the Security Council approved the program, guess what it did? It gave Kofi no option but to take the money from the Iraqis.

"Hell, no." Kofi pushing back after the relentless attacks by the press in 2004.

Kofi then had to convince the Security Council to allow Volcker to look into all aspects of the program, not just the Secretariat's role. There was some resistance, but eventually the Council agreed.

Volcker said at his opening press conference that he would look at the Secretariat first. If they had not done any wrong, he could clear the air; if they had, action could be taken quickly. I believe he wanted the best and fairest treatment for the UN Secretariat. He had to battle a host of US Congressional Committees, which had also launched their own investigations into Oil-for-Food. In the US, there's nothing like a ripe UN scandal to generate lurid interest on the part of officialdom. Only a person of Volcker's reputation could have held them off.

I was in the awkward position of not being able to comment to the media on anything Volcker was investigating. On the one hand, this was easier for me. All I had to say was, "Volcker is looking into this; let's wait for his report." On the other, a spokesperson doesn't look very convincing withholding information, even if it is for a legally justifiable reason.

THE *BBC* AND THAT LITTLE WORD "ILLEGAL"

15 September 2004 was just another miserable day in a miserable year.

Because of all of the negative stories in the press generated by Oil-for-Food, we weren't pushing Kofi to do interviews at his usual pace, which had been averaging about 45 a year since 1999. But I had received a request from a woman at the *BBC* who had interviewed him on the subject of AIDS the year before. She wanted to talk to him this time about general issues, nothing on Iraq, so I passed the request on to Kofi. He liked this woman and he agreed. The day before the interview was to take place, the *BBC* called me to say that the woman had just discovered she had breast cancer and needed immediate treatment. Could they send Owen Bennett-Jones in her place?

Now stupidity is when a person doesn't use their normal smarts, and I stupidly said I would ask Kofi. Owen Bennett-Jones is one of the *BBC*'s top political reporters and this was not the time to expose Kofi to him. But the *BBC* had been very generous to Kofi, had given him lots of airtime and had been consistently fair. Besides, in the past I never had to worry about Kofi with the press. No matter how rough the questioning, he remained cool, dignified and he answered with tact, but also with just enough candor to be credible. And he was always on message; he needed no coaxing. He agreed to talk to Owen Bennett-Jones.

Kofi came out of the door of his office ready for the interview. He put out his hand and I shook it, but he didn't look me in the eye. During this difficult year, I often found him distant. But he could have been formulating his thoughts for the encounter with the *BBC*.

When he walked into the room where the interview was to take place, the crew stopped what they were doing and turned towards him. Kofi not only greeted Bennett-Jones, but, as he usually does, also shook hands as well with the cameraman, the soundman and the producer. Then he settled into his chair.

Bennett-Jones is slick and tough. He started by throwing a hot potato in Kofi's lap. "Are you bothered that the US is becoming an unrestrainable, unilateral superpower," he asked? Great question, but Kofi stayed cool. "Well, I think that over the last year," he began, "we've all gone through lots of painful lessons." Nothing controversial.

Bennett-Jones then asked Kofi whether he thought the resolution passed before the war gave legal authority for the invasion. "Well, I'm one of those who believe that there should have been a second resolution," Kofi said forthrightly, "because the Security Council indicated that if Iraq did not comply there will be consequences. But then it was up to the Security Council to approve or determine what those consequences should be."

"So you don't think there was legal authority for the war," Bennett-Jones asked him?

"I have stated clearly that it was not in conformity with the Security Council — with the Charter," Kofi said.

"It was illegal," Bennett-Jones insisted.

Kofi smiled ever so slightly and inappropriately as he sometimes does when facing a tough question, as if he is saying, I know what you're getting at and now I'm going to give it to you. "Yes," he replied, "if you wish."

Bennett-Jones now had what he wanted, but insisted on nailing it down. "It was illegal?"

Kofi, straight-faced this time, replied, "Yes, I have indicated it is not in conformity with the UN Charter; from our point of view and from the Charter point of view it was illegal."

Off message. Kofi should have stuck to the boring diplomatic wording that the invasion was not in conformity with the Charter. By saying "illegal", he was throwing down a red flag.

Walking down the corridor with him afterwards back to his office, he asked me as he usually did how I thought it went. I said, "I think you're going to get into trouble for using the word 'illegal'." He raised his eyebrows in surprise and then reflected for three or four more steps. "But it's been what I've been saying all along," he said. "But you've never used that word before," I argued back. Several more steps in silence. "Well," he said, with a touch of sadness, not defiance, in his voice, "it's what I think."

BBC ran hard with the quote for days. If Bennett-Jones' intention was to embarrass Tony Blair, he succeeded. And the Bush camp in Washington was furious too. On the other hand, the anti-war faction worldwide, and particularly in the Middle East, was elated that Kofi had come out so firmly against the war. Of course, he had been on the record with that position from the beginning, but with the word "illegal", he made a splash.

When I asked Richard Holbrooke if he thought the "illegal" quote to *BBC* was a political mistake, he replied, "Of course; it was obvious. It was a political mistake, and also a policy mistake. First of all, on policy grounds, in 1999, Kofi had defended Kosovo, which had been structurally similar. So he couldn't argue that the sole legitimate place to justify the use of force was always, and only, the Security Council, and be consistent."

Kofi's closest advisers disagree. "Kosovo and Iraq are apples and cheese," said Kieran Prendergast; "not at all comparable. Kosovo is widely regarded as 'illegal but legitimate'. It was a case of humanitarian intervention. There would have been a large majority in the Security Council in favor, as was demonstrated when the Russians called for a vote to condemn the action after the fact and that failed by a vote of 12 to 3. The reason it wasn't brought to the Council initially was because the Russians had signaled they would veto it. The result was Kofi's speech of September 1999 on humanitarian intervention — one of his very best — which set out clearly the competing imperatives of a complex argument."

"Iraq," Kieran went on, "was neither in accordance with the Charter nor legitimate. It was in no sense a humanitarian intervention. One of the main problems was that the US and the UK kept changing their declared justification for the war — was it Iraq's non-compliance with Security Council resolutions? Or terrorism? Or regime change? There was very little support for the war in the Security Council; the search for a second resolution authorizing military action was abandoned when it became clear that only four members, including the US and the UK, out of fifteen would vote in favor. I think most people now understand that the Iraq operation was not legitimate. No weapons of mass destruction were ever found; there was never any evidence of Iraq's links to al-Qaeda terrorists, and regime change is not an acceptable objective in international law."

THE FALLUJAH LETTER

In late October 2004, Kofi received privileged information that US troops were preparing for an assault on the Iraqi city of Fallujah, a Sunni stronghold. Everyone around Kofi thought this was a bad idea, as did Kofi himself. Kieran Prendergast summed up Kofi's reservations. "His concerns were the inevitable collateral damage, the risk of violations of international humanitarian law, the further damage in the Arab and Muslim worlds to America's reputation, the likely inflammatory effect on the insurgency — rendering the action counterproductive — and the fact that most insurgents in Fallujah had already left for other cities, the Americans having well and truly telegraphed their punch and having failed to seal off the approaches to and the exits from the city."

Kofi did not want to have to deliver this complex argument over the phone; he feared he would be interrupted. So he decided to send a letter expressing his reservations about the military action to President Bush, UK Prime Minister Blair and Iraqi Prime Minister Alawi. Apparently, Iqbal Riza warned about the proximity of the US elections, but Lakhdar Brahimi urged that the letters be sent anyway. The letter to Bush was sent to the US Mission to the UN, as are all routine communications to Washington, except it was faxed, which is unusual for an item of such sensitivity. It went out before the US elections, because that was when the military action was expected to take place.

President Bush was running a tight race for reelection that fall against Senator John Kerry, and Kerry was looking strong. The Bush camp was nervous. "He had left the impression that he was siding with Senator John Kerry in the Presidential campaign," Richard Holbrooke said to me, "and that became even worse with his letter on Fallujah, which they sent by fax machine to the US Mission to the UN. That level of incompetence and stupidity comes very close to willful sabotage. And the people who do that kind of thing in the world I come from should be fired."

On the Fallujah letter, it may well have been a diplomatic blunder to fax the letter for President Bush to the US Mission to the UN, given its sensitivity. Kieran says he was astonished that the letter was faxed, leading the Administration to suspect that we wanted it to leak. In fact, he said, as so often at the UN, the reason was more banal — it was a screw-up, not a conspiracy. And despite the faxing of the letter, it did not leak for several days, and then most likely not from the UN Secretariat.

The leak of the letter could not have been an effort to influence the US presidential elections of that year because the leak happened after the elections, as best I can tell from talking to journalists at the UN. The elections took place on 2 November. The first appearance of the letter in the press was in an article by Maggie Farley of the *Los Angeles Times* on the 5th. Maggie told me she was given a copy of the letter on the 4th and filed immediately.

Second, from what I hear around the press floor at the UN, the leak did not come from the Secretariat, but from a Member Government. As a former spokesperson, I can't ask a journalist about a source, but I allowed myself a half question with a correspondent that I knew well — did it leak from the Secretariat? She told me, "it leaked from a source that wanted to hurt the UN — the US, who else?"

When I asked Irwin Arieff, who wrote that story for *Reuters* and is now retired, he commented, "Our Secretariat sources rarely leaked anything, even when it could make the UN look good."

DEPRESSION?

Prince Zeid of Jordan, who knew Kofi when he was serving in the UN peacekeeping mission in Bosnia, noticed something about him that I had too. His nervous energy is channeled through his legs. Often, at meetings in his conference room, I would sit behind him against the wall. His guests, seated on the other side of the table, saw a calm and composed Kofi, sitting upright, dignified as always, and listening attentively to what they were saying.

But his legs were moving restlessly. I once saw him do a full kick motion, thrusting his leg up till it was parallel to the floor! Luckily, the executive-size conference table gave him plenty of room to swing that leg; otherwise he would have kicked his guest in the shins — or worse.

At the end of 2006, at one of the many farewell parties thrown for Kofi, Prince Zeid offered a toast. Here, in part, is what he said. "Kofi Annan is truly a man of two parts, as all of us who have had the privilege of being seated next to him in conferences only know too well. His bearing in meetings is noble, calming — indeed a monument to stillness — a graceful man, a man utterly in control. At least, in so far as what lies above the conference table.

"Now below it, and particularly if he's anxious about something, Kofi manages somehow to force his anxiety downward, all down into his limbs: his hands, legs and feet. All are in a state of motion. The more anxious he is, the more interesting it becomes, yet kept within the bounds of a sort of rhythm that only an African or a Latin American is capable of. I'm absolutely sure that I once saw him, just prior to his speaking on Iraq, complete a Merengue with the bottom half of his body. And what about that masterful performance of the quickstep during the Oil-for-Food debate!"

An amusing anecdote, and an accurate one. But it was also indicative of the effect that the growing pressure of Iraq was having on Kofi.

Leaving Burkina early

In November 2004, Kofi made a trip that took him to Sharm el-Sheikh, Egypt, for a conference on Iraq and that concluded with a three-day stop in Burkina Faso, West Africa, for the *Francophonie* summit. At home, the drumbeats calling for him to step down were getting stronger. His wife, Nane, I was told, was on the phone to him repeatedly. When I spoke to her two years later, I asked her if she ever thought that the personal price she and Kofi were paying for this job was no longer worth it. She was guarded in her response. "Well, I took my cue from Kofi early on," she said. "For him, what really mattered and has mattered all along is working for the common, the larger good. He felt that there was so much to do that he had to remain focused on trying to find solutions for the larger problems."

In Burkina Faso, Kofi seemed to have hit bottom. With the fire raging in New York, it made no sense for him to spend three days in Ouagadougou. He may also have wanted to be with Nane, who was anguished. On his arrival in Burkina, he attended a dinner in his honor hosted by the President, and then flew home the next morning, leaving behind a senior aide from Senegal to deliver his speech for him.

Elisabeth Lindenmayer, his right hand, made the announcement of the program change; she gave an unconvincing excuse that he needed to return home to deal with pressing matters, without saying what those were. With her eyes, she signaled me there was a problem.

Jean-Marie Guéhenno had joined Kofi in Ouagadougou. "It made me very sad to see a man of his caliber who just wanted to be away," he said. "At a state banquet, he was sitting next to President Compaore at the head table and didn't say three words, not three words during the whole dinner. And then he left the next morning. You could see that things were falling apart and that was the low point."

MORE ON KOJO

On 26 November 2004, Kofi's first day back in New York from Burkina Faso, Claudia Rosett came out with another blockbuster. She reported in the *New York Sun* that Kojo had continued to receive payments from Cotecna as late as February of that year. This seemed to catch Kofi completely by surprise, as it did the rest of us.

Edward drafted a statement for me to read at the noon briefing saying, simply, Kofi had nothing to do with the procurement process and that his son Kojo was an adult working in a totally different sphere and that he, Kofi, had no knowledge of payments that Kojo might have received from Cotecna.

But Kofi himself got the chance to say it in the corridor. That day, he was on his way to give a speech in the building when *CNN*'s Richard Roth called out a question. Kofi promised he would talk to him after the speech. Other journalists began to gather in the corridor. I called Edward on my mobile to alert him, and he came down with the statement he had drafted for me at noon for Kofi to use as talking points with Richard and the others. We sat behind Kofi as he delivered his speech. I whispered to Edward, asking if he had a line in case Kofi was asked if he would resign. He said no, and then scribbled on a pad, "No, I still have very important work to do." I thought that was a little flat, and I scribbled, "It never crossed my mind."

Edward recalls passing the note to Kofi as he left the room and then orally giving him the guidance on the resignation question. "He suddenly flashed me a broad grin," Edward wrote, "which cheered me up considerably."

Kofi approached the journalists and stopped. He took several questions. Regarding Kojo's Cotecna payments, he was asked, "Have you spoken to your son? Are you angry with him?" Kofi then let his hair down and said, "Yes, I have talked to him. Of course, I was surprised and disappointed...."

Now I was really on the defensive. With profound embarrassment, I had to go back to the press briefing room and tell the journalists that, again, what I had said earlier was wrong. Nothing could be worse for a spokesperson, and it couldn't have been a worse time for the UN's official voice to have its credibility downgraded.

In a conversation with Richard Holbrooke in 2006, I was properly upbraided. "And there you are, Fred," he said, "going out and making statements which turn out to be false. Well, I don't understand how you guys could do that. Why did you accept the information that Cotecna gave you and just put it out there as UN statements? Why didn't you double-check first?"

Very good question. In fact, Cotecna had given the information to Lamin and I was authorized to give it to the press by Chief of Staff Iqbal Riza. That's how we work. I had no reason to think it was anything but accurate. But I admitted to him that it hadn't been handled well. Holbrooke continued to hammer away at me.

"Yes, but you made those statements. You issued a UN statement putting forward false information, which hadn't been thoroughly vetted. You had your own reputation to protect, as well as the institution's, as well as the Secretary-General's, and had you said, listen, Kofi, I don't think we should put this out until we have vetted it, or we'll let Cotecna put it out in their name, so they're responsible. But the UN put it out, which gave it the institution's imprimatur and left a legacy out there. Volcker was really angry about that. Everyone wanted to believe you, except the Claudia Rosetts of the world. But it turned out that what the UN said wasn't accurate."

Everything he said was true. Holbrooke is an experienced political operator and his comments made me realize what amateurs we were at the UN in handling the press when under attack.

A Call to Resign

Oil-for-Food was fast becoming a political football in the US. Senator Norm Coleman of Minnesota had been conducting one of the many Congressional inquiries into Oil-for-Food. In an opinion piece in *The Wall Street Journal* on 1 December 2004, he called on Kofi to resign. Minnesota is home to Macalester College, where Kofi got his Bachelor's Degree. *The Minneapolis Star Tribune* came to Kofi's defense, saying in an editorial that Coleman's call was "a sordid move".

"This is really all about Annan's refusal to toe the Bush line on Iraq and the Administration's generally unilateral approach to foreign affairs," the paper's editors wrote. "The right-wingers hate Annan and saw in the Oil-for-Food Programme a possible chink in his armor. They went after it with a venomous fury." Two cheers for the *Star Tribune*. Why didn't *The New York Times* editorial board have the guts to say that?

Jim Wolfensohn, former World Bank President, summed it up this way for me in a conversation I had with him about Kofi in 2006. "The United States is a very strong power that exercises very strong influence on all international organizations," he said. "And if the head of an international organization is visibly seen to be in conflict with the views of the United States, he or she will get savaged. I think that's exactly what happened to him."

Off Balance

To many of us, Kofi seemed not quite right. But different colleagues had different takes.

In Hedi Annabi's view, the campaign against Kofi threw him off balance. "He might have gotten too used to always being treated as a rock star, the secular pope, the Nobel Peace Prize winner," he said. "And the Oil-for-Food scandal destabilized him — it was designed to."

Mark Malloch Brown did not make much of his so-called depression, however, given the strains of the job. "Kofi's greatest disservice to his successors is making this job look easy," he told me in 2006. "Because, in a funny kind of way, there's always been a lot of focus on these rare moments of emotional exhaustion that he has faced. To my mind, this is about as high pressure a job as there is anywhere in the world. And 10 years is a long run at it. It's longer than a full two-term American Presidency and it's at the outer limits of what most elected national political leaders manage to serve. Yet in many ways it's more pressured than any of those jobs, because of the range of pressure points exerted by over 190 Member States and the range of disagreement that bears down on you to resolve. All this comes together with a lack of a clear democratic base represented in the majority in Parliament or a Congress that a national political leader usually enjoys."

"So this sounds perverse," he went on, "but I'm surprised he didn't have more black moments than he did. And I think the reason he survived as well as he did is an absolute vocational passion for the job. I'm sure he views his whole prior life as just a preparation for this position. And he attacked it for 10 years as though every day was the last. You've seen the volume of phone calls he'd make on an average weekend. And although every now and again an issue really gets inside and gnaws away at him, like the Canal Hotel bombing did with the loss of friends and colleagues, he's managed to develop the emotional toughness to keep going, even when there are setbacks."

As Secretary-General, Kofi was playing in the major leagues. I felt he was personally too vulnerable to the kinds of lumps a politician takes every day of his or her professional life. Benny Avni, who reported on the UN for Israeli radio and also wrote for the now-defunct *New York Sun*, gave me a nice example of how a real politician deals with the adversity that comes with the job. "Bibi Netanyahu once told me," he said, referring to the Israeli Prime Minister, 'When I'm attacked, it means I have the microphone'." Now that's a politician.

Louise Frechette saw both Kofi and Nane as vulnerable. "I've said often that Kofi is not a hardened politician, and I think it's all to his credit. He's not a cynical, hardened politician who can take punches easily. Neither he nor Nane were thick-skinned enough to deal with the onslaught of Oil-for-Food. They're very sensitive people who had certainly enjoyed the positive public attention they received but were not really prepared mentally for the personal attacks directed at them. And I think that's what affected him very deeply, the calls for resignation, the terrible articles written about him and all of that."

Despite the talk of depression, many people close to Kofi say they saw no sign of it affecting his performance. I asked Catherine Bertini, his head of management, whether Kofi was always focused when she consulted him on one of her issues. "Always," was her flat reply. And did he ever seem vacant to her or emotionally traumatized? "No," she said categorically.

Kofi's Middle East envoy Terje Roed Larsen's reply was more nuanced. "I was in the Middle East for the worst of the periods, I think, when he was at an absolute low, and I arrived in New York at the end of it." He said to me. "I can tell you one thing — I mean, when I saw him in New York, I could hear in his voice and see in his face the pain he felt, and how difficult it was for him to focus. But he was still extremely supportive — less active, but extremely supportive."

Yet Mary Robinson, the High Commissioner for Human Rights, saw a plus side to his crisis. "I personally feel that when Kofi began to be the butt of very strong criticism from the United States," she said, "especially after that *BBC* interview in which he said that the war in Iraq was 'illegal', that he found his own personal moral strength at that stage in a way that I appreciated. His moral voice became stronger."

His kids certainly noticed, though. When I spoke to Ama and Kojo together in November 2006, and asked about their father's emotional strain, they blurted out a response. "Yeah, he was more withdrawn, pensive," Ama said. "Very unlike him," Kojo added. When I asked them how they thought he pulled it together, Ama began, "He probably realized that other people's problems...," and then Kojo finished the sentence, "...were more important."

"It's what he spent his whole life doing," added Kojo, "worrying about other people's problems. And that was part of what was going on with this Oil-for-Food thing. He's devoted his whole life trying to help others, so why is he getting attacked for things that we all know were totally beyond his control?"

Kojo couldn't help throwing a punch on Oil-for-Food. "My father told me, 'Be a gentleman; keep your mouth shut,' because I wanted to make a lot of noise," he said. "I'm not from that school of thought. And I couldn't understand why, frankly, the UN was so silent on this, why the UN's side of the story wasn't being put out there. I mean, you have a $64 billion program and you found $150,000 in questionable corruption. That sounds to me like one of the cleanest programs in the history of the world."

CHAPTER 21

THE CASE AGAINST BENON

On 2 February 2005, in his first interim report, Volcker zeroed in on Benon Sevan, the chief administrative officer of the Oil-for-Food Progamme. Some of Volcker's investigators seemed to be infected with anti-UN fever or prosecutorial frenzy; he had difficulty controlling them. Members of Congress wanted access to his files for their own investigations; when he refused, the right wing accused him of covering up for Kofi Annan. This distinguished elder statesman saw the integrity he built up during a lifetime of public service being called into question.

Still, he plodded ahead, taking much longer than he expected. Before issuing his final reports in September and October 2005, in which he named the companies and individuals who had paid kickbacks to Saddam Hussein or accepted bribes from him, Volcker produced three "interim" reports in February, March and August. In political terms, this was disastrous for Kofi, because Volcker was making a string of accusations against the Secretariat before the real meat of the investigation — the conduct of Security Council members and the corrupt practices of corporations eager to do business with Saddam Hussein — were dealt with.

Benon is a gregarious Armenian from Cyprus. When he would see me, he would come up to me and say, "Freddy, I love you", and give me a big, wet kiss on the cheek. And the more he saw that it made me uncomfortable, the more pleasure he took in doing it. And then he would look me in the eye and laugh. He was, in fact, a very likeable guy with a long history of distinguished UN service behind him.

What Volcker found was not comforting. Benon, on his annual UN financial disclosure forms, had declared additional income of some $25,000 to $35,000 a year over several years, totaling $160,000. He said it was money he had received from his aged aunt in Cyprus. When Volcker produced a witness who said the aunt didn't have that kind of money, Benon attacked the credibility of that witness. His aunt, he said, who was like a mother to him, had worked all her life and had lived rent-free in an apartment he had bought for her in the 1960s.

But by tracing bank accounts and phone calls and interviewing Iraqis, Volcker constructed a theory that Benon got that money illicitly through the Oil-for-Food program. Benon's name, of course, if indeed it was his, had been on a list of those granted oil allocations by Saddam Hussein's government. Volcker charged that Benon passed these allocations on to a small Panamanian-based company called the African Middle East Petroleum Company (AMEP), headed by a man called Fakhry Abdelnour. An officer of AMEP was Fred Nadler, the brother-in-law of former UN Secretary-General Boutros Boutros-Ghali and a close friend of Benon's. (Volcker found no evidence that Boutros-Ghali was involved in this or benefited from it.)

Kofi suspended Benon in February 2005 following Volker's first interim report, which raised serious questions about Benon's conduct. By the third interim report, on 8 August, which laid out all Volker's evidence against him, Benon had returned to Cyprus where he is today, living in retirement. He was subsequently indicted by the Manhattan District Attorney on 16 January 2007 and on 20 February a Congressional committee asked Cyprus to extradite him to stand trial in the US, which as of this writing hasn't happened and isn't likely to.

"I didn't take a penny"

Throughout, Benon has said he didn't take a penny. His lawyer, Eric Lewis, issued press release after press release, lashing out at Volker's committee. For example, following the first interim report in February, Mr. Lewis charged that the Volker committee "succumbed to massive political pressure" and was seeking to "scapegoat" Benon Sevan. Volcker reported that Benon had asked Iraqi Oil Minister Amer Rashid in June 1998 that an oil allocation be given to AMEP. Fakhry Abdelnour signed a contract with Iraq for the purchase of 1.8 million barrels of oil in September that he then turned around and sold to two other companies for a profit of $300,000.

Benon says that this contract was entered into before he even met Abdelnour. His lawyer said: "There is no evidence to show and it is not credible to argue that Mr. Sevan, who spent 40 years with the UN and ran a $64 billion program, would jeopardize his career for just $160,000; trust a person he had never met to carry out the scheme; and report the proceeds on his UN financial disclosure forms. It never happened."

Volcker went on to charge that through Benon's repeated interventions with the Iraqi Government, AMEP continued to receive oil allocations in 1999, 2000 and 2001, for a total of 7.3 million barrels of oil, which Abdelnour then sold for about $1.5 million more than was paid for it. He also argued that Benon's personal finances were stretched prior to the first sale of oil by AMEP in 1999, after which Benon and his wife Micheline began making cash deposits in their various bank accounts of thousands of dollars each, usually in the form of $100 notes. After the last sale by AMEP in 2001, those cash deposits decreased sharply.

Volcker traced the flow of money from AMEP to a Geneva bank account of Benon's friend Fred Nadler, who was the treasurer of AMEP. He found that Nadler withdrew money when he was in Geneva, just before he went to New York. Cash deposits by Benon in New York followed soon after. As an illustration, Volcker reported that in February 1999 Nadler withdrew $9,500 in two installments. The day after the second withdrawal, he flew to New York. There were several calls between Nadler and Sevan's home or office over the next two days. Benon then made a $1,800 cash deposit in one bank and a $6,000 deposit in another. Two weeks later, he made a third deposit of $1,700 in cash. The total amount of the three deposits made by Benon: $9,500.

In a statement issued on Benon's behalf following the third interim report in August, his lawyer acknowledged that Benon might have "mentioned" AMEP to the Iraqi Government, but that was not the same as "recommending" it. Mentioning AMEP would be entirely normal, he argued, given that the UN was urging Iraq to expand its base of contractors. Volcker had not proven that Benon had "any interest in the company or any motive other than advancing the program." Regarding Volcker's Iraqi sources, the lawyer cast doubt on the veracity of their testimony, saying that most of them were "incarcerated in circumstances strongly suggestive of coercion and mistreatment." The greatest "scandal", he said, is the Volcker Committee's "handling of this matter, which belies any pretense of evenhandedness, objectivity or respect for due process." He did not, however, offer an alternative explanation for the timing of the cash deposits.

Benon seemed to be saying to Volcker, you have spent almost $35 million and have not been able to identify a single penny of income beyond what I reported properly and voluntarily. (The

Volcker inquiry, which was financed out of Oil-for-Food funds, cost over $30 million.) You're just looking to find someone, anyone, to blame.

I e-mailed Benon, who sent me copies of all his press statements issued through his lawyers and closed with the comment, "I want you to know I sleep in peace with myself and I am not ashamed to look in the mirror when I shave." But he never explained the deposits.

CHAPTER 22

KOJO CLAIMS INNOCENCE

When I asked Kofi in the fall of 2006 if I could speak to Kojo, he agreed immediately. Kojo and his sister Ama were visiting Kofi in November, as his second term was winding down. I met with them together at the residence. Kojo came down late. He was wearing a T-shirt with a quote on it by Martin Luther King over his taught frame. He was self-assured and didn't admit for a minute that he had done anything wrong.

"The whole thing is very simple to me," he began. "A lot of the drama was caused by Cotecna, frankly, because they were only giving part truths. They should have come out from day one and said that Kojo stopped working for us full time on such and such a date, but he's still consulting for us in Nigeria and we continued giving him a retainer fee."

"The reality was, there was no scandal," he asserted. "I stopped working for Cotecna full time when we said I did. But they had a Nigeria project, which was their biggest, far bigger than what they were doing in Iraq, which I had been working on for years. So I kept working for them as a consultant strictly in Africa. If you calculate the total figure, it comes to about twenty-something thousand dollars a year — it's not over $3,000 a month. That's what they gave me."

I asked Kojo about Volcker's findings that Cotecna had paid him out of different accounts, as if to hide the amount they were giving him and that Kojo had received payments in different accounts. He stuck to his line.

"Here are the facts," he said. "I got paid, as I said, about $2,500 a month. And over the years, I changed accounts and therefore asked them to send the money to a different numbered account. But the amount didn't change. Cotecna aggregated their payment to me from the beginning, lumping together the monthly fee and reimbursement for expenses. And my expenses were high — air fare, hotels, telephone bills in Africa."

I asked him about his attending meetings with his father while representing Cotecna. "I went to a function where my father was, that's true, and I was getting some contacts for Cotecna," he said. "I did not go to any meeting with my father. He never introduced me to anybody, saying help my son or do this for my son. He's never done that. And you know he wouldn't do that. So, I went to a function where he was once in 10 years. I don't think that's quite the same as me walking the corridors of power."

Kojo and Kofi

I then asked him whether he had been following closely his father's difficulties, which were only aggravated by these reports about him.

"I was following it fairly closely," he told me. "I knew that definitely the issues of me and Cotecna were not helping his cause, but you also have to understand that it was very frustrating for me, because I knew that I hadn't done anything wrong. I had never done any business with the UN.

"You know the father I have. He has never called anybody to assist me. So while I knew I was aggravating everything, there was a lot of resentment on my part, not towards him, but towards the international media. This was just bull, as far as I was concerned, but I had to hold my tongue. It was political. It was all because he said that the war in Iraq was illegal. That's what it was, and that's how I regarded it."

And did he ever tell his father he was sorry?

"Of course I'm sorry for the pain he's gone through," he said, "and for any way that my situation at Cotecna might have contributed to that. And I'm especially sorry if anything I did caused damage to his career. But you have to realize that we're talking about things I did seven years ago. I mean, hindsight is a wonderful thing because if I went back without it I might do the same things again. I've always maintained that I've done nothing wrong and I would not in any way do anything to embarrass my father. I was sorry for what he was going through."

Although Volcker interviewed Kojo once, Kojo afterwards ceased to cooperate with the panel. But Kofi urged Kojo to change course, and Kojo told me that, against the advice of his lawyers and out of respect for his father's wishes, he made a return visit to the Volcker Committee and endured another eight hours of grilling. In the end, Volcker documented through interviews, phone records and bank records that Kojo had received from Cotecna from January 1999 through early 2004 when the consultancy payments ceased, just under $196,000, or about $2,700 a month — just what Kojo said he had been paid.

Volcker expressed concern that in 1998, the year Cotecna won the UN contract, Kojo's phone records indicate he had contact with UN procurement department officials "at critical times". Kojo says these were routine calls to his "Aunty", Diana Mills Aryee, just as he routinely made in uncritical times. Diana was a life-long friend of the Annans who worked in the UN procurement department, and by Ghanaian custom the term "Aunty" is used out of respect. Kojo claims that the calls were purely social.

In the end, Volcker concluded that apart from 1998, the Committee "has not found any further evidence that Kojo Annan engaged in business with the [Oil-for-Food] program."

Kojo's lawyers went after the *Sunday Times of London*, a Rupert Murdoch paper, for having reported that Kojo had lifted oil from Iraq using contacts with Saddam Hussein. In fact, Kojo had never been to Iraq nor had any dealings with Saddam Hussein. Kojo won the suit, and *The Times* paid him a handsome sum in an out-of-court settlement.

Kojo and Coleman

I asked Kojo if his father ever picked up the phone and said, "Kojo, what are you doing?"

"We had a few conversations," he said, "and naturally he was concerned as different revelations came out. But I told him categorically from day one that I never had anything to do with Iraq or this contract and I've stayed by that. My position never changed throughout the scandal. After a while, I wasn't talking to the media anymore, because I was wasting hundreds of thousands of dollars on lawyers. Why am I spending money to protect my name for something I didn't do? Just because certain people are trying to get their five minutes of fame."

And then with a glint in his eye he asked me: "Where's that Norman Coleman chap? Is he still around? Was he re-elected? I saw him at the UN the other day." Coleman, who had called for Kofi's resignation, in fact was not up for reelection that year. But he had attended a General Assembly session and Kojo saw him standing in a group. I asked Kojo if he said hello. "Yeah" he said. "He was shocked. I went to hear my father's final address in the General Assembly Hall and I saw him there. So afterwards I went up to him and said, 'I'm Kojo.' And he said, 'Oh my God, you're the one...' And I said, 'Yes, I'm the one. Nice to meet you,' and I walked off." Coleman lost a reelection bid in 2008.

"No, it was a very tough time for all of us," he went on, "not just my Dad. It was a tough time for me as well. I would be watching TV and these things would come on that made no sense as far as I was concerned. I was a young kid living my life, and they ruined my life for me. I had all my bank accounts shut down. So many things happened to me that weren't reported, because of nothing."

I told Toni Goodale this story. She's known Kofi since Geneva in the 1960s and Kojo since he was a child. She once gave Kojo an internship in her consulting business. "Kojo's got that type of personality — he's a major risk-taker," she said. "I think that's what people have to understand. He's got that outgoing, funny, big personality. I think he took a lot of risks. Hopefully, he learned something from this terrible Oil-for-Food experience."

In the Eyes of His Father's Friends

Kojo was only 25 when Cotecna got the UN contract and yes, Volcker has circumstantial evidence that he abused his UN connections to help the company that was paying him. Kojo categorically denies that. Of course, Cotecna didn't help by not coming forward early with the facts regarding payments to him. But the final judgment against him was nothing like the scandal that the media had portrayed. And yet among many of his father's colleagues, Kojo is often described as having betrayed his father.

I asked Toni Goodale how she thought Kojo felt about that. "It must be unbearable to think that he could have had that much influence on what people thought about his father," she replied. She saw Kojo trading on his father's name. "Kofi And Kojo remain close — I mean, really; he picked him up at school. But when Kojo got past 30, I don't think Kofi knew what his son was doing. He's been a great Dad. But Kojo probably thought, you know, who's going to know about this? I need to get ahead; what do I have? I've got him, his name, right?"

Susan Linnee, who knows Kofi since his undergraduate days at Macalester College, said, "Kofi doesn't understand cynicism. And I think this is one of the reasons he didn't understand his own son; he should have been more of a cynic, because I think that Kojo did not do him any favors. I don't think he gave too much thought to what the reverberations would be or how it would affect his father."

In a conversation with Kofi's younger brother, Kobina, I asked him if he thought that Kojo had any idea how much trouble he caused his father. He laughed and said, "It's a difficult question...". When I told him about my interview with Kojo, in which he continued to protest his innocence, Kobina said, "Yeah. Yeah. Well, that of course is his assessment, I would say. He doesn't probably get the larger picture, put it that way."

Kofi would not talk about Kojo and Oil-for-Food even with his closest friends. Julia Preiswerk, whom he'd known since the 1960s in Geneva, said, "When Kojo's name came up in connection with the Oil-for-Food scandal, he said to me something like, 'I'm under heavy fire, but I don't really understand what Kojo is doing.' It was, sort of, dismay. I think it hurt him enough that he didn't want to talk about it. I don't think he expected it."

And Richard Holbrooke said, "Kofi didn't want to talk about it, but it was clear that it was the most painful thing that could have ever happened to him — betrayed by his own son. It would be to any of us."

David Malone, the Canadian who was head of the International Peace Academy in New York then, sees a link between Kojo's actions and his father's depression. "I think in the larger scheme of things, Kojo's actions aren't terribly important, but in context they provided a scourge for Kofi's ideological and other enemies to beat him with. And Kojo consistently compounded matters by being untruthful with his father, continuing to be untruthful with his father and continuing to abuse his father's name. Thus, Kojo compounded his initial mistakes by being willfully blind to their consequences for his father, and in that sense made a bad situation a great deal worse."

He then added, "And I would say that for any father to be systematically betrayed by bad judgment and bad faith by a child is very hard to bear, and I think contributed to the period in which Kofi seemed to many of his friends, including me, to be quite depressed during the years 2004, 2005."

In the end, I saw no sign of a rift between Kofi and Kojo. To me, Kofi seemed to be guided by a deep, abiding loyalty to, and love for, the boy and despite his early confusion and dismay over Kojo's actions, refused to let the Oil-for-Food flap get between him and his son.

Edward Mortimer, his chief speechwriter, told me, "You remember that he said that he was surprised and disappointed by the revelation that Kojo had continued to receive payments from Cotecna into 2004? And two or three times at various stages during the whole Volcker exercise I tried to put that in the script of his statements so that he should at least repeat that message, and he's always cut it out. I think he felt, don't expect me to go after my own family; that's not the kind of person I am."

In an e-mail to me in May 2007, Kojo said: "They say that you gain strength in adversity, and ultimately I believe the Volcker investigation brought my father and me closer together. Despite all the goings on, family is what you have through thick and thin. Without our strong family base, we would not have gotten through this. We did; and we are a closer, more tightly knit unit for it.

"I always loved my father and I always will."

CHAPTER 23

VOLCKER GETS TO THE MEAT

In his second interim report, Volcker concluded that there was no evidence that Kofi intervened to influence the bidding process on the Cotecna contract, but criticized him for not following up adequately on the conflict of interest charges. Had he done so, he would have uncovered Cotecna's problems in Pakistan and Cotecna's UN contract would not have been renewed. So, management lapses, yes, but no corruption. Frankly, we didn't think it was fair to hold someone at the top of the Organization responsible for a contract decision made by the procurement department, but still, we were relieved.

It wasn't until late October 2005 that Volcker finally got to the real meat, listing more than 2,000 companies and individuals that had paid illegal kickbacks to or taken bribes from Saddam Hussein. The media treated that as a kind of footnote, even though the courts in some nations began following up vigorously. The Australian Wheat Board came under investigation; the Foreign Minister of India had to resign; and a French ambassador was prosecuted.

Why the Secretariat?

David Malone said that he felt it was a mistake on Volcker's part to focus so much on the UN Secretariat. I asked him why he thought they did that. "I think they had a great deal on their plate," he said. "I think that there was a degree of political sensitivity towards questioning too much the role of the Permanent Five, and perhaps other Council members. I've been quite critical in my writing, in my book on Iraq and the Security Council, of the Volcker Commission for giving the Security Council too much of a free ride and focusing excessively on the Oil-for-Food Programme itself. In fact, the Security Council is guilty of a staggering failure of oversight, and that's perfectly obvious when one looks at the facts."

"But it is clear," he went on, "that some of the staffers in the Volcker Commission who were prosecutorial types were more comfortable with issues of financial malfeasance and mismanagement than they were with political direction. So it was easier for them to focus on the first two and to ignore the third. Obviously, that's a personal interpretation because I did not spend a great deal of time talking to Commission staffers. I looked at the outcome, and it struck me as lacking in terms of focus on the Security Council."

Sir Jeremy Greenstock: "Where the political responsibility really lay"

Sir Jeremy Greenstock represented the UK at the UN from 1998 to 2003, and then was posted to Iraq, where he was Her Majesty's Special Representative and deputy to Paul Bremer, the top

US official there. I asked him about Oil-for-Food. "I have always felt that the media," he said, "and particularly the American media, and indeed other personalities in the American scene in particular, did not understand and overestimated the Secretariat's responsibility in the Security Council's running of the Oil-for-Food Programme. It was one of those other areas where the Security Council took responsibility, not just for setting the principles of the policy, but also for the implementation of it."

"The Secretariat had a defined role and the Office of the Iraq Programme was set up for that purpose," he continued. "And I think there was a fairly clear understanding between the 661 Committee [the Security Council body that oversaw Oil-for-Food] and the Office of the Iraq Programme of how things should work. The Secretary-General himself had very little role, in principle or in practice, in implementing that policy. He had general responsibility for the effectiveness of the Office of the Iraq Programme and its staff, and obviously, because it was such a tense political area, would have had responsibility for keeping an eye, a political eye, on the Secretariat's involvement in the whole Iraq saga, which was quite a painful business for the Secretariat in other ways. That task was not done as well as it should have been."

"But it was the Security Council's responsibility to judge what kind of distortion or corruption or diversion or smuggling was going on in and around the Oil-for-Food Programme," he asserted, "and to some extent the Security Council, by design or by accident, was not as careful as it should be in those areas. So the saga of the very large amounts that have been talked about relates mainly to the amounts that leaked out of the Iraq side of the program, not to mismanagement of money by the UN. These leakages were in one sense the result of a decision, active or passive, by the Security Council not to try and contain or control or restrict the smuggling that was going on, mainly by Iraq and its neighbors, under the Oil-for-Food Programme."

When questioned by Paul Volcker, Sir Jeremy said that he gave evidence as to what was going on, namely "that the Security Council, under the influence of its most powerful member, did not make an active decision to try and curtail the Iraqi diversion and smuggling and that he should be very careful about the degree to which his team laid responsibility on the Secretariat side of the UN for mismanagement of the program."

"I think Paul Volcker understood that, but he had some — I didn't really meet them and certainly never talked independently to them — but he had some vigorous young members of his team who by all accounts weren't really prepared to listen to that message," he said. "And there were those influencing that whole approach who clearly wanted this to be a stick to beat the UN with at the Secretariat end and to beat Kofi Annan with, which I always felt to a great degree unjust. And it was very difficult for the Secretary-General to fight back on that because he had the image of being, in overall terms, responsible for the UN as a working body.

"But the fine analysis was not done as to where the political responsibility really lay," he concluded, "and I have always felt, and still feel, that Kofi Annan was treated largely unfairly by the whole saga."

Jean-David Levitte: "Outrage" in the US Congress

Jean-David Levitte was a gifted Ambassador to the UN from France who had been foreign policy adviser to French President Jacques Chirac. He served on the Security Council during part of the time that the Oil-for-Food Programme for Iraq was under way. He was then French Ambassador to Washington, and most recently served as a top diplomatic adviser to President Nicolas Sarkozy. One of the many Congressional Committees investigating Oil-for-Food made the mistake of inviting Jean-David to testify. He readily accepted and asked that he be able to put documents he brought with him into the Congressional record. The Committee said yes; that was their second mistake.

I asked Jean-David what kind of reaction he got when he went before the US Congress. "Outrage," he said, laughing. "Well, you know, I thought that France was being attacked in a very unfair way. So I explained in great detail how I participated in a number of meetings of the Security Council — not the Secretariat, the Security Council — how only the US and the UK had, at their request, received all the documents of each contract for Iraq so that they could review all the details. The other countries just had a summary prepared by the Secretariat and we were satisfied because we had confidence. But for those who were suspicious, they got all the documents.

"And I explained that, to my knowledge, there was an inter-agency process in Washington by which these documents were reviewed and that to my knowledge never, not once, did the US or the UK stop or say that they would like to stop any contract because of kickbacks. Not once. Not once.

"They stopped a number of contracts because of dual use, or possible dual use. For instance, they stopped, I said, vaccines for children because they could be used for soldiers. They stopped the sale of two French bulls, to reproduce cows in Iraq in the French way, because the vaccines used for the bulls could be used by the army. But not once did they stop any contract because of kickbacks. That's a fact, I said.

"And second, US companies were heavily engaged in trade with Iraq, which was not a violation of any law, because it was the implementation of the Oil-for-Food Programme, but they used their subsidiaries in France, and of course in a number of other countries, but for France alone, there were five hundred million dollars registered. And I said this is in my annex; you will see it. And the number one company is, of course, Halliburton. So thank you very much, I said, for publishing that as an official document of the US Congress.

"So there was outrage in front of me. And they said, are you saying that the Oil-for-Food scandal is a US scandal! I said, this is exactly what I just demonstrated, because you were, with the British, the only ones to have all the details in the Security Council. And those taking decisions were the members of the Security Council. And so you accepted all these contracts with a deep knowledge of all the elements of each contract.

"So that was my exchange with them," he concluded. "And after that, France was never attacked again."

Frechette: "If he doesn't understand that…"

The Deputy Secretary-General, Louise Frechette, had these thoughts on the program and Volcker's investigation into it:

"I'm not sure that the reason why the Oil-for-Food 'scandal' happened has ever been explained properly. While the Oil-for-Food Programme was on, the logic was that of sanctions. Sanctions are a political tool used by the Security Council and they are rarely fully enforced. The point was to keep the pressure on Saddam Hussein. The Security Council didn't care whether there were breaches here and there; the point was to keep the pressure on. Once the program was over, it became an issue of corruption and once you move into the logic of corruption, then it's an absolute. There cannot be any tolerance of corruption."

"After the enquiry was over, I heard Paul Volcker say in an interview that he did not understand why the Security Council did not do anything when they saw that oil was leaking to Jordan and Turkey. Well, if he doesn't understand that, he really doesn't understand anything.

"Quite plainly, the Security Council was prepared to tolerate breaches of the sanctions because it didn't want to starve Jordan or ruin the economy of Turkey. It wanted to make sure that the program continued and food got in and if Saddam got a little benefit on the side, that wasn't the main concern."

"You can decide at the end of all this that it was wrong not to apply the sanctions fully, and that it was wrong to tolerate any breach of the sanctions, irrespective of the cost of clamping down on the neighbors or the risk of curtailment of the food distribution program. That's a possible conclusion but that's not the way the Security Council saw things at the time."

Malloch Brown: "As intense as it gets"

I asked Mark Malloch Brown in 2006 how this fight for the survival of the UN compared with other political battles he's fought. "This is just about as intense as it gets," he said, "because it was like a campaign that just went on month after month and every time you thought you were getting to election day, you found you weren't and there were another few months ahead. This was partly driven by the drip, drip, drip of torture of the Volcker Report coming out in different volumes rather than at once; by these different Congressional committees with their escalating investigations of the Secretary-General; and through the spread of the cancerous criticism of the UN through certain right wing media groups from North America to the Murdoch papers in the UK and then to other parts of the English-speaking world."

"And so it's been intense and difficult," he went on, "but also remarkable in its outcome. I think ultimately the reason we prevailed was that we had truth and justice on our side, which always helps in a political fight."

And was he surprised that Volcker spent so much time on the Secretariat and so little on Member States? "You know," he said with some hesitation, "there was already that hint from the time the Security Council okayed what was obviously an investigation commissioned by the Secretary-General. But it was clear that the Council intended to protect itself and walk the Secretary-General out to the end of the plank on this one. On the other hand, Volcker did after all in his conclusions make it clear that there was a huge culpability among Member States and amongst companies and that was where the overwhelming majority of wrongdoing occurred. And his work has led to subsequent investigations, and indeed the fall of political leaders in, for example, India. But there are continuing investigations and inquiries in Australia, France, the UK — I think we have inquiries going on in more than 20 countries. The buck may have taken a long time to reach the company and the country level, but it is getting there."

"But even to the extent he did pursue member governments and companies," Mark concluded, "that wasn't the story, because, you know, after all, so much of the original motivation of this was to fuel a highly political campaign whose target was not Member States but Kofi Annan and the UN."

Stephen Lewis: "It took my breath away…"

Stephen Lewis of Canada was Kofi's UN special envoy for AIDS in Africa. There is never any doubt about what he thinks, and words roll off his tongue with an amazing fluidity and passion. I started by asking Stephen to assess Kofi's influence in the fight against AIDS. He had something else on his mind:

"Right," he said. "Do you mind if I vary from that for a moment?" Not at all, I said: "Let me just tell you that in my experience with Secretaries-General, and Kofi was the third I knew reasonably well, he was far and away the most intelligent and the most decent, the most civilized first citizen of the world that I encountered. And I felt tremendously for him in the attack under the Oil-for-Food stuff and Iraq.

"I thought the attack on Kofi was one of the most unprincipled slanders that I have witnessed in over 20 years of multilateralism. Because all the countries who were undermining Kofi, and in particular the United States, knew exactly what was happening around Oil-for-Food, had themselves been involved in sponsoring corruption — the United States, France and others — and there was the most monumental hypocrisy in the behavior, particularly, of the Americans in attempting, both directly and indirectly, to eviscerate Kofi because they were so mad at him for calling the Iraq war illegal.

"But they were so completely unprincipled about it that it took my breath away. And they were never called to account. This lovely and decent man who shouldered the world's burdens was so wounded by the Machiavellian and deliberate American assault, and no one internationally really took the Americans on, because their hypocrisy knows no limits. Their engagement in corrupt practices in Iraq wildly exceeded anything that the Secretary-General did by way of modest mismanagement of the portfolio. And yet no one took them on.

"Your book is your book, but at some point somewhere the world has to know that this was one of the most gratuitous slanders ever heaped on an international civil servant by an Administration which was, in ethical terms, corrupt to the core.

"And there, I have it off my chest."

J.P. Halbwachs: The CPA's controls were lax

After we closed up the Oil-for-Food Programme and turned over a residual $10 billion to Paul Bremer in Baghdad for deposit in the Development Fund for Iraq (DFI), an International Advisory and Monitoring Board was created to see that that money in the DFI was spent responsibly. The chair of that Board was J.P. Halbwachs, at that time the UN Controller. I asked J.P. what happened with that money.

"This money," he said, "was put in the Development Fund for Iraq together with the receipts from oil sales and was managed by the Coalition Provisional Authority under Paul Bremer. We had an audit carried out which showed that the CPA exercised poor control over the use of the Fund, including inadequate accounting systems, inadequate record keeping, inadequate contract monitoring. This was reinforced by the US Inspector General, who also looked at the CPA management of the Fund, and reported that the CPA provided inadequate controls for some $8.8 billion.

"We also found a number of contracts that were awarded without tender by the CPA, including one for $1.4 billion for Halliburton. We had these contracts audited. We found out that there were about $22 million of expenditure that were made without any proof that services were provided or goods were delivered. We recommended to the Iraqis that they take it up with the Americans to get their money back.

"We also found out that the cost charged by Halliburton to transport fuel from Kuwait to Iraq was exorbitant. In one case, they charged and were paid $694 million to transport $112 million worth of fuel. In today's terms that means they would be charging some $370 dollars to transport a $60 barrel of oil or $8.80 per gallon. Patently absurd."

"They were very lax," he added; "a lot of lax controls."

I asked J.P. about charges of laxity on Kofi's part in the administration of the program. "I don't think there was laxity in the administration of Oil-for-Food," he said. "We took some $63 billion of money during the Oil-for-Food Programme, in the escrow account, and we've accounted for every dollar of it. We've never gotten from an auditor or from Volcker a criticism that we have not accounted for all of this money or that we made improper payments."

"Who was responsible for approving the proposals put forward by the Iraqi Government for its humanitarian supplies? It wasn't the Secretary-General. It wasn't Benon Sevan. It was the Security Council. All we did was put the money aside, contract by contract, and we only paid suppliers after it was confirmed that the goods had arrived and that the details that came into our treasury were identical both in terms of goods and amount to what the Security Council had approved. We had a very tight procedure for this to make sure that this money never went to the wrong guy."

"Who paid the bribes," he asked? "It wasn't Kofi Annan. It was the Australian Wheat Board, and a great number of corporations and individuals, all listed in the Volcker report. You cannot place this at the door of Kofi Annan. The allegations against him were done as a diversion by the American right wing, just because he was against the war. It was very simple."

The story of the unaccounted for $10 billion got very little ink in the American press. JP sent me a *New York Times* article dated 13 March 2010 reporting that the US Treasury Department was looking into massive fraud in the program for the reconstruction of Iraq, which may or may not have included UN money refunded to the US. JP asked me, "Where is Claudia Rosett now?"

Yet the possibility that Benon Sevan took $147,000 over six years was the scandal of the century. The issue was so politicized, that one liberal journal quipped, "If all Benon could steal from a $64 billion program was $147,000, he should have been fired for incompetence."

Kofi: "The Scandal was in the Capitals"

When I spoke to Kofi in late 2006, I asked him if, in his heart, he accepted Volcker's criticism of his management of the Oil-for-Food Programme.

"Obviously," he said, "he had a job to do and a difficult one at that. First of all, the report doesn't make sufficient distinction between the special program, Oil-for-Food, and normal UN activities and management, and uses that to produce a blanket criticism of UN management. So they generalized from the particular, which in fact led quite a few Member States to think that their recommendations were exaggerated. I'm not saying that we couldn't improve our management and our administration. Any organization can improve. We admit our weaknesses and failures and have drawn the appropriate lessons.

"Oil-for-Food was not the UN. It was a very special program with decision centers dispersed, with Saddam selecting contractors bought from and sold to, with the Council approving these contracts and us making sure the paperwork was in order and ensuring fair distribution in Iraq. When you set up a system like that, you're really creating a very difficult managerial situation, for even the best of managers. You cannot hold a manager accountable when the decision centers are out of his hands. There were too many people involved. The [Volcker] committee was rather harsh on the Secretariat and lenient with the Security Council and the Member States."

"And I also believe that even though they were trying to get the Secretariat part of the investigation out quickly, which one thought would take about three months or so, it dragged on for a long time, with rogue investigators leaking things, creating a certain image of the Organization and the Secretary-General. But when the final report came out with the real meat — that was 2,200 companies from around the world whose governments had the responsibility to enforce a Chapter VII resolution and monitor the behavior of their own companies — the story died. In a way, it also became clear, when they discovered only one staff member may have possibly taken $147,000 out of a $64 billion project, that the scandal, if there was one, was in the capitals, not with the Secretariat. But not much hay was made out of that."

Prince Zeid: "Cowardly hypocrites"

Prince Zeid of Jordan thinks it's a scandal that the Security Council didn't hold formal discussions of the Volcker Report, or indeed of any of Kofi's critical reports on peacekeeping.

"You know," he told me in 2006, "the style set by Kofi in addressing Srebrenica and Rwanda was such that if one can be open and honest about the problems that occurred in the past, then it makes it easier to address current problems. And when one looks at the Srebrenica report — you know, Kofi was very courageous in going ahead and releasing the report as it was, because in previous years I can't think of a Secretariat that would have been as brave or as honest in issuing a report as that report turned out to be. And the same with the Carlsson inquiry into the Rwanda genocide. That showed quite a bit of courage and showed an honesty on the part of the Secretary-General which is what really was required of the rest of us and has been lacking."

"The sad thing," he went on, "is that the Member States themselves never properly discussed these reports. There wasn't one discussion of them, or looking at them to try and understand what it is that we had collectively done wrong."

I asked him whether it was Kofi's fault for not throwing these reports back at Member States. "No," he replied. "The sad fact is that we're all cowardly hypocrites. We never properly discussed Srebrenica; we never properly discussed the Carlsson report on Rwanda. After $30 million was expended on the Volcker report on Oil-for-Food, we never had a discussion, not one discussion among the Member States on the conclusions, on what it meant. And today the Security Council is asking what could be done or should be done with North Korea or Iran without any proper understanding of what transpired during that earlier period. We should be aspiring to the basic position that Kofi has taken, and that is, you have to be open and you have to address these issues candidly."

During this entire miserable saga, there were only a few voices of reason getting into print, daring to say the right was wrong. One was an academic from the University of Fairfield, in Connecticut, Joy Gordon, who mastered the complexities of Oil-for-Food and from time to time succeeded in getting an Op-Ed article published. In 2010, she wrote the most detailed and dispassionate analysis of Oil-for-Food in a book called *Invisible War, The United States and the Iraq Sanctions* published by Harvard University Press.

But in the end, my favorite assessment of the program was by James Dobbins, the former US Special Envoy who went to the Rand Corporation, a prestigious think tank in California. "American outrage over the diversion of UN-supervised Iraqi Oil-for-Food money seems to miss three salient points," he wrote in an Op-Ed. "First, no American funds were stolen. Second, no UN funds were stolen. Third, the Oil-for-Food Programme achieved its two objectives: providing food to the Iraqi people and preventing Saddam Hussein from rebuilding his military threat to the region — and in particular from reconstituting his programs for weapons of mass destruction."

CHAPTER 24

THE CARAVAN MOVES ON

TWO PRIVATE MEETINGS

George W. Bush won reelection by a more decisive margin in 2004 and Iraq was just getting worse. Friends started to circle the wagons around Kofi, as he seemed to buckle under the stress. The Deputy Secretary-General, Louise Frechette, hosted a strategy session at her apartment in early December 2004 for about a dozen of us. She told me, "There was a lot of distress among the close advisers of the Secretary-General, who felt that we were drifting badly, that we didn't seem to have a game plan. You know he wasn't well and he was very passive. The meeting was an attempt to try to get a reading of his mind, perhaps try to energize him a bit, but more importantly to try to figure out an action agenda."

Frankly, the prospects were bleak. Edward Mortimer recalled, "We spent most of the meeting being pretty tough, feeling we had to get him to face the need for significant changes in policy, in presentation, in personnel. But he was so passive, said so little, that by the end we were worried he was going to throw in the towel. So we started saying things to buck him up, such as, there was still lots to play for, he had much to be proud of, we were all proud and privileged to work with him, and so on. Shashi then talked about 'the long haul', to which he replied, 'these days one doesn't know how long the long haul will be.' I think we all went home feeling pretty worried that he'd lost the will to fight."

I asked Louise if she thought Kofi was ready to throw in the towel. "There was a cryptic phrase at the very end that could be interpreted that way, and it shocked people. But it was very cryptic. You could not conclude one way or the other. He certainly was not very engaged. I heard subsequently that when he was asked how the meeting went, his answer was, 'well, they got it off their chest'. But at that point, he was just down, I guess."

In my mind, resignation wasn't an option. It would have been the same as an admission of guilt. For the neoconservatives, who were leading the attack against him, the failure in Iraq was their failure. They had their 15 minutes of fame defining US foreign policy and they blew it. Kofi would survive them — if he could get himself together emotionally.

In Holbrooke's Apartment

A few days later, Richard Holbrooke sounded the alarm and hosted a similar meeting of his own. He told me how it happened. "Right after the election, Kofi called me," he said. "It was one of his typically generous, gracious calls. He said how sorry he was that Senator Kerry had lost because it meant I wouldn't be rejoining the Government. And I said, well, you're very kind,

Kofi, but the problem is not mine, it's yours. Let me come see you, right away. I saw him that weekend, on a Saturday afternoon in November, and I said, Kofi, the Administration believes you supported Kerry, and in American politics foreign interference is unforgivable. You're going to have to pick yourself up or else you're not going to get through this thing — like Boutros-Ghali."

Kofi asked if he had any suggestions and Richard proposed a private meeting of a small group of outsiders who cared about him and about the UN. Kofi agreed. Richard proposed that he host the meeting, in his words, "so that you can tell people, if it becomes public — and these things often leak — hat you were just a guest at my house rather than that you convened a meeting." Things involving Richard Holbrooke seem to have a way of leaking to the press.

Kofi and Richard agreed on the guest list — Tim Wirth of Ted Turner's UN Foundation, who brought along his deputy, Kathy Bushkin. Richard proposed Les Gelb of the Council on Foreign Relations, Nader Mousavizadeh, Kofi's former speechwriter, then at Goldman Sachs, and John Ruggie, who had left Kofi's team for Harvard. They had initially decided not to invite anyone from the UN, but at the last minute Kofi wanted his strategic adviser, Bob Orr, to join as note taker. Orr had been Richard's deputy in Washington and Richard had no objections. The meeting lasted almost four hours. "We did not plan it this way," he said, "but it turned out to resemble an intervention."

I spoke to several people who were present, and here is the picture that emerged. John Ruggie had two messages. First, Kofi was losing the confidence of the bureaucracy. Second, he was getting beaten up in the US for wrongdoing, and getting beaten up outside the US for not fighting back hard enough in defense of the Organization.

Nader Mousavizadeh talked about the lack of accountability. At that point, sexual abuse by UN peacekeepers in the Congo was very much in the media and Nader had spoken to Prince Zeid, who had just prepared his report on sexual exploitation by UN peacekeepers. And the Prince told him about the magnitude of the problem and about the lack of interest on the part of senior UN officials, which he found pretty shocking.

Les Gelb was rather brutal, saying, "I'm not here out of any love for this institution, but because I respect you, I want to tell you the Administration's view now is, they're not going to push you out but if you fall, they're not going to save you." One participant observed, "And that had a pretty chilling effect."

The conversation then turned to Kofi's planned trip to Washington. He was confirmed to see Secretary of State Powell, but had not yet heard from President Bush and he felt this was intentional. He worried whether he should go to Washington at all if he couldn't see the President, as that had never happened before. And then Richard came up with what one person said was the quote of the night. "Kofi," he said, "that's the most solipsistic piece of bullshit I've ever heard."

Nader commented. "In seven years of working pretty closely with him I have never been in a meeting where anyone spoke to him like that. And I think that is one of the problems that he faced over time: very rarely did people tell him the truth; very rarely were people not telling him what he wanted to hear to a certain degree. Now I think that happens to every executive and every organization, that the higher up you are the less people are willing to tell you that the emperor has no clothes."

Kathy Bushkin, now Kathy Calvin, of the UN Foundation, was impressed by Kofi's reaction. "My recollection was that he was impressive in his willingness to listen, digest and then act."

Richard, who claims he never said "solipsistic bullshit" to Kofi, summed up the bottom line of the meeting. "Our recommendation was that he had to go to Washington immediately and try to patch it up with the new team." Condoleezza Rice had already been named as Secretary of State at the time of the meeting, which was in early December. The group suggested that Kofi pay a farewell call on Colin Powell and hold an introductory meeting with the Secretary of

State designate. They also suggested that he ask for a meeting with the President, even though they assumed, correctly, that the President wasn't ready to see him.

The second piece of advice they gave him was that he had to make some major personnel changes. "And we singled out Riza," Richard said, "not because we didn't like Riza, but because Riza was blocking any attempts to bring fresh thinking into the process."

FIRING THE FAITHFUL

Iqbal Riza

How could Kofi fire Iqbal Riza? Iqbal had worked selflessly at his side, first in peacekeeping and then as Chief of Staff. He was very good at his job. Kevin S. Kennedy said this about him: "A lot of what goes on in the Executive Office is about trying to structure information and keep processes going. You have to keep oiling that machine and that was one thing that Riza was always very good at. Riza was the guy who never traveled. He never went anywhere. He was not an actor, but truly the behind the scenes guy."

So why get rid of him? Well, I can count two reasons. First, in politics, when you face a scandal, someone has to pay. In the Western world, the most common reaction to scandal in government or the corporate world is to "clean house"; that is, fire people. Kofi was under pressure from Richard Holbrooke and others to fire people, starting with Iqbal.

Second, Iqbal was an extremely refined diplomat, reserved, polite, professional. In short, not really suited to the dirty fight we were in with the American far right — a fight that we were losing badly. Holbrooke's crew had put forward a name to Kofi for the new Chief of Staff — Mark Malloch Brown — to lead the fight back.

Mark is a physically large man, with a large personality and a large presence. He is a born political operator — cunning, I would say, maybe ruthless. He handled press relations for the World Bank, and before that he was a Washington-based communications strategist for companies and politicians, most notably Corazon Aquino, whom he advised in her successful bid to defeat Ferdinand Marcos in the 1986 Philippine presidential elections. Kofi and Mark knew each other from the days when both of them worked for the UN High Commissioner for Refugees.

In July 1999, Kofi picked Mark up from the World Bank and made him head of the UN Development Programme, under unusual circumstances. Kofi had asked the European Union, as the major contributor to UNDP, to send him five resumes of candidates for the top job, which had become vacant. They sent him just one, because they couldn't agree among themselves on more than one, and that one, frankly, was something of a lowest common denominator. Kofi was serious about getting high quality people into the UN, and he wrote back to the EU asking for more resumes. None came. So he ignored the EU and asked his friend Mark Malloch Brown to come up to New York from Washington and shake up UNDP, which he did. Now Holbrooke wanted Mark to shake up Kofi.

"It was unbelievably hard for Kofi," Richard said. "In the two and a half weeks after the meeting in my house, I was on the phone to him almost every day saying, have you moved yet? Have you talked to Mark Malloch Brown? Have you talked to Riza? It was much too much an invasion of an internal process for an outsider to normally do, but I did it because I thought the UN's future was at stake and I really wanted to help Kofi."

Of course, the move could be rationalized in a number of ways. Kofi had a management principle that people at Iqbal's level should not serve more than 10 years or beyond the age of 70. Iqbal turned 70 in March 2004. He told me that he first offered to step down in 2001 at the end of the first term, but Kofi asked him to stay until 2003. He agreed. "When in late 2003 I gave him a list of possible successors, he said I could not leave at a time when Iraq was in flames, and pressed me to stay an extra year," Iqbal told me. "I agreed with some reluctance out of a sense of duty, although my family was unhappy that I had so little time for my grand tots." At that point, Iqbal's younger son had two children.

"In early December 2004," he went on, "we agreed that on 15 January I would hand over to my successor, who was to be Hedi Annabi," the Tunisian veteran of the peacekeeping department who in 2010 was killed in the Haiti earthquake while serving as head of the peacekeeping mission there. "But then Kofi told me of his decision to name Mark Malloch Brown in my place only on the day you announced my departure — 22 December. He had told me he would not announce Mark's appointment before mid-January."

A mid-January announcement was out of the question, in Richard's view. "When Kofi told me that, I said, no, it absolutely won't work. I even said, Kofi, give me a Christmas present. And Kofi called me on his way to Jim Wolfensohn's place for Christmas, and said in his softest voice, 'I'm going to give you your Christmas present; I'm going to announce it tomorrow.' And he did."

The decision was taken so abruptly that I was handed a piece of paper with the announcement as I was in the middle of my noon press briefing on 22 December, so that I learned of the news at the same time that I was giving it to the journalists. And in the announcement I read on Kofi's behalf, he said that it was "with mixed emotions" that he accepted Iqbal's resignation. Edward was away at the time and later said that had he been around, he would have urged Kofi to delete those damning words, which suggested Iqbal had done something wrong.

So at last there was to be a change; Kofi was going to start to defend himself. Mark told me, "Decision-making was at a standstill on the 38th floor, and the attacks, because of Oil-for-Food, were viewed as landing thick and fast without the effective rebuttal that could only be drafted at a senior policy level. We couldn't leave it to you and Edward anymore; there had to be political leadership to fight back."

A few months later, Volcker, in his second interim report, reprimanded Iqbal for allowing his secretary to destroy three years' worth of chron files — 1997, '98 and '99. Chron is short for chronological, and in the UN these are duplicates of outgoing correspondence, which are kept in more permanent files. In fact, an official circular from the UN archives section advises that you destroy your chron files after one year.

Iqbal's secretary, Sita, had requested permission to shred the files for space reasons, as the filing cabinets were full. However, this was just after the Volcker Commission had been created to look into the Oil-for-Food business, and just 10 days after Iqbal had written to all nine UN agencies that had done work through the Oil-for-Food Programme requesting them to "collect, preserve and secure" all documents and files related to Oil-for-Food. Iqbal, in his mind, apparently didn't connect his chron files to Oil-for-Food and told Sita to go ahead and shred.

Volcker didn't buy the explanation that only duplicates were in the chron files. He cited Iqbal's memo to Joseph Connor, the head of UN management, asking him to look into Kojo's relations with Cotecna. That memo was not in the permanent file and possibly could have been in the chron file that was shredded. But in any case, when Iqbal couldn't find it in the permanent file, he went into the hard drive of his computer and printed it out and gave it to Volcker. Still, Volcker found that Iqbal had "acted imprudently" by ordering the shredding.

I must say, given the hostility of the press at this time, I found defending Iqbal's innocence in this matter an uphill fight. It was, at best, poor judgment on his part. Mark commented. "His bewilderment and bad instincts on this illustrated why this good and decent man was out of his depth in the shark-infested waters of Oil-for-Food."

The hostile right-wing press ran with this story with delight. Iqbal saw a long and distinguished career — dealing with the Iran-Iraq war, the Nicaragua elections, the El Salvador peace process, peacebuilding in Bosnia — going down in flames.

He turned bitter. "Having had this personal friendship with Kofi," Iqbal said to me, "when I was savaged by the media for something which I had not done wrong, I was really disappointed that the institution did not stand up and defend me. He obviously was given advice that it was not in his interest to do so and I think he took that advice, which I don't understand. And there was no apology. I apologized to him for having created the problem, but not for what I had done. I hadn't done anything wrong."

Elisabeth Lindenmayer

Elisabeth Lindenmayer of France is petite, but tough, the daughter of a French army officer. She was born in West Africa; growing up, she followed her father to assignments in North Africa, Indochina and Europe. She entered the UN on the management side, and got attached to Kofi in 1987 when he was head of UN personnel. She was one of the people closest to him when he was Secretary-General.

She followed Kofi from personnel to peacekeeping, where she got great satisfaction working on substantive portfolios — Iraq-Kuwait, Somalia, Rwanda. But when Kofi moved to the 38th floor, Elisabeth was made an executive assistant and ended up managing his program. If you wanted to see Kofi, you had to go through Elisabeth. If he went to the Security Council, she sat behind him. She followed him everywhere, was protective of him, was absolutely loyal to him. Even though this work was not substantive, she was good at it; she was a detail person.

She often traveled with him, and when we visited Paris, and called on President Jacques Chirac, the huge Chirac would embrace the little Lindenmayer, kissing her elegantly on both cheeks and greeting her warmly. He awarded her membership in the *Légion d'honneur* in 2006.

We often were on trips together. And on one occasion, Kofi turned to me and in a soft voice tinged with anger said I had not done something well. He had never done that to me before, and in this case what he accused me of was something for which I felt I had no responsibility. I turned to Elisabeth and whispered, "What was that about? That was unfair." She gave me a knowing look, and said, "Welcome to a privileged club. He only does that to those closest to him."

That reminded me of something I was taught in an African cultural anthropology course in the Congo in the 1960s. Some Bantu societies have a custom called, something like, the Laughing Uncle. Boys in the society must have absolute respect for their elders, with one exception — the Laughing Uncle. The boy can abuse one uncle as much as he likes, without punishment, and the uncle has to take it. I wondered if Elisabeth was Kofi's Laughing Uncle. I do suspect that she was on the receiving end quite often. If so, she took it well, laughed a lot and kept her head down at her work. James Traub, in his book on the UN, wrote that Elisabeth spoke of Kofi "with a combination of reverence and mock exasperation, like a nun whose brother has grown up to be an archbishop."

When Iqbal was forced out and Mark Malloch Brown came in, Elisabeth thought she should offer her resignation. She should have; I couldn't imagine her and Mark working together. But she must have thought better of it. Mark told Kofi that many found Elisabeth difficult to work with and he probably didn't want her as his deputy. Kofi said to me on several occasions that he expected his senior people to be able to sort these things out among themselves, and that's what he said to Mark. Mark then told Elisabeth that he hadn't yet decided whether to keep her on as deputy.

Elisabeth wanted the news from Kofi, not Mark; her second mistake. She was about to leave on a trip to Africa with Kofi, and expected to find a chance to talk things through. But throughout the whole trip, not a word was spoken. Finally, as they were waiting to change planes at Paris's

Charles de Gaulle airport to return home, she approached him and asked him about her status. His only reply to her was to speak to Mark when she got back to New York. She must have been devastated. A few days later, we were in our morning meeting with Mark when everybody's blackberries went off with a message from Elisabeth. She had resigned.

Mark said, "We were coming to the conclusion that she had to move, but Kofi had not planned to fire her. Her e-mail, however, put events beyond the point of no return."

Elisabeth expected more support from Kofi. Kofi, however, had bigger problems that he was relying on Mark to help resolve. Still, he probably owed Elisabeth more personal comfort. In the end, he did what he had to do, but it was more painful for everyone than it had to be. Later in the year, Kofi went out of his way to repair the relationship, even inviting himself to Elisabeth's home for Thanksgiving dinner. Eventually, they reconciled. It's hard to stay mad at Kofi for long.

It was Iqbal who had originally advised Kofi to be tough. "I remember saying to him," he told me, "'When you're Secretary-General, you will be overseeing not only the entire Secretariat but the entire system. You've been head of management and personnel, but by nature you're soft and you like to be kind to people. Once you are Secretary-General, you will not be able to do that. You will have to take hard decisions; you will have to take unpopular decisions. And you might have to take decisions that may hurt people, but if it's better for the Organization you must take them.'"

It's ironic that in letting go two of the people closest to him who served him most faithfully, Kofi was taking the kind of hard decision Iqbal was talking about, however badly and unfairly he went about it, and in the process was setting the stage for his comeback.

THE HIGH-LEVEL PANEL REPORT

Kofi set up the High-Level Panel following his "fork-in-the-road" speech in 2003, warning governments that the US invasion of Iraq posed serious questions for the United Nations — namely, was the 1945 concept of collective security valid anymore in an age of international terrorism? Kofi asked 16 former Prime Ministers, Foreign Ministers and other notables to look for answers to this and other pressing questions that some people wished he'd never asked.

One of those notables was Sadako Ogata, the former UN High Commissioner for Refugees. She had this to say about Kofi and the panel. "Kofi saw terrorism in the context of changing global threats and opportunities. Yet he regarded it as just one of the dominant threats of the age, together with nuclear weapons, transnational organized crime, economic and social problems, and particularly poverty. The breadth of his threat perception was remarkable. He instructed us, the members of his High-Level Panel, to reflect on the wide range of threats that he had identified, and then to turn them around as challenges to be addressed. I think he ably steered the UN in the age of terrorism, which dominated the agenda of many powerful states."

The research director whom Kofi selected to work with this panel was Stephen Stedman, a professor at Stanford University in California. Steve and I once ended up sharing a small room at the World Economic Forum in Davos, Switzerland, a place notorious for its shortage of accommodation. Billionaire George Soros was sharing a room with a stranger just next to us. Anyway, Steve and I got to know each other maybe a little better than either of us cared to. I called him in California and asked him to talk about the Panel.

"When I was hired, right from the beginning, Kofi wanted three things from the panel," he said. "He first wanted clarification on whether the Charter and Article 51 was still appropriate in an age when people were talking about pre-emptive and even preventive uses of force. Secondly, he wanted them to take up the question of humanitarian intervention, and he didn't necessarily say it had to be through the Responsibility to Protect. But he clearly wanted the topic of the legality and the normative backing behind humanitarian intervention to be addressed. The third thing that he wanted was Security Council reform. And from the start, those were the three things that he always mentioned to me were his priorities."

I asked Steve to describe how the panel treated the three priority areas.

"On the question of the Charter and the use of force, the panel said that the Charter is still relevant, that the Charter holds up; it's a living document although you probably need a little more imagination in terms of how it's interpreted. But what they said was that when it came to truly pre-emptive use of force, where there was an imminent threat, that there was a long-standing legal interpretation of Article 51 that in fact did give states the legitimate right to the pre-emptive use of force. And Kofi backed that."

"But on the question of the preventive use of force, that is the use of force before a threat had become imminent, our panel said no, there's no way you could consider Article 51 as allowing the preventive use of force. But we argued that in light of some of the discussions today about new threats, it could be that in the future, the Security Council may have to authorize the preventive use of force, but that was the only body that legally could do it."

And was what everyone had in mind there the US invasion of Iraq, I asked him? "Well, yes and no," he replied, "because this was not supposed to be retrospective. I mean, Kofi was not asking for a post hoc judgment about the legality of the war in Iraq and made it very clear this was forward-looking. And that's what we did. We said that over and over again because if the panel had gone into a pissing match over Iraq, we never would have had a report."

On the Responsibility to Protect, the Panel embraced the concept that the international community has the responsibility to protect civilian populations from serious crimes like genocide or ethnic cleansing.

The final priority was Security Council reform. "On this one," Steve said, "Kofi received a lot of criticism saying that the panel never should have looked at Security Council reform. The time wasn't right; the US wasn't interested. It was going to be too polarized. But the fact was, if we had written this report and not addressed Security Council reform, some very important States would have trashed us immediately, including Japan, Germany, Brazil, South Africa and India. And of course we did take it head on and then everybody else wanted to trash us because it was so impossible a task. So we were damned if we did and damned if we didn't."

I then asked Steve what was the report's lasting contribution. "The most lasting impact of the report is the vision it creates of what collective security could be in this era," he replied. "It puts forward a very different vision of collective security from how it was thought of traditionally, certainly at the founding of the UN. That vision, and the analysis behind it, I believe, is a lasting contribution."

A Standing Ovation

Despite Kofi's turning over in his mind the question of resignation, he continued to push his agenda forward, and in December 2004 he received a boost from the Membership. He wanted to pass the report of his High-Level Panel on to the General Assembly. His office had received signals from several Member States that the Assembly wanted to show their support for him. It was decided that he would present the High-Level Panel report in person with a speech.

Lakhdar Brahimi, one of Kofi's most trusted advisers, told me that he gave Kofi the text of Dag Hammarskjold's famous reply to Nikita Khrushchev when Khrushchev called on him to resign. It was in the heady days when Khrushchev, sitting in the General Assembly Hall, banged the table with his shoe. The date was 3 October 1960. Khrushchev accused Hammarskjold, among other things, of being the lackey of the imperialists and called on him to step down. Hammarskjold sensed he had the support of the majority, and he also knew that for him to resign would forever weaken the world body.

He took the podium. "It is not the Soviet Union or, indeed, any other big powers who need the United Nations for their protection," he said; "it is all the others. In this sense, the Organization is first of all *their* Organization, and I deeply believe in the wisdom with which they will be able to use it and guide it. I shall remain in my post during the term of my office as a servant of the Organization in the interests of all those other nations, as long as *they* wish me to do so." Thunderous applause. Khrushchev backed off; a magic moment in UN history.

Lakhdar urged Kofi to deliver a similar message to the Assembly. But whether he was not emotionally strong enough, or whether he made a political calculation that this tack was not right for the moment, I don't know. He did not follow Lakhdar's advice.

I went with Kofi down to the Assembly Hall. When he came out and walked to the podium, the delegates began to clap. Then they rose to their feet and clapped some more. The applause was prolonged. He smiled and modestly acknowledged their tribute with a wave of his hand. I choked up and turned away; the stress of the year was wearing on me too, but my spirits soared for him. Despite his problems with Washington, Member States were collectively telling him, in a public arena, that they wanted him to carry on. Or put another way, as he once said to me, "Don't let the turkeys get you down."

THE TSUNAMI AND THE COMEBACK

The day after Christmas 2004, an undersea earthquake measuring over 9 on the Richter scale occurred off the coast of Indonesia, sending a tsunami raging across the Indian Ocean with waves up to 100 feet high. Over 230,000 people were killed, mainly in Indonesia, Sri Lanka, India and Thailand.

Jean-Marie Guéhenno saw the tsunami as kicking off Kofi's comeback. "I think it was when he visited the countries hit by the tsunami in early 2005 that he gained a new sense of how he would run things. I believe he decided that he would deal with the United States in a certain way; that he took difficult decisions on how he was going to redefine and rebalance that relationship. But as he mobilized the UN relief effort for the Indian Ocean, he became convinced that, yes, there was certainly a lot of space left for the UN in this world, and the UN role in dealing with that natural disaster gave him a sense of purpose."

Before the tsunami struck, Kofi was on a skiing vacation in Montana with Jim Wolfensohn of the World Bank and his wife. On the slopes, he decided he was tired and would return to the chalet. Nane would carry on. He raised his arm to bid her farewell and lost his balance. One of his burly security guards was right next to him, and caught his arm. Snap. There went the rotator cuff. Kofi had to have his arm in a sling; it was painful.

At first he hesitated about visiting the area affected by the tsunami, but in the end he realized he had to go. He cut short his holiday and returned to New York. Before he left for the Indian Ocean, he introduced Mark Malloch Brown to the press as his new Chief of Staff.

On 3 January we flew off to Indonesia. Aceh Province in Indonesia was the hardest hit, and Kofi, accompanied by Nane, visited the provincial capital of Banda Aceh. They flew by helicopter down the coast of Aceh for about an hour — the tsunami had destroyed virtually everything for hundreds of meters inland. From Aceh, they went to Sri Lanka, the Maldive islands and Mauritius. At each step he offered encouragement. In Mauritius, he said: "If any good should come from the upheaval caused by the tsunami, I hope it will be to have proven, once and for all, the need to heed the warning signs, come together well in advance of calamity and sustain a collective effort to end human misery and bring strong foundations for development and peace."

He had found his voice.

Edward Mortimer said to me, "You know, he kind of pulled himself together and he thought, but I've got my agenda, I don't have to be all the time defending myself against what they are saying. And Mark, of course, was very helpful in reminding him of that. Mark said, you know, it's a well-known thing in public relations that if you are in this kind of hole, you have to change the conversation. We cannot be talking all the time on Oil-for-Food. We've got to be talking about 2005 and the agenda for reform. And I think that's where Kofi's instincts were anyway, but I think Mark helped to remind him, saying, come on, we can get through this."

Kofi in Indonesia in January 2005. Edward Mortimer said of him, "You know, he kind of pulled himself together and he thought, I've got my agenda, I don't have to be all the time defending myself against what they are saying."

I would wait for Kofi to arrive at the loading dock every morning, deep in the third basement. After 9/11, he was brought into the UN building that way for security reasons. One morning in the spring of 2005, I was watching him emerge from his car and I tried to judge his mood from whether or not he had bounce in his walk. He approached the six steps leading to the top of the platform where I was standing. And when I saw him take those steps two at the time, I said to myself, yes! Here's the energy I was looking for, the sign I wanted that his inner strength was back.

Egeland leads the response

Jan Egeland was one of those whom John Ruggie called a "modernist", in a famous Op-Ed he did for the *Financial Times* in early 2005. John contrasted the "traditionalists" around Kofi, who were being swallowed up by Oil-for-Food, and the "modernists" like Jan who in an innovative way was coordinating the international response to the tsunami, including working with the accounting firm of PricewaterhouseCoopers to build a web-based financial tracking system to prevent fraud.

Jan's first day on the job was 19 August 2003, the day Sergio was killed in Baghdad. Jan said that experience very much colored his whole experience at the UN. "I saw how the UN went through one of the worst periods ever," he said to me, "and how Kofi Annan went though one of his worst periods ever, starting from the day I arrived."

Despite Kofi's distraction by the major political events of the day, he told Jan that he was free to innovate and he backed him down the line. Jan worked for larger and more predictable funding. Kofi heard him, and put into his 2005 reform report, In Larger Freedom, a call for a Central Emergency Response Fund in order to have cash on hand to take early action to reduce loss of life in international emergencies. The General Assembly approved the idea and more than 60 countries, as well as private donors, have poured over $300 million into the new fund.

Jan also entered into a more intensive partnership with NGOs, going so far as to tap their staff to lead UN humanitarian operations in the field. He brought a vitality and an intensity to the UN's work in the humanitarian field, and his blunt-spoken style often got him in trouble. "You know, I came to the job with the attitude I had in my previous jobs in Norway and in the NGO world of saying things as they are and as I see them," he said. "If you always speak what you regard as the truth, people will expect plain and candid language from you. But, as I soon would learn, it was not necessarily the rule in New York."

In a press conference in late 2004, immediately after the tsunami, Jan called the governments of rich countries "stingy" on humanitarian relief, saying that voters in those countries would support more aid if the governments would take the initiative. That got twisted by the right wing media to say that he was calling President Bush stingy and, even worse, that he was calling for higher taxes. "What I commented on," Jan explained, "was the rich countries' lack of generosity for disaster prevention, development and all of those things that could have prevented the disastrous effects of the tsunami. I did not at all criticize US support for tsunami relief. But some journalists misunderstood what I said and asked President Bush, and he reprimanded me publicly. He was the second Head of State to do so, because President Bashir of Sudan had already complained about me for what I said on Darfur. And then came President Museveni of Uganda, President Gbagbo of Cote d'Ivoire and finally President Mugabe of Zimbabwe, who called me a hypocrite and a liar. So there were many who were after my scalp, both externally and also internally."

But no matter how much hot water Jan got into, Kofi stood behind him. "The one thing I am most grateful for," he said to me, "is that Kofi Annan never, ever censored me and always backed up my right to speak the truth as I saw it, based on my travels in the field and what I heard from eye witnesses on the ground. And that has now, I think, led to something that my successors can also build on. We set a precedent here; we can be outspoken on our ideals even inside the Organization and even inside the Secretariat."

"Hell no"

Kofi clearly had been thinking about whether or not to resign. John Ruggie spoke to him at the residence in early 2005, just before the first Volcker report was to come out. Kofi's lawyer was present. "I said to him that things were going to get bad and ugly over the next few months as the Volcker reports dribble out," he told me. "It will get very personal, so if you're going to resign, do it now and save yourself, Nane and everybody else a lot of grief. He thought for a long moment and then said, 'I'm not resigning'."

In March 2005, Kofi faced the second Volcker Commission report, one that focused largely on his son Kojo. Mark Malloch Brown, who was now taking the lead on Oil-for-Food, convinced him that he should only make a cameo appearance at a press conference on the 29th and leave the rest to him.

During that press conference, a journalist asked Kofi if he felt it was time, for the good of the Organization, to step down. I held my breath. Kofi replied in that low, soft voice of his, "Hell, no". I shook my head and didn't believe my ears. The harshest word I ever heard him mutter was "Gosh", and here he was using a swear word in a press conference. After answering the question more fully, Kofi excused himself and left behind Mark Malloch Brown to take 45 minutes of questions on Oil-for-Food. Mark was cool, in charge and up to the task. But on the other hand, his presence alone at the podium suggested that Kofi was not. The comeback, if that's what it was, was off to a shaky start.

In September of that year, when his personal crisis was largely behind him, Kofi would look philosophically at Oil-for-Food and focus again on his essential work. He summed up his attitude nicely in an interview with Anne Penketh of *The Independent* (London). He said, "The dogs bark, but the caravan moves on. I want to keep going; I have work to do."

Jean-Marie Guéhenno said to me, "Before this whole crisis, his winning the Nobel Prize and all that, the positive press, I mean it's dangerous, because it sort of lionizes you and gives you a sense of omnipotence. It puts you on an elevated pedestal where you can't really stay if you play in the rough and tumble of world politics. And so as a result of this brutal, bruising battle, he may have found that he was not that secular pope who was immune from worldly harm. But he also realized that there was still a job to be done by the Secretary-General of the United Nations. I think he found that balance."

CHAPTER 25

THE RESPONSIBILITY TO PROTECT

R2P

In a speech to the General Assembly in 1999, Kofi asked if the Security Council were deadlocked and large numbers of human lives were threatened or being lost, is intervention without Security Council authorization always wrong? This was right after the unauthorized NATO bombing of Serbia over its treatment of Kosovo. That question went over like a lead balloon.

"The response to that speech was not everything he might have hoped," commented David Malone. "A minority of countries supported his view, but a majority of countries opposed any intervention without Security Council authorization on the grounds that the weak require international law, and a narrow interpretation of international law, as their protection." The next speaker, President Bouteflika of Algeria, put that argument forcefully.

David said that many of Kofi's advisers believed that Kofi was wrong to take this position, that it was simply unhelpful and unnecessarily divisive. "But he was certain, deep down," he said, "that he was right, that human lives, when massively threatened, had to be placed in the balance alongside narrow constructions of international law."

Kofi called David, who was then head of the International Peace Academy, and asked him if he could help study the question of intervention at times of extreme humanitarian distress in a way that might be "creative and break new ground." With financial help from the Canadian Government, David gathered together 8 or 10 of the world's top international lawyers and jurists for two days, and Kofi spent a lot of time with them. But the group deadlocked. They could not agree that there was a basis in international law for humanitarian intervention.

David says that the IPA failure spurred the Canadian Foreign Minister, Lloyd Axworthy, to form an International Commission to study the question. Axworthy named as co-chairs former Australian Foreign Minister Gareth Evans and veteran UN envoy Mohamed Sahnoun of Algeria. Its members spent months in deliberations. This time, there was agreement, and the Commission called its report *The Responsibility to Protect.* Kofi practically walked around with a copy of that report in his pocket.

The Responsibility to Protect crystallized for Kofi, and gave a legal rationale for, the idea that when a government cannot or will not act to stop the gross violation of the rights of its people — violations such as genocide or ethnic cleansing — then it was the obligation of the international community to step in.

Kofi now had to move this concept through the bureaucracy. In the wake of 9/11, he had formed a High-Level Panel to look at the security needs of the 21st century. One of the things he asked that panel to do was to consider *The Responsibility to Protect*. And Kofi had appointed Gareth Evans as a member of that Panel. At the outset, Steve Stedman, the staff director, was not optimistic. "I'll tell you," he said to me, "right from the start, this was one issue that my staff and I never dreamed we would get. We just thought it was impossible." But Gareth Evans pushed, and Kofi pushed, and the High-Level Panel embraced the concept by consensus. It then had to go to the General Assembly. "And the fact that you had a Primakov [former Russian Prime Minister] and a Qian Qichen [former Vice Premier of China] and an Amre Moussa [Secretary-General of the League of Arab States] signing off on this," said Steve, "I think, was instrumental in getting it into the 2005 World Summit document." And that's what happened, making R2P international law.

DARFUR

The classic R2P challenge was in Darfur, Sudan, where conflict over shrinking grazing land pitted nomadic Black Arabs against sedentary Black African farmers. The land conflict got mixed up with a rebel movement in Darfur, resulting in the Government using the nomads, called Janjaweed, as their main counter-insurgency force against the rebels. It is said that between 200,000 and 300,000 people in Darfur have died and 2.7 million have been displaced. In March 2009, the International Criminal Court in the Hague issued an arrest warrant for Sudanese President Omar al-Bashir for war crimes and crimes against humanity, and then in July 2010 charged him with three counts of genocide in Darfur. The decision marked the first time that the world's first permanent war crimes tribunal had issued genocide charges.

At a refugee camp in Chad, Kofi listens as a woman describes bombing raids by Government planes in support of attacks by Janjaweed militia.

Kofi spoke out on Darfur in 2004, but his chief of humanitarian affairs, Jan Egeland, did so even earlier, at the end of 2003, and forcefully. Some key governments did not want to know about it. From a political point of view, the peace talks between north and south in Sudan were at a delicate stage; to drag in the disturbances in the west of the country would just complicate things. But from a humanitarian point of view, women were being raped, people were being killed, villages were being burned and millions of people were being displaced.

"We got very worrying signals from the field at the end of 2003," Jan said. "I myself called it one of the worst humanitarian emergencies of our time, in November, and again in early December. And then in December, Kofi agreed to speak very strongly and publicly on Darfur. With his support, and over the objections of some important members of the Security Council, I briefed the Council twice on Darfur."

Kofi speaking to a recently-returned refugee woman from Ladabo, Darfur, during a visit to Sudan in 2005.

When Kofi asked Jan to lead the first UN inter-agency mission to Darfur, President Bashir wrote a five-page letter to him, blasting Jan and saying that he would not accept him. In the face of Bashir's opposition, Kofi replaced Jan with Jim Morris, head of the World Food Programme. But when Kofi went to Darfur at the end of June 2004, he took Jan along with him. "That was a very important mission in all respects," Jan said, "because it really helped bring a lot of sustained interest to Darfur. And then, people started debating how serious it actually was; some accused us of exaggerating and others said it was a Western issue. But he always came out very strongly on the side of truth there and called a spade a spade. I mean, if there is a scorched earth campaign, if people are massacred, you have to describe it as crimes against humanity and war crimes, and he did."

I traveled with Kofi on that trip to Darfur. The Government claimed it had no control over the marauding Janjaweed militia. Kofi sat down in the dust under a great tree with scores of

Sudanese women displaced by the violence. He waived his Government minders and the rest of us away, and then listened to the women's stories of how the Janjaweed burned their villages, mass raped them and killed their fellow villagers.

By September of that year, the World Health Organization was reporting up to 10,000 deaths a week in the huge displacement camps set up mainly across the border in Chad. Kofi had taken to inviting Security Council members to lunch once a month, to have a chance for a casual off-the-record chat. At the lunch on 15 September, Elisabeth Lindenmayer was with Kofi and told Edward Mortimer that Kofi challenged the Council to act in Darfur under the UN Convention Against Genocide, saying the Members should not fail to act when faced with such direct evidence of genocide.

Kofi then decided to call for such action himself. Of course, this was September 2004 and he was close to his low point over the Oil-for-Food scandal. He stumbled over his text but he delivered it none-the-less and the message was strong. *The New York Times*, under a headline "Annan Urges Prompt Action on Sudan Draft", quoted a European diplomat who said that he thought that Kofi's intervention would make it impossible for China to carry out an earlier threat to veto the measure. China, which is the largest consumer of Sudanese oil and also has a strong belief in national sovereignty, had been one of the main obstacles to Council action against Sudan for what was going on in Darfur.

When the General Assembly plenary opened later in September, Kofi addressed the theme, "the rule of law", and said that fundamental laws were being shamelessly disregarded in Darfur, where "we see whole populations displaced, and their homes destroyed, while rape is used as a deliberate strategy." The newly formed African Union wanted to take the peacekeeping lead in Darfur, and Kofi couldn't say no, but many had profound reservations about their military capacity. "...we all know the present limitations of this new-born Union," he told the Assembly. "We must give it every possible support." And the Government of Sudan wasn't exactly cooperating.

On 18 September 2004, the Security Council welcomed the African Union peacekeeping initiative in Sudan and threatened Sudan with economic sanctions against its oil sector if it didn't cooperate. The following March, the Council created its own Sudan peacekeeping mission to work alongside the AU's. But by the time Kofi left office in 2006, despite the presence of UN peacekeepers, the killing in Darfur carried on. In an Op-Ed in the *Los Angeles Times* on 16 September, 2006, Kofi wrote, "Twelve years ago the United Nations, and the world, failed the people of Rwanda in their time of need. Can we now, in all conscience, stand by and watch as the tragedy deepens in Darfur?"

Despite R2P, apparently we can.

KENYA

R2P can kick in before a genocide takes place, and the African Union seized a chance to put R2P into action in Kenya a year after Kofi left office. He was living in Geneva, where he was setting up the Kofi Annan Foundation as his base of post-retirement operations.

Kenya has a relatively strong economy. Its varied natural beauty and the creation of vast national parks allowed the growth of a developed tourist trade. Its democratic institutions may not be fully functional, but civil society is vibrant and the press relatively free. It was an island of moderation on a turbulent continent, a haven for refugees from crises beyond its tranquil borders. But underneath the calm surface were unresolved problems from colonial times as well as from the period of independence, which began in December 1963. These included tribal tensions, corruption, the need for land reform and power sharing in a political system based on winner-take-all.

The general elections of December 2007 were well organized and well run, according to European Union observers, up to a point. President Mwai Kibaki, a Kikuyu, was going for a second term. His Party of National Unity had won the previous election handily on a promise of reforms that a great majority of Kenyans felt were long overdue. Kibaki had gotten off to a strong start with an anti-corruption campaign and by making primary education free for all children. But he gradually lost steam and many people felt things had returned to bad business as usual.

Raila Odinga, a Luo, headed the opposition Orange Democratic Movement. He is called by his first name to distinguish him from his father, who once sat in Parliament with him, and from his brother, who still does. Raila ran strong in the 2007 elections because of the disappointment with Kibaki, and that's where the problem started. As the votes were being counted, Raila initially looked like the winner. But as the counting progressed, Kibaki gained substantial ground and everyone agrees the election was very close. Each side accused the other of voter fraud. An analysis which Kofi called for later by an Independent Review Committee headed by South African legal expert Johann Kriegler found the electoral process so "grossly defective" and the results so "irretrievably polluted" that it would be impossible to determine who actually won.

The Electoral Commission of Kenya rather abruptly announced that Kibaki was the winner and he had himself sworn in immediately. Raila called foul, declared himself the President of the people, and rioting started. In the town of Eldoret, in the Rift Valley, 50 Kikuyu were reported to have died when a church was set afire. In just a few short weeks, the death toll in ethnic fighting went to a thousand, with hundreds of thousands more displaced from their homes. Tranquil Kenya was beginning to look like just another African basket case.

A Who's Who of African leaders descended on Nairobi to try and calm things down — Desmond Tutu of South Africa, followed by a group of four former Heads of State, then the head of the African Union (AU), President John Kufuor of Ghana, and finally Ugandan President Yoweri Museveni. For various reasons, only one of these visitors met with any success and none stopped the violence. John Kufuor, after meeting separately with Kibaki and Raila, announced that they were prepared to engage in a dialogue led by a Panel of Eminent Personalities named by the AU.

Clearing the Deck

Kufuor wrote to Kofi and asked him to lead the negotiations. The AU named two other members of his team: Graca Machel, the former First Lady of South Africa as Nelson Mandela's wife, and Benjamin Mkapa, former President of Tanzania. Kofi was on his way to Geneva airport on 16 January to take a flight to Nairobi when he was overcome with fever. He had suffered off and on for years from diverticulitis, and this was a fresh attack.

He was rushed to hospital, where the doctors wanted him to stay two weeks. He cut two deals, one with the doctors to release him after one week, then another with the many potential mediators. From his hospital bed, he called one after the other to ask that there be only one set of negotiations — his. They agreed.

Before Kofi left hospital, Kibaki made things worse by hastily filling 16 cabinet positions, none with members of Raila's party, and more violence flared up in the Rift Valley in response. Kofi kept working the phones, asking for political and financial support from key governments, including, of course, from the US and the major African and European players. Secretary-General Ban Ki-Moon called Kofi and asked, "What do you need?" Kofi said, "I need staff." Ban told him to take whomever he wanted from the UN. Kofi reached into the UN's Department of Political Affairs and pulled out Africa specialists with whom he had worked for years, such as Joao Bernardo Honwana of Angola and Margaret Vogt of Nigeria. And he took the head of the

UN's Electoral Division, Craig Jenness of Canada, a veteran of electoral politics, and his colleague Deryck Fritz of Trinidad and Tobago. He then asked the UN Development Programme to handle the administration and the finances of the peace talks.

By the time he touched down in Nairobi on 22 January, Kofi's support staff was in place, administrative procedures were being established, financial support was on the way and he had the strong backing of key Governments. He met separately with Kibaki and Raila, and convinced Raila to call off mass demonstrations that had been scheduled and that could easily have turned violent. Two days later, he met jointly with the two men, and afterwards appeared with them on the steps of Harambee House, the Office of the President; the two shook hands before the cameras. The country exhaled and the violence subsided. But the reconciliation work had hardly begun.

The two sides agreed to appoint negotiating teams, and Kofi's Secretariat produced an agenda, terms of reference and rules of procedure before the process got underway. Kofi regularly talked to the public through the media; he wanted a transparent process. On important occasions, Benjamin Mkapa stood next to him and repeated the same message in Swahili so that everyone got it clearly. Kofi announced a timetable for the process. He told the media that violence had to stop within seven days; short-term issues such as dealing with refugees would be dealt with within four weeks and longer-term issues like land reform and constitutional reform should be resolved within a year.

Talks get under way

The dialogue was formally launched on 29 January. The assassination of two members of Parliament from Raila's party triggered more violence at the very beginning of the process, which was not a helpful start. But in the first days of February, the two sides reached quick agreement on the first two items on the agenda, involving freedom of expression and assembly, investigation into police brutality, return of displaced persons and creation of a South African-style Truth and Reconciliation Commission. That was more promising. The countryside grew quiet.

I had gone to Kofi's office in Geneva in late January to help him set up a press office, but he had left for Kenya by the time I arrived. He called me from Nairobi a couple of days later and said, "I think you better come down here." I jumped into pre-retirement mode and was on a plane that same day. It was great seeing former colleagues again, and to dive into the intensity of negotiations on which so many lives depended. Lamin Sise, Kofi's right hand from the 38th floor, joined us there, as well Kofi's former Legal Counsel Hans Corell, and even Elisabeth Lindenmayer showed up. She was teaching at Columbia University and came with a graduate student. Kofi wanted her to write an academic paper on the peace process and gave her complete access to the talks and the documentation. She later shared a copy of that paper with me, which I used to refresh my memory in writing this account.

We all lived, worked and ate at the Serena Hotel, which was both comfortable and practical. The talks took place in working rooms on the ground floor. We set up a pressroom for regular briefings by Kofi. The delegations moved in and out, frequently stopping in the lobby to talk to the media who were staked out there. Kofi did not want an American as his public spokesperson because the US had been critical of the Government's handling of the elections, so I worked behind the scenes, backing up the UN spokesperson in Nairobi, Nasser Ega-Musa, a Somali, whom we borrowed as spokesperson for the talks. Kofi gave me generous access to the negotiating sessions and I was in a good position to privately brief the foreign press. Nasser and I formed a tight team; he called me "awowo", Somali for grandpa, because I had just learned that my son's wife was expecting my first grandchild. He was a pleasure to work with and knew the Kenyan political situation like the back of his hand.

Since Kibaki considered himself legitimately elected and claimed that this was non-negotiable, and Raila felt that the election had been stolen, a fundamental point was what to do about the December 2007 election results. Recount the votes? Re-run the election? Hold new ones? That's where Kofi used Craig Jenness to good advantage. Craig patiently explained to the two sides that a recount would be time consuming and would not guarantee a fairer result. A re-run in the current political climate would be downright dangerous. New elections would take a year to organize and would just prolong the political crisis. He convinced them to look forward, not back.

If not elections, what? Kofi's next step was to get the parties to agree to a power-sharing formula. Here he reached to Europe, inviting to Nairobi Gernot Erler, the German minister who helped negotiate the power-sharing deal struck between Angela Merkel and Gerhard Schroeder.

Off to Kilaguni

The talks began to drag, and Kofi then used a familiar negotiating tactic — remove the parties from their traditional surroundings and submerge them in intensive negotiation in a bucolic setting without suits and ties. On 11 February, he announced he was moving the talks to an undisclosed location. In great secrecy, we were flown to the Kilaguni Lodge in the Tsavo game park in the southwest of Kenya. Kofi even selected the rooms that the negotiators would sleep in, alternating Kibaki team members and Raila team members to encourage maximum interaction. They couldn't help but bump into each other on the way to breakfast.

Just before leaving for Kilaguni, the parties reached agreement on setting up an Independent Review Committee to investigate the abuses of the 2007 elections and to make recommendations for electoral reform, as Kofi had suggested. That meant at least a temporary end to the argument over who won. Another stumbling block removed.

A major item for discussion at Kilaguni was power sharing, and Minister Erler made his pitch. Power sharing is a pragmatic way that democracies can use to resolve a crisis, he said. He explained to the parties how the German power-sharing deal was negotiated, including agreeing, first, on what ministries would be shared how, then, second, who would sit as Ministers. They listened attentively, but there was skepticism in the room, particularly on the Kibaki side. The exchanges between the two Kenyan parties were more fluid at Kilaguni, but no concrete agreement was reached.

Kofi didn't want to go back to Nairobi empty-handed; he needed to create the illusion of progress in order to maintain calm. With the two sides, he drew up a document detailing agreements reached to date. It was none-the-less impressive: set up an Independent Review Committee on the elections; carry out comprehensive constitutional reform; reform the electoral system; set up a Truth and Reconciliation Commission and tackle legal and judicial reforms.

A Grand Coalition

Kofi gave a press conference immediately on his return to Nairobi. He laid out the progress that had been made in the talks thus far. He mentioned for the first time that talks were under way regarding a "new government". He was recommending that this be a "grand coalition" government. It was premature, given where the talks were at that time, to talk of a "new government", but he was pushing the negotiators forward. Finally, he announced that he was prepared to stay in Kenya as long as it took to reach agreement. There was speculation that he would soon leave. His office in Geneva was canceling day after day of appointments, events that had been scheduled months before, board meetings that were important. But his sense was that if he left Kenya now it would blow up. We called him "a prisoner of peace," which his friend Martin Griffiths shortened to "POP". At one point, he was sitting outside the negotiating chamber reading a draft text and he invited me to read over his shoulder. As I looked down, I saw his shirt heaving from heavy breathing and wondered what kind of a toll this stress was taking on his 69-year-old body.

The two sides were now foot dragging. Kofi called on Hans Corell to lead a Legal Working Group on Governance; in other words, to take a political hot potato — power sharing — and turn it into a technical issue for lawyers. Each side named lawyers to serve on this group. That moved the ball forward. Their draft document described a post of Prime Minister and two Deputy Prime Ministers and the outline of a coalition government. But the full negotiating teams could not agree on the powers to be given to the Prime Minister, presumably Raila, and Kofi was running out of patience and options. On 26 February, Kofi and Benjamin Mkapa went before the press gathered in front of the Serena Hotel and announced that he was suspending the talks. But to calm the country, he insisted that the talks had not broken down. They had just gone as far as they could go with the negotiating teams. It was time to negotiate directly with Kibaki and Raila.

The Crunch

The African Union Presidency had passed from John Kufuor to President Jakaya Kikwete of Tanzania. For Kofi, Tanzania was an interesting example of power sharing between the President and the Prime Minister. So he invited President Kikwete to Nairobi to join him in a face-to-face meeting with Kibaki and Raila.

That meeting took place at Harambee House on 28 February and included just five people — Kofi, Benjamin Mkapa, President Kikwete, Kibaki and Raila. Members of the negotiating teams had pressured to be allowed to sit it, but they were not. They sat with the rest of us in a huge adjoining room, fidgeting. Kofi was determined not to leave until an agreement had been reached, written on paper and signed. President Kikwete reassured Kibaki that under the Tanzanian Constitution the Prime Minister has much more power than what was being considered under the Kenya grand coalition deal, and frankly that didn't bother him at all. Kibaki listened. At one point, when discussing a Constitutional issue, each side briefly brought in their lawyers. Then, after more than five hours of negotiation, agreement was reached. The office of the Prime Minister was described and would be created through a Constitutional amendment. The two parties would each take one post of Deputy Prime Minister, and the rest of the ministries would be shared. And all of that was on paper.

We set up a press event on the steps of Harambee House. Kibaki and Raila each signed the agreement in front of a huge crowd of officials and with the television cameras trained on them. Jubilant citizens could be heard dancing and singing outside the compound. Then each of the two principals spoke. Raila, in his remarks, referred to Kibaki as President Kibaki for the first time since the disputed election. Kibaki's speech was forward-looking and conciliatory. Kofi beamed behind them. *New York Times* columnist Roger Cohen, whom I arranged for Kofi to speak to in Nairobi, wrote that this was "a genocide averted". He was right. R2P had worked and Kofi could now go home.

The parties drag their feet

In international politics, a happy ending can be elusive. The Kenyan parties dragged their feet in implementing the reforms that Kofi had gotten them to agree to. Kofi kept nudging them in the right direction, including calling them together in Geneva for a review of the peace process in March 2009. He invited not only the politicians, but a healthy cross-section of Kenyan civil society and a representative sampling of the Kenyan media. He invited me as well. The interaction was intense and the way forward seemed so clear. And yet when they all returned home, there was once again talk of violence on the horizon as each side positioned itself for the 2012 elections.

When the National Assembly failed, after two attempts, to enact legislation establishing a local tribunal to prosecute those responsible for the violence, Kofi, in July 2009, sent a sealed envelope containing the names of those suspected of being behind the chaos to the International Criminal Court. The ICC, whose creation he had so vigorously supported, would now play a part in Kenya.

Kofi returned to Kenya in October 2009 and said he expected the leaders to lead, and they were not moving fast enough on reform. He then played his civil society card. "Good leaders are also good followers," he told a press conference. I had heard him say that line many times before. Then he added, "and if the leaders can't lead the reform process, then Kenyans should spearhead the reforms."

Then on 4 August 2010, things broke his way. Kenyans turned out in numbers — 71 percent of the voters — and 67 percent of these said "Yes" to a new Constitution that would limit Presidential powers. The 2012 elections were still far away, but the reform process that Kofi had shaped with Kenya's leaders was moving forward.

Today

Kofi and Nane now live on two continents — they have a home in Ghana but also one in Europe. He set up the Kofi Annan Foundation in Geneva, which is essentially a headquarters from which he coordinates his many activities, most focused on Africa.

He has said to me more than once, and often mentioned in his speeches, that he regrets that the Green Revolution of the 1960s bypassed Africa. He is now pursuing this theme through an organization called Alliance for a Green Revolution in Africa (AGRA), of which he is Chairman of the Board.

Following the 2005 G-8 Gleneagles Summit, UK Prime Minister Tony Blair set up the Africa Progress Panel to monitor compliance with aid pledges to Africa. Kofi chairs that panel. One of the many things the APP is focusing on now is climate change on the continent; another is good governance.

Mo Ibrahim is a Sudanese who made a fortune selling cell phones. He set up a foundation that encourages good governance in Africa and gives a cash grant for life to the African leader who gives security, health, education and economic development to the people, then transfers power democratically to a successor. Kofi chairs the panel that makes the selection. (No award was given in 2009 or 2010; draw your own conclusions.)

He is one of The Elders, a group called together by Nelson Mandela to support peacebuilding. They are working on Cyprus, the Middle East, Zimbabwe and North Korea, among other places.

As a peacemaker, he continues to be involved in helping Kenya get on with her reform process. In October 2011 he succeeded, with Sinn Fein leader Gerry Adams and others, in convincing the Basque separatist group ETA to permanently renounce violence and enter into dialogue with Spain and France. And as this book goes to press, Kofi is trying to negotiate an end to the violence in Syria, having been appointed mediator jointly by the United Nations and the League of Arab States.

He is actively supporting the strengthening of criminal justice through the International Criminal Court, in improving the way electoral assistance is being given and helping to do something effective about the illegal use of mineral resources, such as "blood diamonds".

He is Chancellor of the University of Ghana, a Global Fellow at Columbia University in New York and a Professor at the Lee Kuan Yew School of Public Policy at the National University of Singapore.

He sits on the boards of the UN Foundation, the World Economic Forum, the Carnegie Endowment for International Peace, the Carnegie Corporation, the Club of Madrid and the World Organization Against Torture. And that's not a complete list.

After he brought the Kenyan parties to a peace agreement and returned to Geneva, I said to him, "Kofi, when are you going to slow down?" He just looked at his shoes, smiled and said in a low voice, "Yes, Nane says that too."

I was having an e-mail exchange with Nane in March 2010, and she mentioned casually that they were in Singapore. "Singapore!" I shot back. "I thought you were going to get him to slow down."

She answered me in two words. "Tried. Failed."

"The Optimist"

When I returned to Geneva from Nairobi in March 2008, I worked with Lamin Sise at the new Kofi Annan Foundation; Lamin was doing follow-up to Kenya and I was helping set up a press office. It was 8 April, Kofi's 70th birthday. Lamin said, "Let's call him and wish him a Happy Birthday." When Kofi answered, Lamin extended warm birthday greetings, and then waxed lyrical about all of Kofi's accomplishments. Kofi's simple response was, "It's been fun; it's been fun."

It's been fun? I tried to make sense of that; his second term was a misery. 9/11, Iraq, the death of Sergio, Oil-for-Food, Kojo — how could that have been fun? I couldn't help thinking of the Phillip Gourevitch profile of Kofi for *The New Yorker*, "The Optimist".

But I then I said, no. Optimism could not have produced the extraordinary output of the years 1997 to 2006. So what was it then? There is first of all his energy — Nane once said to me, "I think that is a vital part of him, this boundless energy and interest in all and everything, allowing for innovative cross-boundary thinking."

Then there is his strong inner core — the Asante in him. And to this I would add his firm grounding, his innate kindness, his inclination to like and to trust others, his lack of ego, his intuitive political skill, an ability to keep his eye on the big priorities, to lead others naturally and easily in the pursuit of those objectives, an absolute commitment not to give up when he knows he's right and a fundamental respect for the job of Secretary-General of the United Nations.

That then is Kofi Annan. Or at least a part of him.

Optimism could not have produced the extraordinary output of the years 1997-2006.

IV

AFTERTHOUGHTS

1

HOW WILL
HE BE REMEMBERED?

In many of the conversations I had with Kofi's colleagues, as a last question I asked how he would be remembered. Here is a sampling of the responses.

MARTTI AHTISAARI (FINLAND)

I will remember him as somebody who has actually shown what capabilities a person can have when he's given a chance. That's something that he and I have in common. And there are people around us, I think, who will never get that chance.

HEDI ANNABI (TUNISIA)

He has given the job of Secretary-General a profile, a credibility that went way beyond what I've experienced with Secretaries-General since Waldheim. You know, at one point people were even talking about the credibility gap between the Secretary-General as a person and the institution, because he was so revered and respected and had this extraordinary clout and knack for dealing with people.

For example, operation Artemis in Ituri, Congo, is really the result of a single phone call from him to Chirac. That was June 2003, and the Bunia region of the Congo was hopelessly destabilized and we needed to send well-armed troops quickly. France would never have gone in otherwise and of course France agreed to go in on the faith of that conversation. So I think he gave the job a profile that I certainly have never seen before and will be difficult to match.

AMA AND KOJO ANNAN (GHANA)

AMA: I think he did a good job. I think so. And I think he was one of the most popular ones; he put the UN on the map.

KOJO: I'm very proud of him. He rode out the storm. I think that with time the Oil-for-Food scandal will dissipate and I think his legacy will be very strong. As Ama said, he was definitely a very popular Secretary-General. And I think that's because he is a humanitarian. My Dad is the kind of person who, for the security guard downstairs, knows when his daughter's birthday is. He doesn't do that to prove a point to anybody, that's just the kind of human being he is.

What is saddest about the Oil-for-Food scandal for me is that I know he's a man who gave his whole life to help others. He's not a politician. And that's what he did: helped others around the world as best he could, trying to make the world more of a balanced playing field and to let the poor get a better slice of the cake. I think history will eventually tell that's what he did.

HANS BLIX (SWEDEN)

Hammarskjold and Kofi Annan are the Secretaries-General I rate highest. Hammarskjold had perhaps more of a theoretical overview. He was well read in philosophy and in government sciences. I don't know whether Kofi had that theoretical basis for his thinking, but he had certainly a lot of experience and a lot of wisdom in the way he went about it.

Kofi stood up. He did what he could. And he did this very well. The negatives we have heard about him come from people who have other axes to grind. And I think you and I were lucky to work with him.

LAKHDAR BRAHIMI (ALGERIA)

Judgment will be passed by people who know him, and judgment will be passed by people who don't know him. Judgment will be passed by people who will really examine the record; and judgment will be passed by people who will be prejudiced and will not bother to look at the record.

[Laughs.] Those people who hate the UN, who frankly are racists also, will say that this African, we've had to suffer him for 10 years, and now we're really happy he's gone.

But I think he was a very distinguished Secretary-General. He was one of the Secretaries-General who have made a difference. If people don't like every single thing he has done or said, he really put the organization where it should be. And I think that, all in all, his 10 years have been a positive thing for the organization and for himself.

As an African, I think I am very happy that our continent was so well represented at the top of the pyramid of the World Organization. Boutros Boutros-Ghali and Kofi Annan have been great Secretaries-General. The US was very unfair to Boutros. They were not very kind to Kofi, either, starting with the run up to the war on Iraq.

CHRIS COLEMAN (US)

I hope he'll be remembered as a person who took the weaknesses of the Organization and instead of trying to apologize for them, put them front and center for Member States to address, which they sometimes did and they sometimes didn't. But at least he put them out there for them.

And I think he'll be remembered as a genuinely good soul, who understood the challenges of this job, which is pretty much impossible, and preferred to be in the arena to try and make a difference rather than sitting on the sidelines, even though fighting in the arena would inevitably incur real personal costs, as it has. But it was the right thing to do and he did it.

ALVARO DE SOTO (PERU)

He has managed, through a combination of sheer likeableness, his gifts as a communicator and as a networker and his capacity to gain the confidence of people, to make himself into a player at a higher level than was achieved by any of his predecessors. I mean, not even close.

We're talking here about a man who is on a first name, familiar basis with every significant leader on the planet and who moves in the same circles and at the same level. That was quite remarkable.

And I think it had a lot to do with how his image was projected. I have this theory which I'll mention to you, Fred, which is that at the beginning of his term, when he was not as well known, when he was not well-known at all, as a matter of fact, he had somehow managed to take advantage of a passing resemblance to two people. One is Nelson Mandela and the other is Morgan Freeman, the movie actor, both of whom project a kind of image of mellowness.

But what happened is that he acquired such prominence himself over the years that, with the eclipse of Mandela and the growing fame of Kofi Annan himself, he became better known and more prominent and more popular than all of them. He had this image of kindliness and of wisdom. And he had a very stylish way of using his hands on a TV screen, his very elegant hands that he has. And all that, I think, in a curious sort of intangible way that you can't describe properly in words, contributed enormously to this aura that he's leaving office with. It'll be a hard act to follow.

JAN EGELAND (NORWAY)

I think Kofi Annan will be remembered as one of the strongest Secretaries-General ever. With Dag Hammarskjold, he will be up on the top of the list. And he will grow with history. Many may not remember how he brought the UN forward — I was in Oslo when he got the Nobel Peace Prize. I remember. He was unfairly treated by parts of the US and Western press and others in the latter part of his mandate. But history will rectify that.

LOUISE FRECHETTE, DEPUTY SECRETARY-GENERAL (CANADA)

First of all, I think he'll be remembered for the way in which he opened the doors of the UN to all the non-State actors, reaching out to the business community and to the NGOs — his public diplomacy. He really brought in a new approach in the UN that was very effective in mobilizing public opinion on things like the Millennium Development Goals and the AIDS crisis. And I think that's very important for the institution, because the connection to ordinary people is pretty vital.

I think governments will also remember him quite positively. Governments are always a little schizophrenic about the Secretary-General. They want someone who will follow their orders since they're the masters of the House but at the same time, they appreciate someone who is quite pro-active, who's out there ready to take risks. Sometimes they get angry when the Secretary-General takes risks that they don't approve of. But on the whole, I think most governments prefer a Secretary-General who's a little more pro-active than one that is so bland that you don't even know he's there. Kofi was definitely not bland!

You know, even though he was an insider, he still had to feel his way into a role that is really unique. There is no equivalent anywhere. And one of the things that is remarkable about Kofi Annan is how he grew into the job. He filled the shoes; in fact, he made the shoes much bigger.

AMBASSADOR DAN GILLERMAN (ISRAEL)

All in all, I think he will be remembered as one of the most impressive and most effective Secretaries-General. You know, I think there are three categories of Secretary-General. There are the ones the world will forever remember, there are the ones who were pretty mediocre and there are the ones who the world may even forget. And I definitely think Kofi belongs to the first category, the one that will be remembered and respected.

JIM GOODALE (US)

When these crises passed, his last months at the UN were a tour de force. I firmly believe that Kofi was the greatest Secretary-General since Hammarskjöld. The reason was that he found a voice for peace to which the world listened. And he never wavered in his belief in the principles on which the UN was founded and never wavered in telling the world why he thought so.

JEAN-MARIE GUÉHENNO (FRANCE)

The game is taking place on a more level playing field today than when he arrived. And that is a reflection of his work and it's also a reflection of a growing popular engagement. There is a kind of world Town Hall meeting going on. The United Nations is an object of public debate in a way that it never was before Kofi Annan.

So he has made the job for his successors more interesting — and more difficult.

JEAN-PIERRE HALBWACHS (MAURITIUS)

You know, you work at the UN, you sit around New York and you get bombarded by the Claudia Rosetts and all these people. And you move out of here and realize that these people represent a small minority of world opinion, that the rest of the world has a completely different opinion of a) what the UN is worth and b) the contribution and leadership that Kofi gave to this place.

PATRICK HAYFORD (GHANA)

What stands out about him for me is his fundamental decency, and the courtesy and respect he shows to everyone working for him, from the highest to the most junior; his total commitment to the work he's engaged in; his amazing ability to focus with laser intensity on the immediate task at hand, but then immediately switch to another task and focus completely on that. That's quite an extraordinary ability. And his sheer energy; his capacity is prodigious. He has a real concern and keen desire to help Africa in whatever way he can.

RICHARD HOLBROOKE (US)

He enhanced the UN; he became a world figure. And he understood the bully pulpit aspect of the UN, something that Ban Ki-Moon does not understand yet. Darfur is a very good example — you can't do Darfur as low-key, quiet diplomacy; you have to bludgeon the Sudanese into letting those peacekeeping units in.

What are the marks we give Kofi Annan? I'd give him positive marks. He saved the UN. He restored its moral purpose. He inspired and still inspires millions of people around the world, who think he's a beacon of moral authority. But his shining record was seriously hurt, above all, by Oil-for-Food. Still, he will be remembered.

TERJE ROED LARSEN (NORWAY)

I have seen in my time in public life, both international and national, that even the strongest of personalities can become seduced by their public persona. And it kind of kills their private persona and they become unbelievably narcissistic, self-obsessed and after a while they lose any capacity for self-criticism and become impossible people to relate to. I have never seen a trace of this in him. He is incredibly rooted in his own identity. The word that you used, I think, was "centered." Now he's a very integrated personality with an enormously well developed sense of self-criticism. And there is a very genuine modesty in him. He's an enthusiast; he's incredibly energetic; he thinks he can do the impossible; but at the same time there is modesty and humility in him.

And there's also one other side. I've seen people betraying him; I've seen people lying to him. And I see he knows; but he forgives. He has an enormous ability to forgive. I don't think he forgets; but he forgives, which is an admirable quality. He looks these people in the eye and says, mildly, I know you've betrayed me; I know you lied to me. And that's punishment enough. And I think most people shape up when he does this.

And all this displays his tremendous leadership talents. In a way, he was a man of our times in the sense that his leadership style was adapted to the historical context of the House, which he knew inside and out, and the historical context of the world, which he grasped intuitively. And I think he made a difference.

JEAN-DAVID LEVITTE (FRANCE)

Well, his first mandate was a jewel. He will remain, in my view, the best ever Secretary-General since the very beginning of this UN saga. You know, when he was elected, everybody was saying, now we have a Secretary for the UN, and that's what the Americans wanted. And suddenly we saw emerging not only somebody who knew the UN system better than anybody, but he emerged as a kind of Pope, a conscience for the whole United Nations family. He was the incarnation of what the UN should say, should think, should try to achieve. And his first mandate was a magnificent achievement, a great success story.

And then Iraq nearly destroyed everything. And he was attacked in the most vicious way. He nearly was killed — not physically, but intellectually, morally. But he's a strong man; he recovered and he is finishing like he was in his first mandate — the Great Kofi.

MARK MALLOCH BROWN (UK)

Probably the best Secretary-General to date. The only possible competitor, Dag Hammarskjöld, died tragically just as the wolves were circling him as they sought to do to Kofi over Iraq. Yet, the amount of innovation he has introduced in so many areas from human rights, to security and development, together with the extraordinary expansion in the scale of operations during his watch, make him a seminal figure. Oil-for-Food has hurt that but it is ultimately a black mark on a winner's card. This is the man who introduced the Millennium Development Goals, the "responsibility to protect" doctrine, a Human Rights Council, a Peacebuilding Commission, the Global Compact and much else.

He will also be remembered as the warmest, most human – and most culturally global – face the UN has had. His gentle voice calling for peace and tolerance or for behavior change to prevent HIV/AIDS has become the face and voice of the UN to billions.

DAVID MALONE (CANADA)

I think Kofi will be remembered as a very significant norm entrepreneur, as a genuine champion of the humanitarian imperative and of human rights. So I expect his stature to grow steadily in the future, and I expect history to look back on his tenure positively. Although the problems of the second term will undoubtedly be recorded also, they'll be placed in perspective.

Bottom line, I think he did a spectacular job in his first term and will be remembered more for it than for the problems of the second term. The other thing I'd say is that the experience of Kofi Annan should discourage any future Secretary-General from seeking a second term.

CAROLYN MCASKIE (CANADA)

After I spoke to you today, I was really conscious of how much Kofi has accomplished and how strange it is that there is still a class of US press that continues to revile him. It reminds me of the Buddhist philosopher whose validity requires that he suffer persecution; maybe this is what happened to Kofi.

I was struck by how he has made a difference in the whole spectrum of peace: peacemaking (the UN is so often now expected to be one of the players); peacekeeping (it is totally different from what it was 10 years ago); peacebuilding (he launched the process to finally close the gap); and development (the Millennium Development Goals are universally acknowledged as the standard the world is aiming for).

How in the world are there people who say he has not achieved what he set out to do? I believe he has achieved infinitely more than anyone else could have.

His leaving was very emotional for me. We will truly miss him. There's a popular saying from Shakespeare's *Twelfth Night*, "Some are born great, some achieve greatness and some have greatness thrust upon 'em." Kofi embodied all three.

EDWARD MORTIMER (UK)

I think there is a connecting link between humanitarian intervention — the responsibility to protect — and some of his other initiatives, like the Global Compact and the call to action on AIDS. He seemed to say, yes, of course, we have to keep the peace between the States, and I'm available for that when it's threatened, but actually, thank God, that has not been the main problem in our time.

The main problem is what is happening to *people* — more or less irrespective of what State they happen to be living in. We have used from time to time the phrase "human security". That really is the point. You might be living in a stable State with no immediate enemies, but you still aren't secure if you can be thrown into jail or thrown out of your house at any time. And you're not really secure if you're starving, or if every cup of water you drink is likely to give you a deadly disease. So these things have to be thought of as a continuum, not as completely distinct problems.

Of course, people should look in the first instance to their own governments, but government can't do everything. Certainly, one country's government can't do everything by itself. So there has to be somebody representing a collective human interest, which these people can turn to. Now that's a very ambitious program; it probably would not have been realistic to imagine that he could deliver on that 100 percent. But I do think he's got people to think about it in that way, and I think that's very important.

NADER MOUSAVIZADEH (DENMARK)

In Kofi, there was a unique match, temperamentally, between man and mission as Secretary-General. The ability to persuade others to go along with his ideas and initiatives was absolutely critical to his success. I saw, particularly in the early years, how Kofi, over the course of a meeting, would make other leaders think: "How can I help him succeed?" That was enormously valuable to the UN, but as we are likely to see in the future, dangerous to the institution in the absence of a leader with such qualities.

There is no doubt that he will ultimately be remembered as a leader of the UN who was willing to challenge Member States on the issue of sovereignty versus human rights — saying, what they do to their own people within their borders is everybody's business, and I'm going to speak up when people are abused. And nobody liked it, including the United States. I think Kofi will be remembered for this — and should be.

SADAKO OGATA (JAPAN)

Kofi had two very special character traits for which he'll be remembered. First, he was very warm and considerate. Whenever I or UNHCR was in difficulty, he always called to encourage and to advise. His second special characteristic was his balanced judgment. He always tried to get everyone on board. What do I admire in him the most? His warm personality and his broad vision. I hope he will continue to lead all of us and the world, even after he leaves the UN.

YVES OLTRAMARE (SWITZERLAND)

He is a man with a *grande hauteur de vue*, who cut through to the essentials. He is someone who projected an image of the United Nations, of what it should be and could be, that was unique in the history of the Organization. He had his problems of course; we all read about them in the newspapers. But it seems to me that the attacks on him were what we would call in French: *sournoises* [underhanded]. He was Secretary-General during a period of history that was particularly difficult and I think he faced it with great dignity and intelligence.

ROBERT ORR (US)

Kofi Annan made an organization that was global in name into a truly global actor. The UN has long had global mandates that it could only very partially deliver on. Over the last 10 years, Kofi Annan led steadily as UN peacekeeping rebounded from near irrelevance to become the world's pre-eminent peacekeeper, with nearly 100,000 security personnel deployed in all the toughest spots around the globe, a number of personnel second only to the United States.

Over the same decade, the UN became the dominant humanitarian actor globally, more than tripling its presence around the world. Similarly the UN became the world's pre-eminent organizer, supporter, and monitor of democratic elections in over 75 countries. And last, but most certainly not least, under his leadership, the Millennium Development Goals have become the first ever universally accepted framework for addressing the fundamental needs of all people around the world.

He also provided moral guidance and visionary leadership in confronting challenges old and new. He brought nation states into the 21st century, convincing them to adopt the Responsibility to Protect – a truly historic redefinition of nation state sovereignty to include responsibilities as well as rights. He challenged leaders to finally acknowledge and personally commit themselves to fight the catastrophic effects of HIV/AIDS and set up the Global Fund to fight HIV/AIDS, Tuberculosis, and Malaria. And he convinced 192 UN member states to adopt, for the first time, a joint global counter-terrorism strategy — no small achievement.

He will also be remembered as the man who made human rights a real third pillar of the UN, in addition to peace and security and development.

I think he will be remembered as the first real reform Secretary-General, in the sense that he made reform a permanent part of the Organization. I think every Secretary-General after him may be forced to follow his example on that.

Finally I would say he'll be remembered for reaching out to the peoples of the world, and the individual people, not just the states of the world. This is a fundamental shift in the orientation of the United Nations, and Kofi Annan has had more to do with that than any other single person — reaching out to individuals, civil society, and the private sector very directly. And through words and deeds he brought the people of the world closer to the UN and to each other. This is his lasting legacy.

SIR KIERAN PRENDERGAST (UK)

Looking at his record as Secretary-General, he used his very important personal qualities to the full. And because of those personal qualities, and because of his gift of empathy and his ability to get on with people and the fact that in his dealing with leaders, he was curious, respectful and nonjudgmental, I believe he raised the status of the position of Secretary-General very considerably. I can recall many occasions when the Security Council, particularly when they were divided, tended to look to him to try and come up with some formula that might restore their unity, which is not really the role of the Secretary-General.

As Secretary-General he played an important role in opening a window to the world. The UN had really a very government-orientated first 50 years. I mean, when we talk about "we, the peoples", we actually meant "we, the governments". There was a great deal of resistance among the broader membership to opening meetings to any form of participation or even observation by civil society, but he pushed that very consistently and I think the United Nations that emerged after his 10 years as Secretary-General was one that was much more open to participation by, or observation at least by, NGOs, civil society and also the business community.

I don't think he was perfect as a Secretary-General. For somebody who went to MIT as a Sloan Fellow and had an advanced degree in management, I don't think he was that interested in management. He did, as others have acknowledged, do more about reform than I think any previous Secretary-General, but I think he was a little bit inclined sometimes to think "been there, done that" and not follow through on reforms.

But in the overall scale of things, these are minor flaws. There's no such thing as the perfect Secretary-General, who was all Secretary and all General, and I think that our man Kofi was a great Secretary-General, who was a great deal more General than Secretary.

IQBAL RIZA (PAKISTAN)

On the positive side, I think he'll be remembered for his ability to connect with people, not only face to face but in large audiences, including through the media, TV. He connected. I mean, I know people who've just seen him on television and felt a warmth.

His nemesis was, of course, Oil-for-Food, very unfairly, I believe. And there, vicious parts of the media whipped up a complete frenzy, which damaged not only him but the institution. It's going to take decades, I think, before we can recoup the standing we had in public opinion throughout the world.

I think what he'll really be remembered for will be his efforts to improve the UN, strengthen the UN to make it more effective. He reached out to all sectors of civil society. I don't know if he was overreaching or whether he was trying to do too much. And all this while dealing with political crises and powerful governments who have their own interests in these crises which involved such horrendous loss of life in Rwanda, Bosnia, Somalia and then after that, Congo, and now, of course, Darfur.

JOHN RUGGIE (US)

Well, this US Administration's [George W. Bush's] place in history is going to be judged pretty harshly as well. And I think that will probably be taken into account in judging Kofi. The Oil-for-Food thing was an unnecessary self-inflicted wound, and he will get blamed for that, although not nearly the proportion of blame that he's been assigned in that part of the press that you referred to [i.e. the conservative media].

But I would be surprised if in the long run his reputation weren't typically mentioned in the same sentence as Hammarskjold's. The two of them will stand out, at least up to now, as the most important Secretaries-General the UN has had.

And why is he so often compared to Hammarskjold? A tremendous ability to tap into a sense of community that extends beyond national boundaries. And this even more so in Kofi than Dag Hammarskjold; also, an ability to speak for common human interests as opposed to trying to split the difference between competing national interests. I think that is the most profound difference between Kofi and Hammarskjold on the one hand and the other Secretaries-General on the other.

Most of them, when confronted with conflicting national interests, would try to find some way to mediate or split the difference. With Hammarskjold and with Kofi, there was a vision that, as fragile and thin as it might be, there was a broader human community that transcended national interests and it was their role to try to speak for it and to embody it and to institutionalize it.

JEFFREY SACHS (US)

I think without question he has been and remains one of the greatest statesmen of our time. He is admired throughout the world. He went through a terrible period of attack by the political leadership of the most powerful member of the UN, but he came out as standing tall and with his dignity. And I know from my travels all over the world, that he is not only remarkably admired but that he has inspired people all over the world to public service and to achieving crucial global goals, including the Millennium Development Goals.

JIM WOLFENSOHN (US)

I hope he'll be remembered for the fact that he first of all went through a very, very difficult period, that he kept his values, that he didn't panic, he remained very level-headed, even when he was hurting inside. I think he was a first-rate civil servant, and I hope he'll be remembered for being a very constructive and stable person to have at a very difficult time, even though I think he was personally bruised and abused in ways that for a lesser person would have killed him.

He had a terrible time — in relation to his family, in relation to Sergio, in relation to the pressure of events that occurred. He was tested terribly and, by and large, came through it pretty well. A lot of other men would have cracked under that, and I don't know whether it's an African trait or some inherited trait, or something, but it wasn't weakness that got him through, in my judgment. But then, I like the man. Am I wrong?

When you think of his son and the turmoil around that — that was a horrible situation. I don't know where the blame is, but it was a lousy thing to happen. It was a personal test for him. He must have felt that terribly, and I've never dug into it with him, but it couldn't have been anything but tough as hell for him. At the same time, to have all the things going on internationally, and to be taking on the United States, saying the United Nations is not just the United States, which is the biggest thing he did. Now that was really gutsy. And he did it at a time when he wasn't strong. So you have to say "Hats off" to him.

PRINCE ZEID (JORDAN)

In the final measure of things, you want to assume that he'll come out really quite comfortable with what he achieved and what others think of him.

I remember when I was in Zagreb, I was sitting there talking with him about my next career move. And that got me asking him how his own career in the UN proceeded. And he said something very revealing about himself. He said, "You know, I was always good at what it was that I did; never bad, nor brilliant, but good. And I had excellent relations with everyone that I worked with."

I would say he has a great sense of awareness of his space and who he is and what he can contribute. He's a very, very interesting person, and I think, in the end, we're all the richer for having known him or worked with him.

2

HAMMARSKJOLD AND ANNAN

by Sir Brian Urquhart

When Kofi Annan was wrapping up his second five-year term as UN Secretary-General, some were comparing him to Dag Hammarskjold. I worked with Hammarskjold and I find the comparison unhelpful.

Hammarskjold was one of a kind, something of a genius perhaps. He combined messianic feelings about the UN, a vision of how to use and develop it, and a great aptitude for both negotiation and administration. He was a solitary man with little or no appetite for deep personal relationships or for social life. He was a dedicated bachelor and loner. He was self-absorbed. He had a formidable intellect and remarkable powers of political analysis. He was guided by principle in the highest sense, never compromised principle, and was courageous both in action and in not being pushed around by great powers.

Hammarskjold did not seek advice so much as confirmation of his own views. He wrote his most important speeches himself. He put the secretariat, and to some extent the UN itself, on the map as an active organization that if necessary could function effectively in the field by brilliant improvisation. In spite of the constraints of the Cold War, he introduced non-Charter concepts like peacekeeping, and the responsibility of the Secretary-General to work for international peace and security when governments had failed. He was dealing with a much smaller and less complex organization than Kofi Annan was.

A DISCIPLE

Kofi Annan has many human qualities that Hammarskjold did not have. He is outgoing, sociable and consults widely before making a policy decision. It seems to me appropriate to say that Kofi was an enthusiastic successor, admirer, perhaps even disciple of Hammarskjold.

Kofi was the first Secretary-General to come from the Secretariat. This had advantages – he knew a great deal about the UN; and disadvantages – there was a tendency for some analysts to find him limited by the 'culture of the Secretariat', whatever that may mean. It has been argued that a Secretary-General with no previous ties to the Secretariat will find it easier to carry out reforms, but I doubt it.

Although Kofi was the US candidate, he had the misfortune of having had to deal for six years with an ideological US administration that was arrogant and specifically hostile to multilateralism, international organization and international law. For his part Kofi handled himself patiently and with dignity in this very difficult situation, but his obvious disapproval of the 2003 invasion of Iraq enraged US neo-conservatives, who hated him anyway, and they managed to do him serious harm by creating and disseminating widely the mythology of the Oil-for-Food 'scandal'.

It will be a miracle if that 'scandal' does not remain what Kofi Annan is best remembered for, much as U Thant is still remembered, unfairly in my view, for triggering the 1967 Middle East War by withdrawing UN peacekeepers from Sinai, a decision over which he had no legal option. This would be a gross injustice, not only because, as far as Kofi was concerned, the 'scandal' was to a large extent a fabrication, but also because he was successful in his handling of many critical situations, as well as making some major conceptual contributions.

Kofi employed a team of talented speechwriters under the direction of Edward Mortimer and reacted to events with public statements to a far greater extent than any of his predecessors, thus creating a useful precedent for there being a UN world view.

In particular, his formulation of the 'responsibility to protect', eventually approved in principle by the 2005 Summit, set a historical goal, which, like human rights, will take many years to transform into reality.

His proposals for reform were bolder and more far-reaching than those of his predecessors. While governments again and again diluted them or scotched them altogether, he aimed high and what survived of his reform agenda has made the UN stronger.

CHARISMA

Personality and charisma are an important part of a Secretary-General's success or failure. Here Kofi Annan scores very high. He is the only Secretary-General except Hammarskjold who made an impression on the world public, and was someone who would be more likely than not to be recognized walking down the street. In his first term he enjoyed a high reputation for wisdom, calm, unflappability, energy and courage. Sometimes the last quality earned him criticism, as when he visited Saddam Hussein in 1998 and successfully negotiated access to the dictator's palaces for UN weapons inspectors – an agreement, like most agreements with Saddam Hussein, that was soon reneged on.

I sometimes think that some of his staff in the early years were unwise to give the impression to the outside world that Kofi could walk on water. Great first-term success always makes a second term hazardous, as people, and especially the press, long to find fault, feet of clay, personal imperfections etc., in someone universally admired. And in the nature of the job, the Secretary-General cannot hope to succeed all the time.

Kofi cut a dignified and attractive figure, and he and his wife, Nane, made an admirable pair in public. He had a fine public presence and was a sincere, if sometimes soporific, speaker. He was not a great orator, but I suspect that the Secretary-General is better off *not* being a great orator. What he says is more important than how he says it.

It's ironic that the first Secretary-General to have been trained as a manager and who had experience of a range of administrative responsibilities during his previous UN career should be criticized for his lack of management skills. Maybe in its present political form, it is impossible to administer the UN as efficiently as a business corporation or to reform it effectively. It is true that the Oil-for-Food Programme, considering its size and importance, was slackly supervised, as Kofi himself has admitted. Saddam Hussein was about as corrupt and impossible a partner as you could find for such a large and complex affair. The Oil-for-Food Programme carried out its huge task effectively. It fed and assisted the people of Iraq for nearly seven years. It was a triumph of effectiveness and integrity compared to later enterprises in Iraq.

INTEGRITY

For the Secretary-General, integrity is the most essential of qualities. From my limited knowledge, Kofi is a person of complete integrity, and he showed it not only in administration, but in speaking out on matters of principle or importance, and in sticking to his own beliefs and policies in important matters.

To sum up: Kofi Annan was a very good Secretary-General, who left the UN a more valuable organization than he found it.

He was a considerable and constructive innovator.

He enhanced the public reputation of the UN in the world, although the Oil-for-Food 'scandal' damaged it and him.

He was a skillful political operator. (Anyone who can take a strong line in the Middle East, as Kofi did after the 2006 summer war, achieve some results, and keep both Arabs and Israelis more or less on his side, must be a good political operator.)

He was a reasonably good administrator, given the circumstances and the nature of the UN.

He was a world leader of charm and considerable charisma.

He was not an intellectual, but he was sufficiently sure of himself to hire first-class (sometimes intellectual) personal staff and advisers. His main speeches were substantial, important, and often original.

He was honest enough to admit mistakes and report publicly and frankly on the details, as he did on Rwanda and Srebrenica. This was unprecedented. He also tried to learn from those mistakes and not repeat them.

He was someone whose apparently laid-back appearance concealed great energy and stamina. His travels, especially to trouble spots and humanitarian disasters to show the UN flag and rally support for the victims, were heroic.

Like Hammarskjold, Kofi Annan represented the UN to the world very well, and also did a lot of good hard work. Perhaps there lies the essential comparison.

V

SALUTES

I asked a number of world leaders for their thoughts on Kofi Annan. Nelson Mandela was an obvious person to start with. Then I asked a senior person in each of the five governments that sit as Permanent Members of the Security Council. And finally, I asked Javier Solana of the European Union.

NELSON MANDELA

Since I am officially a retired old man now, it gives me great pleasure to speak of a young man who has distinguished himself in service to the world and who has surely earned retirement despite his youth.

Kofi Annan's rich life and career demands more than a few words. He grew up in Ghana in a family of chiefs during a turbulent but exciting time in Africa's history. His childhood was marked by his country's freedom struggles. As he became a man, Ghana became the first African country south of the Sahara to throw off the shackles of colonialism. He was raised on the audacity of hope. It helped him to see, from a very young age, that change was indeed possible — and worth fighting for.

He chose international relations as his own site of struggle. Ten years ago we celebrated when he was elected as Secretary-General of the United Nations. We were personally gratified to see the position going to another African, after Egypt's Boutros Boutros-Ghali. We celebrated again when he was elected to a second term.

We watched with pride when he and his organization won the 2001 Nobel Peace Prize. Again, we watched with pride as he threw himself into efforts to stop another war in Iraq. Despite his trademark cool and calm style, it was mentioned at the time that he behaved more like a general than a secretary! And when the United Nations was defied and Iraq was invaded, he dedicated himself to making peace in that troubled land.

Kofi has walked a long road, and he has made an outstanding legacy. We salute him, and wish him well in whatever ventures the future holds for him.

COLIN POWELL
Excerpts from a conversation with the former Secretary of State of the United States of America

I had to remind my colleagues frequently that Kofi was not the commander of the UN, he was the Secretary-General of the United Nations and he was the agent of the Security Council. So he was us. And we had to keep in mind that he had a responsibility to the 15 members of the Security Council and to the 192 members of the General Assembly.

He was extremely helpful as we worked our way through a number of issues: for example, in Haiti, Liberia and Sudan. So many of these crises that sometimes start out in a unilateral or a coalition-of-the-willing way, end up then being handed to the UN to bring to fruition. And that is repeated lots of places.

In our work on HIV/AIDS, the United States and Kofi collaborated to create the Global Health Fund some five or six years ago. And I think if it hadn't been for our cooperation with Kofi and initial funding, it might not have gotten the start that it did.

I found it useful to keep Kofi informed, to get the benefit of his leadership, his wisdom and his incredible contacts around the world where he is so respected.

And did we have disagreements? Sure, we had serious disagreements over Iraq. He would have preferred to keep the inspections going longer and was very troubled at the disarray that occurred within the United Nations Security Council as we approached the issue of the second resolution. We had a different point of view. And even though there may be some in the United States Government who directed their animus toward Kofi, I never did. Even when we disagreed, we always did it in terms of how do we get along, how do we move forward, how do we solve the problem, not how do we bash each other.

The Oil-for-Food Programme was a serious problem, and the UN was finally forced into doing something about it. And I think that will not look well for Kofi over time. It will always be something of an item in the deficiencies column.

We were perhaps more aggressive than the UN or Kofi might have liked with respect to the need to reform, and the reform of the management system of the UN is still under way.

So there were disagreements with Kofi, but there's always been tension between the United Nations and Washington. I was National Security Adviser to President Reagan in 1988 when Reagan decided it was time to start funding the UN again. And it took us many years to catch up on our arrears, but I'm pleased to say that as Secretary of State I always believed it was in our interest to support the UN and not just take the easy road of criticizing it as a debating body sitting in New York and not accomplishing much.

So the relationship between Washington and the UN during Kofi's 10-year tenure was sometimes strained. But I think he goes out with the respect of the Administration.

I consider him a friend, a dedicated public servant, somebody who served the United Nations well. He was a good Secretary-General, an advocate for peace; he always tried to find a peaceful solution to the challenges of the world, a policy that I too have tried to follow in my life. I don't look for wars; I try to avoid wars. That's what Kofi always did. He's very highly regarded throughout the world, and, even in the United States you will find some in the political spectrum who would share my high admiration for him.

JACQUES CHIRAC
former President of France

Kofi Annan was at the helm of the United Nations during a time when it was necessary to have the courage to insure that multilateralism prevailed, the determination to promote unfailingly the UN Charter and genuine vision in order to confront the major challenges of the 21st Century.

He led the UN effort not just for peace, but also for human rights and economic development. He unceasingly called attention to the common bonds that link these three pillars upon which the United Nations was founded.

Without raising his voice, he made himself understood. The world will remember his courageous statements against the illegitimate use of force, his sounding of the alarm over Darfur and the Millennium Development Goals to which we are all committed.

We were in constant contact, and a sense of mutual confidence and friendship quickly formed between the two of us. He knew he could count on France, as was the case in the Ituri region (of the Democratic Republic of Congo) in 2003 when civilian populations were seriously threatened. I also knew that I could count on his support, which was essential in finding innovative sources for financing economic development.

There were those who sought his downfall. He resisted their attacks. France was always at his side.

He finishes his mandate respected by all. I am convinced that he will be remembered throughout the course of history as a great Secretary-General of the United Nations.

TONY BLAIR
former Prime Minister of the United Kingdom

Kofi has made sure there is not only a will but a way for the international community to improve its partnership with Africa. He has reminded us, repeatedly and tirelessly, not only that we *should* work to help Africa address the problems it grapples with every day, but also that we *can* actually, collectively, make a massive difference to the lives of millions of Africans across the continent.

His leadership contributed to the agreement of the Millennium Development Goals in 2000. And in 2005, he played a key role at the G8 Summit at Gleneagles in July and the UN Summit in September that delivered new commitments for Africa. That is why I was delighted that Kofi will co-chair the Africa Progress Panel, which will work to ensure that the world keeps the promises it has made to Africa.

Responsibility to Protect encapsulates much of what has made Kofi's stewardship of the UN so significant and so widely admired: a clear sense of the duty of the international community to help and if necessary act to protect citizens who are denied protection by their own governments. His leadership has been invaluable in re-affirming, strengthening and attempting to implement this principle, which is one that the British Government strongly endorses. Responsibility to Protect will be one of the policies most closely associated with his tenure as Secretary-General.

SERGEY LAVROV
Minister of Foreign Affairs of the Russian Federation

Kofi Annan was at the head of the United Nations for 10 difficult years, during a period when, following the euphoria generated by the end of the Cold War, the world entered a complex and contradictory period.

During this troubled time, he worked effectively with the Security Council to resolve a number of prolonged violent conflicts and, in my view, realized a crowning achievement at the Millennium Assembly when he put forward his vision of harmonizing the international community's development efforts by citing the specific goals and target dates contained in the Millennium Development Goals.

Unfortunately, during Kofi's tenure we also witnessed the emergence of new conflicts and threats, massive violations of human rights and the unilateral use of force.

In these difficult circumstances, his greatest accomplishment as United Nations Secretary-General was his aspiration to strictly abide by the principles of international law, respect for the UN Charter, and implementation of UN organs' decisions. His outstanding energy and motivation contributed much to strengthening multilateral diplomacy and to the growing demand for UN involvement in international relations.

Kofi will also be remembered for his sweeping reform of UN peacekeeping, a subject he knew well from his years at the head of the peacekeeping department. The chaotic growth of this essential UN activity, both in numbers of personnel and complexity of mission, called out for a rethinking of the UN's policy in this area. The reform of peacekeeping is a major contribution, and one that will contribute to world stability well into the future.

Kofi's energy, integrity and moral judgment have always been highly valued by the Russian Government. He enriched the Organization with valuable ideas, gathering governments under the tree, in African style, to seek a collective solution to the world's problems.

I have warm memories of my longstanding relationship with him. Together, I feel, we worked for the higher good, sometimes succeeding, and all the while maintaining a collaborative friendship.

Kofi laid the foundation for a more inclusive, a better managed, and a stronger United Nations for the new millennium. That, in the end, is his legacy. I am confident that it is a solid foundation that his successors can build on, and for that I and my government are grateful to him.

LI ZHAOXING
former Minister of Foreign Affairs of the People's Republic of China

Kofi is an old friend of mine.

He is affable yet candid, warm and composed, gentle but firm. He loves people and has dedicated the best time of his life to the United Nations, the largest intergovernmental organization, and to the cause of peace and development of mankind. He has thus won respect both for his country and the African continent.

During the 10 years when he worked in his office on the 38th floor of the UN headquarters building, Kofi faced both historic opportunities and challenges. Enduring tremendous pressure, he made every effort to put the UN spirit into practice.

A proponent of UN preventive diplomacy, Kofi has worked so hard to mediate for peace. He put forward the Millennium Development Goals, declaring war on poverty, disease and illiteracy. His hope is for everyone to live in dignity. He is dedicated to making human rights one of the pillars of the United Nations, and he advocates mutual respect and harmonious coexistence among civilizations. Committed to reform, Kofi instilled a new momentum in this organization in its efforts to respond to global challenges. In particular, he urged the international community to address the needs of Africa and helped forge a partnership between the United Nations and Africa. Kofi has much credit to claim for the hard-won progress of the United Nations and the world.

Kofi is a great individual, a good colleague, and a Secretary-General whom I hold in great admiration.

A Conversation with JAVIER SOLANA

The European Union worked alongside the United States, Russia and Kofi as the so-called Quartet in search of Middle East peace. The EU often takes a common position in the UN, and its voice worldwide was Javier Solana, who had the title of High Representative for the Common Foreign and Security Policy. I interviewed him in his office in Brussels at the end of January 2007.

I started by saying that Kofi Annan had no diplomatic training, then by asking Javier Solana whether he thought that was a hindrance or a help to him as Secretary-General.

"The qualities of a man are the qualities of a man," he replied, "regardless of what his training is. And the qualities of Kofi Annan were extraordinary, in particular the dignity with which he handled problems and his profound commitment to making this world a better place.

"I met him for the first time in Bosnia, when he was head of UN peacekeeping, and since then we have built a friendship that I would call profound. We talk on the phone regularly, sharing our thoughts, and I have to tell you very honestly that with rare exceptions, very rare, I was in agreement with his analysis and his positions. So for me it has been a great pleasure to have had the opportunity of working with him."

And how was he viewed in the European Union?

"In the European Union, he was viewed as a friend," he said. "But I don't have to tell you the importance that the European Union attaches to the United Nations system. We are ourselves a multilateral organization, therefore for us effective multilateralism is at the core of our vision of the world. And so as a matter of principle we have great respect for the person who heads the United Nations, which is the center of gravity of the multilateral system.

"But in the case of Kofi, he was something else, because he was not only respected in principle, he was respected because of who he was — his personality. He had a great relationship with, and a great empathy for, all the leaders of the European Union, regardless of their ideology. And not just the leaders. I think Kofi was listened to by the European people themselves with great attention and great sympathy.

"I think that one of Kofi's most important virtues is his moral capacity to speak his mind and his heart about the many global problems that we face and to speak critically at times. He is somebody who can mobilize the minds and hearts of people and point them in the right direction.

"I remember his last visit to the European Union in the summer of 2006 when the resolution on ending the war in Lebanon was about to be taken up. He and I agreed to have a meeting here in order to try to quickly unblock the deployment of forces for an enlarged UN force in Lebanon. And for that, he knew, and I knew too, that without the European component this enlarged force would not be viable, the resolution would not be adopted and the war would not end. And we succeeded. You know, people sometimes think that Kofi is somebody who was not results-oriented, but it's not true. He is very much results oriented, as for example in the way he dealt with Lebanon.

"Now let me tell you about Kofi and the Quartet on the Middle East. We felt that it was necessary at that time to organize a group of people, of countries, with the Secretary-General, to give the Middle East peace process a fresh boost. And the first meeting was in Kofi's office. At that point it was a trio — the Secretary-General, Colin Powell and myself were there. And that was the beginning, really, of what we call today the Quartet. Later we invited the Russians and they were keen to join. For him, Middle East peace was a fundamental objective and he threw himself into it."

How do you think he'll be remembered?

"Well," he said, "I think he will be remembered as a great Secretary-General of the United Nations. And I think that the fact that the United Nations through him was awarded the Nobel Prize shows very clearly the respect that so many people in the world have for the institution, but also for him. He is sensible, he is cool-headed but at the same time with a warm heart. And that is what gave him this dignity that you can feel when you talk to him.

APPENDIX

Most often, sources who are quoted multiple times are cited by their full names initially and by their first names thereafter. If you don't know these people, you can quickly get lost. So here is an alphabetical list by first name, followed by short biographies alphabetically by last name, to help you keep track.

Afsane (Bassir-Pour)

Ahmad (Fawzi)

Alvaro (de Soto)

Ama (Annan)

Andrew (Arkutu)

Andrew (Gilmour)

Andy (Mack)

Annika (Savill)

Barbara (Crossette)

Benon (Sevan)

Benny (Avni)

(Sir) Brian (Urquhart)

Boutros (Boutros-Ghali)

Carlos (Lopes)

Carolyn (McAskie)

Catherine (Bertini)

Chinmaya (Gharekhan)

Chris (Christopher Coleman)

Chris (J. Christer Elfverson)

Craig (Jennis)

Dan (Gillerman)

David (Harland)

David (Malone)

(Lord) David (Owen)

Darko (Mocibob)

Denis (Halliday)

Edward (Mortimer)

Elisabeth (Lindenmayer)

Evelyn (Leopold)

Farhan (Haq)

Francis (Bartels)

Friederike (Bauer)

Georg (Kell)

Georges (Abi Saab)

Gillian (Sorensen)

Hans (Blix)

Hans (Corell)

Hedi (Annabi)

Ibrahim (Gambari)

Ingvar (Carlsson)

Iqbal (Riza)

Irwin (Arieff)

Isel (Rivero)

Jan (Egeland)

Jean-David (Levitte)

Jean-Marie (Guéhenno)

Jean-Pierre (« J-P ») (Halbwachs)

Jeff (Jeffrey Sachs)

(Sir) Jeremy (Greenstock)

(Chen) Jian

Jim (James Goodale)

Jim (Wolfensohn)

Joachim (Hutter)

Joanna (Weschler)

John (Ruggie)

Julia (Preiswerk)

Kevin (S. Kennedy)

(Sir) Kieran (Prendergast)

Kobina (Annan)

Kojo (Annan)

Lakhdar (Brahimi)

Lamin (Sise)

Louise (Arbour)

Louise (Frechette)

Marcel (d'Hertefelt)

Maggie (Farley)

(Lord) Mark (Malloch Brown)

Martin (Griffiths)

Martti (Ahtisaari)

Mary (Robinson)

Maurice (Baril)

Michael (Moller)

Michel (Lavollay)

Nader (Mousavizadeh)

Nana Essie (Annan)

Nane (Annan)

Nick (Nicholas Panzarino)

Nitin (Desai)

Noeleen (Heyzer)

Patrick (Hayford)

Paul (Keteku)

Peter (Piot)

(Gen.) Philippe (Morillon)

Rachel (Mayanja)

Richard (Holbrooke)

Robert (Orr)

Rob (Watson)

Rolf (Knutsson)

Sadako (Ogata)

Salman (Ahmed)

Shashi (Tharoor)

Stéphane (Steph) (Dujarric)

Stephen (Lewis)

Steve (Stephen Stedman)

Susan (Linnee)

Tamrat (Samuel)

Terje (Roed Larsen)

Thorvald (Stoltenberg)

Tom (Thomas Franklin)

Toni (Krissel Goodale)

Viru (Virendra Dayal)

Warren (Hoge)

Yves (Oltremare)

(Prince) Zeid (Ra'ad Zeid Al-Hussein)

I wish also to thank the many others who helped me and who are not quoted directly in this book, especially, Hassen Fodha (Tunisia), Vladimir (Volodya) Gratchev (Russia) and Joe Sills (US).

BIOGRAPHIES

1. GEORGES ABI SAAB *(Egypt)*: An international legal scholar whom Kofi met at Geneva in 1961 when they were both students at the Graduate Institute of International Studies. Today he is Professor Emeritus at the Institute.

2. SALMAN AHMED *(United States)*: Political officer in the UN Department of Peacekeeping Operations who co-authored with David Harland the internal study on the Srebrenica massacre and who worked with Lakhdar Bramimi on the report on peacekeeping reform. He is now working at the US State Department as Chief of Staff for US Ambassador to the UN Susan Rice.

3. MARTTI AHTISAARI *(Finland)*: Diplomat who headed the UN Peacekeeping Mission in Namibia, wrote the controversial assessment of the humanitarian effects of the 1991 invasion of Iraq to liberate Kuwait, worked with Cyrus Vance and Lord Owen on the Yugoslav peace talks in Geneva, served as President of his country, was Kofi's envoy to talks on the final status of Kosovo, did the critical security assessment for Kofi of the attack on UN headquarters in Baghdad, negotiated the peace agreement between Aceh rebels and the Indonesian Government and won the Nobel Peace Prize in 2008.

4. HEDI ANNABI *(Tunisia)*: Involved in the Cambodia peace process from 1982 to 1991 as Special Representative of the Secretary-General, then helped set up the UN peacekeeping mission there in 1992. Kofi brought him into the Peacekeeping Department in 1993 as head of the Africa Division and then appointed him Assistant Secretary-General in the peacekeeping department in 1997. Kofi intended to name him successor to Iqbal Riza as Chief of Staff in 2005, but under pressure from the Oil-for-Food scandal instead named Mark Malloch Brown to that post. Hedi was head of the UN peacekeeping mission in Haiti and died in the 2010 earthquake there.

5. AMA ANNAN *(Nigeria/Ghana)*: The daughter and first child of Kofi Annan and Titilola Alakija of Nigeria.

6. KOBINA ANNAN *(Ghana)*: Kofi's younger brother, Ghana's Ambassador to Morocco until his retirement in 2009.

7. KOJO ANNAN *(Ghana/Nigeria)*: Kofi's son and second child with Titilola Alakija.

8. NANA ESSIE ANNAN *(Ghana)*: Kofi's half-sister, the eldest of five children sired by Kofi's father, Henry Reginald Annan.

9. NANE ANNAN *(Sweden)*: Kofi's wife since 10 September 1984, a lawyer turned artist whom he met when both worked as single parents at the Office of the UN High Commissioner for Refugees in Geneva. She is the daughter of the distinguished jurist, Gunnar Lagergren, who arbitrated the Taba boundary between Israel and Egypt. She has a daughter Nina by her first marriage. As UN First Lady, she worked for broader public knowledge about and action against HIV/AIDS and also advocated the rights of women.

10. **LOUISE ARBOUR** *(Canada)*: As Chief Prosecutor for the Yugoslav and Rwanda Tribunals from 1996 to 1999, she indicted Serbian President Slobodan Milosevic in 1999. She was named a justice of Canada's Supreme Court that same year, a job Kofi convinced her to give up in 2004 to become UN High Commissioner for Human Rights. She stepped down as High Commissioner in 2009 and is currently President of the International Crisis Group in Brussels.

11. **IRWIN ARIEFF** *(United States)*: Veteran reporter for the *Reuters News Agency* who worked at the UN with bureau chief Evelyn Leopold from 2000 to 2007.

12. **ANDREW ARKUTU** *(Ghana)*: A prefect at Mfantsipim, the elite private secondary school in Ghana, when Kofi was a student there.

13. **BENNY AVNI** *(Israel)*: Reporter for *Israel Radio* and then for the now defunct *New York Sun*.

14. **FRANCIS BARTELS** *(Ghana)*: The director of Mfantsipim, Kofi's secondary school in Ghana, and a close friend of Kofi's father, Henry Reginald Annan. Later, he was Ghanaian Ambassador to Germany, and eventually worked for UNESCO in Paris, where he lives in retirement today. In his honor on his 100th birthday, Kofi established a foundation in his name in Accra, Ghana.

15. **AFSANÉ BASSIR-POUR** *(France)*: Iranian-born French journalist who was bureau chief at the UN for the French daily *Le Monde*, and then bureau chief for the same publication in Geneva. She received the *"Prix des Yeux d'Or"* award for her coverage of Kofi's trip to Baghdad in 1998. She is currently Director of the UN Regional Information Centre in Brussels.

16. **GENERAL MAURICE BARIL** *(Canada)*: A 40-year veteran of the Canadian Armed Forces, General Baril was UN Military Adviser from 1992 to 1995 when Kofi was head of peacekeeping. In 1997 he was named Chief of Defence Staff in Canada and retired in 2001.

17. **FRIEDERIKE BAUER** *(Germany)*: The former foreign editor of the *Frankfurter Allgemeine Zeitung*, she wrote the first book on Kofi in 2005, titled *Kofi Annan, Ein Leben*.

18. **CATHERINE BERTINI** *(United States)*: Distinguished herself as the head of the UN World Food Programme from 1992 to 2002. (She was awarded the World Food Prize in 2003.) Kofi named her Under-Secretary-General for Management in 2002; she resigned in 2005. She was a Senior Fellow at the Bill and Melinda Gates Foundation. She now teaches at Syracuse University and is a Senior Fellow at the Chicago Council of Global Affairs.

19. **TONY BLAIR** *(United Kingdom)*: British Prime Minister from 1997 to 2007.

20. **HANS BLIX** *(Sweden)*: The former Foreign Minister of Sweden who served as Director General of the International Atomic Energy Agency from 1981 to 1997, and whom Kofi named chief UN weapons inspector in Iraq in 2000. He served in that capacity until UN inspections ended with the US-led invasion of Iraq in March 2003.

21. **BOUTROS BOUTROS-GHALI** *(Egypt)*: UN Secretary-General from 1992 to 1996.

22. **LAKHDAR BRAHIMI** *(Algeria)*: Former Algerian Foreign Minister who held a series of important UN posts, including head of the UN mission in South Africa that oversaw the elections that brought Nelson Mandela to power in 1994. He then led the UN peacekeeping mission in Haiti in 1994, conducted a ground-breaking study on the reform of UN peacekeeping in

2000 and was Kofi's special envoy in Afghanistan, where he led negotiations to form a national government following the fall of the Taliban in 2003. Kofi then sent him to Iraq in 2004 as Special Representative, following the attack on UN headquarters in Baghdad that killed 22 UN staff members.

23. INGVAR CARLSSON *(Sweden)*: Former Prime Minister of Sweden (1986-1991) whom Kofi asked in 1999 to conduct an independent investigation into the UN's role during the Rwandan genocide of 1994.

24. CHEN JIAN *(China)*: Kofi's Under-Secretary-General for General Assembly Affairs and Conference Management, responsible for documentation, translation, interpretation and meeting servicing of not just the General Assembly, but also the Security Council and the Economic and Social Council. He was a member of China's first delegation to the General Assembly in 1972 and Assistant Minister of Foreign Affairs from 1996 to 1998. Today he teaches at universities in Beijing and Shanghai and is President of China's UN Association.

25. JACQUES CHIRAC *(France)*: President of the French Republic from 1995 to 2007.

26. CHRISTOPHER (CHRIS) COLEMAN *(United States)*: Kofi spotted Chris, an academic specialist in UN peacekeeping, at the International Peace Academy and hired him as a one-man think tank in the peacekeeping department. He subsequently worked in the Executive Office of UN Secretary-General Ban Ki-Moon and now heads Policy Planning and Mediation Support in the Department of Political Affairs.

27. HANS CORELL *(Sweden)*: Kofi's Legal Counsel and Under-Secretary-General for Legal Affairs from 1994 to 2004. Before that he had been Under-Secretary for Legal and Consular Affairs in the Swedish Foreign Ministry and Chief Legal Officer of the Ministry of Justice. From 1962 to 1972 he served in the Swedish Judiciary and was appointed Judge of Appeal in 1980.

28. BARBARA CROSSETTE *(United States)*: *New York Times* bureau chief at the UN from 1994 to 2002 after having reported for that same paper from Asia. Author of several books on Asia and distinguished commentator on UN affairs.

29. VIRENDRA (VIRU) DAYAL *(India)*: Under-Secretary-General and Chief of Staff to UN Secretary-General Javier Perez de Cuellar and briefly for Secretary-General Boutros Boutros-Ghali, who headed the mission to Baghdad that Kofi also went on to negotiate the release of UN hostages just prior to the US-led invasion to free Kuwait in 1991.

30. NITIN DESAI *(India)*: Kofi named him Under-Secretary-General for Economic and Social Affairs in 1997 after folding three UN departments into one. Kofi also asked him to serve as Secretary-General of the 2002 World Summit on Sustainable Development in Johannesburg. As Senior Economic Advisor to the Brundtland Commission from 1985-87, he had introduced the concept of sustainable development. He retired from the UN in 2003.

31. STÉPHANE (STEPH) DUJARRIC *(France)*: Former *ABC* television producer whom I hired as Associate Spokesperson for Kofi in June 2000, and then was named my successor in 2005. In 2007, he became Director of Communications for the UN Development Programme before returning to the UN Information Department as Director of News.

32. JAN EGELAND *(Norway)*: Kofi named him Under-Secretary-General for the Coordination of Humanitarian Affairs in 2003, in which capacity he coordinated the international response to the tsunami that swept across the Indian Ocean in December 2004. He also served as UN envoy to Colombia from 1999 to 2002. Before these UN assignments, he was Secretary-General of the

Norwegian Red Cross and, from 1992 to 1997, Norwegian State Secretary for Foreign Affairs, working among other things on the 1993 Oslo Accords between Israel and the Palestinians.

33. **J CHRISTER (CHRIS) ELFVERSON** *(Sweden)*: Chris was de facto deputy to Benon Sevan in the Office of the Iraq Programme that oversaw the Oil for Food Programme. As such, he was responsible for overseeing all reporting to the UN from Iraq as well as for the implementation of the program in the Kurdish north of Iraq. Today he is the Senior Diplomatic Adviser to Concordia 21 and affiliated organizations.

34. **MAGGIE FARLEY** *(United States)*: UN Bureau Chief for the *Los Angeles Times* from 1999 to 2008.

35. **AHMAD FAWZI** *(Egypt)*: Former *Reuters* television journalist whom Kofi called on from time to time to assist with travel to and press relations in the Middle East. He was brought into the UN as deputy spokesperson for Secretary-General Boutros Boutros-Ghali and served as director of the UN Information Centre in London before becoming a senior director in the UN information department. He was attached to Lakhdar Brahimi as spokesperson twice, once during the Afghanistan negotiations in Bonn in 2001 and again in Iraq in 2004. He was media adviser to Sergio Vieira de Mello during the elections in East Timor in 2000 and spokesperson for Sergio in Baghdad in 2003 until just before the attack on UN headquarters there in August of that year.

36. **THOMAS FRANKLIN** *(United Kingdom)*: Senior UNICEF official who was director of the UNICEF program in Rwanda from 1991 to 1994, and was evacuated at the beginning of the massacres.

37. **LOUISE FRÉCHETTE** *(Canada)*: Former Canadian Deputy Minister of Defense whom Kofi hired as the UN's first Deputy-Secretary-General in 1998. She was his right hand, leading the UN reform process, facilitating coordination throughout the system and helping with any problem that cropped up. She chaired for Kofi the Iraq Steering Group to coordinate the UN system's role in Iraq after the US invasion of 2003.

38. **IBRAHIM GAMBARI** *(Nigeria)*: Former Nigerian Foreign Minister (1984-85) and Ambassador to the UN (1990-1999), he was named by Kofi Adviser on Africa in 1999, chief of the UN mission in Angola (2002-2003) and finally Under-Secretary-General for Political Affairs in July 2005, succeeding Kieran Prendergast. Secretary-General Ban Ki-Moon subsequently named him Special Adviser, in which capacity he continued the diplomatic work with Myanmar that he started under Kofi and also led UN efforts on the implementation of the International Compact with Iraq.

39. **CHINMAYA GHAREKHAN** *(India)*: One of three Under-Secretaries-General who worked closely with UN Secretary-General Boutros Boutros-Ghali. He was responsible for reporting to the Security Council.

40. **DAN GILLERMAN** *(Israel)*: Named Israeli Ambassador to the UN in 2003 and voted Vice President of the UN General Assembly in 2005 as a result of Israel finally being accepted as a member of a regional group by which the Assembly organizes its business. The last Israeli to be so honored was Abba Eban 54 years earlier.

41. **ANDREW GILMOUR** *(United Kingdom)*: Deputy Political Director in Kofi's office, dealing mainly with the Middle East, a position he continued to hold under Secretary-General Ban Ki-Moon. Prior to that, from 2003-2006, he was senior political adviser in the UN Office in West Africa, based in Senegal. He also had Mideast experience, in both Gaza and Jerusalem,

as a political section head under Terje Roed Larsen, Special Coordinator of the Middle East Peace Process (2000-2003). After Kofi stepped down, he served for two years as Deputy Special Representative of the Secretary-General in Iraq and at the end of 2009 was appointed Representative of the Secretary-General in Belgrade.

42. JAMES [JIM] GOODALE *(United States)*: The New York first amendment lawyer who married Toni Krissel, a friend of Kofi's in Geneva in the 1960s when Kofi and Toni were both students there. Jim was Vice Chairman of *The New York Times* and advised Kofi privately on media relations when Kofi was Secretary-General.

43. TONI KRISSEL GOODALE *(United States)*: Met Kofi in Geneva while on a Junior Year Abroad as a student at Smith College in Massachusetts. They stayed closely in touch over the years. She later introduced Kofi to her husband Jim Goodale, who also became a close friend of Kofi's. She heads her own fund raising consulting firm in New York City, Goodale Associates.

44. SIR JEREMY GREENSTOCK *(United Kingdom)*: The UK's Ambassador to the UN from 1998 to 2003; and from September 2003 to March 2004 was the UK Special Representative for Iraq, where he worked alongside Ambassador Paul Bremer, the American who headed the occupation administration there. After retiring from the Foreign Service, he became Director of The Ditchley Foundation.

45. MARTIN GRIFFITHS *(United Kingdom)*: Founding Executive Director of the Centre for Humanitarian Dialogue (HD Centre) in Geneva from 1999 to 2010, Martin previously worked for UNICEF in Asia and was Director of the UN's Department of Humanitarian Affairs. Through HD Centre, Martin was instrumental in helping Kofi set up and run the Kenya mediation of 2008.

46. JEAN-MARIE GUÉHENNO *(France)*: Senior French diplomat whom Kofi named Under-Secretary-General for Peacekeeping Operations in 2000. He served in that capacity, overseeing over 100,000 UN soldiers, police and civilian staff serving abroad in UN peacekeeping missions, until the end of Kofi's mandate in 2006.

47. JEAN-PIERRE HALBWACHS *(Mauritius)*: Kofi named this experienced UN administrator who joined the Organization in 1973 UN Controller in 1997. When the International Advisory and Monitoring Board was created as a watchdog over the Development Fund for Iraq, including funds transferred by the UN from the Oil-for-Food Programme to the US-led coalition in Iraq, Kofi nominated " J-P" as a member and he was subsequently appointed Chairman.

48. DENIS HALLIDAY *(Ireland)*: The experienced UN official named by Kofi as the first UN Humanitarian Coordinator for Iraq in 1997. He resigned in 1998 in protest over the impact of UN sanctions on the innocent Iraqi population.

49. DAVID HARLAND *(New Zealand)*: While serving as a relatively junior UN official in Bosnia during the war there, David considered himself a « dissident » because he believed the UN was appeasing the Bosnian Serbs. He was surprised when in 1999 Kofi asked him to conduct an internal inquiry into the Srebrenica massacre that took place in Bosnia in 1995. His report was extremely critical of the UN Secretariat and the leadership of the UN peacekeeping mission in the former Yugoslavia.

50. PATRICK HAYFORD *(Ghana)*: Former Ghanaian Ambassador to South Africa whom Kofi named Director for African Affairs in his Executive Office from 1999 to 2005.

51. MARCEL D'HERTEFELT *(Belgium)*: Cultural anthropologist and leading specialist on Rwanda and the Great Lakes Region of Africa who taught at universities in Africa and at the

University of Texas at Austin. He was attached to Belgium's Royal Museum for Central Africa at Tervuren and is the author of several books on Rwanda. He now lives in retirement outside of Brussels.

52. NOELEEN HEYZER *(Singapore)*: This research officer for the International Labour Organization and director of the gender and development program of the Asia Pacific Development Centre became head of the UN Women's Fund (UNIFEM) in 1994. In July 2007, she was named Executive Secretary of the UN Economic and Social Commission for Asia and the Pacific.

53. WARREN HOGE *(United States)*: UN Bureau Chief for *The New York Times* from 2004 to 2008. He is currently Vice President for External Relations of the International Peace Institute in New York.

54. RICHARD HOLBROOKE *(United States)*: Veteran US diplomat who served as US Ambassador to the UN from 1999 to 2001. He and his wife Kati were close friends of Kofi and Nane's. In 1995, he successfully negotiated an end to the war in Bosnia at the peace talks held in Dayton, Ohio. He died of a heart attack in December 2010 while serving as US President Barack Obama's special envoy to Afghanistan.

55. JOACHIM HUTTER *(Germany)*: Director in the UN peacekeeping department, responsible for operations in Asia (1994-2001) and then Europe (2001-2003).

56. CRAIG JENNESS *(Canada)*: Election expert and head of the Electoral Division of the UN Department of Political Affairs from June 2006 to the present. Kofi called on him in February 2008 to advise him on electoral issues in the Kenya negotiations.

57. GEORG KELL *(Germany)*: The former head of the New York office of the UN Conference on Trade and Development hired by Kofi in 1997 to advise him on the UN's relations with the private sector. He worked with John Ruggie to create the Global Compact, and was director of that program from 2000.

58. KEVIN S. KENNEDY *(United States)*: A UN veteran, Kevin served under Sergio Vieira de Mello in the UN peacekeeping mission in Kosovo. He worked in Kofi's Executive Office from 2000 to the end of his mandate, when he joined the peacekeeping department. Between 2007 and March 2011 he led the Headquarters team responsible for the UN mission in the Democratic Republic of the Congo, where he also served on assignment as Director of Information. He now heads the UN's peacekeeping training service.

59. PAUL KETEKU *(Ghana)*: A member of Kofi's extended family who once lived in the Annan household in Ghana.

60. ROLF KNUTSSON *(Sweden)*: This UN veteran joined the Organization in 1969 and served in the UN Development Programme in Jordan, Ecuador and Tanzania. He worked abroad in several UN peacekeeping missions — Lebanon, Jerusalem, Central America and Western Sahara. He was Kofi's Director of Political Affairs and Deputy Chief of Staff and later his Personal Representative in Lebanon. Before retiring, he was named Executive Secretary of the UN Compensation Commission for Iraq in 2000.

61. TERJE ROED LARSEN *(Norway)*: Middle East specialist who was a central player in the Oslo peace process on the Middle East. In 1994, Secretary-General Boutros Boutros-Ghali named him special envoy to the occupied territories. As Secretary-General, Kofi named him special coordinator for the Middle East peace process in 1999 and subsequently special envoy for the Lebanon-Syria issue in 2004. He became President of the International Peace Institute (IPI) in New York in 2005, a position he continued to hold when Kofi called on him once again in 2006 to be special envoy to Lebanon to help negotiate a cease-fire between Israel and Hezbollah. He continued in that special envoy role under Secretary-General Ban Ki-Moon while concurrently remaining President of IPI.

62. MICHEL LAVOLLAY *(France)*: One of the first clinicians involved with HIV/AIDS, Michel worked with the World Health Organization's Programme on AIDS in the late 1980s. He was also one of the first specialists sent to Iraq in 1997 to set up the Oil-for-Food Programme. He is married to Afsané Bassir-Pour.

63. SERGEY LAVROV *(Russia)*: Former Russian Ambassador to the UN who was named Foreign Minister of his country in March 2004.

64. EVELYN LEOPOLD *(United States)*: Veteran *Reuters* correspondent, who was UN bureau chief from 1990 to 2007. She is currently UN contributor to *The Huffington Post*.

65. JEAN-DAVID LEVITTE *(France)*: Former French Ambassador to the UN at Geneva from 1988 to 1990. He was diplomatic advisor to French President Jacques Chirac from 1995 to 2000 and then Ambassador to the UN from 2000 to 2002 and to the US until 2007. From May 2007 to May 2012, he served as diplomatic advisor to French President Nicolas Sarkozy.

66. STEPHEN LEWIS *(Canada)*: A former labor mediator, columnist and broadcaster, Stephen served as Canadian Ambassador to the UN from 1984 to 1988. As a senior UNICEF official in New York from 1995 to 1999, he helped draw attention to the world AIDS crisis. Kofi then named him special envoy for AIDS in Africa, a post he held from 2001 to 2006. In 2003, he set up the Stephen Lewis Foundation to assist AIDS victims in Africa.

67. LI ZHAOXING *(China)*: Foreign Minister of China from 2003 to 2007.

68. ELISABETH LINDENMAYER *(France)*: Born in West Africa to a French Army officer, the Sorbonne-educated Elisabeth first worked for Kofi in the UN personnel department in 1987, then followed him to the peacekeeping department, where she specialized in Iraq-Kuwait, Somalia and Rwanda. Kofi made her his personal assistant when he became Secretary-General, in which capacity she managed his program. She organized most of his trips abroad and travelled with him. French President Jacques Chirac named her to the *Légion d'honneur* in 2006. She now teaches at Columbia University.

69. SUSAN LINNEE *(United States)*: Met Kofi in November 1960 when he was at Macalester College in St. Paul, Minnesota and she was at the University of Minnesota. She has stayed in touch with him since. She became a reporter for *Associated Press* and her last posting before retirement was as *AP* bureau chief in Nairobi, Kenya.

70. CARLOS LOPES *(Guinea Bissau)*: In September 2005, Kofi brought this widely published development economist into his office as director in charge of political affairs. In March 2007, Secretary-General Ban Ki-Moon named him Executive Director of the UN Institute for Training and Research in Geneva. In March 2012, he was named Executive Secretary of the UN Economic Commission for Africa.

71. ANDREW (ANDY) MACK *(Australia)*: Andy Mack was Kofi's Director of Strategic Planning from 1998 to 2001 and worked with John Ruggie drafting Kofi's report to the General Assembly on the Millennium Development Goals. He left the UN to spend a year at Harvard in 2001 and is now based at the new School for International Studies at Simon Fraser University in Vancouver where he directs the team that produces the highly regarded Human Security Report.

72. LORD (MARK) MALLOCH BROWN *(United Kingdom)*: A former journalist for *The Economist*, Mark joined the Office of the UN High Commissioner for Refugees in the early 1980s, where he first met Kofi. He then worked as a communications consultant in Washington, D.C., advising Corazon Aquino in her successful bid to defeat Ferdinand Marcos in the presidential elections of 1986. He became Vice President for External Affairs of the World Bank in 1994 and served in that capacity until Kofi named him Administrator of the UN Development Programme in 1999. At the height of the Oil-for-Food scandal, December 2004, Kofi asked Mark to be his Chief of Staff and then in March 2006 named him Deputy Secretary-General, succeeding Louise Frechette. He joined the UK government in 2007 when Prime Minister Gordon Brown named him Minister of State for Africa, Asia and the United Nations, a position he resigned from in 2009.

73. DAVID MALONE *(Canada)*: Academic and diplomat who was Canadian Ambassador to the UN from 1992 to 1994. He was head of the International Peace Academy (now the International Peace Institute) from 1998 to 2004, after which he returned to government service, overseeing Canada's multilateral and economic policy as Assistant Deputy Minister for Foreign Affairs and Trade. He served as Canadian High Commissioner to India from 2006 to 2008 and is currently President of Canada's International Development Research Centre.

74. NELSON MANDELA *(South Africa)*: Leader of the anti-apartheid movement, who was freed after 27 years in prison and served as President of his country from 1994 to 1999.

75. RACHEL MAYANJA *(Uganda)*: Lawyer and UN administrator who served in UN peacekeeping missions in Namibia (1989-90) and Kuwait (1992-94), and whom Kofi named Special Advisor on Gender Issues and the Advancement of Women in 2004.

76. CAROLYN MCASKIE *(Canada)*: Veteran diplomat whom Kofi named deputy Humanitarian Coordinator in 1999. She then served as head of the UN peacekeeping mission in Burundi from 2004 to 2006 and when Kofi's proposal for a UN Peacebuilding Commission was approved by the General Assembly in late 2005, he made her head of the Secretariat unit that services the Commission. She is now retired.

77. STANLEY MEISLER *(United States)*: UN correspondent for the *Los Angeles Times* from 1991 to 1997 who wrote two books on the UN, *United Nations: The First Fifty Years* in 1995 (updated as *United Nations, A History* in 2011) and *Kofi Annan: A Man of Peace in a World of War* (2006).

78. DARKO MOCIBOB (Bosnia-Herzegovina): A political officer in the UN Department of Political Affairs who worked on the Oil-for-Food Programme for Iraq under Benon Sevan.

79. MICHAEL MOLLER *(Denmark)*: A senior director in Kofi's Executive Office from 2001 to 2005, handling, on and off, the Iraq portfolio. Kofi then appointed him Special Representative in Cyprus at a time when the island's two factions hadn't been speaking for two years. He got them back to the table and laid the foundation for the current negotiations. After leaving the UN, he joined Kofi in Geneva in September 2008 as Executive Director of the Kofi Annan Foundation. He is now retired.

80. PHILIPPE MORILLON *(France)*: General in the French Army who served as commander of the UN forces in Bosnia and Herzegovina and who traveled to Srebrenica to negotiate between the Muslim and Serb forces in the region, briefly becoming a hostage there. He was elected to the European Parliament in 1999, served for 10 years and did not stand for re-election in 2009. That year he was named head of the European Commission's Electoral Observation Mission in Afghanistan.

81. EDWARD MORTIMER *(United Kingdom)*: Journalist at *The Times* (London, 1967-85) and then *The Financial Times* (London, 1987-98); Kofi named him chief speechwriter in 1998. He not only shaped Kofi's messages but helped shape policy as well, particularly in the area of human rights. He stayed until the end of the second term in 2006, and then became Senior Vice President of the Salzburg Global Seminar.

82. NADER MOUSAVIZADEH *(Denmark)*: Former associate editor at *The New Republic*, he joined the UN in 1996 as a political officer in Bosnia and in 1997 became a speechwriter and de facto political advisor to Kofi, a post he occupied until 2003 when he left to join the investment banking firm of Goldman Sachs. In 2009, he founded Archipelago Partners, a geostrategic advisory firm based in London and in 2010 was named CEO of Oxford Analytica.

83. AMRE MOUSSA *(Egypt)*: Foreign Minister of Egypt from 1991 to 2001 and from 2001 to June 2011 Secretary-General of the League of Arab States.

84. SADAKO OGATA *(Japan)*: Former Dean of the Faculty of Foreign Studies at Sophia University in Tokyo, she represented her country at the UN Commission on Human Rights in Geneva and at the Permanent Mission to the UN in New York. She became UN High Commissioner for Refugees during the turbulent 1990s, when she expanded the role of her Office in Bosnia, Cambodia and other crisis spots. After leaving that job in 2000, she was named President of Japan's International Cooperation Agency in 2003.

85. YVES OLTRAMARE *(Switzerland)*: A philanthropist and former private banker who served for 30 years on the Investment Committee of the UN Pension Fund and who was befriended by Kofi in 1997.

86. ROBERT C. ORR *(United States)*: Was Director for UN Affairs at the US National Security Council in the White House when Kofi was elected Secretary-General. He was later deputy to US Ambassador to the UN Richard Holbrooke, heading his Washington office, in which position he was instrumental in securing $1 billion in arrears payments to the UN. In 2004, Kofi named him head of his strategic planning unit, and he continues to advise the current Secretary-General on his policy priorities — from climate change to food security and global health.

87. LORD (DAVID) OWEN *(United Kingdom)*: Foreign Secretary of his country at the age of 38, David and US Secretary of State Cyrus R. Vance drew up the Anglo-American proposals for the independence of Rhodesia, now Zimbabwe. David was co-founder of the Social Democratic Party in the UK in 1981 and Leader from 1983-90. He was the EU negotiator working alongside UN negotiator Vance and then Thorvald Stoltenberg in the Yugoslav peace talks in Geneva 1992-1995.

88. NICHOLAS (NICK) PANZARINO *(United States)*: UN security officer in charge of the Secretary-General's detail under three Secretaries-General, from Javier Perez de Cuellar to Boutros Boutros-Ghali to Kofi.

89. PETER PIOT *(Belgium)*: A medical doctor and specialist in microbiology, Peter was the co-discoverer of the Ebola virus in Zaire in 1976. Professor at several universities in Europe and Africa, he put in place the first international anti-AIDS program in Africa in Kinshasa, Democratic Republic of the Congo (previously Zaire). In 1995 he was named head of UNAIDS, a responsibility that he kept throughout Kofi's two terms. He is presently Professor and Director of the Institute for Global Health at Imperial College London, UK.

90. COLIN POWELL *(United States)*: US Secretary of State from 2001 to 2005.

91. JULIA FALVY PREISWERK *(United States)*: On a Junior Year Abroad in Geneva from Smith College in the 1960s, Julia Falvy bumped into Kofi at the UN Library. He then introduced her to his best friend Roy Preiswerk. She and Roy were married in 1963 and Kofi became godfather to their first child, a son, Frank. She remains in Geneva today as a practicing psychoanalyst.

92. (SIR) KIERAN PRENDERGAST *(United Kingdom)*: British diplomat who served as UK Consul General to Israel, High Commissioner to Zimbabwe and Kenya and then Ambassador to Turkey. As Under-Secretary-General for Political Affairs from 1997 to 2005, he was one of Kofi's principal political advisers.

93. ISEL RIVERO *(Cuba)*: UN career included working in the Department of International Economic and Social Affairs, the Department of Peacekeeping Operations and the Department of Public Information. In peacekeeping in the 1990s, she was desk officer for Rwanda and later in Kigali was the Special Assistant to the Special Representative of the Secretary-General for Rwanda.

94. IQBAL RIZA *(Pakistan)*: In UN service from 1978, Iqbal served as Director of the Office for Special Political Affairs from 1983 to 1988, where he was a senior member of the team for the political negotiations related to the Iran-Iraq war, and also head of the special team which undertook several missions to the front (1983 to 1987) to investigate the use of chemical weapons in this conflict. He then distinguished himself in Central America, first as chief of the UN observer mission for verification of the electoral process in Nicaragua in 1989-90 and then as Special Representative of the Secretary-General in El Salvador in 1990. Kofi recruited him as deputy in the peacekeeping department from 1993 to 1996. In 1996, he served as Special Representative in Bosnia and Herzegovina. Secretary-General Kofi Annan then named him Chief of Staff in 1997, and he served in that capacity until early 2005, when Kofi named him Special Adviser to the Secretary-General, a position in which he continues with Secretary-General Ban Ki-Moon.

95. MARY ROBINSON *(Ireland)*: First female President of her country (1990-1997), she served as UN High Commissioner for Human Rights from 1997 to 2002. She is Honorary President of Oxfam International, Chair of the GAVI Alliance Board and a founding member of the Council of Women World Leaders. She is President of the human rights NGO in New York, Realizing Rights: The Ethical Global Initiative, which she founded in 2002.

96. JOHN RUGGIE *(United States)*: Austrian-born former professor of international political economy at the University of California at Berkeley and then Dean of the School of International Affairs at Columbia University, John was named as Kofi's first director of strategic planning in 1997. He directed Kofi's reform effort, wrote key speeches for him and worked on two other major projects for him — the Millennium Development Goals and the Global Compact. He left the UN in 2001 to teach at Harvard University's Kennedy School of Government. In 2005, Kofi appointed him Special Representative for business and human rights.

97. JEFFREY D. SACHS *(United States)*: Economist who taught at Harvard University for 20 years before moving to Columbia University's Earth Institute, where he became director in 2002. While at Columbia, Jeff was Kofi's head of the UN Millennium Project, charged with following up on governments' performance in meeting the Millennium Development Goals.

98. TAMRAT SAMUEL *(Eritrea)*: Political officer since 1989 in the Department of Political Affairs specializing in Asia and the Pacific. From 1992 to 2000, he was in charge of the Secretary-General's good offices mission to East Timor.

99. ANNIKA SAVILL *(UK/Sweden)*: Former journalist with the *Associated Press, Reuters* and *The Independent* newspaper (London), where she was Diplomatic Editor, Annika was deputy head of Kofi's speechwriting team from 1997 to the end of his second term in 2006. She continued as lead speechwriter for Secretary-General Ban Ki Moon before being named in 2008 as Deputy Executive Head of the United Nations Democracy Fund.

100. BENON SEVAN *(Cyprus)*: A Cypriot-Armenian, he was special representative of Secretary-General Javier Perez de Cuellar for Afghanistan from 1998 to 1992. Kofi named him director of the Office of the Iraq Programme in 1997, in which capacity he oversaw the Oil-for-Food Programme for Iraq. In August 2005, Paul Volcker accused him of having taken kickbacks from Saddam Hussein; Kofi had relieved him of his functions in February of that year when the allegations first came to light. He resigned and retired on 7 August 2005 and remains in Cyprus under indictment by US courts, although he continues to claim innocence.

101. LAMIN SISE *(Gambia)*: Did his BA, MA and Ph.D at Johns Hopkins University and then got an LL.B at Cambridge University. His first UN job was as deputy legal adviser with the UN Conference on Trade and Development in Geneva; he eventually became a legal officer at UN Headquarters in New York. Kofi recruited him into the peacekeeping department, and when Kofi became Secretary-General, Lamin was one of a handful of people that followed him from peacekeeping to the 38th floor. He served Kofi there for two full five-year terms. Starting 2008, he advised Kofi during the Kenya negotiations and monitored the Kenya portfolio for him at the Kofi Annan Foundation in Geneva.

102. JAVIER SOLANA *(Spain)*: The former Secretary-General of NATO (1995 to 1999), he served as the European Union's High Representative for Common Foreign and Security Policy from 1999 to 2009.

103. GILLIAN SORENSEN *(United States)*: Gillian handled NGO relations for Secretary-General Boutros Boutros-Ghali. Kofi named her Assistant-Secretary-General for External Relations, also asking her to handle dozens of celebrities who participated in Kofi's Messenger of Peace program. She went on to work for Ted Turner's UN Foundation in 2003.

104. ALVARO DE SOTO *(Peru)*: Brought into the UN in 1982 by Secretary-General Javier Perez de Cuellar, Alvaro led the 22-month negotiations that ended the decade-long war in El Salvador in January 1992. While Assistant-Secretary-General for Political Affairs overseeing the Americas, Europe and Asia and the Pacific, he was Special Envoy for Myanmar from 1995 to 1999. Kofi then put him in charge of the Cyprus negotiations from 1999 to 2004 where he produced a meticulously detailed peace agreement, which, in the end, was not accepted by both sides. Kofi then assigned him to Western Sahara from 2003 to 2005, another Mission Impossible. Finally, Kofi made him UN Middle East negotiator. He ended that assignment and left the UN at his own request in May 2007. His confidential end-of-mission report, which was leaked to the *Guardian* newspaper in London, laid out in stark clarity the contradictions in UN policy toward the Middle East. He is currently Associate Fellow at the Geneva Centre for Security Policy, Senior Fellow at the Ralph Bunche Institute, and a member of the Global Leadership Foundation.

105. STEPHEN STEDMAN *(United States)*: Professor of Political Science at Stanford University in California whom Kofi named as staff director of the High Level Panel he set up to assess the security role of the UN in the 21st century.

106. THORVALD STOLTENBERG *(Norway)*: Prominent Norwegian politician who served as Minister of Defense from 1979 to 1981 and Minister of Foreign Affairs from 1987 to 1989.

He was appointed UN Ambassador in 1989 and in 1990 was named UN High Commissioner for Refugees. He succeeded Cyrus R. Vance as UN negotiator alongside European Community negotiator Lord (David) Owen in the joint UN-EC peace talks on Yugoslavia held in Geneva from 1992 to 1995.

107. SHASHI THAROOR *(India)*: Shashi first met Kofi at UNHCR headquarters in Geneva in 1980 and later moved to Secretary-General Javier Perez de Cuellar's peacekeeping unit in 1989 as Special Assistant to the Under-Secretary-General. When Secretary-General Boutros Boutros-Ghali set up a separate Department of Peacekeeping Operations in 1992, Kofi joined its staff as Assistant Secretary-General. When he became head of it in 1993, he invited Shashi to remain as his Special Assistant. When Kofi became Secretary-General in 1997, he named Shashi Executive Assistant, and then Director of Communications. In 2002, Kofi made Shashi, then only 46, Under-Secretary-General for Communications and Public Information, one of the youngest-ever to hold the rank of Under-Secretary-General. In 2006, as Kofi was stepping down, India proposed Shashi as Kofi's successor, but he lost to Ban Ki-Moon of South Korea. In 2009 Shashi was elected to the Indian Parliament and was named Minister of State for External Affairs, a post he resigned from in 2010. On the side, he is a widely published author of novels and historical analyses as well as a frequent commentator on current affairs.

108. SIR BRIAN URQUHART *(United Kingdom)*: After serving six years in the British Army during the Second World War, he became one of the first people hired to join the Secretariat of the new United Nations in London in 1945. He worked closely with the first five Secretaries-General, helped define modern peacekeeping with Secretary-General Dag Hammarskjold, and wrote penetrating biographies of both Hammarskjold and Ralph Bunche. He is a distinguished commentator on global affairs and a frequent contributor to *The New York Review of Books*.

109. ROB WATSON *(United Kingdom)*: *BBC* veteran of 25 years and longest-serving *BBC* Bureau Chief at the UN, from 1994 to 1999. If he had to add a personal description of himself, he said immodestly, it would be, "Rob is a very fidgety, witty and warm hearted and somewhat neurotic but a very hard working *BBC* hack dedicated to the cause of fair and honest reporting".

110. JOANNA WESCHLER *(Poland)*: Human rights expert who has conducted human rights investigations in countries on five continents. She was a researcher for Poland for Helsinki Watch, researcher for Brazil for Americas Watch and director of Human Rights Watch's Prison Project. She then became the first UN representative of Human Rights Watch at the United Nations, serving from 1994 to 2005. She is currently research director for the publication *Security Council Report*, affiliated with Columbia University.

111. JAMES (JIM) WOLFENSOHN *(United States)*: Australian-born President of the World Bank from 1995 to 2005 who became a close friend of Kofi's. He subsequently founded the Wolfensohn Center for Development, a think tank based in Washington, D.C., and has a consulting business in New York. He is also an accomplished cellist and is President Emeritus of Carnegie Hall.

112. PRINCE ZEID RA'AD ZEID AL-HUSSEIN *(Jordan)*: Began a UN career as a political officer in the UN peacekeeping mission in Bosnia and Herzegovina from 1994 to 1996. He became Jordan's Ambassador to the UN in 2000, and from 2002 to 2005 was the first president of the governing body of the International Criminal Court. In 2005, Kofi, as Secretary-General, asked him to prepare a report on sexual abuse by peacekeepers. In 2006, Jordan nominated him to succeed Kofi as Secretary-General, but he lost to Ban Ki-Moon. He was subsequently named Jordan's Ambassador to Washington and then returned to New York as UN Ambassador in 2010.

THANK YOU...

— to Kofi Annan, for making me his Spokesperson and giving me so many wondrous stories to tell the next generation, and to Nane, whose spirit buoyed mine.

— to my son Jan, the computer genius to whom this volume is dedicated and who toured Vukovar with me in August 1992 (he was crazy about the band Megadeath and I wanted him to see what that meant in Yugoslavia), and his wife Julie, for having helped store all the data electronically and for having solved myriad technical problems for me.

— to my wife Kathryn Gordon, the formidable former editor of the United Nations Yearbook, for correcting many of my spelling errors and for putting up with me.

— to Edward Mortimer, a generous spirit, for having spent hours with me on individual chapters and also for having shared his notes with me.

— to Sir Kieran Prendergast, for having patiently guided me through the most politically complex portions of the book.

— to Sir Brian Urquhart for help with the peacekeeping chapter and for both contributing the Preface and sharing his thoughts on Hammarskjold and Kofi in a wonderful essay.

— to Jim Sutterlin, my first mentor at the UN, for his wise counsel.

— to David Finn for agreeing to publish this book and for sharing the manuscript with Ashbel Green.

— to Knopf editor Ashbel Green for providing crucial guidance.

— to the more than one hundred persons who contributed to this work by talking to me and critiquing drafts.

— to the UN Security team who shared their thoughts with me, especially Nick Panzarino and Mark Hoffman.

— to Michael Moller, for his help from the Kofi Annan Foundation, and Marie Heuzé, for moral and practical support, both in Geneva.

— to the A-Team in the UN Spokesperson's Office in New York for answering with patience and grace my 4,000 e-mails with small, factual questions.

— to the members of the UN press corps for helping me live through interesting times.

PHOTO CREDITS